WHAT PRICE CHANNEL 4 NOW?

EDITED BY

JOHN MAIR, FIONA CHESTERTON,
NEIL FOWLER, DAVID LLOYD,
IAN REEVES, RAYMOND SNODDY
and
RICHARD TAIT

Revised Edition

Published 2021 by Abramis academic publishing

www.abramis.co.uk

ISBN 978 1 84549 788 0

Typeset in Garamond

Abramis is an imprint of arima publishing.

arima publishing
ASK House, Northgate Avenue
Bury St Edmunds, Suffolk IP32 6BB
t: (+44) 01284 700321

www.arimapublishing.com

Contents

Part one: The 2021 edition

Part two: The 2016 edition

Acknowledgements

This book was never expected to need a revised and expanded edition. By the time our first edition had been published in June 2016 the government had unexpectedly answered our question *What Future for Channel 4?* by abandoning its plan to sell it off, settling for more modest changes, including moving more of its operations out of London. Like Margaret Thatcher in 1988 and John Major in 1997, David Cameron had looked at privatisation and rejected it. We – and most readers – made the assumption that Channel 4's future had been settled for at least a decade.

But when, just five years later, the Johnson government revived the idea of privatising Channel 4, it was clear that many of the arguments of principle in the original book were still very relevant. And we had also set out to do more than cover the ownership debate. We had wanted to analyse this unique institution through contributions from some of the key producers and executives from its early days to the current battle over its future.

So this book has two parts.

Part One brings the controversy about the status of Channel 4 up to date with analysis of the government's new proposals and the current debate they have provoked. Part Two, the original book, covers the 2015-16 arguments, which are now being largely re-run today, and analyses Channel 4's distinctive history and culture.

The editors hope combining all this in one book will make a timely and useful contribution to the passionate arguments about the future of such an important force in British broadcasting. Our thanks as always to Richard and Pete Franklin at Abramis for making it possible with their customary speed and good humour.

John Mair, Oxford
Fiona Chesterton, Cambridge
Neil Fowler, Northumberland
David Lloyd, London
Ian Reeves, Kent
Raymond Snoddy, London
Richard Tait, London

Introduction
By Raymond Snoddy

The future is still to be decided

When *What Price Channel 4?* was published in 2016, with the subtitle *Would privatisation be a disaster, an opportunity or a rebirth?* the impact and sales were muted.

It may have been published just in time to have an influence on the outcome, a decision by David Cameron's Conservative government not to go ahead with plans to privatise a channel like no other in the world – a public service broadcaster, with public service obligations wholly funded by commercial means.

The fact that the 'battle' for Channel 4 had been won unexpectedly early inevitably meant it became a book for very specialised media cognoscenti.

What Price Channel 4 Now? is not a second edition of the original. It is far more important than that. The decision was taken to reprint the entire original unchanged, as a guide to what was believed and argued at the time, but with added contributions contributing an up-to-date dimension.

In the face of Boris Johnson's apparent determination to move a Conservative government towards privatisation – yet again – the new version leads off with 11 completely new chapters, the first by the current chief executive of Channel 4, Alex Mahon opposing privatisation, as did her predecessor David Abraham in the original edition.

Lifelong broadcasting executive David Elstein argues the case for privatisation, as he did last time and is opposed, once again, by marketing and management academic and author Patrick Barwise, professor emeritus at the London Business School.

There is, however, a much more surprising chain of continuity than the appearance of a number of familiar names.

Changes in the broadcasting world

Since the publication of the original there has been a profound transformation in the world of broadcasting and communications – the rapid rise of the streaming giants of California such as Netflix and Disney + accompanied by the arrival of tech companies such as Apple and Amazon in the world of the media and not least the social media companies such as Facebook and Google.

It is a phenomenon that overall has put pressure on both the ratings and finances of public service broadcasters everywhere and yet, helped in part by the Covid-19 pandemic, there has been a new appreciation of the social value of public broadcasters in the face of a surge online of fake news and dangerous delusions, not least from anti-vaxxers.

The most remarkable thing of all is how little the arguments about the future shape of Channel 4 have changed, even intensified, in face of the apparent threat from trillion-dollar companies.

It is the widespread, though not universally held, view throughout the UK broadcasting and creative economy that the case for retaining Channel 4's public status, as opposed to becoming just another commercial channel among hundreds, has been strengthened rather than weakened by the events of the past six years.

In her contribution Alex Mahon argues that in the face of the disruption of the streamers Channel 4 can come out fighting, and winning on its own turf. 'There is no reason why our gargantuan external competitors, international groups offering content that appeals in dozens of countries, must become the dominant retailers in our own, British market,' Mahon comments.

An independent Channel 4 rather than one 'beholden to shareholders' would continue to offer more to British viewers. At the same time, if Channel 4 were to be owned by ITV, the enlarged quoted company could then be quickly snapped up American investors.

If that happened all of British broadcasting, apart from the BBC, would be under foreign ownership.

Mahon would like the future of Channel 4 to be determined as part of a wider look at the future of public service broadcasting in the UK.

'Or, to use a more C4 metaphor, are we not asking bakers to 'on your marks get set …bake' without telling them whether they are to make a sandwich, a loaf or a showstopper?'

In my chapter I argue that the case put forward by the government for a 'new ownership model' is weak and driven more by ideology than any obvious need for change. Most of the advantages claimed for a private Channel 4 can be, and in many cases already is, being achieved under its current ownership structure.

Former culture secretary Oliver Dowden, for instance, claimed a private Channel 4 could be more agile in its investments. It is, however, difficult to think of a better example of agility than a public Channel 4 moving within 24 hours to secure the live rights to show Emma Raducanu's triumph at the US Open tennis on free-to-air television.

If the government wants to help Channel 4, how about ensuring that the programme schedules of all of the UK's public service broadcasters are prominently displayed on all devices? It could also increase its borrowing limit, modestly, or allow the channel to keep a small portion of the rights to programmes it commissions and broadcasts.

Mrs Thatcher's role

Stewart Purvis, former ITN chief executive and Ofcom partner for content and standards, looks back and reveals that although Channel 4 was created under prime minister Margaret Thatcher she was always a sceptic of it being a publicly-owned channel.

Although Mrs Thatcher accepted reluctantly the idea of a public Channel 4, in 1988 she was still trying to combine Channel 4 and Channel 5, before it had even been licensed, to create a third force to rival the BBC.

Purvis, writing initially before the sacking of John Whittingdale, media and data minister, and a long-time supporter of privatisation, warned that if this plan goes ahead what has been called variously Channel 4's role as 'this creative greenhouse' and the R&D lab of UK television, would, in effect, disappear.

Maggie Brown, distinguished media journalist and historian of Channel 4, also takes the long view, and notes that there have been four attempts to privatise the broadcaster, including the present most significant one, and all under Conservative governments.

Her second 'dawning revelation' is that the small scale of Channel 4 and its 'no jobs for life model,' with no less than seven chief executives, all external, may have created an inbuilt ability to refresh.

Brown believes all is not lost. Channel 4 has millions of fans who like its programmes, there is fierce opposition from independent producers and some Conservative MPs are highly critical. She concludes: 'Channel 4 now needs to buttress its opposition with new hits. Programmes that make you think. Content that has a reminder of its special DNA. It has been done before.'

Straying from its remit

Broadcaster and media executive David Elstein believes that in theory each of ITV, STV, Sky, Viacom or Discovery might be interested, and depending on the terms of the contract, be prepared to pay £1bn, perhaps even more.

While the channel is not in immediate financial danger, its £74m surplus was achieved by cutting programme costs by £138m while still claiming to have fulfilled its remit. Channel 4 thereby confirmed 'what has been obvious to us for many years: the famous remit is as long (or short) as a piece of string.'

Elstein argues this has been so since the 2003 Communications Act led to the abolition of many of Channel 4's old programme quotas. The channel's latest annual report showed that repeats took up 70 per cent of its schedule and until recently Channel 4 claimed to be broadcasting more than 50 hours a week of education 'an absurd and false boast'.

Elstein says that Channel 4 has strayed so far away from its original public service remit – it thinks the *Great British Bake Off* should be classified as public service content – that the only way of re-imposing control is by selling to a private owner. There is considerable potential for internal savings, and small independents could be protected by having their own quotas.

For Elstein privatisation offers an opportunity to correct the flaws in the Channel 4 business model, extract the synergies that the Channel has failed to deliver, or even pursue, and deploy those resources to strengthen the channel's output by putting greater emphasis on public service content.

And, after all, the independent producers now so opposed to privatisation are all privately owned businesses themselves.

Patrick Barwise, emeritus professor of management and marketing at the London Business School, argues that none of the claimed privatisation benefits, such as combining the advertising sales houses of ITV and Channel 4, actually requires Channel 4 to be privatised.

Setting policy, Barwise argues, is often about striking a balance between different views and stakeholders. In this case the government has achieved the rare distinction of being opposed, not just by the usual suspects but by reputable independent analysts, some Conservative MPs, Channel 4 itself and all three sets of stakeholders – organisations representing viewers, independent producers and advertisers.

Barwise also notes that the government's consultation questions are all designed to encourage pro-privatisation responses. 'As far I know this is unprecedented in a public consultation,' concludes Barwise, who fears that despite such widespread opposition 'the signs are that the government plans to force it through regardless.'

A distinctive news voice

Matt Walsh and Stephen Cushion of Cardiff University's School of Journalism, Media and Culture argue that for 40 years Channel 4 News has broadcast original, impartial, hard-hitting journalism that has held power to account.

Recent academic studies show that Channel 4 News is not only distinctive but different from the news output of other public service broadcasters, with a higher proportion of international news and a greater emphasis on hard news, including politics, and public affairs.

The Cardiff academics note that on nightly news bulletins on BBC, ITV, Channel 4, Channel 5 and Sky News roughly a third of items included at least one instance of a journalist challenging or questioning a government decision. Channel 4 had the highest amount with almost six in 10 items including some interrogation of policy, with Channel 4 featuring the most robust and explicit questioning.

Walsh and Cushion argue that if Channel 4 is to be privatised then mechanisms should be put in place similar to those brought in to protect Sky

News when the Sky group was bought by Comcast in 2018. They should include guarantees on funding with the creation of an independent editorial board.

'Given Channel 4 News's distinctive contribution to the UK's broadcast ecology, in our view, any buyer should be required to undertake a legal commitment to protect and enhance the news service both on television and online,' they say.

Richard Tait, a co-editor of this book and a professor of journalism at Cardiff University, warns that the history of broadcasting regulation in the UK shows that promises in broadcasting are easily made and not always kept.

Communications regulator Ofcom could indeed be asked to implement a ring-fencing of the Channel 4 news budget and guarantees along the lines of the Sky News Comcast deal.

Yet there is nothing in the current remit to say Channel Four News should be an hour long and broadcast at 19.00 on weekdays. It is impossible to say at this stage, Tait points out, what Ofcom would do if new owners of Channel 4 subsequently decided they did not want to continue with a loss-making hour of news in a valuable slot.

The former editor-in-chief of ITN argues: 'If the final agreed price is seen as low, the charge will be that a public asset has been given away – if high, the new owners will need to make changes which will start appearing on screen and elsewhere.'

He concludes: 'And no matter what the deal says, privatisation puts shareholders and managers, not regulators in the driving seat long term.'

The importance of documentaries

Lorraine Heggessey, chair of the trustees of The Grierson Trust and the Trust's managing director Jane Callaghan, wrote a letter directly to culture secretary Oliver Dowden, which will probably land on the desk of his successor Nadine Dorries, emphasising the importance of Channel 4 to the pre-eminence of British documentary making.

The Grierson Trust, which celebrates the best documentary filmmaking in the UK and around the world, makes it clear Channel 4 had brought creative innovation, dynamic support, diverse voices and new talent to the industry. Such aspects of Channel 4's work were critical for the UK's world-leading documentary industry to thrive.

The societal value of Channel 4 'is unlikely to be sustainable in a for-profit model in which ratings and revenue and shareholders are prioritised,' Heggessey and Callaghan argue.

They add: 'It is critical that the conditions of any sale would be explicit and measurable in order to ensure that these core values, so sustaining to UK business, creativity and culture, and even global standing, are retained.'

Fiona Chesterton, the first commissioning editor for daytime programmes at Channel 4, accepts that the market will continue to supply a wealth of content for the wider under-35s audience. It comes down, she believes, to whether you think entertainment is all that young people need and deserve, and whether you think that something will be missing for teenagers- especially those still at school.

How much, Chesterton asks, would producers feel it was worth investing in challenging, domestically-focused content, when they need to raise co-production money from internationally-focused services? 'In particular, how much would be focused on under 16-year-olds, living say in Dudley, with a broader purpose than merely entertaining them?

'This is a question that the DCMS does not address in its very unspecific and less than watertight assurances, in its consultation document,' she believes.

She emphasises that adults, and parents in particular, are nervous of the Wild West of internet content and favour not just regulation but the historic values of public service broadcasting. They do not want those values washed away in a tide of globalised content, however slick and well produced it might be. 'In sum they want their kids hearing more Dudley accents than LA ones,' she insists.

Buyers in the wings?

John Mair, co-editor of both Channel 4 books and who has edited no less than 42 'hackacademic' volumes, asks the key question – who are the runners and riders if the government pushes ahead with the privatisation of Channel 4?

Mair raises the possibility of a management buy-out of the channel, closely followed by ITV and the Viacom-owned Channel 5, which would both benefit from a combination of advertising sales houses. An equally serious candidate to buy Channel 4 would be Sky, which would thereby acquire a useful terrestrial 'barker' channel for a price that what would amount to little more than peanuts for the Comcast-owned business.

Mair believes that attention from the streamers like Netflix and Disney+ are unlikely as is any interest from either Google or Facebook.

Since its inception, Channel 4 says it has invested £12bn in UK-produced material and last year commissioned 274 production companies.

The question marks over its future ownership comes amidst turmoil on both the Ofcom and the Channel 4 boards with a re-run of the search for a new Ofcom chairman and a new chairman needed for Channel 4 from January 2022.

According to Mair, whatever happens 'the cards seem well and truly stacked against the status quo ante. With Channel 4 change is coming. The questions are: Who will own it as its enters its fifth decade and just what will they own?'

This mission is bigger than just saving Channel 4

By Alex Mahon

Channel 4's chief executive officer argues that it can grow its impact and become even more of a catalyst for the health of the UK's creative economy

Let me be clear about one thing from the start: I do not want to save Channel 4.

Yes, you read that correctly.

I know that people throughout British society are desperate to save C4. The extraordinarily creative people who make its programmes want to save it. Politicians who recognise the irreplaceable value of its unique status want to save it.

And most of all, millions of people who love its news, its documentaries, its comedy, its drama, its programmes that fit in no easy genre, want to save it. An audience that relishes, even if they do not know of, its remit to represent the unrepresented and give voice to the unheard, wants to save it. (At least, those who are aware of the proposals to change it want to and we have published the data that shows that.)

But I'm not interested in salvation. It's not enough.

Why I am not looking to be a saviour.

Let me explain. I share the government's view: it is crucial to the future of the UK's creative economy – which is in turn crucial to the future of the UK's overall economy and to its standing in the world – to take a long view of C4. Those who care about this country should certainly look over a distant horizon to find the best way of doing the amazing, the matchless, things that C4 does, far into the future.

But let me be clear in case I am misunderstood: my confidence in the future of this organisation means that I do not want to 'save' Channel 4 because 'saving' it is not enough.

I am only interested in growing our impact, making more, doing more for British audiences, and being even more of a catalyst for the health of the UK's creative economy.

Together with the board and executive of C4, I want to take it far, far forward, not just build a wall around it and preserve it. Change comes naturally to us because it is the inevitable result of our remit and our place in the landscape.

They say that if there is one benefit to the prospect of execution it is to concentrate the mind on life to date and the immediate future. While we are assured by government that we are not in peril of our existence, nonetheless we have concentrated our minds. But in doing so we have also looked way out into the future, confident that there will be a very bright one. We have looked at what C4 does now and what it could do if, instead of looking at how it can be 'saved', we now plan for it to be, simply, more.

As part of its consultation document and in a number of subsequent statements, the government has made it clear that it wants to protect and assure the future role of C4. And it has said that C4 goes beyond being what it is now: a critical part of Britain's much-admired, never-matched television industry.

What is this Chanel Fo(u)r?

So we looked, to begin with, at what C4 is for.

I am sure the government would agree with me that Britain's creative economy needs C4 for some of the same reasons that it did when the broadcaster was founded in 1982: first, as a foil to the BBC's power and influence as a news source, and to the dominant position in production and ideas that it enjoyed only four decades ago; second, as a dilution of the monopoly position on advertising that ITV enjoyed at that same time.

These needs are normally expressed as 'keeping the BBC and ITV on their toes', the former creatively, the latter commercially.

We also need to work alongside those great institutions, pooling our strengths where that is the best move to maintain the greatness of British telly. In any case, we need to have competition in order to make co-operation count.

But, of course, it is not just about the BBC and ITV. It is not just about a need to find the best way to prevent a reversion to old ways from which only a few powerful stakeholders – the audience not being among them – benefited.

Because, as no sentient person could possibly ignore, there is so much more than the BBC and ITV for us to compete with.

How has the channel evolved?

Some of what has changed since C4 was born and what has shaped its continual, joyful and energising process of constant evolution is undoubtedly good for British audiences. The appearance of Sky and Channel 5 broadened choice enormously, increased the size of the production sector that C4's existence had created and offered audiences more choice of shows.

The expansion of digital giving us Freeview and Freesat brought new channels into every home with greater choice from companies such as UKTV or Discovery or QVC, for early adopters of shopping from the sofa.

But as is the case in every corner of the digital revolution, disruption seems to follow the Second Law of Thermodynamics: like entropy, in an irreversible system of change, disruption increases.

The disruption of streamers such as Netflix, Amazon and Apple or the conglomerating ranks of American broadcasters is a battle that in some ways is being fought thousands of feet above our head. But the effects on us, as an industry and as a creative economy, are inevitable and unmistakeable.

Yet I do not understand the perception that we should just hunker down, reduce our exposure to loss and save what we can. Why, when we know we can come out fighting and indeed winning. We can show that, small as we might be by comparison to them, this is our turf and it's what *we* do here that counts.

There is no reason why our gargantuan external competitors, international groups offering content that appeals in dozens of countries, must become the dominant retailers in our own, British market.

I have heard it said that Brits care more about television and its quality than almost any other people. Certainly, with such a long and distinguished history of public service broadcasting, the supply of high-quality programmes has always been around. That stimulates further demand and further supply in a virtuous circle that may explain why we were able to construct such an extraordinary industry.

A new law of TV thermodynamics? Maximum width, minimum depth

But, as competition for 'content' – its nature selected and driven by algorithms – grows, is it inevitable that quality rises? Or is it more likely that quality falls as quantity rises? Creative choices made on the back of algorithmic choices will not be enough to satisfy British tastes. What works for the world is not enough for our audiences.

Indeed, it is right there where opportunity lies, not just for us, but for that vast supply chain we rely on and which relies on us.

We already exploit that opportunity of course, with shows such as *Gogglebox,* or dramas like *It's A Sin*. These are quintessentially British: made by Brits, for Brits on issues that resonate with Brits. Local telly that in each case can also go global. A multinational streamer makes things from the other way round: maximum width and minimum depth.

Naturally, we have to find ways to make the right investments, build the right technologies and support the right makers so that our beautiful British garden of creation is not strangled by invasive species.

And we are already doing it. Not for profit. For the value it adds to our offer, an offer to all, for free and universally available. The US Open tennis final deal with Amazon in September was a significant investment, for instance, but it allowed everyone in Britain the chance to be in on a conversation that otherwise would have been closed and exclusive – in the worst meaning of that word.

While others commercial broadcasters may quake at the prospect of reliance on advertising income, we don't.

Our progress on transforming from airtime to digital advertising markets is, to borrow a phrase, world-beating. I doubt anyone would be warning Facebook and Google that their business models are in danger from disruption, yet they rely on advertising for almost all of their revenue. It is, as always in this industry, about your share. We are growing our share and we are confident that the trend in that is up, not down. Most analysts agree with us.

Save the British creative industries!

So you can see why I believe that merely 'saving' C4 is not going to be enough. It won't be enough to maintain our creative industries as the UK's fastest-growing sector, nor of British video production being both our fastest-growing export sector and also our most effective, persuasive, influential accent in the cacophony of global conversation.

Indeed, I would go as far as to say that there is only a limited value in a future C4 unless it becomes something that is bigger and better than it is now; unless it continues its evolution into something that leads where others follow; unless it remains a vital contributory force in keeping Britain at the top of a worldwide industry tree in a model that is all too rare in the 21st century.

If that is best done with C4 in private hands or under some different, bespoke and imaginative ownership structure, then that is a decision for government and eventually for Parliament. One thing I know for certain is that, given the right conditions and the right ambitions, this organisation can do so much more for Britain and its people.

It has been hard to answer that 'if' question at the beginning of that last paragraph. The simple reason being that we do not, at the time of writing and therefore at the time the consultation on the future status of C4 closed, know for certain what the government's ambitions for public-service media (PSM) will be.

Does DCMS want to 'save' PSM? We don't yet know how the government will react to Ofcom's PSB review nor to the conclusions of the panel that has met privately to offer further insights.

Obviously, we all hope that a future PSM landscape will be wider and give us more than what we have, more value in every sense: money, social cohesion, a broader base of industrial growth, soft power.

Because the sort of questions that this vibrant industry of limitless potential has been asking itself in these uncertain times are the same questions the government appears to be asking itself on a broader, national, level.

Would a Britain without a stronger PSM sector be richer or poorer? Would it have a bigger influence on world events or a smaller? Would it be within its own borders more inclusive or more exclusive? More or less tolerant and embracing of diversity? More or less level? More or less free of unwelcome foreign influence? More or less British?

These are the questions we ask at C4 about our own role in the future of the UK television industry and of the entire country. We know the answers we can give to those questions: an independent C4 rather than one beholden to shareholders is far more likely to offer more to Britain in answer to each question.

Who will buy C4 and what will they give in return?
Yet what makes C4 so attractive to buyers is not giving more to Britain.

If they are a domestic buyer, it is the prospect of a taking out costs through combination-cuts and having a monopoly position on advertising, which in turn would make a combined UK commercial PSB incredibly attractive to the global aggregators of content. I'm not sure many people have noticed the potential danger of losing everything but the BBC to foreign ownership if there were an ITV-C4 combination, for instance. It would probably not cost a US giant more than a few months' revenues to pull off.

If the proposed buyer is alternatively one of those US 'content-farmer' megaliths, the appeal of buying C4 is getting a ready-made audience of young Britons, of an edgy brand, backed up by the most advanced approach to digital advertising in the world.

So C4's market value depends either on the value of monopoly, which in turn depends on abandoning the principles on which advertising air time is sold, or on continuing the remit exactly as it is today: because, make no mistake, our points of difference which have created the young audience, the edgy brand, even the success of our digital ad business, are all inextricably bound to that remit to be different and innovative.

So you can see why we think that these decisions are of profound importance to the UK media landscape. And why, without a clear wider vision for PSM that only a government can provide, whether it's really possible to decide what the most effective future status of C4 ought to be?

To use a more C4 metaphor, are we not asking bakers to 'on your marks, get set…bake' without telling them whether they are to make a sandwich, a loaf or a showstopper?

About the author
Alex Mahon has been CEO of Channel 4 since 2017. She started her career as a PhD physicist and then a strategy consultant at Mitchell Madison Group. She held senior positions in Talkback Thames, Freemantle Media Group and RTL, before becoming CEO of Shine and then of Foundry. She has been chairman of the Royal Television Society Programme Awards, a non-exec on the Edinburgh International Television Festival, and a member of the government's DCMS advisory panel on the BBC.

Game over for Channel 4 before it starts?

By Raymond Snoddy

There is little in the government's new master plan for Channel 4 to like

The consultation period on the future of Channel 4 closed, dramatically, at 23.45 hours on Tuesday September 14, 2021. Unfortunately, the most interesting question of all was whether there had been any point in taking part, given the government's previously expressed attitude.

As the executive summary of the government's consultation document states unambiguously: 'The government's preferred option is to facilitate a change of ownership of Channel 4,' which is a euphemism for the 'P' word – privatisation.

In his foreword the then Culture Secretary Oliver Dowden, who was replaced by Nadine Dorries in the September 2021 reshuffle, put some flesh on the bare bones of the planned privatisation.

'It is our current view, to be tested through this consultation, that a new ownership model for Channel 4 would be the best means of ensuring its future success and sustainability as a public service broadcaster and its continued contribution to the UK creative industries,' Dowden argued.

He added that there were constraints that come with public ownership and a new owner could bring access and benefits, including access to capital, to strategic partnerships and to international markets. Private investment would also mean more content and more jobs and the channel could be more agile as a result, he argued.

You could be forgiven, therefore, for thinking this is a done deal and the consultation process mere window dressing, particularly as merchant banks are thought to be already lining up for the privatisation fees with a White Paper planned for later this year.

A different, more democratic way?
A truly open process would have set out three equal and perfectly rational options for the future of Channel 4 – maintenance of the status quo, modification of the status quo to give the channel greater freedom to raise capital and own a higher proportion of its programme rights, plus privatisation,

which in such a more balanced context might then have looked like a potentially disruptive tearing up of nearly 40 years of public ownership. Instead the witnesses were led and a sale or privatisation already looked like a *fait accompli*.

This will inevitably seem to some as naïve, but just for a moment set aside all conspiracy theories and take the government at its word that it genuinely believes that 'a new ownership model' would best protect the future of Channel 4 as a public service broadcaster.

After all, it is an incontrovertible fact that national public service broadcasters everywhere are coming under intensifying financial and ratings pressure particularly from the rise of the international streaming giants such as Netflix and Disney+ and the financial power of their subscription bases spread across the world.

It is an equally incontrovertible fact that since 2002 Channel 4's audience share has fallen from 9.8 per cent to 5.9 per cent in 2020. Channel 4's portfolio of channels share has also fallen, but only from 10.6 per cent to 10.1 per cent now – a reasonable performance you might think in the face of such vastly increased competition.

Yet set aside ideology – that Conservatives usually prefer private to public ownership on principle –and former media minister John Whittingdale, replaced in the reshuffle by a fast-rising young woman Julia Lopez, has been in favour of privatising Channel 4 for at least 25 years, and had to be restrained from pushing ahead with it six years ago when he was culture secretary.

For now, forget political malice as a motive and the revenge against a stringent Channel 4 News, coverage in which ministers will not appear regularly and when a melting block of ice was used to represent Johnson when he failed to take part in a leaders' debate on climate change during the last general election campaign.

Also ignore any money that might come to the Treasury as the result of a sale. Accept that the government is sincere in wanting to stick roughly to the channel's existing remit to be diverse and innovative and, above all, broadcast around 208 hours of news a year at peak time plus 208 hours of current affairs (80 at peak) and the sums raised will inevitably be relatively trivial.

Complete with full existing obligations plus custom and practice that does not appear in the channel's licence, Channel 4 could be worth little more than £300m to £500m – say up to £1bn with reduced obligations, although then it might no longer be recognisable as Channel 4.

The key question remaining is whether or not a change of ownership, which the government seems so enthusiastic about, is the best way of protecting the future of Channel 4?

It looks as if the government is determined to impose its 'help' on the channel whether its executives and directors want it or not, and they have made clear this is not the sort of help they think they need.

It still looks like a solution to a problem that either does not exist or appears manageable without a change of ownership.

Sale of the century?

The Channel 4 business will probably produce revenues of more than £1bn this year, after coping well with the pandemic crisis during which, remarkably, it had a record surplus although this was achieved by cutting the channel's programme budget.

The risks of a sale are considerable. Obviously at the moment earnings are ploughed into programme making and a private owner would expect profits. Even if a new owner proved to be benign, and Viacom/CBS has turned out to be good owners of Channel 5, there is always the danger of drift towards greater commercialism. Any weakening of obligations in spirit or in fact would be difficult to define let along overturn by regulation.

The impact on jobs in the creative economy and the supply chain of independent programmes was set out in independent analysis by consultants EY, formerly Ernst and Young, in a September 2021 study commissioned by Channel 4.

EY found that privatisation would cut Channel 4's economic contribution to the supply chain by around 30 per cent, particularly in the nations and regions of the UK. Around £2bn would be transferred from the creative economy and regions to a new private owner as a result, the consultants estimated.

Contradicting the government's optimism on job creation, EY modelling concluded there would be a drop of 26 per cent in jobs overall – as much as 35 per cent outside London and the south east. Smaller independents, particularly outside London, could seriously lose out.

Blowing up Thatcher's experiment?

Such forecasts are serious enough but the greatest risk of all is probably the most intangible. Privatisation could undermine a culture created by a unique experiment, unequalled anywhere in the world, that has proved to be very successful, funding a robust public service broadcaster by commercial means, when C4 was set up in 1982 by Margaret Thatcher's government.

The other major problem with the government approach is that most of the benefits it is claiming can be gained through a 'new ownership model' can already be achieved under public ownership.

Channel 4 has already proved it can be innovative in the digital sphere and recently signed an extensive commercial collaboration agreement with Sky. Other international deals are perfectly possible in future, including with some of the main acquisition candidates.

By coincidence of timing a remarkable example of how swift-footed Channel 4 can be came only three days before the government's consultation ended.

In the government document, one of the arguments advanced for a 'different' ownership model was that Channel 4 would have the ability to invest 'in an agile manner' as a result.

It is difficult to currently think of a more agile broadcaster than Channel 4 when faced with an historic sporting first, the 18-year-old British qualifier

Emma Raducanu reaching the US Open women's final in Flushing Meadows, New York.

Culture secretary Dowden helped by appealing to the owner of the TV rights, Amazon Prime, to make them available to free-to- air television. It was, however, Channel 4, which negotiated a seven-figure deal within 24 hours to broadcast the final in UK prime time, and was rewarded with one of the finest women's tennis matches ever.

A peak of more than 9.2m were able to see the Raducanu victory on the Channel on a Saturday night. Public service in tandem with US media capitalism.

It was the highest audience that Channel 4 had attracted since the London Paralympics in 2012, another bold C4 broadcasting coup that might have left a more commercial, private broadcaster, nervous at the outset.

At the very least the Raducanu broadcasting triumph raises questions about the government's assertion that commercial ownership was necessary to make Channel 4 more agile.

If the government seriously wants to protect the UK's public service broadcasters, including Channel 4, from the advance of the California tech giants, the first step would be to guarantee prominence of their programme guides on all devices.

As for Channel 4, how about giving it access to new capital by increasing its borrowing limits from the present £200m to say £300m? This would be an almost invisible pinprick in the enormous pile of public debt compared with the UK's current total of £2,224bn.

The government could also allow Channel 4 to own more of its programme rights. Other public broadcasters are required to commission at least 25 per cent of their output from independent producers.With C4 it is 100 per cent. How about inverting that percentage in the case of Channel 4 and allow it either to make or own the rights to up to 25 per cent of what it broadcasts?

There are many ways of improving Channel 4's competitive position without the risk of potentially tearing up much of what has made the channel so successful.

Game set and match to ideology

Overall, it is difficult to escape the conclusion that the evidence for the imposition of a new form of ownership on Channel 4 is weak and the outcome potentially damaging not just to Channel 4 but the structure of the UK's public service broadcasting system and the overall British creative economy.

It is also difficult to escape the conclusion that the government motivation rests more with ideology, with political malice as a distinct possibility, than any overwhelming desire to safeguard the future of Channel 4 as a successful public service broadcaster.

For those who thought the risk of a new ownership model is too great to take, and who still suspect that the government approach is being driven by ideology and political pique, it would have been best that they remembered the September 14 deadline for submissions.

The government's mind may already have been made up, but at least it will have been warned of the dangers of potentially undermining one of the more imaginative creations of Margaret Thatcher's time in office.

It is difficult to know what the position of Nadine Dorries on the future of Channel 4 will be, although she has been a trenchant critic of the BBC, even less the views of Julia Lopez.

The working hypothesis still has to be that they will line up behind established government policy in favour of privatisation – although, with fresh eyes, you never know entirely.

About the author

Raymond Snoddy OBE worked on local and regional newspapers, before joining *The Times* in 1971. Five years later he moved to the *Financial Times* and reported on media issues before returning to *The Times* as media editor in 1995. He is now a freelance journalist writing for a range of publications. He is a co-editor of this book.

Unfinished business?

By Stewart Purvis

**Margaret Thatcher may have created the fourth channel, but by 1989
she was prepared to privatise it. She thought she had a better idea – a
merger with Channel 5. Now, more than 30 years on, her vision of a
privately owned Channel 4 – as part of a 'Third Force' to rival the BBC
and ITV – may be about to be realised**

When the Downing Street policy unit wrote to tell Margaret Thatcher in April
1989 that 'the Home Secretary rejects a privatised C4', she scribbled back one
word: 'Why?' When she lost that battle with Douglas Hurd, her policy adviser
wrote: 'As Channel 4 has successfully resisted privatisation, the government
should not hand it over to the broadcasting fraternity for them to run as they
wish'. She endorsed this vigorously with double strokes of her pen. When
Channel 4 pushed back over a new board structure she wrote tersely 'Parliament
decides, not Channel 4.'

Her political secretary throughout this and other broadcasting battles in the
1980s was John Whittingdale, still in his 20s, who worked with her for several
hours a day. By 1996, when John Major was prime minister, Whittingdale was an
MP, asking the DCMS Secretary if he would consider the privatisation of
Channel 4 'at the first opportunity'. By 2015 Whittingdale was the DCMS
Secretary himself. He tried to make privatisation happen. Now, in 2021, it seems
difficult to avoid the conclusion that John Whittingdale, now the former
minister of state for media and data, set out to complete Thatcher's and his own
unfinished business. Ironically, for the second time, he was reshuffled out of his
post before he could complete the task. But so far it appears that this time his
successors will set out to finish the job for him.

The government's document for an 'open consultation' states a preference for
a 'change of ownership of Channel 4'. The ideological core is summed up by
Whittingdale: 'It's worth asking the question why we need two publicly-owned
broadcasters'. In effect he is saying that we can stomach one public intervention
in the broadcasting industry (a BBC restrained as much as possible by its
funding and its Charter) but not two.

Masterclass years

Over the past three decades I've watched this debate mostly from the upper circle but occasionally from the front row of the stalls. The masterclass years were Michael Grade's performances on the party conference fringe when, at over-cooked English breakfasts at fading seaside hotels, the chief executive of Channel 4 would imply but never actually express political sympathy for each different political party. This became a must-see ticket for those invited.

The anti-privatisation cause was helped by influential figures such as Grade's chairman in 1996, the Tory donor Michael Bishop, who sent a 'Dear John' letter to John Major which is credited with seeing off that year's push for privatisation. A decade later Bishop, by then Lord Glendonbrook, was saying 'Britain doesn't need two publicly- owned broadcasters' and Michael Grade, by then Lord Grade, was arguing for privatisation.

Each time the policy debate is re-opened a new rationale is required. The rapid changes in technology have provided regular pegs. Today it is the growth of the 'streamers' such as Netflix, although Channel 4's most recent accounts show that the current model is robust enough to cope with not only multiple digital revolutions but also a global pandemic. Channel 4 is clearly sustainable. Indeed, the current chairman Charles Gurassa says the broadcaster is in 'demonstrably robust financial health', with a 'strong, debt-free balance sheet and access to the capital we need for investment'.

'The last bastion of restrictive practices'

What is different this time is that in order to achieve their ideological goal by finding a buyer, the government may be prepared to sacrifice something very special about C4 that Margaret Thatcher created.

Forty years ago, she saw the creation of a publicly-owned publisher-broadcaster, funded by advertising but not allowed to make its own programmes, as a way of attacking what she called 'the last bastion of restrictive practices': the ITV companies and the technicians' union ACTT.

In her own terms the launch of C4 was a great success not only as an attack on the ITV companies, which eventually lost their advertising monopolies, and the ACTT, which lost its closed shops but more positively because it created a whole new industrial sector of 'independent production' (the 'indies') which had barely existed in television until then.

The UK became a global leader in the production and format market and all these industrial policies were achieved without a penny of public money, while providing the UK audience with some great television. The subsequent new terms of trade that independent producers could keep more rights to the programmes they made strengthened their negotiating arm and the wealth of some owners. The yacht steered by one leading indie arouses great envy amongst broadcasters who commission programmes from him.

The rise and rise of independent production

After nearly 40 years of helping small companies grew and create wealth – how Thatcherite can you get? – the latest data show it still works with many more production companies than any other commercial broadcaster . C4 had 274 across film, tv and digital in 2020 compared to ITV's equivalent of 86 and C5's of 111 in 2019.

As for any off-setting benefit from the arrival of the streamers, Ofcom figures show that in 2018 they produced 182 hours of original UK content compared to a total of 32,000 hours from Channel 4 and the other UK public service broadcasters.

Yet one of the six questions in DCMS's consultation document is 'Should the government remove the publisher-broadcaster restriction to increase Channel 4's ability to diversify its commercial revenue streams?'

The government's reasoning is quite simple: some of those companies who might consider buying C4 – even those who do some business with independent producers – also have their own in-house production companies. Owning Channel 4 would offer new synergies and opportunities for these insiders which they are bound to want to exploit to recover the cost of purchase. Keeping the publisher-broadcaster model intact would inevitably limit the number of bidders and the size of their bids.

Chris Curtis of *Broadcast* magazine points out that if you allow a new C4 player 'to own IP, launch in-house production or expand internationally, you can only do so at the expense of the indie sector. Attempting to stabilise a British broadcaster by undermining British production seems like an odd step'.

When *Broadcast* launched a 'Not 4 Sale' campaign, 100 bosses of indies signed up. John McVay, CEO of their trade body Pact, said: 'I think it's shameful that the public interest doesn't appear at all in this consultation document'. The former Conservative leader in Scotland, Ruth Davidson, said selling off C4 was 'preposterous' and changing its remit risked putting indies out of business. The media analysts, Enders, concluded that if Channel 4's current remit was preserved it posed 'little attraction to a buyer for more than a modest amount' and 'for a profit-oriented buyer, there would be motive and opportunity to game the current remit'.

Does news have a future?

Suddenly the government's rationale for change was becoming a recruiting sergeant for scepticism and opposition. Among the possible 'new freedoms' which the document could be a relaxation of the requirements for news.

In an interview with C4 News' Krishnan Guru-Murthy, John Whittingdale said; 'I like C4 – it has served the purpose it was created to do brilliantly'. But when Guru-Murthy asked him whether C4's obligation to provide an hour of news in prime time a day could change if privatisation went ahead, Whittingdale said: 'I have no preconception that would change.' Less than a reassuring answer.

The Channel 4 licence that sets out that the news obligation could be changed in the same way that Channel 5 is currently asking to change its news schedule. If it came to budget cuts remember no broadcasting regulator has ever intervened to protect a news budget.

On top of all this potential room for post-privatisation flexibility the government has deliberately created a situation where nearly half of the non-executive directorships on the Channel 4 board, including the chairmanship, will be vacant by the end of 2021. Since those directors will appointed by Ofcom 'in agreement with the Secretary of State for Digital, Culture, Media and Sport' the chance will be there for the government to begin to install a board for whom privatisation is a given.

The job of these new directors would not be overseeing the running of a publicly-owned broadcaster or to resist privatisation, it would be to make the transition to a new private owner as smooth as possible.

That likelihood was reinforced when the DCMS added the following words to their job advertisement for new directors: 'We also now invite all candidates to indicate if they have experience of having led or been part of a board stewarding a business through a significant corporate transaction'. I wonder what such a transaction might be.

Return of the 'Third Force'?
Looking back to the 1980s, Margaret Thatcher accepted the original idea of Channel 4 but then thought she had a better idea. In a Downing Street document from October 1988 she indicated her support for the creation of a 'Third Force' to rival the BBC and ITV by 'combining C4 and C5'.

The fifth channel had not yet been licensed but the prime minister was already looking ahead. The Broadcasting White Paper of 1988 floated the idea but nothing came of it.

However, it could just be one of the outcomes of this review. The consultation document points out that 'Channel 5 has thrived following its sale to ViacomCBS' and some see the American company as the most likely bidder. Tory MP Andrew Griffith, an adviser to Whittingdale when in office, appears to want C4 to merge with ITV, C5 or Sky and a 'glide path' away from the current terms of trade.

If that happens Margaret Thatcher's ambition may finally be realised by John Whittingdale but her most valued TV legacy, this 'creative greenhouse' as C4 once called it, the 'R&D' lab of UK television, will disappear.

This article first appeared in the September 2021 edition of the British Journalism Review.

About the author
Stewart Purvis has been connected with Channel 4 for much of its history as editor of Channel Four News, ITN chief executive, Channel 4 consultant and a non-executive director of Channel 4 for the seven and half years ending in May 2021. He has also been Ofcom partner for content and standards, Visiting Professor of Broadcast Media at

Oxford University, the first Professor of Television Journalism at City University, London and advisor to the House of Lords committee on communications.

What price Channel 4? The long history of attempts to privatise it

By Maggie Brown

Can the challenge of privatisation inspire reform and a better service for viewers, or will it result this time in a sale to a private owner? Can past battles and positive responses, which allowed Channel 4 to plough its distinctive path since 1982, be a guide to the future?

In the process of writing Channel 4's history I've noted two patterns weaving their way through the four decades.

The first is the questioning of its strange publicly-owned status, which started bubbling away in 1988 as it found its feet. It is a threat that has never subsided but never delivered. The second is my dawning recognition that the small scale and no-jobs-for-life model has an inbuilt ability to refresh itself, which works. There have been seven chief executives so far.

Not one since founder Jeremy Isaacs has there been an internal candidate. It is clear this combination of threat and turnover can (usually) be a key strength.

There have been four attempts to privatise Channel 4 counting this one, all put in train by Conservative governments, kick started by Margaret Thatcher in 1988.

The link?

John Whittingdale, the Conservative MP for Maldon, Essex, is the link between the other three, including this, the most serious to date.

Channel 4 was founded by Thatcher's regime but she never loved it. Anthony Smith, the brains behind the victory which beat ITV's claim, to make an ITV 2 was able to convince Sir Keith Joseph that a publisher-broadcaster would inspire enterprising small new media businesses – living out the Tory manifesto. This spawned the UK's independent production industry, within a decade that became an organised lobby, now growing from a national to global force.

The infant fourth channel was under the protection of regulator the Independent Broadcasting Authority, holding shares on behalf of the public. Start-up costs (around £200m) and annual income were provided and guaranteed by the ITV companies, which in return sold C4's commercial breaks until 1993. This early model was a far cry from today's Channel 4, battling for ratings and revenue.

Round one

In the run up to the 1990 Broadcasting Act Channel 4 privatisation was seriously debated for the first time. Justin Dukes, deputy chief executive to Isaacs was a firm supporter of it, as was Michael Grade, briefly, until he succeeded Isaacs.

But high-level political lobbying resulted in an outcome less harmful than might have occurred in that decade of huge media shake ups. Thatcher, after rounding on the BBC, then moved on ITV, imposing a destructive highest-bidder auction for their franchises. She chaired the cabinet committee on broadcasting that decided the terms of the 1990 Act.

Channel 4's fight took place largely in private meetings with top decision makers away from the newspapers, 'not to mention a number of trips through the dustbins of Downing Street,' said Grade. I was shown the range of six options for change (not published at the time), which Channel 4 drew up as early as 1988, recognising it had to save itself. The initiative worked.

That Act took a moderate path as far as Channel 4 was concerned: it was not required to bid competitively for its licence, it was not sold off, the programme remit was technically unchanged. It was regulated by the new Independent Television Commission.

The key was winning the right to sell its own advertising from 1993, which also commercialised the culture. But it was forced to pay ITV for a guarantee against trading losses (which never occurred), a rough repayment scheme for its 1980s start up support. That ended in 1999.

That 1988-1990 campaign was headed by C4's chair, Sir Richard Attenborough, a master charmer who hit it off with Thatcher, as did his deputy, industrialist Sir George Russell (he organised the retiling of Number 10's kitchen). Michael Grade oversaw a more 'professional' Channel 4 schedule (bespoke children's programmes an early casualty) and recruited a skilled advertising force.

This is the first, biggest adaptation galvanised by a privatisation threat. Channel 4 morphed into a self-reliant broadcaster devising a golden ad formula based on younger audiences, and upmarket viewers. The surplus funded the Horseferry Road HQ. *Film 4* took off.

Airline entrepreneur Sir Michael Bishop was hand-picked by Attenborough as his successor. A committed Conservative and friend of Prime Minister John Major

Round two

The second attempt to privatise Channel 4 occurred in 1996. John Whittingdale, a former aide to Thatcher attempted to insert a clause into the Digital Broadcasting Act to do it.

Bishop believed privatisation was 'only a whisker away' because the government was desperate for cash. A price tag of £1bn was mooted. He wrote a private Dear John letter, with Grade's approval. This argued that 'Channel 4 is not a suitable case for this treatment.'

Noting the downmarket poor content 'of the vast majority of satellite television and increasingly similar trend within the ITV network it is only too clear what happens when conventional shareholder pressures are applied to the TV industry,' he wrote. 'Quality and choice are diminished. For Channel 4, with new shareholders seeking to maximise profits, money for dividends would have to be taken directly from the screen, at viewers' expense.

'Second, an important qualification for privatisation has been the targeted corporation required access to government funding. Channel 4 has never required or sought financial support from the government. I believe such a philistine approach towards an organisation that has contributed to bringing the arts, music, education, film and current affairs to a vast new wider audience at no cost to the public purse would elicit widespread condemnation(including) strong supporters of the government'.

'We canned it,' Bishop said. But he knew much of Channel 4's programming did not serve such elevated tastes. ITV called it derisively 'Channel Three and a Half' for abandoning its remit with bad taste shows.

Bishop's team scouted for fresh creative leadership and digital channel experience and in 1997 appointed Michael Jackson, the third chief executive. He had run BBC2 with aplomb. Jackson introduced a drastic overhaul, new waves of comedy including Ali G, classic 8pm programmes including *Grand Designs,* cricket and…. *Big Brother.*

The lesson from 1996 again underscored top-level access to decision makers, a protective regulator and producer/advertiser allies. Channel 4 survived as a statutory corporation, erased from the 'red book' of privatisation. In July 1996 Tony Blair pledged in writing: 'Channel 4 is a success and I believe it would be wrong to place in jeopardy its achievements by privatising it.' (Channel 4 was also required in 1999 to re-commit to the programmes including religion, education, current affairs and multi-cultural).

Labour was in power 1997-2010 and, with the 2003 Communications Act, introduced a liberalising agenda under powerful regulator Ofcom which pushed the public service broadcasters beyond digital channels into online, introducing data based PSB reviews, deregulation beyond news and current affairs, bestowing ownership of IP-programme rights to independent producers (hitting C4 hard).

Channel 4 experienced the full blast of competition and sudden advertising downturns in 2001 and 2008. It began a begging bowl strategy which failed. Kevin Lygo, the inspiring programme director offset *Big Brother's* sprawl with large dollops of fresh programming. Andy Duncan, the fifth chief executive, finessed digital expansion and the venture into 4 on demand (4OD), but failed with radio and was sacked in 2009.

Round three

David Abraham, the first CEO to have run an American network and an advertising agency founder, was selected to succeed him because of his organised business approach. His first act in 2010 was a (failed) bid for Channel 5. He then threw himself into 'self-help', mining audience data to drive digital and targeted advertising and All4.

Any threat of privatisation was neutralised in 2010 because David Cameron's coalition relied on the Lib-Dems who pledged support for Channel 4's status quo. But C4 was on red alert from 2014 onwards as the 2015 election neared. Chair Lord Burns drew up a scheme to turn it into a public trust.

Round four

Cameron's 2015 outright victory saw John Whittingdale appointed Culture Secretary. By September 2015 his ambition to privatise Channel 4 was out in the open, though this was not an election pledge.

Whittingdale instantly dismissed the Burns plan and launched a review of Channel 4's business in November. An irate Abraham called in the external company lawyer to remind board members of their loyalty to Channel 4. The new C4 chairman, Charles Gurassa, decided the C4 model worked. Cameron resigned after the Brexit referendum and incoming prime minister Theresa May changed tack fast and C4 became part of a levelling up industrial strategy.

Karen Bradley, MP became Culture Secretary. The compromise agreed in 2017 is the current partial move out of London, which Abraham failed to seal, finished by outsider successor Alex Mahon doing the final negotiations and reorganisation.

Now for the knockout blow?

When Boris Johnson won the 2019 general election with an 80-strong majority Channel 4 was back on the agenda. Whittingdale, was appointed Culture and Data Minister, prepared the ground with a formidable ally, Conservative MP, Andrew Griffith, former chief operating officer at Sky Television.

Whittingdale had polished arguments for Channel 4 being too small to survive, rushed a consultation over the 2021 summer holidays and is minded to seek change. Though he was removed from government in the September 2021 reshuffle.

Lessons from history are clear. All is not lost. Channel 4 has millions of fans who watch its programmes.

There is fierce opposition from independent producers with the rallying call 'kick up as much fuss as you can.' The model is seen by this powerful lobby as the best way of delivering funds to invest in the successful production sector.

Some Conservative MPs are highly critical, and the House of Lords has engaged in the debate. Defenders of public service broadcasting from Church of England bishops to the Voice of the Listener and Viewer are springing to the defence. The rush to legislation can be slowed.

Channel 4 has moved to defuse the stand-off between Channel 4 News and the Conservatives. In a detailed rebuttal on September 6, after a successful Paralympics, Mahon launched a detailed new strategy to fend off privatisation, including its financial strength and a list of initiatives, including new spending on remit programmes. But she has kept the temperature deliberately low.

Channel 4 now needs to buttress its opposition with new hits. Programmes that make you think, content that has a reminder of its special DNA. It has been done before.

About the author

Maggie Brown is a media journalist and historian. She is a Bristol University history graduate with a postgraduate journalism MA from Cardiff University School of Journalism. Her career includes roles at the *Birmingham Post & Mail*, Reuters, and *The Guardian*. She was a founder of *The Independent* 1986 where she was its first media editor and then a contributor to *Media Guardian, The Observer, PR Week, Media Week*, and *The Stage*. She is the author of *A Licence to be Different: The Story of Channel 4 2007* and *Channel 4: A History from Big Brother to the Great British Bake Off 2021*.

The case for privatisation
By David Elstein

Channel 4 was always a cultural, rather than a business, opportunity. Is the wool being pulled over our eyes in the great Channel 4 privatisation debate? Are the facts not being allowed to spoil a good story?

Let's deal with the simple issues first. Are there any buyers for Channel 4 out there, and what would they pay?

It would be pointless for any potential acquirers to show their hand before a White Paper or sale proposal is published. But in theory, each of *ITV, STV, Sky, Viacom or Discovery* might be interested and – depending on the terms of any actual contract – might be prepared to pay up to £1bn or even more.

Would viewers actually notice a difference from a change of ownership? That would depend in part on the specifics of a sale contract, but given that even under the present ownership at least 100 new programmes appear in the schedule every year, change is inevitable.

The more complex issue is why, after so many failed attempts, the government should want to privatise Channel 4, and why it might think it would succeed, especially after the entire Department for Culture, Media and Sport ministerial team was removed in the September cabinet re-shuffle.

The stated view from ministers was, before they were all removed, that Channel 4 has too narrow a revenue base – primarily TV advertising, which is in long-term decline – to compete with fast-growing subscription services like Netflix in securing the most high-profile projects. To some extent, Channel 4 agrees: it recognises that its major strategic risk is in competing for the best content and talent.

How much such a risk matters is open to debate. Certainly, Channel 4 is right to claim that it is no immediate danger. As we saw last year, even during a savage downturn in advertising, it can simply cut its programme budget: so much so that it actually reported a £74m surplus by year-end, and even an uptick in audience share.

The remit

But that downside resilience also exposed Channel 4's Achilles heel. Despite slashing programming costs by 23 per cent – £138m – it still claimed to have 'fulfilled its remit', so confirming what has been obvious to some of us for many years: the famous remit is as long (or short) as a piece of string, and has been ever since the Communications Act of 2003 created a new media regulator, Ofcom, and in the process abolished almost all the old programme quotas that the old ITC had enforced with some rigour.

The most damning statistic in Channel 4's latest annual report was that repeats took up 70 per cent of its schedule: something unthinkable in the pre-2003 days, when the maximum permissible was 40 per cent. In 2012, the figure was 52 per cent; in 2016 56 per cent. So lax is the remit that in theory repeats could constitute 95 per cent of the schedule, and there is nothing Ofcom could do about it.

Remit core and cost

The only 'hard' obligations are for 4 hours a week of peak time news, and the same amount of current affairs, of which only half has to be in peak (and one-third of which is currently repeats).

There are a number of 'percentage quotas', but there is no fixed baseline against which to measure them. Apart from that, the remit consists of aspirations: Channel 4 chooses these, and decides for itself whether it has met them. They are unquantified and unenforceable. The remit could be fulfilled at a cost of less than £50m a year. That would not scare a maiden aunt, let alone the likes of Sky, Viacom, Discovery or ITV.

Some people like to say of Channel 4 that 'it costs us nothing'. Of course, that is not true. Apart from £200-300m of Treasury subsidy of Channel 4's launch costs and of its own launches of failed businesses, the channel has always enjoyed privileged access to gifted terrestrial spectrum, as well as precious prominence on electronic programme guides. Although the value of spectrum and prominence has faded, the benefit from them has probably averaged £20-30m a year since launch, or perhaps £800m.

For many years, these benefits were justified by Channel 4's output of public service content: seven hours a week of education, three hours a week of multicultural programming, 330 hours a year of schools and one hour a week of religion, in addition to the obligatory news and current affairs output. On top of those licence requirements, the channel also supplied six hours a week of documentaries and five hours of arts.

After the passage of the 2003 Act, as most of the fixed quotas disappeared, so too did the programmes they were meant to protect. Schools were shuffled off to video, and multicultural content, such that remained, subsumed under the heading of 'diversity' (alongside sexuality, disability and any religion that might sneak into the schedule: none of it prescribed in terms of volume). Arts programmes, once so prominent, became a rarity.

Education – once at the core of the schedule, representing 15 per cent of the channel budget – is now allocated just half a percent of the budget, which delivers some 18 hours of content a year, half of it, inexplicably, accounted for by the teen drama, *Ackley Bridge*. The 2003 Act calls for Channel 4 to make a 'significant contribution of programmes of an educational nature and other programmes of educational value'. Ofcom seems – like Channel 4 itself – to have lost sight of this statutory obligation.

Bizarrely, until recently, Channel 4 claimed in its annual reports to be broadcasting more than 50 hours a week of education: an absurd and false boast that induced no comment from Ofcom – nor from other oversight bodies, including parliamentary committees.

How many suppliers? What is PSB?

This is not the only example of Channel 4 misleading the public. Its references in its annual reports to working with more than 300 'producers' every year has persuaded unwary commentators to believe that this refers to qualifying independent producers: the category of supplier from which Channel 4 (and other terrestrial broadcasters) is required to source at least 25 per cent of its commissions. For the last five years, this figure has fluctuated between 160 and 170. The '300' includes an assortment of 'producers': but of fillers and promotions, not actual programmes.

Another claim in the latest annual report is that the schedule for the youth-oriented sibling channel, E4 includes 'original commissions and acquisitions'. There are almost no first-run original commissions, and even the repeats of such series as *Gogglebox* are heavily outnumbered by US comedies. Fifty episodes a week of *The Big Bang Theory* is by no means unusual.

If Channel 4 were a food manufacturer, it would face prosecution under the Trade Descriptions Act. E4 is also in permanent breach of the most basic Ofcom requirement, that its schedule comprise at least 50 per cent European works.

Channel 4 tries to conceal how far it has drifted from its original public service role by claiming a figure for investment in public service content that is inflated by including drama and comedy: never previously considered by any regulator a public service category (they are news, current affairs, regional, education, children's, arts, religion and documentaries). The true figure is about £80m a year, or 12 per cent of its total content budget.

Given the halving of Channel 4's audience share in the last decade, such expenditure delivers about one minute a day of public service content consumption by the average adult. These days, Channel 4 makes little obeisance in the direction of public service: its mission statement is 'change the world through entertainment'. It claims that *The Great British Bake Off* should be classified as public service content!

What is to be gained by a new owner?

It may seem paradoxical, but in practice, ministers can only re-impose control on Channel 4, tighten up its obligations, and make them legally enforceable by selling the broadcaster to a private owner, binding it by contract to comply or face financial penalties. It is pointless fining a publicly owned body.

The key incentive for a buyer is the scale of synergies available from acquiring a standalone broadcaster. It has been obvious for decades that Channel 4's standalone business model is inherently inefficient, with annual savings of between £100m and £200m available from merging back office functions with another broadcaster.

Channel 4's employees currently cost on average £100,000 a year each: by far the most expensive in the media industry. The top 792 cost over £110,000 each. With hundreds of people in finance, marketing, IT, transmission and corporate affairs, the room for savings is extensive. The programming department is ten times larger than its equivalent at Five.

The board of Channel 4 seems oblivious to potential savings. Indeed, last year, when the programme budget was slashed by 23 per cent in the face of a temporary loss of advertising, the staff payroll rose from nine per cent of total costs to 11 per cent. When board members tell us that privatisation will lead to a trade-off between profits/dividends and 'the remit', they ignore the huge opportunities for internal savings. As for 'the remit', knowledge of its tenuous nature does not deter the chairman from warning the government of his board's concern that uncertainty over privatisation might affect its ability to 'deliver the remit'. Really.

Indies and the C4 PSB

Channel 4 and its main lobbyists, the independent production sector, seem to believe that private ownership and public service delivery are incompatible. Yet ITV has been privately owned since its inception 65 years ago, and during the 1980s and 1990s delivered vastly more public service content than Channel 4 currently offers. The issue is not ownership, but regulation.

It is, of course, ironic that independent producers, all of which are privately-owned, profit-seeking enterprises, should assume the worst of private ownership, going so far as to condemn potential buyers of Channel 4 as 'profit-maximising' (a boo word also used by Channel 4 itself). How many indies would admit to cutting quality in order to increase profits? How many would expect to stay in business by alienating their customers in doing so?

One leading creative has warned that 'as soon as we privatise Channel 4 everything will be about what can attract American money'. One might ask him: is the schedule of privately-owned ITV driven by American money? Is there the slightest evidence that Five – which is American-owned – is driven by American money?

This kind of wolf-crying is also to be found in Channel 4 public statements, such as that claiming the nation's TV production sector would face 'irreversible' damage from privatisation. Why would a new owner reduce the number of programmes produced (even assuming the sale contract did not forbid that)?

As it happens, Channel 4 commissions currently amount to well under 10 per cent of the production sector's turnover. Even if we just focus on qualifying independents (those not controlled by other media companies), last year, Channel 4 spent just £155m with them. Even if ITV were to buy Channel 4, and replace some of the output currently sourced from independents with in-house productions, qualifying independents would still be protected by the 25 per cent quota.

To what extent competitive tension between potential bidders allows ministers to extract desirable programme commitments as part of a sale process remains to be seen. Ring-fencing the news budget and introducing an independent news supervisory board (as was required before Comcast's bid for Sky was approved) should be a high priority.

Other objectives could be a quota for smaller independents within the 25 per cent minimum; a restoration of real public service content requirements; a strict limit on repeats; minimum levels of spend on programming; minimum levels of spending in the nations and regions; and perhaps a quota for companies owned by ethnic minorities. Scrutiny of performance by the National Audit Office should be annual; and escalating financial penalties should be built into the contract to punish non-compliance with its terms.

Look to a bright future

Privatisation offers an opportunity to correct the flaws in the Channel 4 business model; extract the synergies that Channel has failed to deliver (or even pursue); deploy those extra resources to strengthen the channel's output; put more emphasis on public service content; and perhaps use the proceeds of a sale to revitalise public service broadcasting more broadly (as the Conservatives pledged when they proposed privatisation 20 years ago).

Not to give every opportunity for that better outcome to prevail would be a serious dereliction of duty.

About the author

David Elstein was a leading activist in the 1970s and 1980s in campaigning for the fourth channel to be allocated to a publisher/broadcaster owned by the IBA, rather than to ITV for a junior service. After Channel 4 was launched, his production company became one of its main suppliers. He subsequently became Director of Programmes at Thames TV, Head of Programming at BSkyB and launch CEO of Channel Five. He has been chairman of the British Screen Advisory Council, the National Film and Television School, Open Democracy and the Broadcasting Policy Group.

A bad idea whose time may have come

By Patrick Barwise

Privatising Channel 4 has been proposed and rejected many times, most recently in 2016. It is opposed by C4 itself, all the relevant stakeholder groups and many Conservatives. But the government seems determined to push it through regardless

In 2016, the Cameron government dropped the idea of privatising Channel 4 when it realised that the proceeds would be small, the claimed benefits largely illusory, and privatisation would risk damaging UK independent producers and weakening C4's delivery of its public service programming remit.[1] All these factors still apply today.

I was directly involved in 2016 as co-author[2] of a report for C4 on the likely consequences if it were privatised.[3] We focused on the investment case for a prospective (media or telecoms) buyer. This investment case drives the potential proceeds and other likely impacts of privatising C4.

The potential proceeds and the government's dilemma

Assuming a buyer (i) able to extract some synergies[4] and (ii) willing to honour C4's public service programming remit, we estimated a maximum price in 2016 of £400-500m – a drop in the ocean. The equivalent figure today might be even lower because technology and market trends have reduced the value of free-to-air commercial broadcasters, while telecoms companies – among the potential buyers in 2016 – are now, rightly, moving out of TV.[5]

Our £400-500m included £220-225m from raiding C4's cash reserves and squeezing its suppliers, mainly independent producers, by paying them later. Excluding these questionable sources of 'value', the likely proceeds while still honouring the remit would have been only £200-300m. Anything much above that would have to come from getting more 'bang for the buck' (revenue per pound) from C4's content budget by getting around its public service programming remit. We identified seven ways in which its new owner could do this, by reallocating its content budget:

1. From UK commissions to (mostly US) acquisitions;

2. From loss-making to profitable genres, especially during peak viewing hours;

3. From programmes developed for UK viewers to those with international appeal;[6]

4. From newer, riskier programmes to safer, more mainstream ones, with longer runs and more repeats;

5. From finding and nurturing new talent to mostly working with established talent;

6. From commissioning from hundreds of independent producers of all sizes across the UK to using fewer, bigger, mainly London-based suppliers;

7. From paying the full first-run cost of new commissions to deficit financing (as well as paying later).

All of these would conflict with C4's mission and role within the UK broadcasting ecology, especially outside London.[7] Assuming the government wishes to prevent them, it will need to make C4's remit more quantifiable and enforceable.[8] However, its dilemma was and is that *to attract a suitable buyer, it will almost certainly need to abandon, or significantly weaken, C4's publisher-broadcaster model and public service programming remit and how strictly the latter is enforced.*[9]

Depending on who the buyer is, the synergies and savings may now be somewhat more than we estimated in 2016. But there are no credible scenarios in which the privatisation proceeds are material, i.e. billions of pounds.

C4's unique – Conservative-developed[10] – model has worked well for almost 40 years: at minimal cost to the taxpayer,[11] it broadcasts universally available, free-to-air programmes; provides creative competition to the other public service broadcasters (PSBs) and a home for alternative voices and new ideas;[12] supports independent producers of all sizes across the UK; and gives advertisers additional ways to reach younger and minority viewers. All with just 900 employees, with more than 30 per cent already based outside London.[13]

Why would a Conservative government put all this irreversibly at risk?[14]
The main claimed reason is that C4's model is said to be no longer sustainable because of ever-growing competition: for *viewers*, from subscription video on demand (SVoD) and social media; and for *advertising*, mainly from Facebook and Google.[15] But these trends were already well known in 2016 and, despite them, C4 keeps defying the doomsayers, delivering its remit, winning awards and still covering its costs.[16] And, anyway, a commercial owner would be *less* committed to the remit as it would need to maximise the return on its investment.

The government says privatisation would give C4 access to capital to invest in the (presumably profitable[17]) digital innovation it needs to adapt to these challenges. But C4 hasn't asked for its £200m borrowing limit to be raised – and, if it did, its current owner, the UK government, has better and cheaper capital market access than any potential acquirer.

Media minister (until the September 2021 reshuffle) John Whittingdale[18] has revealed the real problem here: the Treasury's refusal to let C4 borrow more because it would – *very* marginally – increase reported public sector borrowing.

If true, this is economic madness, unless Treasury officials really believe that a privatised C4 would automatically be better at generating and executing digital investment opportunities – somewhat implausible, since C4 is currently *ahead* of the private-sector commercial PSBs (ITV, C5 and STV) in digital development.[19] It means the government is refusing to give C4 the capital the same government says C4 needs for essential, profitable investment, while simultaneously saying the number one benefit of C4 privatisation will be access to capital! Confused or what?

Similarly, the suggestion that privatisation might enable ITV and C4 to cut costs by combining their advertising sales operations[20] wrongly assumes that this could not happen with C4 still in public ownership. Combining the ITV and C4 sales operations may or may not be a good idea[21] but this has little if anything to do with C4 privatisation.

In fact, *none* of the claimed privatisation benefits[22] actually requires C4 to be privatised!

Policy is often about striking a balance between different views and stakeholders. But in this case the government has achieved the rare distinction of being opposed not only by what it might see as the usual suspects,[23] but also by many Conservatives,[24] reputable independent analysts such as Enders Analysis,[25] C4 itself,[26] and groups representing all three sets of stakeholders: VLV (viewers),[27] Pact (independent producers)[28] and ISBA (advertisers).[29] It's certainly rare for a policy proposal to be opposed by groups representing *all* the affected parties.[30]

If privatising C4 is a bad idea, why might its time have come?

But if privatising C4 is such a bad idea, why do I think '[its] time may have come'? Four possible reasons.

First, Covid has badly hit the public finances. The Treasury has never been sympathetic to public service broadcasting.[31] It won't worry much about C4's remit if selling it off might raise, say, half a billion – a mere rounding error in the national accounts,[32] but 'every little helps' and there are doubtless bankers talking up the potential value in the hope of earning some fees.

Second, the proposal may be payback for C4's perceived hostility to the prime minster.[33] In 2019, Dorothy Byrne, C4's then head of news and current affairs, described him as a 'known liar'[34] and then C4 News replaced both him and Brexit party leader Nigel Farage with melting ice sculptures when they refused to appear with the other party leaders in a climate change debate.[35]

Third, it may be part of the PM's wider culture war, led by his senior advisors, power couple Dougie Smith and Munira Mirza.[36] According to well-placed sources, ministers such as former culture secretary Oliver Dowden are 'not blowing a dog whistle, it's a Dougie whistle. We're all culture warriors now' and

'Dougie has Dowden on a string.'[37] The government's 'war on woke' seems unlikely to abate under Dowden's successor Nadine Dorries, an enthusiastic culture warrior.[38]

Finally, privatising C4 has long been a pet project of the now former media minister John Whittingdale. In 2015, when – as Culture Secretary – he last proposed it, his media special advisor was Carrie Symonds, now married to the PM. Whittingdale and Mrs Johnson are said to be still in touch, so perhaps the idea now has another inside track at Number Ten, in addition to 'Dougira'.

The government's consultation

By the time you read this, the government *may* have published the results of its consultation on this matter. I say 'may' for two reasons. First, the Johnson government is strikingly resistant to independent democratic checks and transparency.[39] Typically, the advice it will be receiving from its Public Service Broadcasting Advisory Panel will remain confidential. Secondly, the evidence is that it has already made up its mind to privatise C4 regardless and has, therefore, actively sought both to bias the consultation responses and to minimise their number:

- The consultation is being run over just ten weeks over the school summer holiday;
- The consultation document doesn't even mention that privatisation has been repeatedly rejected, most recently just five years ago by a Conservative government, and says nothing about what has changed since then to justify reviving the idea now. Instead, it absurdly focuses on how much has changed *since C4's launch in 1982*, giving the clear – highly misleading – impression that this is the first time privatisation has been considered, when in reality it has been looked at and rejected many times;
- The consultation questions are mostly worded to encourage pro-privatisation responses;[40]
- Every question asks respondents to provide 'supporting evidence' with their response, the implication being that the views of those unable to provide such evidence won't be given much weight. As far as I know, this is unprecedented in a public consultation.

Privatising Channel 4 has been proposed many times, most recently in 2016, and always rejected because of the damaging likely consequences. It is opposed by C4 itself, all the relevant stakeholder groups and many Conservatives. But, at the time of writing (September 2021) the signs are that the government plans to force it through regardless. By the time you read this, you should know the outcome.

Notes

[1] As a 'publisher-broadcaster', C4 commissions most of its programmes from UK independent producers, supplemented by selected acquisitions such as *Walter Presents* foreign language drama series. Its remit prioritises innovative programmes for younger and more diverse audiences, using the financial surplus from popular hits such as *The Great British Bake Off* and *Gogglebox* to subsidise *C4 News* and other loss-making public service programmes.

[2] With Dr Gillian Brooks (then at Oxford University, now at King's College London).

[3] Patrick Barwise and Gillian Brooks, *The Consequences of Privatising Channel Four*, Channel Four, May 2016, https://www.channel4.com/media/documents/press/news/Desktop/Barwise_final%204May'16.pdf. Chapter 4 in the 2016 section of this volume summarises our analysis of the likely impact on UK independent producers.

[4] Cost synergies, revenue synergies (cross-selling etc) and 'soft' synergies (exploiting C4's relationships with other parties).

[5] It's been suggested that now is a good time to revisit privatisation because broadcasters are consolidating to combine their programme libraries. But C4 isn't allow to own content rights, so it doesn't have a programme library. And if, to attract buyers, ministers drop or water down this part of its remit, that will risk seriously damaging the independent producers.

[6] Especially if, as the Government seems to be planning, C4's 'publisher-broadcaster' model is abandoned or weakened, allowing it for the first time to retain foreign rights in the programmes it commissions.

[7] EY estimates that privatising C4 would lead to a reduction of up to 26 per cent in the number of jobs in its UK supply chain, rising to 35 per cent in the nations and regions: EY, *Assessing the impact of a change of ownership of Channel 4*, September 2021, report commissioned by C4.

[8] Claire Enders, Tom Harrington and Abi Watson, *Channel 4 privatisation: Valuation, buyers, problems* [2021-085], Enders Analysis, 1 September 2021.

[9] It may also need to reassure prospective buyers about C4's future prominence and the length of its licence, and that it will not introduce new restrictions on TV advertising (eg for gambling sites or HFSS foods): ibid.

[10] C4 was launched by Margaret Thatcher and Home Secretary Willie Whitelaw in 1982 to offer competition to the BBC and ITV.

[11] In return for its public service commitments, C4 – like the other PSBs (BBC, ITV, C5 and STV) – benefits from free spectrum and EPG prominence, both of which have a continuing opportunity cost to the Treasury. Privatising it would, presumably, not affect these privileges. David Elstein notes that establishing C4 also cost the taxpayer roughly £200m in the 1980s (setup costs and foregone revenue from the ITV levy) and that the Treasury then lost an additional £84m from its share of the cost of C4's failed new ventures. (David Elstein, 'There's no good reason to stop a sale of Channel 4', *Daily Telegraph*, 22 July 2021 and Chapter 7 in the 2021 section of this volume). However, these historic sunk costs, too, are irrelevant to the current privatisation question, which is about future costs, benefits and risks.

[12] Such as its transformative coverage of the Paralympics since 2012.

[13] This proportion is set to grow as more staff move to, or are recruited in, C4's new offices in Leeds, Bristol, Glasgow and Manchester.

[14] Especially since C4 privatisation was not mentioned in the 2019 Conservative Manifesto.

[15] *Consultation on a sale of Channel 4 Television Corporation*, DCMS, 6 July 2021 https://www.gov.uk/government/consultations/consultation-on-a-change-of-ownership-of-channel-4-television-corporation/consultation-on-a-potential-change-of-ownership-of-channel-4-television-corporation.

[16] Despite Covid, it reported excellent results for 2020, including an 11 per cent increase in digital advertising revenue: https://www.channel4.com/press/news/channel-4-annual-report-2020-record-financial-surplus-and-significant-digital-growth. This was *before* the recent recovery in TV advertising, which is expected to continue through 2022 and beyond: Omar Oakes, 'AA/Warc upgrades UK ad market forecast to record 18% growth', *Mediatel News*, 29 July 2021.

[17] 'Presumably profitable' because why else would the new owner make these investments?

[18] Interviewed by Damian Tambini at the Oxford Media Convention, 19 July 2021.

[19] Tom Harrington, Abi Watson and Jamie McGowan Stuart, *Channel 4: Privatisation, here we go again* [2021-067], Enders Analysis, 22 June 2021. See also Tom Harrington, Jamie McGowan Stuart and Gill Hind, *ITV H1 results: Back to 2019* [2021-076], Enders Analysis, 2 August 2021.

[20] Andrew Griffith MP, Fireside Chat with Claire Enders, 13 July 2021. Enders Analysis, https://vimeo.com/570235165/0b83cbea2d.

[21] There would be cost savings and the combined operation would be better placed to compete against Google and Facebook. But it would have a dominant market share of around 70 per cent of UK TV advertising, raising difficult issues of market definition and market power. There is also no guarantee that ITV would be the highest bidder for C4 in an auction with a level playing field. Similar comments would apply to combining the Sky sales operation (the only other sales point) with C4's, with the additional issue that Sky is now part of the US media giant Comcast.

[22] Strategic partnerships and acquisitions, international expansion, 'agile' investment, revenue diversification. See page 6 of the consultation document.

[23] Such as the opposition parties (Dame Angela Eagle MP, Westminster Hall debate, 21 July 2021, https://www.parallelparliament.co.uk/mp/angela-eagle/debate/Commons/2021-07-21/debates/4144D532-677E-4F33-BA29-DA389645D941/Channel4Privatisation) and 38 Degrees (https://you.38degrees.org.uk/petitions/stop-the-privatisation-of-channel-4).

[24] Karen Bradley, 'Channel 4 means more to the British people than an empty sell-off', *The Times*, 26 July 2021; Ruth Davidson, 'No Tory should want to privatise Channel Four', *Daily Telegraph*, 8 July 2021. See also Andrew Mitchell MP and Sir Peter Bottomley MP, Westminster Hall debate, op cit.

[25] Tom Harrington, Abi Watson and Jamie McGowan Stuart, op. cit.

[26] Christopher Williams, 'Channel 4 attacks government's "very harmful" privatisation plans', *The Telegraph*, 20 July 2021.

[27] *Channel 4 Privatisation Briefing: Putting Profit Before Public Service?*, Voice of the Listener & Viewer, August 2021.

[28] *Pact statement on Government review of Channel 4 ownership*, Pact, 23 June 2021.

[29] Hannah Bowler and Alex Farber, 'Major advertising body pans C4 privatisation', *Broadcast*, 30 July 2021.

[30] Obviously, proposals to cut public funding are always opposed by the directly affected stakeholder groups. But the Government claims that its aim in privatising C4 is to *benefit* it and its stakeholders.

[31] As Voice of the Listener & Viewer has shown, the 2010 and 2015 funding deals imposed on the BBC by Chancellor George Osborne had, by 2019, already cut its real public funding by 30 per cent – far more than most people realise – in a market with rising real content costs, bid up by the likes of Netflix and Amazon: https://www.vlv.org.uk/news/vlv-research-shows-a-30-decline-in-bbc-public-funding-since-2010/. The Government is now said to be planning a further cut in the BBC's much reduced real funding over the next five years: Steven Swinford, 'Ministers reject plea for licence fee to keep up with inflation', *The Times*, 31 August 2021; Enders Analysis (In Brief), *BBC licence fee settlement: A diminished TV ecology*, 10 September 2021 discusses the likely negative impact on the wider UK TV ecology. With annual inflation now running at 3-4 per cent, the cumulative impact of any further licence fee freeze will be hugely damaging.

[32] Enough to buy 1.6 miles of the HS2 line or 2.6 F35B Lightning planes (but, in both cases, with no contribution to operating costs): Nils Pratley, 'At £307m per mile of track, can the cost of HS2 be justified?', *The Guardian*, 3 February 2020; https://www.forces.net/news/what-you-need-know-about-f-35b.

[33] Ben Woods, 'Channel 4 goes to war over privatisation plan', *Daily Telegraph*, 23 June 2021, https://www.telegraph.co.uk/business/2021/06/27/channel-4s-battle-remain-independent/.

[34] That the PM is indeed a 'known liar' is not, as far as I know, disputed: he has twice been fired for lying and there are many other documented examples of his lies: Peter Oborne, *The Assault on Truth: Boris Johnson, Donald Trump and the Emergence of a New Moral Barbarism*, Simon & Schuster, 2021). But pointing this out will not have made C4 popular at Number Ten.

[35] Jim Waterson, 'Tories threaten Channel 4 after ice sculpture takes PM's place in debate', *Guardian*, 28 November 2019, https://www.theguardian.com/politics/2019/nov/28/ice-sculpture-to-replace-boris-johnson-in-channel-4-climate-debate.

[36] Ben Woods, 'Channel 4's battle to remain independent', *Sunday Telegraph*, 27 June 2021, https://www.telegraph.co.uk/business/2021/06/27/channel-4s-battle-remain-independent/.

[37] Tim Shipman, 'How the Tories weaponised woke', *Sunday Times*, 13 June 2021, https://www.thetimes.co.uk/article/how-the-tories-weaponised-woke-jlmwh0p36.

[38] Tony Driver, 'Nadine Dorries planning a war on 'crackpot' BBC programming, minister suggests', *The Telegraph*, 16 September 2021.

[39] Institutions it has ignored, attacked, defunded or undermined include Parliament, the judiciary, the civil service, the BBC, the Electoral Commission, unhelpful Westminster

lobby correspondents, the Intelligence and Security Committee, the Charity Commission, the independent advisor on ministerial standards, the commissioner for public appointments and the independent assessment panel for candidates for the Ofcom chairmanship.

[40] For instance, rather than asking 'Should C4 be privatised?', Q2 asks if it would be 'better placed to deliver sustainably against the government's aims for public service broadcasting if it was outside public ownership'. Similarly, Q5 asks if the Government should 'remove the publisher-broadcaster restriction' to 'increase Channel 4's ability to diversify its revenue streams'.

About the author

Patrick Barwise is emeritus professor of management and marketing at London Business School, chairman of the Archive of Market and Social Research, former chairman of Which? and co-author, with Peter York, of *The War Against the BBC* (Penguin, November 2020).

Impartial, independent and informative

By Matt Walsh and Stephen Cushion

How distinctive is Channel 4 News in the UK's broadcast ecology? Research shows it does more than other bulletins to hold the government to account and the high standards of its journalism run the risk of being undermined by privatisation

For almost 40 years Channel 4 News has broadcast original, impartial, hard-hitting journalism that holds power to account.

In the past five years alone, it has won 228 industry awards for its work, including exposing the Cambridge Analytica scandal, investigating systemic electoral bias against black American voters, and revealing ExxonMobil's lobbyists attempts to water down climate change regulation.

It was even nominated for an Oscar for its documentary film co-production *For Sama*, which reported on the brutal siege of Aleppo in Syria. Despite the characterisation of some critics, viewers find it both challenging and impartial.

Recent academic studies have drawn attention to Channel 4's distinctiveness An Ofcom (2020: 32) representative survey of the UK public found Channel 4 was considered a more impartial broadcaster than its terrestrial competitors, including the BBC. to the UK's broadcast news ecology, demonstrating its impartial, independent and informative journalism.

In 2019 Ofcom commissioned Cardiff University to examine the range and depth of UK news programming (Cushion 2019, 2021). The study categorised news according to whether it reflected a hard or soft topic. This was based on conventional definitions of these categories of news, which, broadly speaking, defined such politics, international news, education, and health were categorised as hard news, and crime, celebrity/entertainment, the royal family, sport, and weather were coded as soft news.

The study found that while the editorial selection of news was broadly similar across TV channels, there were some subtle and significant differences that demonstrate the distinctiveness of Channel 4 news.

Hard news agenda

The findings revealed that the BBC *News at Ten* supplied a harder news agenda than ITV's and Channel 5's evening bulletins, with 85.7 per cent of its time spent on topics such as politics, the economy and international affairs, compared with 80.6 per cent and 79.4 per cent for the respective commercial broadcasters.

But, above all, Channel 4 dedicated the most time to these topics, with 93.5 per cent of its total share of output considered to be hard news. International news made up 30.9 per cent of airtime on Channel 4 News, whereas for BBC News at Ten it was 26.0 per cent on BBC *News at Ten* and 25.1 per cent on ITV News at Ten. Channel 5 spent just 6.7 per cent of its total news agenda covering this category.

Compared to a previous study of UK television news in 2012 – which used the same definitions of hard and soft news and covered a five-week period (25 days) (Barnett et al 2012) – the findings also revealed Channel 4 increased its hard news agenda compared to 2009 (Barnett et al, 2012). Its reporting of politics and public affairs, for example, rose by 12.2 per cent over ten years.

Overall, the Ofcom-commissioned study demonstrated that Channel 4 provides a distinctive window on the world compared to other nightly news bulletins, with an emphasis on covering hard news topics including politics, public affairs, and international issues.

The importance of being distinctive was emphasised by the former long-standing Head of News and Current Affairs at Channel 4, Dorothy Byrne, who said in an interview for the Ofcom study that:

> *Everything we cover should be important, but they don't have to slavishly follow the same news agenda as other people. In fact, and you may have found differently, if they do the same stories every night as the BBC or ITV, we're not doing our job, because we are there to bring alternative ideas and alternative stories to light. And so in both our news and current affairs, we aim to cover stories that other people might neglect and groups who get neglected. So some of the stories will be whatever everybody else is covering and some will be nobody else is covering. I sort of judge it over a period – do I feel we've got a bit too mainstream, or do I feel we've gone a bit too far off a sort of core news that people need to know, so it's a balance* (cited in Cushion, 2019).

Distinctive coverage of the pandemic

In a study about UK television news coverage of Covid related reporting in April and May 2020, a comparative content analysis of 1259 items found Channel 4 also played a distinctive role in covering the pandemic (Cushion et al., 2021).

In the nightly news bulletins on BBC, ITV, Channel 4, Channel 5, and Sky News, roughly a third of items included at least one instance of a journalist or source challenging or questioning a government decision.

But Channel 4 had the highest amount with almost six in 10 items including some interrogation of policy. Moreover, the study found Channel 4 featured the most robust and explicit questioning of government decisions. For example, this live two-way with the Channel 4's political editor showed how directly they challenged government decision making:

> *The government is really quite reluctant to talk about exit strategy in part, of course, because there isn't one fully worked out, there isn't a file, it's not completed work. But mainly because they are deeply worried about the idea that if they go around talking about a relaxation...people will stop their compliance with the rules. And as they stood themselves accused of mixed messaging before the shutdown happened, they are acutely aware of the dangers of mixed messaging* (Channel 4 News, 16 April. Cited in Cushion et al., 2021).

Overall, the study found that while most UK television news bulletins did not regularly feature any questioning or challenging of government policy by journalists or sources during a key moment in the first phase of the pandemic, the clear exception was Channel 4 News which most robustly held the government to account.

Protecting Channel 4's journalism

Given independent academic studies have demonstrated the unique democratic value of its journalism, the question then is not should Channel 4 News be saved – that is self-evident. But how can it best be protected should the government proceed with the sale of Channel 4?

The UK government's consultation document suggests that it is of the view that 'Channel 4's existing obligations relating to a high provision of news and current affairs content, should be broadly retained in any potential reform.' It is our opinion that this is too loose a definition and could lead to the high standards of Channel 4's journalism being undermined after privatisation.

Safeguards should be put in place to ensure that Channel 4 continues to broadcast no less than 208 hours of news per year at peak time, plus 208 hours per year of current affairs, 80 of those hours at peak.

Channel 4 News's budget of just shy of £30m a year should be protected, as should its remit for high quality television journalism, editorial independence, along with its prime-time transmission time.

This could be monitored and regulated by Ofcom, which should be tasked with a specific responsibility for an annual review of the resources available and the quality of Channel 4's news provision, in addition to the more general ad hoc reviews of public service broadcast news, which it presently conducts.

There is a precedent for this. When Sky was bought by Comcast in 2018, the American company entered a legally binding commitment to guarantee the long-term funding of an editorially independent Sky News. It guaranteed a decade of inflation adjusted funding for the 24-hour TV news channel and established an independent editorial oversight board.

The government could choose to do something similar to protect the future of Channel 4 News. Given Channel 4 News's distinctive contribution to the UK's broadcast ecology, in our view, any buyer should be required to undertake a legal commitment to protect and enhance the news service both on television and online.

References

Barnett, S., Gaber I. and Ramsay, G. (2012) From Callaghan to credit crunch: changing trends in British television news 1975-2009. London: University of Westminster.

Cushion, Stephen (2019) The Range and Depth of BBC News and Current Affairs: A Content Analysis. London: Ofcom

Cushion, S. (2021) 'Are public service media distinctive from the market? Interpreting the political information environments of BBC and commercial news in the UK', *European Journal of Communication*, Ifirst

Cushion, Stephen, Morani, Marina, So, Nikki and Kyriakidou, Maria (2021) 'Why media systems matter: A fact-checking study of UK television news during the coronavirus pandemic', *Digital Journalism*, Ifirst.

Ofcom (2020) Ofcom's Annual Report on the BBC 2019/20. London: Ofcom. https://www.ofcom.org.uk/__data/assets/pdf_file/0021/207228/third-bbc-annual-report.pdf

About the authors

Matt Walsh is the head of the School of Journalism, Media and Culture at Cardiff University. He became an academic in 2014 after more than 20 years as a working journalist. He currently sits on the executive board of the Broadcast Journalism Training Council and the Standards Code committee at the press regulator, Impress.

Stephen Cushion is a professor at the Cardiff School of Journalism, Media and Culture at Cardiff University. He has carried out four impartiality reviews for the BBC Trust (between 2009 and 2016) about BBC News and commercial media coverage of devolution and the use of statistics and was commissioned by Ofcom in 2019 to examine the BBC's range and depth of news and current affairs programming.

Promises, promises?

By Richard Tait

As the government pushes on with the next stage of its privatisation plan, much may depend on the credibility of the regulators in guaranteeing that any new owner could be trusted to maintain 'a strong commitment' to public service broadcasting. But we may have seen this movie before

If Boris Johnson gets his way (and prime ministers with a majority of more than 80 usually do), the current debate over the future of Channel 4 is less likely than in the past to end with the government abandoning its plan quite early in the process in the face of strong and broadly based opposition to the idea.

Not many people have changed their views since 2015 in either direction – certainly Channel 4 itself, and its supporters in broadcasting and journalism, still believe that privatisation is a terrible idea. But this time, the battle is probably going to move from a debate over the *principle* of privatisation to a much more concrete examination of what in *practice* privatisation would really mean.

How much would prospective purchasers actually pay for the business? How much of the key current public service commitments would they promise to keep? And perhaps most importantly of all, how to ensure, if privatisation is pushed through, they keep those promises? How convincingly those questions are answered may determine whether this campaign to sell off Channel 4 is any more successful than the previous attempts.

An enormous amount would depend on regulation. Rather oddly, the actual word is absent from the government's case for privatisation (DCMS 2021). However, the government's view appears to be that many of the most important parts of Channel 4's remit are non-negotiable and that the new owners, whoever they may be, will cheerfully sign up for maintaining them. But these commitments could cost a lot of money – and that will have to be reflected in the purchase price. The government talks expansively about privatisation bringing new money and opportunities – 'access to capital', 'strategic partnerships' and 'international markets' – but any company thinking of bidding for control of Channel 4 is first of all going to go through the business's cost base and schedules with a fine tooth comb.

Long before the Treasury and the bankers start taking soundings on price, prospective purchasers will want to have a very clear idea of what they can do and in particular where the potential savings can be made – in the remit, schedules, programme budgets, terms of trade, buildings, staff costs and advertising sales. Can they close Leeds, merge their sales operations, make their programmes themselves? Do they really need that hour of news, losing money in the middle of the schedule, that seems to hack off the government and its supporters?

1990 and all that

Regulation matters because what is being proposed is the biggest change in British public service broadcasting since the 1992 franchise round transformed independent television. And although so much has changed in the last 30 years in broadcast technology and markets, there are still some suggestive similarities with, and perhaps lessons from, the past.

The 1990 Broadcasting Act was partly driven by a belief in the inherent superiority of market solutions and partly by political score-settling. Margaret Thatcher despised the way independent television was being run, as she saw it, as a cosy cartel (Thatcher, 1993: 634-7) and bitterly resented some of its journalism, such as *Death on the Rock* (Bolton, 1990). She replaced a system of awarding Channel 3 licences on the basis of programme promises for a competitive tender process where whoever bid most got the franchise, subject to a baseline 'quality threshold'.

Thirty years on, the Johnson government has an equally radical plan. It takes a similarly clear ideological position – that there is no justification for a second publicly owned PSB – the market will do a better job. And again, rows over journalism are playing too prominent a role.

Channel 4's chances of survival have been seriously weakened by No 10's hostility to Channel 4's journalism, not helped by Channel 4's then head of news and current affairs, Dorothy Byrne, calling the prime minister a liar at the Edinburgh Television Festival in 2019 and the decision to put a melting ice sculpture in his place when he declined to take part in a Channel 4 election debate on the environment (Brown, 2021:266).

While the government case for privatisation is almost effusive in its praise for much of Channel 4's output, it says absolutely nothing about the quality and importance of its journalism. Its sole paragraph on journalism merely states that 'the government is currently of the view that Channel 4's existing obligations relating to a high provision of news and current affairs content, should be broadly retained in any potential reform' (DCMS, 2021).

Changing the rules

In the 1990 Act, regulation was meant to be the safety net to maintain at least the basics of a public service and ensure the winning companies kept the promises they had made. Some hope. The ink had not dried on their new licences before the companies embarked on a determined and largely successful campaign to undermine the whole basis of the system as a network of regional and national licences.

Raymond Snoddy, one of the editors of this book, tells the wonderful story of Michael Green, fresh from winning the London weekday franchise (replacing Thames, who had made *Death on the Rock*) and before his company Carlton had started broadcasting, lobbying senior conservative politicians at their party conference for the regulators to allow the companies to cut their costs by changing the rules on consolidation (Snoddy, 1996: 219).

He soon got his way and the companies embarked on more than a decade of successful lobbying for more and more mergers and takeovers, ending in 2003 with Carlton and Granada, by then controlling all the licences in England and Wales, merging to form a single company – ITV plc. The companies were equally assiduous in pushing, usually successfully, against what they rapidly decided were unaffordable licence obligations (Fitzwalter, 2008).

There are plenty of criticisms of the effectiveness of regulation elsewhere in this book – David Elstein thinks they have let Channel 4 off lightly: Stewart Purvis points out that no broadcasting regulator has ever intervened to protect a news budget; Liz Forgan argues against putting too much trust in remits: in another chapter I look at what the regulators allowed to happen to ITV's news heritage and how its recent revival is down to management decisions rather than regulatory intervention.

But, in allowing all this, the regulators were simply going with the flow and taking their lead from the politicians – for the last three decades the conventional political and industry wisdom has been that regulation would fall away as technology and audience expectations changed. That view was backed by relentless lobbying, led by the UK's most influential media mogul.

In 1989 Rupert Murdoch argued for broadcasting to be 'freed from the bureaucrats of television' (Murdoch, 1989) and he and his newspapers have been campaigning for the lightest of regulation ever since.

Of course, Murdoch had a point – the tight regulation that was appropriate to the age of spectrum scarcity had to change and continue to change with the revolutionary developments in multi-channel, and then in online and on-demand. The real issue was much more about how far and how fast. And recently, arguments over the desirability of some level of regulation seem to making a comeback. Whereas once it was a given that you cannot regulate the internet, now the debate is how much you should, with Ofcom being given responsibility recently for regulating harmful online content (Ofcom 2020).

And the abandonment of the fairness obligations in US broadcast journalism has helped create the horrific situation where lies and deranged conspiracy theories are scarcely challenged by Fox News, one of the most powerful television news organisations in the world (Tait, 2020).

A third of Americans think that Donald Trump won the election; most Republican voters believe that the Capitol riot of January 6, 2021 was a 'false flag' operation by the left to discredit Trump (Moore, 2021). Suddenly, further de-regulation in the UK does not seem such a brilliant idea. Murdoch's son James, who had attacked regulation as close to creationism and used to argue that only the market would guarantee editorial integrity (Murdoch, 2009) resigned from News Corp, owner of Fox News, in October 2020, saying 'a contest of ideas shouldn't be used to legitimise disinformation... at great news organisations, the mission really should be to introduce fact to disperse doubt – not to sow doubt to obscure fact, if you will'(Dowd, 2020).

Protecting Channel 4 News

So the debate over regulation is likely to be about what, realistically, can the regulator do. Ofcom has proved itself an effective regulator of content standards – protecting freedom of expression despite political pressures. It is also good at setting and monitoring quantitative targets such as diversity and regional production.

Ofcom could certainly be tasked to implement the excellent idea floated by Deborah Turness, ITN's chief executive (and supported in this book by David Elstein and by my Cardiff colleagues Matt Walsh and Stephen Cushion), that Channel 4's news budget should be ring fenced and guaranteed on the lines of the 2018 deal where Comcast, as a condition of being allowed to take over Sky, signed up to a 10 year guarantee of the Sky News budget and an independent editorial board (Turness, 2021).

There are other areas where a quantitative regulatory approach could work – in relations with independent suppliers, for example, the amount of in-house production, the terms of trade with independents, regional quotas and the encouragement of start-ups could all be agreed, measured and monitored.

Could that agreement stretch to the duration of the news and its scheduling? There is nothing in the current remit to say Channel Four News should be an hour long and that it should be scheduled at 19.00 on weekdays.

Recently, Ofcom has been considering a request from Channel 5 to be freed from one of its last significant licence obligations – to broadcast 120 hours of news a year in peak time (18.00-22.30). Ofcom is minded to agree to this as Channel 5 is proposing to lose its current 18.30 bulletin and run an hour-long programme from 17.00-1800 – on the basis that there is already a block of high-quality news available from BBC, ITV and Channel 4 covering the whole of the 18.00-20.00 period (Ofcom 2021).

It is impossible at this stage to say what Ofcom would do if new owners of Channel 4 subsequently decided they did not want to continue with a loss-making hour of news in a valuable slot.

Successive Channel 4 managements have seen the news at 19.00-20.00 as key part of the brand (Brown 2021: 215-216). In theory, Ofcom could make it a non-negotiable part of the new remit. It is, in fact, quite hard to see where else an hour of Channel 4 News could be scheduled in peak without undesirable overlaps with BBC and ITV.

The crucial problem is, will the prospective buyers agree? Comcast's commitment to Sky News was a price worth paying in the context of a £30bn deal (Mayhew, 2018). The Channel 4 privatisation is not in the same league, but if a new owner is serious about keeping the best of the existing service, it cannot be a deal-breaker to ask it to commit to Channel 4 News.

But reaching agreement on the regulatory structure could involve complex negotiations and trade-offs, with the perhaps unworthy suspicion at the back of the mind that history shows us promises in broadcasting are easily made and not always kept. If the final agreed price is seen as low, the charge will be that a public asset has been given away – if high, the new owners will need to make changes which will start appearing on screen and elsewhere. And no matter what the deal says, privatisation puts shareholders and managers, not regulators, in the driving seat in the long term.

Running out of bandwidth?

The more you look at the *process* of selling off Channel 4, in terms of the politics, the draft legislation, the commercial negotiations and the agreements on future regulation, the more complex, detailed, controversial and time-consuming it becomes.

Civil servants like to talk about 'bandwidth' to define a government's capacity to undertake a number of complex tasks simultaneously. This winter and spring there are surely likely to be a quite a few areas which will inevitably take priority over privatising Channel 4 – Covid, the NHS, the economy and education are all going to be in the public mind a long way ahead of a controversial change in the structure of public broadcasting. The September reshuffle is said to reflect the prime minister's 'boosterish vision for the country', with a focus on delivery and levelling up. It is not immediately evident how Channel 4 privatisation – complex and contentious, with not much obvious public appeal – plays into that message (Shipman, 2021).

And DCMS itself is now under new political management, with the unexpected departures in the reshuffle of culture secretary Oliver Dowden and minister of state for media and data John Whittingdale. Few MPs have been as enthusiastic for Channel 4 privatisation as Whittingdale; even people in broadcasting who disagree with his conclusions would concede few MPs understand the issues in all their complexity as well as he does.

Given the economic importance of the creative industries in the UK and the battering they have had during the pandemic, where does selling off a currently very successful broadcaster (which says it doesn't need any help) really fit in this government and this prime minister's priorities? It will not be long before we find out.

References

Bolton, Roger (1990) Death on the Rock and other stories, London: WH Allen.

Brown, Maggie (2021) Channel 4 A History: From *Big Brother* to the *Great British Bake Off,* London: BFI/Bloomsbury.

DCMS (2021) Consultation on a potential change of ownership of Channel 4 Television Corporation, 8 July 2021. Available online at https://www.gov.uk/government/consultations/consultation-on-a-change-of-ownership-of-channel-4-television-corporation, accessed 10 September 2021.

Dowd, Maureen (2020) James Murdoch: Why I pulled the ripcord and resigned from News Corp, *The Independent,* 15 October 2020.Available online https://www.independent.co.uk/news/media/james-murdoch-rupert-murdoch-interview-news-corp-resignation-b992518, accessed 10 September 2021.

Fitzwalter, Ray (2008) The dream that died: The rise and fall of ITV, Leicester: Matador.

Moore, Robert (2021) January 6 and the challenge to American television journalism, Mair, John, Clark, Tor, Fowler, Neil, Snoddy, Raymond, Tait, Richard (eds), Populism, the pandemic and the media, Bury St Edmunds: Abramis, pp 5-9.

Mayhew, Freddy (2018) Comcast stands by pledge to maintain funding for Sky News over ten years and create new editorial board with safeguards for independence, Press Gazette, 25 September 2018. Available online at https://www.pressgazette.co.uk/comcast-stands-by-pledge-to-maintain-funding-for-sky-news-over-ten-years-and-create-new-editorial-board-with-safeguards-for-independence/, accessed 10 September 2021.

Murdoch, James (2009) MacTaggart Lecture, 28 August 2009. Available online at http://image.guardian.co.uk/sys-files/Media/documents/2009/08/28/JamesMurdochMacTaggartLecture.pdf, accessed 10 September 2021.

Murdoch, Rupert (1989) MacTaggart Lecture, 25 August 1989. Available online at http://www.thetvfestival.com/website/wp-content/uploads/2015/03/GEITF_MacTaggart_1989_Rupert_Murdoch.pdf, accessed 10 September 2021.

Ofcom (2020) Ofcom to regulate harmful content online, 15 December 2020. Available online at https://www.ofcom.org.uk/about-ofcom/latest/features-and-news/ofcom-to-regulate-harmful-content-online, accessed 10 September 2021.

Ofcom (2021) Consultation: Request for change of licence conditions relating to the provision of news output on Channel 5, 30 June 2021. Available online at https://www.ofcom.org.uk/consultations-and-statements/category-3/licence-change-request-for-news-output-on-channel-5, accessed 10 September 2021.

Shipman, Tim (2021) Time for Tiggers: reshuffle delivers Boris Johnson's 'boosters', *The Sunday Times,* 19 September 2021.

Snoddy, Raymond (1996) Greenfinger, The rise of Michael Green and Carlton Communications, London: Faber and Faber.

Tait, Richard (2020) Impartiality's Last Stand?, Mair, John, Clark, Tor, Fowler, Neil, Snoddy, Raymond, Tait, Richard (eds), Populism, the Pandemic and the Media, Bury St Edmunds: Abramis pp 240-248.

Thatcher, Margaret (1993) The Downing Street Years, London: Harper Collins.

Turness, Deborah (2021) The Media Show, 6 August 2021. Available online at https://www.bbc.co.uk/programmes/p09rk7s4, accessed 10 September 2021.

About the author

Richard Tait CBE is Professor of Journalism at the School of Journalism, Media and Culture, Cardiff University as well as being a co-editor of this book. From 2003 to 2012 he was Director of the School's Centre for Journalism. He was Editor of *Newsnight* from 1985 to 1987, Editor of *Channel 4 News* from 1987 to 1995 and Editor-in-Chief of ITN from 1995 to 2002. He was a member of the 2004 Neil Review of the BBC's journalism after Hutton. He was a BBC Governor and chair of the Governors' Programme Complaints Committee from 2004 to 2006, and a BBC Trustee and chair of the Trust's Editorial Standards Committee from 2006 to 2010. He is a fellow of the Society of Editors and the Royal Television Society and a Board member (and former Treasurer) of the International News Safety Institute. He was adviser to the 2016 Lords committee on communications inquiry, 'A privatised future for Channel 4?'

Letter to the minister: Documentaries need protection

By Lorraine Heggessey and Jane Callaghan

This letter, from The Grierson Trust to the DCMS secretary of state, underlines the huge importance of Channel 4 to British tradition of documentary and factual programme making

Dear minister

The Grierson Trust is one of the leading voices in the UK documentary and factual television industry. We are writing to you to express our views on the proposed privatisation of Channel 4 and, in particular, to highlight the things that we would like to see protected or enhanced if there were to be a change in ownership of Channel 4.

Our organisation was established 49 years ago to celebrate and champion the documentary genre, and to commemorate the work of the documentary pioneer, John Grierson, by holding the annual British Documentary Awards, which are widely regarded as the Oscars of the documentary world.

Since 2012 we have focused on bringing diverse and under-represented voices into the industry through our annual training programmes, Grierson DocLab. We provide an entry point for those who would otherwise find the industry inaccessible including those facing geographic or socio-economic challenges.

We would like to draw your attention to the significant impact Channel 4 has on the documentary sector through:

- the number of hours of factual programming it commissions;
- its drive for innovation and diversity;
- its commitment to commissioning from companies based in the nations and regions;
- its support for many small and relatively unknown companies;
- and its willingness to take risks.

We would like to see the contribution Channel 4 currently makes in the documentary industry included in its remit going forward. Ideally, we would like to see a greater commitment to documentary programming and commissioning from small production companies, as well as new entrants, throughout the UK.

There are three areas where Channel 4's public service broadcasting (PSB) remit has tremendous value to a range of stakeholders, which we believe are unlikely to be top priorities if the organisation's not-for-profit status is changed, and which we would be concerned to see maintained or strengthened under privatisation:

Investment in the nations and regions

Channel 4's work outside London is extensive – both in terms of financial investment and the creation of job opportunities: it currently supports 3,000 jobs across the UK, and more than 50 per cent of its spend in 20/21 was outside London. The broadcaster already has commitments in Leeds, Bristol, Glasgow and Manchester representing 400 jobs. This has been highly beneficial for the documentary sector in bringing a range of stories, perspectives and voices to the screen.

It also provides pivotal support and investment for start-ups and small independent production companies including through its Indie Growth Fund, having already invested £12bn in the sector. It has been a catalyst for the creative industries outside the capital and has fuelled plurality of voices, commissioning more than 300 production companies to make more hours of TV than any other commercial PSB, of which factual commissions outnumber any other genre in terms of independent production.

Its factual commissions involve more independent production companies than any other genre. We believe this demonstrates that Channel 4's role in the factual production eco-system is a vital part of its contribution to the long-term sustainability and growth of the UK's production sector.

This commitment to spend outside London and to commission from a wide range of companies based throughout the UK is something we would like to see retained under any future ownership, as it contributes to excellence and innovation in the documentary genre, keeping it relevant and vibrant.

The wider impact of this on our work is significant. Since 2012, the Grierson DocLab training and mentoring scheme has supported individuals from under-represented backgrounds to break into the industry. This includes:

- Outside of London: 64 per cent of trainees are from outside of London;

- Gender representation: 64 per cent female; 33 per cent male and 3 per cent non-binary;

- Cultural diversity: 60 per cent of trainees describe themselves as coming from diverse backgrounds;

- Disability: 16 per cent of trainees describe themselves as being disabled.

To deliver our training, we work very closely with a wide range of independent production companies across the UK, which provide vital bursary supported work placements. Many of them have benefitted from investment by the

Channel 4 Indie Growth Fund, specifically Lightbox, Popkorn, True North, True Vision and Voltage TV.

Others have grown through commissions from Channel 4 including: Blast! Films (London), Century Films (London), Lion TV (Glasgow), Minnow Films (London), Plimsoll Productions (Bristol), Testimony Films (Bristol), The Garden (Leeds and London) and Wise Owl Films (Leeds).

This in turn, feeds job opportunities, employment prospects and key skills outside London.

A gateway for young people

Channel 4 is also a place for young people – as audiences, contributors and creatives. More than 90 per cent of 18-34s are reached by Channel 4's portfolio of channels, putting it ahead of LadBible, Disney and the BBC; 80 per cent are signed up to streaming platform All4. It has also led the way in innovation and platform partnerships with YouTube and TikTok, taking its content direct to its audience.

For creatives, the broadcaster commits to skills building and industry training – more than 5,000 people have benefitted since 2015, providing vital talent pipelines for the sector and a way in for newcomers to the industry. In doing so it helps to sustain and diversify the documentary workforce in the UK across geography, gender, ethnicity, social background and more.

Channel 4's factual department has made a specific commitment to fostering and nurturing early career creatives such as documentary directors in its First Cut strand as well as working with NFTS to support 20 female producer/directors from under-represented backgrounds.

A number of Grierson DocLab alumni have gone on to receive Channel 4 commissions and funding themselves. Notably Bristol-based Michael Jenkins' fledging company, Blak Wave Productions, was awarded a discretionary C4 Emerging Indie Fund award as well as commission as part of the *Take Your Knee Off My Neck* series. Dershe Samaria's company, Nuwave Pictures, was selected for the first Channel 4/The TV Collective Indie Accelerator scheme which pair black, Asian and minority-ethnic-led indies with commissioning heads of department for unscripted genres. Poppy Goodheart had her directorial debut, *The Boy Who Can't Stop Dancing* on Channel 4, having been selected for its First Cut scheme for new directors.

Channel 4's commitment to young people is also demonstrated in its commissioning strategy designed to connect with its young audiences: Channel 4 is more successful with the demographic than any other UK PSB. Twenty-two of the top 25 young shows were on Channel 4 last year. It is also committed to developing new on-screen talent from Chidera Eggerue (*Bring Back the Bush*) to Yinka Bokinni (*Damilola: The Boy Next Door*).

Giving voices to the unheard

Finally, Channel 4 provides an important framework for improving diversity within the industry and ensuring that the future of the documentary genre involves a rich variety of voices. Notably, the channel is at the forefront of driving change through dedicated and bold programming initiatives such as its Black to Front initiative.

However, this is only one element of its representations of broader diversity, embedded within its corporate culture. Its current role and remit as a PSB means that its metrics for success go way beyond simply measuring viewing figures, which allows Channel 4 to commission riskier programming, providing a platform for innovation as well as for complex and specialist pieces.

In addition to providing important funding streams for black, Asian and minority ethnic-led indies through its Accelerator scheme, which specifically seeks different perspectives, Channel 4's wider factual programming portfolio has embraced diversity – from the Paralympics and *Undateables*, which redefined programming involving people with a disability to its engagement with social issues such *Hair Power: Me and My Afro, Damilola: The Boy Next Door, Ramadan in Lockdown* and *Davina McCall: Sex, Myths and The Menopause*.

This societal value to Channel 4 is unlikely to be sustainable in a for-profit model in which ratings and revenue and shareholders are prioritised. It is critical that the conditions of any sale would be explicit and measurable in order to ensure that these core values, so sustaining to UK business, creativity and culture and even global standing, are retained.

We believe that one of the reasons British documentary makers are recognised as world class is the unique broadcasting landscape and ecology of the UK television sector.

Channel 4 has a distinctive role in this, which is different to the licence-fee funded BBC and to the commercial ad-funded PSBs – ITV and Channel 5 – which have to deliver a profit for shareholders rather than putting any profits back into programming.

The fact that Channel 4 sits alongside not just the other PSBs but also a flourishing range of channels from providers such as Sky and more recently from the streamers, such as Netflix and Amazon Prime, brings a richness to the documentary sector that would be lost if Channel 4's remit is not preserved.

Programming brings creative innovation, dynamic support, diverse voices and new talent to the industry, which we regard as vital elements for the wider industry's development and future.

These aspects of Channel 4's work are critical for the UK's world-leading documentary industry to thrive and The Grierson Trust seek your assurance that these attributes will be protected and enhanced whatever the future shape of Channel 4.

Yours faithfully

Lorraine Heggessey, chair of trustees

Jane Callaghan, managing director

About the authors

Lorraine Heggessey is chair of The Grierson Trust. She began her television career in current affairs with *Panorama*, *This Week* and *Dispatches*. She edited *QED* and then became head of BBC Children's Television, and then director of programmes and deputy chief executive of BBC Production. From 2000 to 2005 she was controller of BBC1, then chief executive of Talkback Thames, executive chairman of Boom Pictures and chief executive of the Royal Foundation.

Jane Callaghan has worked for The Grierson Trust for 20 years, becoming Managing Director in 2014. Prior to that she was a director of Multimedia Ventures, a digital media consultancy business whose clients included the European Commission, the Department of Trade and Industry and the Heritage Lottery Fund.

The Big Fat Teenage Challenge – revisited

By Fiona Chesterton

Bespoke content to meet the needs of older children and younger adults in the UK has been an important part of Channel 4's remit and needs preserving if the government's desire for privatisation succeeds

As I sat down to write this chapter, hundreds of thousands of teenagers all over the country were preparing to go back to school, no doubt hoping that the coming year will be rather different from the past two. As the summer holidays drew to a close, Channel 4 was reminding them what the last school Covid-disrupted year was like, with a documentary series, launched in prime time, called *Sixteen: Class of 21*.

This series featured Year 11 pupils at an academy in Dudley, in the West Midlands. There was football-mad Callum – too easily distracted from his online maths class by looking at girls as well as footie on his mobile phone. There was head girl Aaminah and best friends Sade and Kara, all filming themselves, as they went through the ups and downs of preparing for their GCSEs, much of the time spent at home rather than in the classroom.

The series was produced by Label One, the same production company which made the remarkable documentary series called *Hospital* for the BBC, and, it should be noted, supported by the BBC's long-standing educational partner, the Open University. This managed to get right inside the NHS before as well as during its biggest crisis. One felt that if they had made this school series for the BBC, there might have been more attention on the struggles of the teachers to keep this perilous show on the road, more of the wider context of the examination system and dealing with the endless and ever-changing orders coming down on high from Whitehall. Here, the focus was very much on the young people themselves, and that, surely, was no accident. Channel 4's mission – part of its remit indeed – is to reach young people, partly by holding up a mirror to them.

As the Channel 4 annual report describes their youth strategy, the 'focus was on popular mainstream programming that reflects their lives and interests and helps them to better understand the world around them.' Last year another classroom-set series *The School that Tried to end Racism* was another example of this genre.

The end of an era?

So the question now is –would such programmes be commissioned if Channel 4 were privatised, or without a sufficiently robust public service regulatory framework? Does the government think that the provision of non-fiction programming like this, targeted at teenagers and made primarily for a UK audience, is worthwhile and needs future-proofing? Can they point to examples of where the streaming services, let alone other UK-based commercial commissioners, have run shows like these?

It is hard to be confident from the DCMS' own statements in its consultation document on Channel 4, where it asks the British public to agree with its preferred option to privatise the channel. Firstly, I would point out, that by referring to Channel 4, we must also include its portfolio of services, particularly E4, 4Music and the currently free video-on-demand (VoD) service, All4, which also have special appeal to a younger audience, and which seem to be subsumed in the discourse around the main channel.

Yes, the government says of a privatised but regulated Channel 4, it 'sees the value of delivery of broadcast content appealing to young and diverse audiences' along with a 'more risk-based approach to content' and 'is minded to retain such obligations.'

There is a big but though. 'It will be important to ensure its remit does not prohibit Channel 4's future sustainability and its ability to broadcast relevant and quality content given the developments in the media landscape – with young audiences increasingly likely to consume content on non-linear platforms such as VoD services…' This apparently regardless of the fact that C4 has its own rather successful VoD service.

What then in the end does this commitment to specific not-necessarily-commercially-driven services for young people amount to? Does the DCMS see that there is a big difference, not least in commissioning intent, between *Sex Education*, a school-set drama series, produced in the UK but commissioned by Netflix, and programmes like *Sixteen* and *The School that tried to end racism?*

Deconstructing the DCMS consultation

For a start, let's drill down into that phrase – 'appealing to young and diverse audiences.' This is a phrase that trips off the tongue of media folk as well as the DCMS pretty easily these days. It generally refers to a wide demographic of viewers, encompassing people from sixteen to thirty-five.

Most 35-year-olds are parents, so hardly comparable in life stage with Callum and Kara in Dudley. The younger end of this wide spectrum is hard to reach and also of less commercial value, as long as they have a limited income and purchasing-power.

There is little doubt that the market will continue to supply a wealth of content for the wider under-35s audience. It comes down to whether you think entertainment is all that young people need and deserve and also whether you think that something will be missing for teenagers – especially those still at school.

Yes, a privatised Channel 4, would no doubt wish to continue reaching the under 35s – but surely would judge that drama and entertainment were the best genres with which to reach them.

How much, if at all, would it continue to commission non-fiction programming with a serious intent? How much would producers feel it was worth investing in developing challenging domestically-focused content, when they needed to secure co-production money from internationally-focused streaming services?

In particular, how much would be focused on under-16-year-olds, living, say in Dudley, with a broader purpose than merely entertaining them? This is the question that the DCMS does not address in its very unspecific and less-than-watertight assurances in its consultation document.

Is 2021 any different from 2016?

At the time in 2016 when I wrote the original chapter, 'The Big Fat Teenage Challenge' with Karen Brown, there was plenty of concern amongst politicians and the regulator, Ofcom, about the decline of programming for older children and teenagers across the spectrum.

As recently as the summer of 2018, Ofcom raised concerns about what it described as the lack of programmes specifically made for older children across all genres, including provision of age-appropriate news and programmes that 'reflect diverse, younger audiences' lives' and asked ITV and Channel 5, as well as Channel 4, to come up with plans to meet this challenge. The DCMS also promoted a new initiative called the Young Audiences Content Fund (YACF), designed to provide additional funding for children's programming, with a multi-million- pound budget, to be managed by the British Film Institute.

At that time, the YACF was widely welcomed by producers specialising in children's programming – particularly the promised additional investment of £57m over three years. With Covid disruption to production in 2020, it may be too early to judge how successful this initiative will be. Still, the evidence so far does not convince that this would fill the gap left by a privatised Channel 4, nor this very specific market failure. Far from it.

The Year 1 evaluation (www.BFI.org.uk) shows that the fund's managers made awards of just £12.5m in the first year, with commitments to just seventeen projects in production, the majority of awards being for development.

Looking in detail at these projects in production, it is hard to be convinced that these will meet the challenge Ofcom identified, particularly to meet the needs of older children. Of the seventeen projects listed in the BFI's report, just six are designed for older children, three of which were destined for broadcast on the fourth channel in Wales, S4C (so by definition not for a UK audience). Another two were for C4 and E4 and the sixth, an estimable initiative by Sky to provide a weekly news programme for children. While I welcome Sky Kids *FYI* show, it's a shame that C4 seems to have abandoned this territory, once pioneered by them with *First Edition*. Don't teenagers deserve a choice?

What is more concerning is that already the DCMS has quietly removed 25 per cent of the original budget of £57m. according to the Children's Media Foundation. What the DCMS gives, the DCMS can take away it seems.

Some will say that such top-down initiatives are doomed to fail, if the audience itself doesn't demand it. Young people have moved on and away, they say. Eyeballs are still fixed on screens but not the traditional ones.

What place for regulation and PSB values?

Of course, this is true, but it also remains true that adults – and parents in particular – are nervous of the Wild West of online content, and believe there is still a need, not just for regulation, but for the social and cultural values that the public service broadcasting framework embodied over the past hundred years to continue. They do not want to see this washed away in a tide of globalised content, however, slick and well-produced it might be. In sum they want their kids hearing more Dudley accents than LA ones.

Channel 4, which celebrates its 40th birthday in 2022, has not grown middle-aged. Its brand is still cooler than the BBC's. It is still working very hard to meet the needs of the domestic young audience. It is, for example, busy developing what it calls a digital-first service for 13 to 16-year-olds, including a dedicated Channel 4 branded You Tube channel. This will be run out of its new and growing operation in Leeds. Its early commissions suggest a continuing focus on the well-trodden path of identity and relationships, but give it time to grow, won't you DCMS?

About the author

Fiona Chesterton was the first Commissioning Editor for Daytime programmes at Channel 4, and in a long career in public service broadcasting, was also Controller, Adult Learning at the BBC and Director of TV for Skillset.

As well as being co-editor of the original *What Price Channel 4*, she has contributed to several books on media issues, most recently *The Virus and the Media: How British Journalists covered the pandemic(pub Bite-Sized Books, 2020)*. Her first book, *Secrets never to be Told* has just been published by the Conrad Press.

Who will buy it?

By John Mair

Channel 4 was always a cultural, rather than a business, opportunity. Is the wool is being pulled over our eyes in the great Channel 4 privatisation debate? Are the facts not being allowed to spoil a good story?

Assuming that the Johnson government uses its landslide majority to push through some form of privatisation, then who are the runners and riders to be the new owners?

To this observer, it looks almost a near certainty that Channel 4 will be put on the market. How much for? What conditions and who are the runners and riders in the C4 stakes? The situation is still cloudy but getting a little clearer.

Firstly, price. Any sale will not dent the UK public sector borrowing requirement (PSBR) by much. Chancellor Rishi Sunak has nearly £300bn to try to recover from excess Covid pandemic spending on economic support for individuals and businesses, vaccines development and purchase, test and trace and other contingency spending by the NHS.

Any sale of Channel 4 will net somewhere between a low £300m (the Barwise lowest estimate) to £500m (the *Daily Telegraph* estimate) to £600-1500m (the Enders Analysis estimate). That's between 0.1 and 0.2 per cent of the pandemic extra spend.

The most valuable C4 assets are the terrestrial frequencies and their places on the electronic programme guide (EPG); their investment in digital audience targeting and advertising, where they are ahead of the game; the myriad physical properties around the UK – in London, Leeds, Bristol and Glasgow – they presumably either own or lease (some they were strong armed into creating as part of their previous fight against privatisation in 2016)

A Leeds national headquarters at the old Majestic Cinema was opened in September 2021 but C4 owns precious little Intellectual Property (IP). That has long gone to the independent production supply companies. It is the engine of their businesses not Channel 4's. In 2020, C4's annual revenue was close to £1bn and it returned a profit of £74m. That was re-invested into programmes as is its normal practice.

Close to home and further away

When (and if) privatisation occurs, the cleanest option may be a management buy-out. That would need an injection of private equity funding. The UK is currently seeing a rash of private equity deals to buy out national companies and institutions. A private Channel 4 would be the latest.

The other two big UK commercial PSBs (public service broadcasters) – ITV and Channel Five – will also have their eyes firmly on the Horseferry prize. The great advantage is combining their advertising sales. One estimate is that amalgamation could save the buyer £200m per year on 'back office costs' – administration, advertising, transmission and more. Any initial capital investment might thus repaid in less than three years in the case of the lowest estimated market price. Pretty much a bargain!

On advertising, Channel Five is not as far down the digital advertising and targeting road as C4, so would gain that from any merger. It may be hard to remember that C4 was first mooted as 'ITV 2' before setting up as a self-standing channel in 1982 and the (then 15) ITV companies sold its advertising space for the first four years, after which C4 was forced to pay a levy to ITV on its advertising revenue until 1998. It went only after a public battle. So, if ITV plc buys C4, it is back to 1982.

A Channel 4/Five merger was put forward by Mark Thompson in 2004 when CEO of the former and later in the decade by Andy Duncan, the then C4 CEO. The idea did not fly on either occasion. The biggest regulatory hurdle for both ITV and C5 post-merger could be the joint share of the television advertising sales market they will control. Anything over 40 per cent should generate referral to the Competition and Markets Authority – the old Monopolies Commission – but there are those already out there rolling the pitch for that threshold to be raised.

Sky UK is also likely to be in the market for C4. The two already have a strategic partnership on advertising sales. Comcast paid £30bn for the company in 2019, so the market price (even at £1bn) of C4 is spare change for them.

Sky News was left ring fenced for a decade in that deal. Combining Sky News and a revamped Channel 4 News would deliver many economies of scale. To counter arguments about C4 news survival and bias, the DCMS could midwife a similar arms-length arrangement for C4 News. There are those who say the main ideological driver for C4 privatisation anyway is the Johnson government's distaste for the tenor of the news service.

The C4 terrestrial spectrums might also provide a shop window/a barker slot for Sky and other non -terrestrial broadcasters' products, which do not currently break through. Sky, for example, spends millions on drama which gets little press or critical reaction. The transmission of the cricket world cup final in July 2019 (the rights were owned by Sky) achieved a 4.5m audience on C4 alone. Likewise, the USA women's Open tennis final in September 2021 (the rights were owned by Amazon Prime), which Emma Raducanu won, garnered an audience of 9.2m on a Saturday night for Channel 4.

Will the American multi-national network broadcasters – such as CBS, NBC, Discovery, and 21st Century Fox– show any interest in C4 ? That is doubtful. Some already have interest in the UK in Channel Five and Sky but it is difficult to see they would want their terrestrial portfolio expanded.

One group which the DCMS has been touting as possible buyers – the VSOL or 'streamers' – are also unlikely to show any interest. Their markets in the UK and worldwide are well carved out and booming.

Netflix now has more than 15m subscribers in the UK and by 2020 more than half of British households subscribed to at least one streaming service. Their revenue model is based on conditional access and subscriptions. No room in that for a terrestrial PSB broadcaster. Channel 4 long ago abandoned its own subscription model with the demise of a paid-for Film 4 in 1996.

The social media companies like Google and Facebook are also unlikely to show much interest in purchasing C4.They have their own channels like YouTube and have precious little to gain from a micro niche channel in the UK. The C4/Google relationship is that of the supplicant and the elephant rather than vice versa.

Conditional access to buying C4

There are two big questions that face any potential buyers. What are the conditions they are expected to meet? Will they have to keep Channel 4's remit, though in reality that's more myth than substance. Since the 2003 Communications Act, the Channel is just legally obliged to transmit news in prime time, education programmes, be distinctive, innovative and culturally diverse plus to buy in all their programming from independent producers.

C4 was set up as a publisher broadcaster not a programme maker. The proportion of programmes to be bought in by any new owners from independent producers is a major hurdle. That is currently close to 100 per cent and many have got fat on the proceeds of that strategy.

Put simply, the channel pays for the cost of production – plus a production fee – in return for limited domestic showings of the programme or series. The intellectual property is kept by the production company and has been since 2005/2006.

Format and foreign rights are how the indies make their real money. Think *Big Brother* or *The Great British* (substitute as appropriate to market) *Bake off.* The big independents and their trade association Pact are trying to draw red lines in the sand for any new owners as part of any sale legislation. Do they have the power?

The shape of the independent production sector has changed considerably since 1982. The days of the small back room/kitchen table one-man companies (like mine!) nurtured by the Jeremy Isaacs C4 regime in the early days has gone.

The minnows have been swallowed up by bigger fish and even they by whales and sharks, some of them big multi-national companies. The number of companies has halved, the survivors are bigger and more can now be (and are) controlled by broadcasters. Since its inception, Channel 4 says it has invested £12bn in UK-produced material and last year it gave commissions to 274 production companies – a much smaller number that it the good old days.

Any merger will still have to jump over that bar of competition policy enforced by the Competition and Markets Authority. There is a 40 per cent threshold of share in any market which leads to referrals to the CMA. Certain potential buyers like Sky are now engaged in rolling the pitch so that the advertising market is widened to include not just TV advertising but other forms as well such as outdoor advertising. If that easing happened, then any C4/ITV or C4/Sky merger becomes a much more viable proposition.

Keeping the new C4 on the straight and narrow

How will any of this be enforced? Ofcom, the broadcasting industry regulator, is best described as being in a state of flux at the moment. They should have a new Chair appointed in late 2021/early 2022 after the fiasco of the failure to shoehorn Paul Dacre, the former editor of the *Daily Mail* and a man with little broadcasting experience plus a distaste for some broadcasters, into the chair.

The race is being re-run but the winner may still be Dacre. Channel 4 too will have a new chair and two new board members in January 2022 when Charles Gurassa and others leave office. Any newbies are likely to be much more sympathetic to the government's wishes.

Whatever happens, the cards seem well and truly stacked against the status quo ante with Channel 4. Change is coming. The questions are: Who will own it as it enters its fifth decade and just what will they own?

About the author

John Mair is one of the editors of this book and the previous volume. His tiny company Mair Golden Moments had a small number of Channel 4 commissions. In the last decade, he has edited 42 'hackademic' books, mainly on media and journalism subjects. The latest are *The BBC at 100 –Will it Survive?* and *Populism, the Pandemic and the Media*, both published in July 2021.

Preface:
Without Channel 4, I'd still be naked

By Jamie Oliver

Fifteen years ago in early 2001, I took an idea for a new documentary series to Channel 4 hoping they would give me a chance. I'd had some early success with the BBC and the three *Naked Chef* series but I felt it was time for a change, a new challenge.

I wanted to shake things up a bit and move on from the 'cheeky chappy' image. I wanted to start a London restaurant that not only served incredible food but also had a brilliant apprenticeship programme so that professionals could train young people to become the next generation of great British chefs. And they would not be just any young people; I would be looking for disadvantaged young people, perhaps including some who had struggled with homelessness or crime. I wanted to push myself and I needed a broadcaster that would challenge me.

That's where Channel 4 came in. I went to them asking whether they would take a punt on a documentary series where there was only a small chance of a successful result.

To be honest, they pushed me more than I was expecting because they wanted authentic, warts-and-all television and not just 'The Naked Chef opens a Restaurant'. They were absolutely right to do that, and I truly don't think I would be the man I am now had it not been for that key decision.

And that, to me, is the Channel 4 way: brave, risk-taking, demanding – but also nurturing, dynamic and caring. They're like the best sort of parent; you know they love you but they also want to help you reach your full potential and sometimes that means some tough conversations. For the right reasons, of course.

It's been fifteen years since we started filming *Jamie's Kitchen*, which led to the opening of Fifteen restaurant in London and we're all still here – me, Channel 4 and Fifteen – all doing well, all still shaking things up, all taking risks and reaping the rewards.

Channel 4 is now almost 35 years old but to me it still maintains that edginess that it had on day one.

When I look back at all the programming I've done for them, it's really quite an amazing and diverse list. We've made travel programmes like *Jamie's Italian Escape*, *Jamie's America* and *Jamie Does....*; we've done straightforward cooking shows like *30-Minute Meals*, *15-Minute Meals* and *Money Saving Meals*, helping millions of people to get back into the kitchen and cook using fresh ingredients; we've done one-off campaigning specials like *Eat To Save your Life*, *Jamie Saves Our Bacon* about the pork industry and *Jamie's Fowl Dinners*, which overnight changed the way Britain buys chicken and eggs.

And, of course, we've made series and specials that have launched campaigns and changed government policy. Together, Channel 4 and I have created real change.

The series about school food shocked the nation's parents, media and – eventually – policy makers into focusing on the dire state of our children's meals. When I started making the programmes, I couldn't get an appointment to see anyone from government to discuss this issue. By the time we'd finished the series, I was sitting down with Tony Blair discussing the creation of the School Food Trust and a £280 million investment to implement improvements in school food across the UK, with another big investment to come just years later.

In the same way, our series *Ministry of Food* shone a light on the lack of cooking skills amongst adults and led to Ministry of Food Centres in the UK and Australia that have taught thousands of people to cook over the past seven years.

More recently, of course, the *Sugar Rush* documentary in the summer of 2015 was in effect the starting gun for a huge campaign backed by doctors' groups, dentists' groups, education campaigners and the health lobby which continues to push for tighter regulation and stronger policies to tackle one of the main causes of our obesity epidemic and the spread of diet-related disease, particularly among children. This culminated in George Osborne's surprise announcement of a tax on sugary sweetened drinks in his 2016 budget.

Channel 4 is a terrific platform for reaching millions of smart, well-informed and vocal viewers. Its people are not afraid to take risks and as a result they get a lot of flak – and so do I – for some of the programmes we make together. But they keep the faith in me and I keep the faith in them, whether it's for a series on endangered fish species or the crazy thing we make with Jimmy Doherty on the end of Southend Pier, *Friday Night Feasts*. Channel 4 is as comfortable being playful as it is being provocative.

Most importantly, I guess that for the past fifteen years it's felt like home. The people at Channel 4 have been nurturing, encouraging, caring, and when I say 'people', I mean everyone from the top down. Yes we've had the odd disagreement – that happens in every home – but we've always come out of them stronger, and that's the sign of a great relationship. Thanks for caring, Channel 4.

March 2016

Introduction:
Spirit and purpose

By Jeremy Isaacs

What was Channel 4 going to be like? I was asked before we went to air. Cartoonists had a ball. Mark Boxer's Stringalongs in Hampstead were worried it was going to be 'too much our kind of channel'. Mel Calman's little man hoped 'it won't be too good for me'. The best target I could manage was 'a channel all would watch some of the time, and no-one for all of the time'. Viewers would pick and choose.

Kelvin MacKenzie's *Sun* persisted in tagging C4 as 'The channel that nobody watches'. I wrote to warn him that he was doing what an editor should never do – telling his readers what they knew from their own experience to be untrue. Many *Sun* readers, lured by *Countdown* or *Brookside* or a raft of *Golden Oldies* or NFL's *American Football*, were watching us appreciatively. He took the point and asked me to lunch.

In an early edition of *Voices*, Al Alvarez chaired a discussion on 'The Arts under Dictatorships', with Mary McCarthy, George Steiner and Joseph Brodksy. Claus Moser, Warden of Wadham College, Oxford, and Chairman of the Royal Opera House, wrote to thank me: 'Jeremy, that was exactly what television is for!' Well, up to a point, dear Claus. Everyone has their own idea of what television is for.

C4 owed its existence to what, for some, seemed a miraculous conception: a closely argued, lengthy dialogue between senior officers in the Independent Broadcasting Authority, Colin Shaw and Brian Young, and their equivalents in the Home Office. The crucial notion of the broadcaster as publisher, rather than programme producer, came from Anthony Smith. But the channel's structural relationship to ITV was forged by the IBA/Home Office partnership, and was to find expression in Willie Whitelaw's Cambridge speech in 1979.

Q: 'Mr Whitelaw, what proportion of the channel's programming do you expect to come from independent producers?'

A: 'The largest practicable.'

In the legislation that followed, Channel 4 was to pursue 'innovation and experiment in the form and content of programmes' and to provide 'a distinctive service'.

In November 1982, it came into being. Foreign broadcasters, amazed, flocked into Heathrow to find out how it had happened; could we, they wondered, have one too? What amazed them was that it was the government's doing, and a Tory government at that. And Mrs Thatcher approved. 'Stand up for free enterprise, won't you, Mr Isaacs!' she urged. I told her some of our programmes would. 'Not nearly enough!' she complained later. But she knew by then that hundreds of entrepreneurial programme makers had found a living by it, and was grateful.

It would be odd, ironic and regrettable, if another Conservative government put an end to that.

Channel 4 has always been about programmes – their endless, pluralistic diversity.

David Rose, cheered on by David Puttnam – 'The important thing is to get the film running through the camera' – gave us *Film on Four,* beginning with Stephen Frears' *Walter,* proceeding to *My Beautiful Laundrette* and beyond.

Naomi Sargant, responsible for the 15 per cent of our airtime that had to be educative, launched series after series of what she called 'life-skills' programmes: sewing, gardening, baking, building etc. You can see her mark everywhere today. *Quilts in Women's Lives,* denounced unseen by some who should have known better, remains a landmark.

Mike Bolland, hopping from youth programmes to new comedy, brought entertainment that I, for one, never expected to see on the screen. *Saturday Night* was 'Live' indeed.

Liz Forgan expertly helped grow ITN's *Channel 4 News,* and the current affairs shows that attended it. People told me that an hour-long news would never work. I knew they were wrong; a near-prototype existed on PBS in the United States. After a dreadful start, it was kicked into running order by Stewart Purvis and has never looked back; it's a far better thing today than it ever was then, offering a different take on what's happening to those offered by Sky or the BBC.

But the main thing is that this range of output happens outside the building, and has many different makers, of all shapes and sizes.

The channel has grown and prospered under every – well nearly every – succeeding chief executive. It is in excellent hands today. Michael Grade, who now believes that the time for privatisation has come, distinguished himself in office, combining skilfully with his Chairman, Sir Michael Bishop, to fend off a previous move to sell the channel off. For that, we are in his debt. And now? 'Perhaps', someone said to me, 'Grade wants to buy it?'

For me the most painful blemish in the channel's offering over the years was the hugely popular and lucrative *Big Brother* from Endemol. (Stand up, Peter Bazalgette and take your bow.) Tim Gardam did well to commission it. The first few years brought an involving novelty to our living rooms. Two, three years, fine; five years, well, ok. Seven years? That was enough, surely.

Big Brother went on and on for thirteen years and spread, like a rapacious weed, over the schedule in peak-time, seven nights a week, for thirteen weeks a year, keeping, as became apparent, lots of other possibilities off the screen. The channel became known as *The Big Brother Channel*. The tail was wagging the dog. When the belated great axe swung, C4 came to life again.

Of course it is a good thing for our society if we take a long hard look at Channel 4 today, and ponder whether, in a fast changing world, the channel should alter also. But it is doubtful that the spirit and purpose that still distinguishes it could survive ownership by a body that aims at dividends for share-holders, properly entitled to expect maximum profit. It is not clear how that spirit, if the transformation were effected, could possibly be protected. Many will say outright that it could not.

What is certain is that no drastic step in that direction should be taken without a wide-ranging public debate, collecting the voices and opinions of those who watch it, and, also importantly, of those who make a living by it.

Well, here we are. With this series of essays, let's begin.

Sir Jeremy Isaacs was the founding CEO of Channel Four from 1981-1987. He is one of the great television programme makers, 'The World at War' (1973) his masterpiece. Before Channel Four, he was Director of Programmes for Thames Television (1974-78), and subsequently General Director of the Royal Opera House (1987-1996). He is 83 and lives in Suffolk and on the Isle of Skye

Section 1:
What future for 4?

Introduction by Richard Tait

It is one of the paradoxes of British television that, despite the past two decades of rapid change driven by new technology and new players, the UK, to the surprise of some, still has a uniquely successful public service broadcasting system (PSB). As well as the BBC, which has (so far) avoided death by a thousand cuts and the deadly embrace of state control, we have a popular and successful commercial network in ITV which still believes in high quality journalism and drama; and we have Channel 4, a happy accident of public policy from the Thatcher years – a public corporation, funded commercially and with a remit dedicated to producing distinctive, risk-taking programmes and attracting under-served audiences.

This summer two key components of that system face their biggest challenges since the deregulation of commercial television in 1992. The BBC's Charter and Agreement are up for renewal and the jury is still out on whether the corporation will retain the resources and the independence to do its job properly. And the government has signalled that it is thinking seriously about privatising Channel 4. This book reflects the passionate arguments for and against a privatised Channel 4 – the politics, the business case, the impact both on the UK broadcast sector and on its audiences.

Privatisation has been mooted – and rejected – on at least four occasions in the past. This time, writes the doyen of media correspondents Raymond Snoddy, it could be different. He unpicks the complex and unpredictable politics of privatisation and reports that the government even thought about introducing privatisation in the March Budget, leaving less opportunity for debate. He also reveals the tensions in the Cabinet between John Whittingdale, the Culture Secretary, and George Osborne, the Chancellor. Add to the mix Whittingdale's position as a long-standing advocate of Brexit and it is no surprise Snoddy believes 'the picture for Channel 4 will only become clearer after the 23 June referendum, and its consequences, have worked their way through the political system'.

But the advocates of privatisation believe their case is compelling. David Elstein has held top jobs at Thames, Channel 5 and Sky. He is critical of Channel 4 management's mistakes in the past and not over impressed by their current performance – losing audiences faster than other PSBs in recent years. He believes that his detailed analysis of the channel's output suggests too little is being spent on truly distinctive content. David estimates that the cost savings and synergies from the takeover of Channel 4 by a major international broadcaster such as Sky, Viacom or Discovery could free up as much as £200 million a year, allowing Channel 4 to do more, not less, distinctive programming. His conclusion is that a carefully managed privatisation (with tight regulation) 'might deliver considerably more public value than the status quo'.

Opponents of privatisation have two main arguments. The first is that Channel 4 is a sound business and in no need of being 'rescued' by private ownership. Toby Syfret, head of TV at Enders Analysis, one of Europe's top media research companies, is not convinced that Channel 4 faces serious financial problems either now or in the future or that it cannot afford to continue to make distinctive programmes. He argues that 'financial sustainability and remit sustainability can go together, and Channel 4 is today performing strongly on both fronts'.

The second objection to privatisation is that the remit – the distinctive (but often unprofitable) programmes which make Channel 4 different – would not survive a privatised company's focus on the bottom line and that the UK independent production sector which makes so many of those programmes would suffer. Channel 4 commissioned two leading economists, Professor Patrick Barwise of London Business School and the LSE and Dr Gillian Brooks of the University of Oxford, to estimate what the impact of privatisation could be for Channel 4's investment in programmes. Their conclusion is that a privatised Channel 4 would be most likely to cut costs and commission a more commercially profitable schedule. The impact on the independent production sector would be significant: 'a 44% cut in Channel 4's UK content investment'.

One of the first signs that the government was serious about privatisation was when in September last year the respected Channel 4 chairman, Lord Burns, was not asked to stay on for a further year. Lord Burns had advocated as an alternative to privatisation the mutualisation of Channel 4 as a mutually owned not-for-profit company. In his 'Exit' interview with the House of Lords Select Committee on Communications, part of which we publish here, he stressed the benefits of stability which that option could bring and warned of the potential downside of privatisation: 'There would be less risk and less innovation. I characterise this as a situation where the more value you want to extract from it in a sale, the more you have to compromise the channel's public service obligations'.

Lord Burns has been joined in opposing privatisation by David Abraham, Channel 4's chief executive since 2010, having previously run UKTV. He is convinced that privatisation is 'a solution in search of a problem'. He is proud of Channel 4's current performance and sees the four key elements at the heart of the remit to be to stimulate public debate; to reflect cultural diversity; to champion alternative points of view; and to nurture new talent. He believes that Channel 4 'continues to make an economic, social and cultural contribution of a kind I simply cannot imagine a shareholder-owned company being able to match'.

Liz Forgan was one of Channel 4's founding commissioning editors, famously hired on the spot by chief executive Jeremy Isaacs after she had come to interview him for *The Guardian*. She went on to be Channel 4 director of programmes for nearly a decade. She accepts that there is perfectly good argument for privatising Channel 4, but is not convinced by it, advising her readers: 'put not your trust in remits'. The remit has worked because the people running Channel 4 wanted it to work. A privatised company would see things very differently. 'The remit could appear in letters of gold at the top of the Memorandum and Articles and it would make no difference to a CEO bound to a different master'. Her conclusion is that 'what it is not possible to believe is that a privatised Channel would deliver as wide a range of programming or take as many risks with new talent and new ideas'.

The intense arguments in this section – and in the rest of this book – reflect just how much is at stake. Public service broadcasting remains a key part of our culture as the most popular source of entertainment and has an even more key role in our democracy as the most used and most trusted source of impartial, accurate journalism. The future of Channel 4, whether in public or private ownership, is not just a matter of media policy. It matters to us all as viewers and citizens.

Through political channels

By Raymond Snoddy

As the Culture Secretary dithers over the politics of privatisation, the future of Channel 4 may yet be decided by wider issues – not least the Brexit vote

It is entirely possible that Channel 4 could by now have been well on the way to privatisation. It would have caused enormous controversy and allegations of bad faith, but the privatisation announcement could easily have been buried in the Spring budget statement.

Naturally the move would have come without warning, except for the usual, detailed leak in *The Sunday Times*, a few days before. It would have appeared like a bolt-out-of-the-blue and amounted to a *fait accompli*, just one measure among dozens in the Budget.

The controversial news would have been swamped by the headlines on George Osborne's tax plans and would have slipped effortlessly into the current narrative that we live in the most uncertain times since the crash and that difficult decisions were inevitable. And even though with Channel 4 we are only talking about a mere billion pounds or so – tiny in the scale of things – further efforts were needed to reduce the deficit and anyway this was a measure to safeguard the channel's long-term future.

The potential route map was very clear. The privatisation of Channel 4 after 33 years as a public corporation would come through the Money Bill that turns the Budget proposals into law. So far as the Government was concerned, the Money Bill would have been the ideal vehicle for a swift legislative conclusion to the rather tricky Channel 4 issue.

It is secondary legislation, so there is no need for messy instruments like white papers or broadcasting bills, and as the future of Channel 4 was scooped up with vital financial measures, there would be little opportunity for extensive debate.

A Money Bill also has one important characteristic that would make it particularly suitable for privatising Channel 4, from the Government's point of view.

Any broadcasting bill trying to carry out such a thing would run into extensive cross-party opposition in the House of Lords, including from former broadcasters and even former Culture Secretaries.

In contrast a Money Bill is a magic device that once certified as such, effectively whizzes into law. Under the Parliament Acts, once a Money Bill passes through the House of Commons it becomes law after one month, with or without the approval of the House of Lords.

What a neat way for Culture Secretary John Whittingdale to make his mark on the broadcasting history of the UK.

Is this a conspiracy theory or just plain conspiracy?

Such an approach would certainly carry echoes of the way the Culture Secretary tried to bounce the BBC into accepting the full, immediate £700 million cost of funding free licence for the over 75s without any negotiation – or was made to try.

Then there was no warning; simply Monday morning telephone calls from Whittingdale to the BBC director-general Lord Hall and Rona Fairhead, chairman of the BBC Trust, proclaiming that the decision had been taken and any 'mitigation' would have to come considerably later in the discussions on the renewal of the BBC's Royal Charter.

It was only when Lord Hall warned Chancellor George Osborne, who had taken over the issue from Whittingdale, that, as a result he would have to announce the imminent closure of BBC 2, BBC Four, all BBC local radio stations and the national news services of Scotland, Wales and Northern Ireland, that the hard line softened. In particular the over 75s charge on the BBC will now be phased in over a number of years.

Shotgun wedding

Claire Enders, founder of research group Enders Analysis, whose work on Channel 4 privatisation has gone to both Whittingdale and the Treasury, is convinced that the Budget route – 'a shotgun wedding' – was a serious policy option despite some obvious obstacles. There was a view, from Whittingdale and his civil servants, that a standalone Channel 4 might become unsustainable in future, apparently based on a misreading of Channel 4 accounts, and that privatisation could provide the solution. The original impetus for the privatisation plan, however, almost certainly came from the Treasury.

Apart from the ensuing political row, the obstacles to using the Money Bill manoeuvre included the fact that Channel 4's licence runs out in 2024 and any significant changes to its remit *would* require primary legislation.

'What we (Enders Analysis) have achieved so far is that a shotgun wedding on the wrong basis – that Channel 4 was unsustainable – that was going to be shuffled through in this budget through a Money Bill and therefore secondary legislation, has been kicked down the road,' Enders explains.

'The Budget route was definitely Plan A,' insists Enders, a former ITV executive.

David Abraham, chief executive of Channel 4, was very aware of the Plan A thesis which he believes could only have worked as 'a very aggressive approach from a Cabinet that was united to do something.'

Abraham did not however think it plausible because of what he believes is the absence of that unity, between Chancellor Osborne, Whittingdale and Business Secretary Sajid Javid.

The Channel 4 chief executive was, however, concerned enough to ask Channel 4's lawyers to look into the issue.

The judgement of the lawyers was that the Budget Money Bill approach was perfectly feasible politically, if the privatisation had been in the Conservative manifesto.

'If something isn't in the manifesto, and if there is something so big and noisy as Channel 4, to stage it in this way would piss off a lot of people,' Abraham was told.

'Quite a lot of Tories would get very angry if they weren't given the opportunity to have a proper discussion. It would be regarded as railroading,' he added.

Not only was Channel 4 privatisation not in the manifesto, its executives had also been assured before the last election by Culture Minster Ed Vaizey that there were no plans to privatise the channel.

Abraham treated ministerial denials of privatisation at the time with caution, because he and his team were starting to hear other things off-stage, and started to prepare for a battle just in case.

Whittingdale, Abraham claims, has been 'talking out of both sides of his mouth,' denying the privatisation threat in public and then 'telling his journalistic mates at parties that he was coming after it.'

Then came the spectacular public leak in September 2015.

On Wednesday, 26 August, Whittingdale had told the Edinburgh Television Festival that 'the ownership of Channel 4 is not currently under debate,' though naturally he refused to rule out all circumstances in which such a thing might happen.

Similar weasel words were spoken, at least in public, at the Royal Television Society's Cambridge Convention a few weeks later.

Then on 24 September a senior civil servant was photographed – or more precisely the heading of a 'commercially sensitive' document peeping out of his briefcase was photographed – as he walked into Downing Street.

The damning document, or the part of it inadvertently made available to the public, read: 'Work should proceed to examine the options of extracting greater public value from the Channel 4 corporation, focussing on the privatisation option in particular.'

Some have argued that the leak must have been a deliberate trial balloon designed to gauge public reaction.

After all, so many civil servants and ministers have been caught by the power of long range lenses to blow up the wording of casually-held documents as they walk into Number 10 that by now everyone must be aware of the danger. Mustn't they?

The cock-up theory is more likely on this occasion because there is evidence of pandemonium after the leak. Whittingdale was caught coming close to lying, or at the very least being very economical with the *actualité*, and all went quiet on the issue for a month or so.

At the very least the Government's public cover was blown and any chance of staging a coup via the Budget, probably a long shot in the real world, was gone.

Abraham thought that was that, but now believes that Whittingdale went back to Cabinet and got permission to undertake a review. Depending on interpretation of the murky world of inter-departmental politics, this was either an attempt to breathe new life into the plan or even possibly an attempt to kick Channel 4 privatisation into the long grass – or at the very least delay its implementation.

Too much negative talk?
But where did the idea of privatisation this time come from, who was behind it and what is likely to happen now? In a theoretical sense the idea has been around for a couple of decades. The Treasury keeps a list of public assets that could be sold and Channel 4 has always been on it. When it looked as though it might reach the top of the list, the concept ran into powerful opposition, most notably in the Major years from Michael Grade when chief executive and his chairman, the dyed-in-the wool Tory and founder of the British Midland airline Sir Michael (later Lord) Bishop.

During the 'begging bowl' phase, when Andy Duncan was chief executive and Luke Johnson chairman, the worry was less about privatisation than finding a way to do something about the £100 million deficit that was mysteriously forecast but which never materialised.

Everything was explored from Government subsidies and mergers with Channel 5 to increased co-operation with the BBC, a merger with BBC Worldwide and even giving Channel 4 a slice of the licence fee.

Endless talking came to nothing, and in the case of the BBC some animosity, with Johnson and the then BBC chairman Sir Michael Lyons almost coming to blows over the failure of partnership conversations.

All the negative talk from Channel 4 helped to seed the idea that a single stand-alone broadcast channel, albeit it with offshoots such as More 4 and Film on Four, could not survive alone in the modern world of international media giants.

Privatisation was not just about free market ideology, or raising a relatively small sum of money for the Treasury, it was both necessary and sensible for the future good of Channel 4 – or at least that's the way the argument was deployed.

There is no single cause for the current interest in (if not outright enthusiasm for) privatisation, in some sections of the Conservative Party. Rather it is a 'witches' brew' stirred up from a mixture of the personal and the political.

The privatisation idea may have come to the surface again when Sajid Javid was in charge at DCMS. In June 2015 the then chairman of Channel 4 Lord Terry Burns, a former permanent secretary at the Treasury, picked up rumours of a possible privatisation from Treasury contacts. The plan for a rapid privatisation may have originated in the Shareholder Executive, part of the Treasury responsible for managing government corporate assets. The Executive had been involved in the plans to privatise the Post Office.

Certainly there were signs in July 2015 that a rapid privatisation of Channel 4 was very much on the political agenda.

According to Chris Bryant, former Labour shadow Culture Secretary, privatisation is a 'personal obsession' of John Whittingdale, who once worked in the Downing Street Policy Unit and was a special advisor to Norman Tebbit.

'He hopes this will be his legacy – a strange sort of legacy I would say,' says Bryant, who notes that ministers often want to meddle even if, in the case of broadcasting, things would be better left alone. The incentive for Whittingdale, according to this line of argument, has intensified because he was blocked in his aim of taking more radical action against the BBC.

The political background is a Conservative Government which in its ideological stance is as Thatcherite as any since Thatcher herself in thinking the market knows best in most things. Even leaving aside the issue of whether Channel 4 can stand on its own two feet, there is a feeling among opponents that it is 'not on top of its game' in terms of delivering on its remit to offer innovative programmes that are both diverse and appeal to minorities.

A senior public relations executive with expert knowledge of both the media and the Conservative Party sees it as 'a classic example of Tory history bumping up against Tory ideology'.

'Despite its rather glossy marketing exterior the Conservatives have never had a more Thatcherite government than the one that's in power now. From an ideological point of view why not privatise Channel 4?' the executive argues.

The Key Influence

In the debate over privatisation one person has been particularly influential. According to Claire Enders, whose view is supported by a former Culture Secretary speaking only for background, that is Ray Gallagher who worked at Rupert Murdoch's Sky as director of public affairs for 15 years. Gallagher went on to become advisor to the Culture, Media and Sport select committee, chaired for a decade by Whittingdale, and then was appointed the Culture Secretary's special advisor in June 2015. 'Ray Gallagher is the leading proponent (of privatisation), working for John and John has to have ideas,' says Claire Enders.

Elstein's views on Channel 4 are set out in Chapter 2 of this book, but his approach could not be more clear. It includes the argument that public ownership has not bequeathed commercial wisdom and that 'Michael Jackson (former C4 chief executive) and his successors squandered nearly £300 million on non-core activities.'

Being acquired by a large media group would mean savings of £200 million a year, not least from the fact that the new owners 'would be able to dispense with at least 500 of its 808 staff.'

Add in the headquarters building, worth around £85 million, along with Channel 4's reserves of £250 million, and serious money would be involved.

Against such a financial background, according to Elstein, a buyer could be persuaded to accept a legally enforceable stronger remit, including the creation of a public broadcasting fund which would lead to more arts and education programmes than Channel 4 broadcasts at the moment.

He accepts, however, the main thrust of an Enders Analysis paper that there is no pressing need to sell Channel 4 and that the channel is not in any foreseeable danger of failing.

'All that may be true, but does not affect the central calculation. If Channel 4 can survive – even thrive – indefinitely in public ownership, thanks to a weak remit, then it is all the harder to justify leaving money and a stronger remit on the table unrealised, especially if a proportion of the money raised can be used to provide a contestable public service content fund,' Elstein argues.

Enders Analysis, by contrast, believes there is no current case for privatising C4 at all. The channel was delivering its remit with great success, was commercially sustainable and promised both to remain highly sustainable and grow its public service broadcasting contribution through its current licence ending in 2024.

'Reforming' Channel 4 by placing it in private hands 'requires the Government to somehow conclude that it is unsustainable with its current remit, and that in relation to minorities, British independent film, investigative journalism, news plurality, comedy and innovative social documentaries and market impacts on independents outside the M25, its unquestioned significant social impacts will fall away anyway,' argues Enders Analysis.

The researchers Toby Syfret and Claire Enders go one stage further and say that any conclusion of unsustainability by DCMS, echoed at least initially by Whittingdale, flew in the face of the manifest evidence of the past 33 years. 'No sane person could support it let alone publicly defend it through the entire legislative process,' Enders argues.

In the battle of the heavyweight reports Patrick Barwise, emeritus professor of management and marketing at the London Business School, has a similar view.

Barwise notes that John Whittingdale told the Commons Select Committee in January that the main reason he was considering privatisation of Channel 4 was not, as widely assumed, to raise money.

Instead it was to "ensure (C4) can continue to deliver the remit, in what is to become a very-fast changing and challenging environment."

Even without the detailed information that only a green and white paper can provide, Barwise is convinced that privatisation would almost certainly damage UK independent production.

Barwise and co-author Gillian Brooks (details in Chapter 4 of this book) envisage a 58 per per cent projected rise in real (inflation-adjusted) content spend by 2025, implying a big increase in Channel 4's ability to deliver the remit.

The US candidates

Barwise believes, almost certainly correctly, that if Channel 4 is privatised it will be bought by a large company moving into, or expanding its operations in the UK.

The main candidates are US media companies such as 21st Century Fox, Comcast/NBC Universal, Disney, Discovery, Liberty Global, Scripps, Sony Pictures Television, Time Warner and Viacom.

Few if any have any experience of public service broadcasting, most would regard UK television as over-regulated, and as broadcasters and production companies themselves would spell the end of the C4 publisher-broadcaster model.

Unless there is a significant cut in programme budgets and a move to more mainstream programming Barwise sees 'realistic, perhaps optimistic' savings and synergies in the £20-£40 million range – and a realistic maximum valuation of between £220 million and £440 million, considerably less than most current speculation.

As the debate on the channel's future developed, a couple of particularly surprising supporters of privatisation emerged – Lord Grade and Luke Johnson, both of whom vehemently opposed a sale when they held high office in Channel 4.

C4 CEO David Abraham decided to take each to lunch separately to try to understand where they were coming from. 'In Michael's case he is very clever and very charming but the bottom line of the lunch was: "listen dear boy the game is up. You really ought to throw your lot in with an IPO (initial public offering) and you could do very well out of it",' says Abraham. 'I spent the lunch telling him why that couldn't work and that personally I wasn't interested.' Lord Grade then wrote a letter thanking Abraham for lunch and arguing that it would be better for Channel 4 to be in private hands.

Abraham said nothing in public until Grade 'chose to blab his mouth off' at a Broadcasting Press Guild lunch at Pinewood Studios and told journalists that Abraham's position defied commercial logic.

The Channel 4 chief executive showed Grade's letter to a journalist.

As for Johnson he had appeared at Edinburgh by video asking whether or not Channel 4 should be in the private sector despite being against such a thing in the past.

'Over lunch he said I should not be shutting down the debate. I am not in a position to shut down the debate. I don't own Channel 4. Politicians decide,' Abraham explains.

Johnson replied that the politicians definitely want to look at this and that he (Abraham) should be open to discussion.

In fact Abraham emphasises hundreds of staff-hours have gone into preparing all the numbers, plans and future projections for the visits of civil servants from both the DCMS and the Treasury.

It was against the background of the two lunches that Abraham attacked Lord Grade at a conference in March for 'changing his mind more often than he changes his socks' and advised him to go off and enjoy his Channel 4 pension.

Johnson was accused of 'getting out the begging bowl' on behalf of Channel 4 and had flip-flopped on his view of the channel's future.

Their changing positions had made them, Abraham said: 'the flip and flop of British broadcasting.'

Privatisation, he added, was a solution looking for a problem.

As the discussion evolves there will be clear differences often, but not always, breaking along party lines. Two of the most effective Heritage/Culture Secretaries have been David Mellor, Conservative and Lord Chris Smith Labour.

Mellor can see no case whatsoever for Channel 4 remaining in the public sector and for him the idea that the channel is a necessary part of the fabric of public service broadcasting in the UK is quite wrong. 'They see themselves as a commercial broadcaster putting out stuff like *Big Brother* (2000-2010) and trawling along the bottom of the aquarium in terms of public taste. I think they should be privatised and the sooner the better – though this Government is so infirm of purpose across a whole range of things I wouldn't be at all certain,' says Mellor.

The 'boiling frog' theory

Lord Smith is equally passionate in the opposite direction. Channel 4 is a sometimes quirky, sometimes infuriating broadcaster, he says, but in an ingenious and remarkable way and without costing either the taxpayer or the Government a penny.

Is it possible to create a strong regulatory regime to protect the public remit of a privately owned Channel 4?

'I think that's a load of baloney. You can start out with that intention and you can have all the assurances in the world that that will happen but gradually, bit-by-bit, it will be eroded away. It will be a boiling frog [supposed not to notice gradual heating] and suddenly we will realise it is dead,' explains the former Culture Secretary, who will oppose privatisation in the House of Lords should a Bill on the subject ever get there.

Ultimately the fate of Channel 4 could be determined by neither broadcasting not financial issues, but the larger political context.

In short, the channel could be saved from privatisation by the Brexit debate.

John Whittingdale is one of the 'gang of seven' in the Cabinet who have come out in favour of the UK voting to leave the European Union in the June 23 referendum. He is not the most prominent, or the most vociferous advocate of Brexit, and is not a recent 'betrayer' because he has long been a Eurosceptic.

In March he did choose to write a relatively moderate Thunderer column in *The Times* arguing that he had hoped Prime Minister Cameron would have been able to negotiate a new relationship with the EU.

What the Prime Minister produced 'falls a long way short of the new arrangement I would like to see', Whittingdale argued.

If, as seems more likely than not, the UK votes to stay in the EU by however small a margin, the outcome for the Culture Secretary's political career could be grim.

Mellor knows the ways of the Conservative Party and has no doubt what will happen next. 'There will be a night of the long knives. It's perfectly obvious that a lot of Cameron's people in Downing Street are thirsting for blood. There will be people too big to get rid of. John Whittingdale is not one of them,' says Mellor.

His very lack of front-line importance, or scale of betrayal, might work in the opposite direction, unless Cameron wanted to get rid of the embarrassment of someone so apparently keen on privatising the Channel 4 of Willy Whitelaw and Margaret Thatcher.

John McVay, chief executive of PACT, the independent producers group, predicts that Whittingdale might just get 'a Caesar's pardon' although as things stand privatisation, he believes, is now looking less likely.

The Culture Secretary may have deliberately, or by implication, helped to save the channel from privatisation by insisting that its current remit should be protected in any privatisation process.

In August 2015 the Culture Secretary told television executives at the Edinburgh International Television Festival: 'The remit of Channel 4 is a priority and it's not going to change.'

Was such a commitment an example of Whittingdale's economic naivety – that you can have privatisation *and* the remit – or part of a cunning plan to put a spanner in the Treasury's privatisation plans in the knowledge that the full remit would make Channel 4 relatively unattractive to potential buyers? Under the 'benign' Whittingdale theory on the C4 issue his survival in power would be important in opposing Treasury privatisation forces.

Whatever the political fate of Whittingdale, he or his successor will also have a number of options to consider that fall short of for-profit privatisation, whether through a sale to another broadcaster, or the most drastic and potentially damaging option of all – purchase by venture capitalists.

There is the mutualisation/ or non-profit equity option from Lord Burns, an option fully explained in Chapter 5 of this book.

The former Treasury mandarin is in general in favour of privatisations – but not this one.

The Dyke plan

Former BBC director-general Greg Dyke has come up with another option. He was at a health farm recently feeling a bit bored and starting thinking about Channel 4…

What if you borrowed a lot of money at current low interest rates and gave it to the Government? Channel 4 would simply pay the interest on the loan not the capital enabling Channel 4 to continue as presently constituted.

Dyke talked about the plan with his old ITV colleague, the Labour Peer Lord Hollick, and then with the chairman and chief executive of Channel 4. They thought they could manage such a deal while running Channel 4 in the public interest.

'We would go to the Government and say look we can get you between £700 million and £1 billion and leave Channel 4 as it is. Surely that would be good for you. It would be disaster if Channel 4 went to any of the private equity people sniffing around,' says Dyke.

He and Lord Hollick are waiting to see the fallout from the EU referendum before deciding whether to push ahead with the idea.

Dyke, now chairman of the Football Association, believes it would be impossible for a privately-owned Channel 4 to retain a public purpose remit.

'If it goes to anybody whose major interest is maximising profit that will be the end of Channel 4 as we know it and that is what we are against,' says Dyke.

Claire Enders has set out a variant of the idea as part of her strategy to take a longer term approach and kick the can down the road rather than going for a simplistic 'shotgun wedding'.

The longer term Enders approach involves persuading the Government to extend Channel 4's licence to 2030 and revalue the stake it is holding on its books at £450 million. 'It's a no-brainer,' she says. 'They revalue that asset in their books and if they really want to they could get a dividend stream that would prove it was worth it. There is nothing wrong with £50 million a year.' Enders adds that establishing a dividend flow might even make the company more interesting to potential buyers in future.

The researcher is convinced that the can really has been kicked down the road at least for now, and that the debate about the future of Channel 4 will continue through this Parliament and probably into the next.

David Abraham fears that despite protestations in private, Whittingdale will never give up on Channel 4, although he might not last long enough to take the privatisation forward. The question might them depend on who becomes the next Culture Secretary and whether they cared enough to try to push the controversial issue through.

'We keep hearing that it is Osborne's calculation that the pain against the gain is simply not worth it. He's going around making speeches about the importance of the creative industries,' Abraham notes.

Against that, the Conservatives could be going into the next election facing a weakened opposition and there would be little to stop them putting Channel 4 privatisation into the next manifesto, and perhaps even announcing it in a future budget if they had another election victory.

Damaging uncertainty

The Channel 4 chief executive is most angry about the current behaviour of John Whittingdale, holding on to all his options, damaging the very asset he might yet privatise through the uncertainty he continues to create.

'What I need is for him definitively now to say "I am not privatising Channel 4 for the rest of this Parliament". We need clarity. That is the thing they owe us,' Abraham insists.

When he addresses staff meetings Abraham has no idea what to tell them. When he meets WPP chief executive Sir Martin Sorrell, the advertising boss wants to know what the Government's plans are before signing any long-term deal with the channel.

Even worse, the Channel 4 chief executive has to sit down with partners UKTV in the knowledge that the 50 per cent owners of the group, Scripps, have made it clear they are interested in bidding for Channel 4 if it was to become available.

'It's a bloody impossible position to be in. Whittingdale is doing great damage because he doesn't know how to run a commercial channel. It's been fine up until now but it's not fine indefinitely,' says Abraham.

Yet despite conflicting theories about where the push for privatisation came from, Whittingdale remains interested, at least in public. In March he told Richard Brooks in a *Sunday Times* interview he still favoured privatisation: 'I'm looking at the options, but would argue that Channel 4 is being restrained by not being privatised. It means it has less deep pockets.' Whittingdale claimed he would safeguard the channel's news, current affairs programmes and Film4 and try to do something about its lack of children's programmes. 'I'm separately looking at its remit which is rather fuzzy,' Whittingdale added.

Meanwhile a former Culture Secretary believes there is little chance of privatisation this year and only a minor chance next year. Yet the battle between Tory history and ideology could yet take a skip in the direction of the latter, amid signs that John Whittingdale is not completely isolated from the Conservative Government hierarchy – at least on the privatisation of Channel 4 and if the Treasury did indeed provide the initial impetus who knows what might yet happen.

The picture for Channel 4 will only become clearer after the 23 June referendum, and its consequences have worked their way through the political system.

About the author

Raymond Snoddy is a journalist, author, television presenter and one of the country's most respected media commentators, having covered the news industry for more than 35 years. He began his career on the *Middlesex Advertiser*, and worked for *The Times*, where he was the paper's first media editor, and the *Financial Times*. His books include a biography of media tycoon Michael Green and *The Good, The Bad and The Ugly*, about ethics in the newspaper industry. Raymond was the presenter of Channel 4's award-winning *Hard News* series, and of the BBC's *Newswatch*. He was made OBE for his services to journalism in 2000.

The case for privatisation

By David Elstein

Current ownership has not served the original remit as well as many believe. The option of privatisation – coupled with tougher regulation – could deliver better public value

On his last day of six years in office as chairman of Channel 4, that wisest of owls Lord (Terry) Burns told listeners to BBC Radio 4's *The Media Show* that 'you can have the Channel 4 remit, or you can have privatization, but you cannot have both'.

The logic behind this pronouncement has a respectable history. A previous chairman, Sir Michael (later Lord) Bishop, of impeccable Tory credentials, warned then Prime Minister John Major against any idea of privatisation in 1996: 'When conventional shareholder pressures are applied to the TV industry... quality and choice are diminished... with new shareholders seeking to maximize profits, money for dividends would have to be taken from the screen.'

A very similar formula was expressed by the channel's current chief executive David Abraham in 2015: shareholders would expect a 20% annual return on their capital after buying Channel 4, and that could only come from taking money out of the programme budget and abandoning the channel remit.

Other critics of the notion of privatisation (notably, the excellent paper from Enders Analysis published last December) have followed a similar line. With EA, the working assumption is that an acquirer would look for a 20% profit margin, even if it were not distributed as a dividend. Normally, that would be true. However, in a carefully managed auction of an asset that may benefit a rival, to your disadvantage, if you fail to bid the full price, that margin may be eroded down to 1 or 2%.

Clearly, there is abundant evidence that this is not a binary choice between content and dividends. Indeed 15 years ago, a policy paper issued by the Conservative opposition, in advocating privatisation, noted that the average dividend paid by the largest broadcasters quoted on the London stock market was well below 2%. ITV plc today still yields less than 2%, and both News Corp and 21st Century Fox less than 1%. Of the likely bidders for Channel 4, Discovery and Liberty do not pay dividends, and Viacom pays a bare 3%.

The kind of situation where new shareholders require large dividends is typically a private equity transaction. If one thing is certain in this whole affair, it is that there will not be a sale to private equity. A sale only makes sense to an existing media player – one that can extract synergies and savings from ownership of Channel 4.

The fallacy in the Burns/Bishop argument is the assumption that revenues and costs are fixed such that only a reduction in spending or a significant devaluation of the remit can release value for a new owner. Yet I know from my own experience of running Channel 5 that this is completely untrue. I proposed to Channel 4 in 2000 that we merge all our back office functions (finance, administration, HR, transmission, accommodation, airtime sales, acquisition and so on), leaving the programming and marketing staff entirely independent, in order to make savings of between £130 million and £190 million a year between us.

As it happens, Channel 4 rejected the approach (though, ironically, they subsequently tried to buy Channel 5): but the scale of savings that might be achieved by a buyer such as Sky, Viacom (owner of Channel 5), Discovery or Liberty Global (owner of Virgin Media) must easily run to £200 million a year by now. Currently, that is public value going to waste.

The formula so often used by leaders of Channel 4 – that we make a valuable contribution to the creative economy 'at zero cost to the taxpayer' – is simply wrong. Allowing that £200 million to go begging every year, when public service broadcasting is in long term decline, cannot be the right answer. We have ample evidence from Channel 4's own behaviour (including the attempted purchase of Channel 5) that a stand-alone public service channel is a sub-optimum proposition, unless – as was the case when Channel 4 was originally designed and launched – there is a guaranteed level of revenue and complete protection from the vagaries of the marketplace.

In 1982, this took the form of an annual payment from ITV, which in return derived all the benefit from selling Channel 4's airtime – and, incidentally, was able to write off its Channel 4 subscription (with the level set by the regulator at the time, the IBA) against the levy on excess profits which prevailed in those days: in effect, the bulk of the cost of Channel 4 in its initial phase was borne by the Treasury.

The removal of this ITV guarantee followed the recommendation from the 1986 Peacock Committee that Channel 4 should sell its own airtime, so as to create more competition for advertisers in the airtime market-place – a conclusion based on the well-founded assumption that ITV was effectively suppressing the true value of Channel 4 airtime. As the Thatcher government pushed this change through, the board of Channel 4 considered its future options – including merger with the yet-to-be-launched Channel 5, and privatisation (which senior board executive member Justin Dukes favoured).

The trade-off

The debate inside Channel 4 was rather similar to the current argument: once you had to earn your keep, how far might your 'remit' – your attempts to innovate, and your commitments to public service content of all kinds – be compromised? Of course, the 'remit' that the early Channel 4 set out for itself was largely composed internally: the Broadcasting Acts setting up the channel were remarkably bare of detail, other than a requirement to be 'innovative', be an alternative to ITV (and only ITV), include a suitable proportion of material of an educational nature, and commission a substantial proportion of output from producers independent of ITV (a proportion that Whitehall interpreted as 15%).

It was Jeremy Isaacs and his launch team who decided upon much of what we now regard as the core Channel 4 remit: serving minorities, sexual as well as ethnic; targeting younger audiences; committing to education both formal and informal; supporting filmed drama (both for cinema and TV screens); finding alternative voices and opinions; and growing the share of output commissioned from independents to a clear majority.

What has notably disappeared today from the Isaacs version of Channel 4 is a strong commitment to education, to the arts and to ideas: evidence that the nature and strength of a remit is not in itself dependent upon a particular level of income, even under public ownership. The programme budget for Channel 4 today is 50% higher – even allowing for inflation – than that for 1982, though of course the sheer scale of competition facing the channel is vastly greater.

For Isaacs, the tension was between fulfilling his public service objectives and winning a large enough share of audience to keep ITV happy in its role as sales arm and supplier of a guaranteed budget (he aimed at 10% in a 4-channel system, but never actually exceeded 8% in his six years as chief executive). Cheap imported sitcoms, quizzes and a home-grown soap were required in order to fund the arts, schools, films, current affairs, minority programmes and early evening news that he had chosen to commission.

It is crucial to understand that this trade-off has remained at the heart of the Channel 4 conundrum, however often the dice have been rolled in terms of the underlying financing. This was true of each successive formula adopted by ministers and regulators in an attempt to underpin the Channel's remit.

So, to begin with, the extra cash that flowed into Channel 4 once it started selling its own airtime seemed to have proved Peacock right. The programme budget grew but so did the overhead, as some 60 airtime sales staff – paid high salaries and strongly incentivized through bonus schemes – arrived (there are now nearly 200 in the sales team): a change that decisively and permanently shifted the channel's culture.

Inevitably, senior non-sales staff began to ask why their salaries – and other benefits, such as company cars – did not match those of the airtime team. When the 1991 ITV franchise round approached, Michael Grade – who had succeeded Isaacs as chief cxecutive – persuaded the board to offer the channel's key managers (including him) golden handcuffs in the shape of large cash payments to compensate them for declining to take part in any of the bids for ITV licences.

In his six years at Channel 4, Isaacs earned a total of £250,000: soon, his successors were earning that every year, then twice as much every year (as with Grade's successor, Michael Jackson), then three and even four times as much. At one point, the three top managers at Channel 4 earned £4.8 million between them in two years – more than twice as much as the organisation's total profits.

Today, the average annual salary at Channel 4 for the 800-plus employees (four times the number required when Channel 4 launched – at one point the total grew to over 1200) is more than £75,000, and the employment cost to the channel adds another £5,000 per head.

From public service broadcaster to media corporation

One of the reasons that Channel 4's payroll has swollen so far is that economic logic, changing priorities and an expansive vision of the future have inexorably pushed it that way. It was not just an airtime sales team that Channel 4 had to hire: marketing and lobbying became key departments within the channel, the first to maximize the value of the Channel 4 'brand', the second to squeeze yet more concessions out of the political class.

The negotiation to induce ITV to give up selling the channel's airtime (and walk away from the nominal losses incurred in setting up the channel) had resulted in ITV being allowed to claim half the income earned by the newly-independent business, once Channel 4's income exceeded 14% of all net TV advertising revenues (anything beyond 18% was excluded). The formula further required Channel 4 to allocate half its own share of any surplus generated to a Treasury reserve, with even the remaining half being subject to ministerial approval before it could be used for anything other than the channel budget.

It took some years, but Channel 4 managed to overturn all these restrictions. It emerged as a stand-alone entity (the Channel Four Corporation), no longer controlled directly by the IBA, with a primary duty to protect the main public service channel, but with the freedom to explore other activities, provided these were 'incidental or conducive' to that primary purpose.

In effect, Channel 4 could launch anything it liked: ministers had allowed a determined management, supported by the powerful independent producer lobby and an array of well-wishers, to drive a coach and horses through the original legislation and design of the channel.

Some of that support had been secured by Channel 4 making a series of promises to spend all the money it retrieved (including the £84 million in the Treasury reserve) on new programmes: it even listed the genres and the associated cost. But most of these were forgotten as the channel embarked instead upon a strategy of diversification – naturally, presented as the best way to fulfil Channel 4's objectives.

Michael Jackson, who became chief executive in 1997, went so far as to announce that the whole concept of public service broadcasting was old-fashioned. He decided to shape the new Channel Four Corporation as a multi-faceted media business. He launched pay channels – Film4 and E4 – but on terms (extracted by carriage provider BSkyB) which ensured they could never be profitable: they lost a cumulative £160 million before reportedly reaching break-even, and then being converted to free-to-air services.

By the time Jackson resigned in 2001, the Channel Four Corporation had fallen into losses for the first time in a decade. In the five years from 1996 to 2001, Channel 4 had gone from an operating profit of £134 million to a loss of £28 million – a turnaround of £162 million.

Film production and distribution companies set up by Jackson were closed by his successor, Mark Thompson, after losing £40 million. As Thompson put it in the 2002 Annual Report, 'some operations – notably the feature film production unit – were pursuing failing strategies'. He announced that 'we have put Channel 4 itself back where it should be – at the centre of everything we do,' cutting nearly 100 jobs and £21 million of costs in his first year. Yet Thompson persisted with Attheraces, which cost Channel 4 £23.3 million before it withdrew from the venture.

Thompson's successor Andy Duncan also bought and invested in third party businesses: £29 million went on a half share of EMAP's music channels (later disposed of); £500,000 on a website that closed after 8 months; £3.6 million on Life One Broadcasting (promptly written off – Channel 4 had just wanted its EPG slots); £500,000 on Ostrich Media (written off); £200,000 on Popworld; £1.5 million on Fingertip Software; £1 million on a failed speech radio station; and undisclosed millions on a digital radio venture.

At least Channel 4 was not alone in writing off £6.4 million on Project Kangaroo, a video-on-demand joint venture with BBC Worldwide and ITV, who lost £24 million between them after the Competition Commission ruled against the venture (it was eventually taken over by Arqiva, who lost another £15 million before finally admitting defeat).

One way and another, Jackson and his successors squandered nearly £300 million on non-core activities – virtually all the reserves and profits accumulated by Channel 4 and the Treasury since it started selling its own airtime – in just 17 years. That does not even include the £5 million lost when it was deposited with a dodgy bank that then went bust.

I rehearse this awkward history because it would be wrong to imagine that public ownership automatically protects Channel 4 from misguided adventures and flawed strategies on the part of its managements and regulator-appointed non-executives.

Perhaps a commercial company, with real shareholders and their chosen non-executive directors, might have staunched this flow of failed projects, or at least challenged the strategy. Yet the underlying lesson is that all this activity was directly or indirectly designed to underpin Channel 4 as a public service, once the ITV guarantee had been removed.

Building the broader base

Two more important precedents need to be cited before we can directly address the issue of privatisation. The first is the series of attempts to deliver what I had offered Channel 4 in 2000: a larger structure which would generate both savings and new revenues, thereby providing Channel 4 with a cushion against advertising recessions, audience fragmentation and intensifying media competition.

The amount Channel 4 bid for Channel 5 in 2010 – when RTL finally admitted it did not know how to make Channel 5 profitable – was only narrowly beaten by Richard Desmond's £104 million offer. In the same year, Channel 4 made another £100 million bid, for the Living TV portfolio of channels, which were eventually bought by Sky. The second of these attempts to broaden Channel 4's base (and make the kind of efficiency savings I had offered a decade earlier) would have left the public service channel surrounded by up to 20 commercial services.

The strategic significance of trying to broaden its economic base by deploying the last of its reserve funds was underlined by that fact that the Channel 4 board was at the same time warning Ofcom and DCMS ministers that it faced a medium-term prospect of a revenue shortfall of £100-£150 million a year, which would force a significant cut-back in 'remit' programming.

Channel 4 annual reports at the time showed that it allocated just £153 million to what it called 'core' public service genres, such as news, current affairs, documentaries, arts, education and religion – about a quarter of its total content spend.

Ofcom and its former chief executive Lord Carter (by then the minister in charge of the Labour government's digital strategy) took the pleas of economic vulnerability seriously, though working to the lower figure of £100m figure for the annual deficit, rather than Channel 4's pessimistic estimate of £150m. Efforts were made to induce BBC Worldwide to enter into some form of partnership with Channel 4, but these were eventually abandoned with no public statement of either the rationale behind such a deal or the reasons for its failure.

Given that there was very little overlap between the two enterprises, it would seem that the object of the exercise was simply to underwrite from BBC cash-flow and assets any shortfalls that might occur in Channel 4 revenues: so scarcely a strategic approach – rather, a sticking plaster remedy.

In the event, the financial plight Channel 4 had forecast for itself never materialised: one reason may be that the amount spent on 'core' public service genres has dropped from £153m to £85m. The whole episode has been airbrushed from memory: indeed, in its paper on Channel 4 privatisation Enders Analysis declared that 'financial sustainability has never been an issue throughout the course of Channel 4's 33-year history under successive leadership teams'.

Of course, even if that declaration had been true, it would not have signified much. Channel 4 can always be 'sustainable' one way or another, by simply compromising further in the constant tension between commerciality and public service. To that extent, nothing has changed since 1982. Indeed, the direction of travel over the last decade tells its own story.

The economics of Channel 4

Essentially, Channel 4 has managed to maintain a flat revenue profile for the past decade: total income in 2006 was £937m, and £938m in 2014, with the average for the past five years being £929m. This has been achieved by relying increasingly on its digital channels to supplement the declining audience share of the main service. In 2006, Channel 4 contributed an audience share of 9.6% to the total portfolio share of 11.9%; in 2014, it was 5.6% out of 10.9% (according to the Ofcom Communications Market Report of 2015, the 5.6% is actually 4.8% for the main channel, plus 0.8% for its +1 delayed version).

Of course ever since the launch of multi-channel television, there has been a recognised phenomenon of audience fragmentation. The 'heritage' broadcasters – BBC, ITV and Channel 4, later joined as a terrestrial analogue channel by Channel 5 – worked hard to offset the threat from the hundreds (over 500 currently) of new channels available to viewers, by launching and promoting their own digital services.

The effect of fragmentation on the five PSB channels has been dramatic, with a decline in their combined audience share in all homes from 73.8% in 2004 to 51.2% in 2014. The most marked decline has been in Channel 4's audience share, down over 50% (followed by BBC2 and Channel 5, down by 39%, then ITV, 35% and BBC1, 12%).

But in multi-channel homes, the PSBs fought back. Their new digital channels have almost trebled their audience share in those homes to 20.7%, effectively replacing nearly all the losses by the main channels. The other 500 channels on cable and satellite have actually lost a fifth of their audience share since 2004, as the PSBs and their portfolios captured 71.9% of all viewing in all homes. The satellite attack has been comprehensively repelled. The key to that success has been the allocation to the PSBs and their portfolio channels of all the best transmission frequencies and EPG slots on the Freeview system.

However, the performance of the components in the various portfolios has been markedly different. BBC1 and BBC2 have more than held their combined audience share, rising from 26.2% to 27.8% in multi-channel homes between 2004 and 2014, with their digital add-ons (BBC3, BBC4, BBC News, CBeebies, CBBC, BBC Alba and BBC Parliament) only contributing a 2% increase as part of an overall a rise from 29.5% to 33.1%.

ITV (along with ITV+1) has declined by 17% in those homes in those years, but its portfolio (ITV2, ITV3, ITV4, ITV Encore, CITV and ITVBe) has doubled its share, from 3.2% to 6.4%: so overall, a standstill at 22%. Channel 5 has seen a modest combined rise, from 5.1% to 5.9%, with a slight decline for the main service being compensated for by the portfolio channels (5*, 5USA) jumping from 0.2% to 1.5%.

The Channel 4 position is completely different. For the 20 years from the launch of Sky TV, between 1988 and 2007, Channel 4's audience share averaged 10%, with a low of 9% and a high of 11%. From the 9.8% share in 2006, Channel 4 has fallen away to 4.8% in 2014: a drop of 51%.

Because Channel 4's digital channels were originally pay services, it makes best sense to measure their relative performance from when they all became free to air. From 2006 to 2013, the Channel 4 portfolio audience share in multi-channel homes averaged 11.2%, dipping last year to 10.9%, but there was a dramatic shift in the balance between the main channel and the add-on channels (Film4, E4 and More4, together with their +1s, 4seven and 4Music).

In 2014, Channel 4's share was 4.8% out of that 10.9 portfolio total: a ratio of 44:56. If the +1 share is added to that 4.8%, the ratio rises to 51:49. The BBC1/2 ratio to its digital siblings is 84:16; ITV's 71:29; and Channel 5's 75:25.

Why should there be such a huge discrepancy? It may be partly because Channel 4's demographic profile (16-34, up-market) is more prone to the rapid shift in media use from TVs to other devices, and from linear viewing to on-demand viewing. But that alone cannot be a sufficient explanation, as the audience share for E4 – which has a much younger profile than Channel 4 itself – has risen: tolerance – even encouragement – of the shift must have played a part.

Why does it matter? After all, isn't this outcome a belated validation – following all the misfires and failures – of the diversification strategy? The Enders Analysis paper sees this high reliance on the digital channels as a sign of strength. Sadly, such a comforting thought misses the point. The portfolio channels are nominally part of the Channel 4 remit, which 'applies across all services and genres', according to the Annual Report. But the fact is that anything recognisably public service about Channel 4's output is almost exclusively confined to the main channel.

As the proportion of the main channel's content devoted to core public service declines, and the audience for the channel subsides, we can safely say that much less than 1% of the portfolio's 10.9% audience share is attributable to public service content: with £900m flowing through the Channel 4 Corporation every year, what we have is a very small dog wagging a very large tail.

Although you will not find the figure in the Channel 4 Annual Report (which contains a mass of detail, but not this), the Ofcom Communications Market Report (CMR) of 2015 tells us that the proportion of total Channel 4 Corporation revenue earned by advertising on Channel 4 itself in 2014 was just £483 million: 56% of the total £860m in advertising and sponsorship that the channels portfolio as a whole brought in (sales of rights earned a further £78m).

Also missing from the Channel 4 Annual Report is any breakdown of the balance of earnings between online and sponsorship sales, as between the main channel and the rest of the portfolio. The CMR tells us that the non-advertising revenues for ITV, Channel 4 and Channel 5 combined were £273m. Somewhere between 20% and 22% is probably Channel 4's share: say, £55m.

Likewise, the CMR shows £653m as the commercial PSB portfolio channels' revenue, with the Channel 4 portfolio's share probably close to £300m. Online revenue and commission from sales house activities on behalf of third party channels (a gross amount of £135m was earned) accounts for the balance of the £860m.

It would seem that the main channel's contribution to the income line is between £540m and £550m. On the expenditure side, according to the Annual Report, £492m was spent on the main channel in 2014, with £110m allocated to the digital channels and online content. The Annual Report gives us no clue as to what allocation of overheads can be made, as between the main channel and everything else. Even where such figures have been reported in the past, the document draws a discreet veil.

For instance, in the 2002 Annual Report, under the heading 'transmission and regulatory costs', we are clearly told that analogue transmission of Channel 4 cost £24.6m and digital transmission £14.1m, with transmission costs for the digital channels coming to £5.9m. Today, analogue transmissions have ceased, but the Annual Report compresses all transmission and regulatory costs into one number: £104m. As regulatory costs cannot be much more than £2m a year, it would appear that transmission costs have multiplied by five in 12 years, with no explanation given; and the split between Channel 4 and the portfolio channels has been concealed.

By contrast, the BBC declares the transmission costs for every one of its nine television services. The total of £111.8m includes £46.2m for BBC1 and £24.2m for BBC2 – both requiring complex transmitter arrangements to allow regional and local variations in output. That does not apply to any of the Channel 4 portfolio channels, which use a single content feed (though their advertising slots can vary regionally). The only reason for secrecy on the part of Channel 4 I can imagine would be to disguise the true balance between the cost of sustaining the main service and the rest of the corporation.

My working assumption is that the main channel is quite delicately poised. If the government were to pursue its privatisation option, all the underlying figures would have to be declared to potential buyers. They would then have to address the issue of the remit: and the truth about the remit – which may surprise some observers – would then be fully exposed.

The truth about the remit

The original Channel 4 licence conditions from the 1980 and 1981 Broadcasting Acts had quite limited provisions: essentially, most of the characteristics of Channel 4 that are most familiar today were actually nothing to do with legislation, but were introduced by the first, Isaacs-led, management team. In 1982, there was no bar on in-house production, and for many years Channel 4 produced the weekly answer-back programme, *Right to Reply* (an element much missed from the schedule of today).

The sheer volume of proposals from the independent sector ensured there was no need to build up an internal capability. Now, there is actually a legal bar (though the current management would like to change its relationship with the sector, either by retaining more ownership in content it commissions, or by acquiring equity in production companies). Likewise, the commitment to British film was an Isaacs initiative (much encouraged by Channel 4's first deputy chairman, film-maker Richard Attenborough).

The lengthy document that constitutes the present Channel 4 remit incorporates certain changes flowing from the 1990 and 1996 Broadcasting Acts, which were then extensively re-shaped during the passage of the 2003 Communications Act. The licence issued in 2004 has seen some minor changes subsequently, but is essentially cross-referenced to two dozen clauses of the 2003 Act. We are currently on to the 17th 'variation'. Then, in 2010, the Digital Economy Act required Channel 4 to deliver to Ofcom an annual statement on media policy.

That there may be some confusion today over what constitutes the Channel 4 remit is largely down to the central feature of the 2003 Communications Act: the creation of a single media regulator, Ofcom. When the various telecoms and media regulatory bodies were merged in 2003, one crucial level of expertise in the old IBA (which had become the ITC by the time merger occurred) that was lost was quality control.

Licence holders under the old ITV system (pre-1993) were inured to annual meetings with the IBA, where their record of compliance with detailed quota requirements was accompanied by a lengthy interrogation of quality of output, both locally and (where relevant) for the network.

These were no mere formalities. Before licences were auctioned, licence holders were primarily judged on quality, and cumulative negative annual reports could put the licence at risk. IBA officials were experienced and knowledgeable: they were confident of their judgements and not afraid of issuing yellow cards.

That has all gone, of course. Ofcom lacks any staff with quality control experience, which is why it would need to beef up its Content Board significantly if it were to take over quality control for the BBC. If that were to happen, a much more pro-active version of its current relationship with Channel 4 might become possible.

In the meantime, Ofcom has advanced an elaborate – but ultimately pointless – set of definitions of the purposes and characteristics of public service broadcasting. I say 'pointless' because they tell you nothing useful: not whether, and to what extent, designated PSB services (BBC1, BBC2, ITV1, Channel 4 and 5) are consonant with those purposes and characteristics, nor how to make them consonant if they are not, nor why it matters if they still fail, nor what then to do.

Indeed, since 2003, Ofcom has charted a steady decline in the delivery of public service content and of originated programming, without ever suggesting how this depressing trend might be reversed. As far as Channel 4 is concerned, the main changes by Ofcom have been to loosen public service obligations, not tighten them.

As for the 2010 Act, that has simply given statutory weight to a set of aspirations which Channel 4 is expected to pursue. There is no established measure of success, nor any prescribed penalty for failure. The tests for whether they are being met are devised by Channel 4 itself, and presently show commendable achievement. But if these – or other – tests showed lesser success, or even failure, there is no provision for any remedial action. The requirement is to *state* the aspirations, not *fulfil* them in an objective fashion.

If we look at the quantitative obligations, failure here could result in cash penalties (though the point of fining a publicly-owned corporation for failing to meet its business objectives is not clear). In fact, the hard quotas are remarkably few in number. The peak-time news hour introduced by Isaacs has become enshrined in law: Channel 4 must offer high quality news bulletins (but then, so must ITV and Channel 5), at lunchtime and in the early evening each weekday, and in the early evening on Saturdays (the Sunday early evening bulletin sometimes turns up very early in the evening). There is no requirement as to how much Channel 4 must spend on news, even as a percentage of the channel budget (it actually spends £25m, or 5%).

There must also be 4 hours of current affairs every week, of which a proportion must be transmitted in peak viewing time (between 6.30pm and 10 pm). Channel 4 slightly over-delivers on current affairs (an average of 5 hours a week, 3 in peak), but not on news.

According to the Channel 4 Annual Report, it is required to supply 1 hour of schools programmes *every year* (actually, the Ofcom website says half an hour). That this absurd minimum requirement is satisfied by the provision of four hours a year – *a year!* – begs the question as to what Ofcom is trying to achieve.

The end of education
In 1987, Channel 4 had taken over transmission of ITV's schools programming (it being accepted that it was unfair on ITV to maintain that obligation whilst being denied the right to a second channel, which is where the BBC's schools programmes were shown at that time). The original obligation was 330 hours a year, broadcast during school hours, which also became Channel 4's financial responsibility in 1993, after it won commercial independence from ITV.

The service became known as Channel 4 Schools, and then Channel 4 Education and finally 4Learning, in 2000; and programmes continued to be broadcast through to 2009. But by then, the morning slots on the schedule had become commercially valuable, and schools programmes were first shunted off to the night hours, for recording and subsequent use by schools, and then out of the schedule altogether, as Channel 4 persuaded Ofcom that non-linear distribution would be much more flexible and economical. By then, the budget for education had been cut to £6m a year, and that resource was primarily re-deployed online.

In 2010, the last head of education at Channel 4, Janey Walker, was made redundant, and although the budget for education remains at £6m, there is no longer any 'remit' requirement for actual transmissions. 4Learning itself was sold in 2007 to Espresso Group, and re-named (confusingly, but no doubt deliberately) Channel 4 Learning. When Isaacs launched Channel 4, one of his most powerful commissioning editors was for education – Naomi Sargant – with 15% of the channel budget and 400 hours of transmissions in her portfolio.

Even in 2000, Channel 4's remit included 7 hours of education every week, in addition to the schools obligation of 330 hours a year. But Ofcom has simply abandoned that, despite the 2003 Act requiring Channel to make a 'significant contribution of programmes of an educational nature *and* other programmes of educative value' (note the '*and*'). Also abandoned have been the requirement for one hour of religion each week and the 0.5% training and development levy, along with three hours of multi-cultural content each week.

The licence still speaks of the need to reflect a 'culturally diverse society', but the most recent Annual Report finessed that requirement by offering 'diversity' instead, and treating the many hours broadcast from the Sochi Paralympics as Channel 4's contribution to diversity. I applaud Channel 4's sustained commitment to disability issues: but disability is *not* synonymous with culture.

Under Isaacs, arts and ideas had been a central ingredient of the schedule. A transmission of Schoenberg's opera *Moses and Aaron* in peak-time would be unthinkable today. The brilliant array of programmes commissioned by Michael Kustow is a distant memory. Kustow himself did not survive the transition from Isaacs to Michael Grade, but Grade could still place a season of sixteen Allegro Films music documentaries in peak time on Saturday nights for the whole of the Autumn schedule.

Under Jackson and Thompson, there were not only live broadcasts from Glyndebourne, but commissioned operas, such as Jonathan Dove's *When She Died: Death of a Princess*. Today, the arts are barely visible on Channel 4, and neither the IBA nor its successors – the ITC and Ofcom – ever saw fit to require an arts quota.

Even the fixed quota obligations that seem firmest have soft edges. The most basic – origination – used to be 70% in peak and 60% across the schedule. The 60% is now 56%, and Channel 4 comfortably delivers the requirement. However, this is not a '*first-run*' obligation: 9% of the peak-time delivery of 77% is repeats. Across the schedule, 29% of the 63% delivery is repeats. Channel 4 could meet these quota obligations *without commissioning a single first-run programme* other than news and current affairs.

Before Ofcom took over enforcement of the quotas, there was indeed a 'first-run' requirement: 80% in peak, 60% across the schedule. Last year, 43% of Channel 4 transmissions were first-run: that is, 57% repeats. The current remit is scarcely likely to strike fear into the heart of a maiden aunt, let alone major media players like Discovery and Viacom.

Only two quota requirements have edged up. The quota for independent commissions 'outside the M25' was raised to 30% (in 2002, pre-Ofcom) and then 35%, as a proportion of both money spent on commissions and hours independent commissions transmitted. It is being met with some comfort, and could easily be raised to 40%.

Within the 35%, a 3% quota for 'the nations' was introduced – 3%! – rising to 9% by 2020 (Channel 4 was given 7 years' notice of this change). Even that would be a very low level, compared to the populations of 'the nations' (18% of the UK). The current spend is £21m in Scotland, Wales and Northern Ireland, or 5.5% of the budget. No wonder a former Channel 4 director of programmes described the channel's performance in Scotland as 'dreadful'.

The only other fixed quotas – independent productions (25%), European independent production (10%) and European origin (50%) – are relatively straightforward for Channel 4 to fulfil, given its publisher-broadcaster status. Subtitling, signing and audio description quotas are in the same category: readily fulfilled by all the targeted broadcasters.

The Enders Analysis paper includes a table presenting the licence obligations for Five (as Channel 5 is now called) alongside Channel 4's, implying there is a major difference. In fact, nearly all the measurable quotas imposed on Channel 4 are imposed on Channel 5, even if sometimes to a lesser extent. Contrary to the Enders paper, 5 is obliged to provide a range of high quality programming and impartial news, as well as current affairs, along with all the quotas for independent production, origination (in peak and across the schedule) and commissioning outside the M25. It so happens that 5 continues to supply a large volume of children's programming (24 hours a week), even though that is no longer a licence requirement (but is 24 hours a week more than Channel 4 supplies).

The 'soft' targets

Of course, there is a major difference: the 'feel-good' attributes that Channel 4 (but not 5) is meant to pursue – being innovative and distinctive, reflecting alternative views and cultural diversity, offering educational content, helping to inspire change and nurture talent, stimulating debate, espousing partnership and investing in high quality content.

Self-evidently, most of these objectives lack any means of objective quantification. All credit, then, to Channel 4, in making a thorough meal of its 'statement of media policy' in response to this obligation: 90 pages of evidence, compared with the single page of reporting on fixed quotas (though admittedly that is published twice, in separate parts of the Annual Report).

Yet when you prod this prodigious apologia, you find that 'innovation' seemingly comes primarily through 'commissioning programmes' – something all broadcasters do (this also fulfils the 'nurturing talent' objective).

Diversity is partly expressed through the number of 'suppliers' (338), which one unwary analyst interpreted as independent production companies. In fact,

Channel 4 commissioned actual programmes from just 207 independents (exactly half the number as were used in 2002 – but you will find no suggestion from Ofcom that, as a result, Channel 4 was failing on the 'diversity' front). Also tucked into 'diversity' (along with programmes on multiculturalism and same-sex marriage) was 'religion'.

In the same vein, reporting from overseas apparently counts as 'seeking alternative views' – sadly, this category declined 23% in 2014, partly because of the absence of *Hugh's Fish Fight*; again, seemingly nothing to worry Ofcom.

Another indicator of 'diversity' is cited from the Film 4 schedule: a screening of Kurosawa's *Seven Samurai*, 60 years after its first release, and after several dozen previous television broadcasts. Quite why this should be mentioned ahead of the genuinely laudable premiere for a peak-time transmission of the first film from a Saudi female director – *Wadjda* – is hard to understand. Meanwhile, 'stimulating debate' is delivered by the hard quota of news and current affairs (so no different from Channel 5, except that main current affairs output from that channel is an actual live debate).

Impressively, Channel 4 shows up well ahead of the other PSB channels when it comes to public perceptions of which of the five is best at offering diversity and alternative opinions; challenging prejudice; showing minority viewpoints; encouraging people to think differently; tackling difficult subjects and adopting a different approach to them; taking risks and being experimental. This is admirable, but has its limitations.

First of all, Channel 4 has spent 33 years building on its statutory obligation to 'be different', with a constant marketing message. As it compares itself with three channels launched decades before it, 'taking a different approach' is scarcely the most demanding of tasks. Indeed, when 5 – which makes no attempt to market itself in these terms, but just happens to be a newcomer on the scene – turns up as Channel 4's nearest competitor (however distant) in several of these measurements, it is a sign we need to take them with a degree of scepticism.

Once Channel 4 reverts to actual hard facts to demonstrate its commitment to innovation, by comparing its number of one-off new programmes in peak time with what its competitors do, it reveals a 27% decline year-on-year, still in second place to BBC2, but at a much more respectful distance.

This change, we are told, is a result of the 'maturing' of Channel 4's renewal strategy, leading to 'a much stronger spine of returning series' than in recent years. That might be marginally persuasive, but for the evidence in the Ofcom CMR showing that, over the last five years, the average proportion of spend on new commissions as opposed to returning series has been 28% on Channel 4, compared with 30% on Five and 34% on the BBC.

Lord Burns pointed out in last year's Channel 4 Annual Report that Ofcom's latest PSB review had said that the channel's 'number of new and one-off programmes delivered compares favourably with other PSBs' – ignoring Ofcom's less flattering observation on returning series (as above, in the CMR).

Burns also notes Ofcom's highlighting of 'the resilience of Channel 4's portfolio audience share', even though the CMR says it is the *least* resilient of the PSB portfolios.

None of this is to denigrate Channel 4's performance and current leadership. It commissions and broadcasts many outstanding programmes. It reaches younger audiences better than other PSB channels, and ethnic minority viewers almost effectively as does Five. It wins many prizes, deservedly (even if we don't really need to be told that one of its productions had made the 'best ten' list of the Boston Online Film Critics, and another that of the Central Ohio Critics Circle).

But we need to be clear-eyed about what its true significance is, and how viable that significance would be under private ownership. For instance, its critical role in supporting the independent production sector – which barely existed when it launched – has now to be seen in the light of that sector's growth. Channel 4 was once responsible for 90% of the sector's revenues: now the £279m it spent with qualifying independents in 2014 represents 10% of sector revenues (and just 56% of Channel 4 expenditure).

And although Channel 4 remains reasonably distinctive, such is the imitative nature of the television industry that the lauded distinctiveness is often blurred. For instance, last December, I asked some colleagues to pick out from the Christmas schedules which ten programmes emanated from Channel 4 and which from Five:

Britain's Favourite Christmas Songs	*Britain's Favourite Children's Books*
The Rich Kids of Instagram	*Can't Pay? We'll Take It Away*
How The Rich Live Longer	*On Benefits: Cashing In For Christmas*
A Primary School Nativity	*Inside Lego At Christmas*
Greatest Ever Christmas Movies	*Britain's Best Loved Double Acts*
My Crazy Christmas Lights	*My Crazy Christmas Obsession*
The World's Greatest Spy Movies	*Building The Ice Hotel*
Million Pound Motors	*The Millionaire Party Planner*
A Frozen Christmas	*Help! I'm Snowtrapped*
The World's Most Expensive Food	*Most Shocking Christmas TV Moments*

You'll find the answers at the end of this chapter.

Channel 4's transparency

Another worrying feature of today's Channel 4 is its tactical avoidance of transparency. It is not just that its expenditure headings (such as 'transmission costs') and its revenue statements (the actual split of income from the main channel and the digital channels, and between advertisements, sponsorship and online) are irritatingly opaque.

It also sets out programme expenditure under two separate and non-comparable sets of headings. The first, on page 16 of its Annual Report, is Channel 4's preferred design, whilst the second – relegated to page 164 – appears to reflect historic reporting practices.

According to the latter table, the largest single area of output for Channel 4 in 2014 was 'education', with 2,622 hours, costing £98m. This is surely a (Freudian) misprint for 'factual'. Channel 4's commitment to education is actually minimal – £6m of spend, and 9 hours of origination across the portfolio. As it happens, in addition to what should have been labelled 'factual', this table also includes 'other factual' (£25m, 165 hours), and 'documentaries' (£25m, 274 hours): three categories totalling £148m and 3,061 hours.

On page 16, we are offered tables setting out spend (but across the portfolio, not just the main channel) and broadcast hours (but on first-run origination across the portfolio, not all output on the main channel). Here we learn that portfolio spend on 'factual' is £169m, and portfolio first-run origination hours 1,174. Obviously, Channel 4 could easily reconcile these confusing different sets of figures, but it has chosen not to do so. Some might regard this as deliberate obfuscation.

At least with drama, we know that the full £100m spent across the portfolio was all on the main channel, but that only 160 of the 579 drama hours broadcast were first-run origination. Likewise, the £22m sport budget all went to the main channel, generating 616 hours of first-run origination (and 198 hours of repeats).

By contrast, £84m is declared as being spent on film, which sounds impressive. But only half of that amount went to Channel 4 (generating a meagre 17 hours of first-run origination, as compared with 961 hours of repeats and acquisitions); the rest went, presumably, to the Film4 channel. The actual spend on film production and development was a modest £16.9 m.

Entertainment, as per the lay-out on page 164, seems to incorporate comedy (which is separately listed in the page 16 version); conversely, quiz and game shows, and music and arts, are separately listed on page 164, but not on page 16, so presumably are incorporated in the definition there of 'entertainment'. The combined cost across the portfolio of 'comedy' and 'entertainment' is stated on page 16 as £167m, of which £134m appears to be for Channel 4 (according to page 164).

News provision and cost is the same on both lay-outs: £25m cost and 242 hours (in other words, everything is on the main channel). Channel 4 carries all the costs of current affairs (£20m, delivering 145 hours of first-run origination and 238 hours in all), and of sport (£22m, delivering 616 hours of first-run origination and 814 hours in all). None of this detail matters very much, however tiresome it is to analyze (and for patient readers to peruse): but then the sting is in the tail.

In the page 16 lay-out, there are entries for 'education' (£6m spend, 9 hours of first-run origination across the portfolio) and 'older children' (£2m, 4 hours) – a hangover from a previous, belated decision to provide some children's content, after decades of no provision for children. There is no mention of these categories in the Channel 4 transmissions list on p164, suggesting that those hours are not actually broadcast on Channel 4. Similarly, the listings for 'arts and music' (£8m, 92 hours), and 'religion' (£1m, 11 hours) on page 164 are not mentioned in the table on page 16, listing (we are told) *all* the portfolio origination spend.

Brazenly, Channel 4 offers a group of genres which it claims constitute its contribution to core public service broadcasting: news, current affairs, education, schools, comedy, drama, arts and religion, on which it spent £172m in 2014 (or 28% of total portfolio spending). The inclusion of drama and comedy is startling: no annual report a decade ago would have dreamed of trying to squeeze those into the 'endangered species' core definition. If we just focus on the other categories, and add in 'documentaries' (not listed on page 14, but identified separately on page 164) and 'older children', we come up with a cost of £85m, or 14% of all Channel 4 spend. This delivered 876 broadcast hours: exactly 10% of Channel 4's total transmissions.

The average amount of viewing of Channel 4 each day is 10.5 minutes. As public service content almost certainly attracts less viewing than entertainment content, it seems safe to say that *Channel 4's contribution to the viewing of core public service content is less than one minute per day per person in the UK.*

Perhaps for some people that induces simply a shrug of the shoulders. Isn't box-ticking public service broadcasting a very 1990s concept? Shouldn't we embrace the fuzzy feel-good definitions that the Digital Economy Act, the Communications Act, Ofcom, the BBC and Channel 4 have set out?

What do we really need?

I can only speak for myself. In my view, the issue with Channel 4 is not privatisation, but how to enhance its central public service broadcasting role. I would like to see Ofcom re-instate all the old Channel 4 quotas, other than for schools programming (for which there is no longer a meaningful broadcasting responsibility).

So: 7 hours of education every week (validated by suitably qualified and specially hired staff at Ofcom); 1 hour a week of religion and ethics; 3 hours of multi-cultural programming every week; 80% of Channel 4 transmissions to be first-run in peak and 60% across the schedule; with 70% of such transmissions to be origination in peak and 60% across the schedule.

All the current requirements for news and current affairs, for independent production, and for signing, sub-titling and audio-description should be maintained, and the training levy re-instated.

In addition, I would introduce a requirement for 1 hour a week of arts, with at least half of all arts output in peak; and for 40% of all commissions to be from outside the M25, and 10% (as from 2018, 15% as from 2020) from the Nations. A new requirement would be for at least 300 qualifying independent production companies to receive commissions each year, of which at least 20 would have annual turnover of less than £1m; and for at least 2 hours a week (from 2018) of programming, sourced from at least 10 companies, where either the director, the producer (of which there should not be more than two) or the executive producer (of which there should not be more than two) is BAME, such that at least 50 different such individuals are identifiable each year.

I would also impose a requirement that the current budget for Channel 4 be ring-fenced and inflation-proofed, along with the budget for news and current affairs.

In exchange, I would excuse Channel 4 the rigmarole of the annual statement of media policy, though it would be welcome to continue with it if it so chose.

Much of the criticism of the government's exploration of possible privatization of Channel 4 has started from the Burns premise: you can have privatization or the present remit, but not both.

I have not the slightest doubt – having examined the reality of the 'remit' – that any number of purchasers could deliver the present 'hard' quotas and a version of the 'soft' (but anyway unenforceable) targets. It therefore does not surprise me that the government has been able repeatedly to assure us that the 'remit' would be strengthened within any privatization.

Interestingly, that is exactly what the Conservatives promised in the document I cited earlier, from January 2001, when putting forward a detailed proposal for Channel 4 privatisation, 'with an enhanced remit to deliver high quality drama, current affairs, news and minority programming on its core channel'.

Perhaps just as importantly, that document pledged to use the proceeds from any sale to create an arts and culture endowment. There is obviously an opportunity today to do something similar, in the shape of a public service content fund, as proposed by – yes! – Lord Burns 10 years ago in his report to Tessa Jowell on the future of the BBC.

I see no evidence that privatization is being pursued for irrational or ideological reasons: the 2001 document is not confused, nor self-contradictory, let alone insane, as some critics have alleged. The test of the sanity of the proposal will come as and when the Treasury tries to find would-be buyers at the desired valuation, who are willing to take on a much tougher remit and regulatory regime.

The 2001 document was confident that a sale of Channel 4, even with a strengthened remit, would raise at least £2 billion. The reasoning is not complicated. The present Channel 4 headcount of 808 includes 214 in programming, 192 in sales, 110 in marketing, 69 in finance and HR, 66 in rights exploitation, 51 in transmission and engineering, 40 in IT, 36 in corporate affairs, 17 in strategy and 13 in talent support. Clearly, a large media company buying Channel 4 would be able to dispense with at least 500 of these, saving some £30-40m a year.

Even larger savings would be available from absorbing accommodation, transmission, acquisition, financing, HR and administration costs. For most acquirers, folding their airtime sales function into Channel 4's would add a welcome premium to the value of their advertising inventory, without inflicting any significant damage on other ad-funded broadcasters. For some, there would also be tax efficiencies.

The value of all these elements would surely be in the range of £200m a year, to which can be added the value of the Channel 4 premises (£85m) and the cash reserve maintained by Channel 4 (£230m), which a larger company could simply pocket, given its capacity for funding all Channel 4 operations out of its broader cash flow.

Would a buyer accept a stronger remit? We have evidence from the recent sale of Five to Viacom. During the Ofcom approval process for the sale, Viacom offered (note: Ofcom itself did not suggest) stronger quota requirements in three of the licence requirements. Ofcom sensibly accepted them, and re-issued the licence with the new terms. It should learn from that outcome.

There is one factor that might justify a reduced sale price and even a delay in imposing all the new quota requirements: the need to reverse the decline in Channel 4's audience share. We should never lose sight of the fact that the object of the exercise is to ensure that we use available public resources to enable the creation and consumption of core public service content. How a purchaser proposed to take Channel 4 back to a 6%+ share should be a factor in any negotiation.

The Enders Analysis paper rightly argued that there is no pressing need to sell Channel 4: the proceeds would make barely a dent in the UK's debt obligations, and Channel 4 is not in any foreseeable danger of failing. To support that argument, the analysts presented forecasts for advertising revenue that show a real degree of comfort.

All that may be true, but does not affect the central calculation: if Channel 4 can survive – even thrive – indefinitely in public ownership, thanks to a weak remit, then it is all the harder to justify leaving money, and a stronger remit, 'on the table', unrealized, especially if a proportion of the money raised can be used to provide a contestable public service content fund, thereby reversing the long term trends Ofcom has tracked in its successive reports on PSB.

Ofcom has told us that in 2014 spending by the PSB channels (BBC1, BBC2, ITV, Channel 4 and Five) 'on new UK originated programmes has fallen by

15% in real terms since 2008, to £2.5 billion (of which £500m is on sport) – the same level as in 1998'.

Specifically, says Ofcom, spend on arts and classical music has fallen by 25% (32% since 1998), while 'provision has all but ceased of religion and ethics (down 26% since 2008, 58% since 1998) and formal education (down 77% since 2008, 70% since 1998)'. That Ofcom itself has failed to impose an arts quota on Channel 4, and has allowed the quotas for religion and education to be abandoned, is a painfully ironic comment on its adequacy as a regulator.

If there is to be a sale process, Ofcom – and especially its content board – needs to be meaningfully strengthened, so that any new remit can be vigorously enforced. The legislation provides for cash penalties for failure to perform, which – even if they are pretty useless with regard to a publicly-owned Channel 4 – can certainly be deployed with a private owner. The maximum penalty is 5% of relevant turnover – or £25-30m – but lower penalties of £5m or £10m could be imposed for repeated failure to meet key quota requirements under a strengthened remit.

There might also be a case for a retrieval mechanism, whereby persistent failure by the new owner to observe the key terms of the new remit would result in the loss of transmission spectrum and associated carriage privileges; and perhaps the brand name, too.

A new regime should also encompass quality judgments from Ofcom, along the lines of those issued by the BBC Trust in relation to the BBC service agreements. The retreat into woolly generalities needs to be halted, and reversed.

It is possible that the present Channel 4 board will volunteer to adopt the tougher remit proposed here, in order to fend off privatisation. If so, well and good: after all, Ofcom floated the idea of auctioning the licences for ITV and Five before they were renewed last year. At the very least, the government would then have a base line of requirements for any privatisation process.

I fully understand that many people would be nervous of privatising Channel 4 – even if that delivered a much stronger remit and a public service content fund – simply because of distrust of the outcome, or even distaste for private ownership. I spent many years of my life campaigning for Channel 4 to be launched as a publicly-owned enterprise, rather than the fourth channel being assigned to an ITV2. 11 years ago, when publishing *Beyond The Charter: The BBC After 2006*, I rejected any suggestion of privatising Channel 4.

So I am conscious of a certain irony in now believing that a carefully managed privatisation might deliver considerably more public value than the status quo. 11 years ago, the collapse of the Channel 4 audience had not begun, and the remit was still robust. I can live with the irony: the needs of public service broadcasting must prevail.

About the author

David Elstein's 50-year career in broadcasting includes production (*This Week*, *The World At War*, *Panorama*), executive roles (chief executive, Channel 5; head of programming, BSkyB; director of programmes, Thames TV; managing director, Brook Productions and

Primetime Productions) and non-executive chairmanships (British Screen Advisory Council, National Film and Television School, Commercial Radio Companies Association, DCD Media plc, Screen Digest, Sports Network plc, Sparrowhawk Media, Luther Pendragon). He has been a visiting professor at the universities of Oxford, Stirling and Westminster and is currently chairman of open Democracy and the Broadcasting Policy Group. He was a founder member of the 76 Group, the Channel Four Group and the Association of Directors and Producers, all of which campaigned for the establishment of an independent Channel 4.

'Spot the remit' quiz answers

Britain's Favourite Christmas Songs (Five)	*Britain's Favourite Children's Books* (C4)
The Rich Kids of Instagram (C4)	*Can't Pay? We'll Take It Away* (Five)
How The Rich Live Longer (C4)	*On Benefits: Cashing In For Christmas* (Five)
A Primary School Nativity (Five)	*Inside Lego At Christmas* (C4)
Greatest Ever Christmas Movies (Five)	*Britain's Best Loved Double Acts* (Five)
My Crazy Christmas Lights (C4)	*My Crazy Christmas Obsession* (Five)
The World's Greatest Spy Movies (C4)	*Building The Ice Hotel* (Five)
Million Pound Motors (C4)	*The Millionaire Party Planner* (C4)
A Frozen Christmas (C4)	*Help! I'm Snowtrapped* (Five)
The World's Most Expensive Food (C4)	*Most Shocking Christmas TV Moments* (Five)

Notes
All information in this article is drawn from:
Channel 4 Annual Reports
Ofcom reports on public service broadcasting
Ofcom 2015, Communications Market Report,
Enders Analysis (2015), 'Channel 4: Sustainability and Privatisation', December 16
Conservative Central office news release 'Conservatives to Privatise Channel Four' (January 21 2001)
Gardam, T (2000) speech 'Channel 4's Public Service Role', December 13.
Brown, M (2007), ,A Licence To Be Different'(2007)

Greater detail on the diversification strategy of Channel 4 can be found in my Beesley Lecture (September 24 2009), available at http://www.theguardian.com/media/2009/sep/24/david-elstein-beesley-lecture

Sense and sustainability

By Toby Syfret

Channel 4 may have lost overall viewing share, but detailed analysis reveals many reasons to expect a very positive outlook for revenues – and for the remit – over the next 10 years

It was not clear precisely why the government was examining Channel 4 privatisation options when news broke in September 2015 that it was actively exploring them. Then all became clear in February 2016, when the parliamentary news web site *PoliticsHome* ran an interview with Secretary of State for Culture, Media and Sport, John Whittingdale, in which he ruled out the Treasury interest in selling assets: 'One thing I would say is that the reason for doing this is not because George wants some money'. (Schofield 2016)

Instead, it had all to do with the decline in viewing. 'The truth is,' said Whittingdale, 'Channel 4's market share has been falling every year for the last four years. It's still delivering good content and it's still delivering the remit and covering its cost but my concern is whether it can still do that in five or 10 years.'

The concern is perfectly reasonable. Reported TV viewing has seen a marked decline during the past few years, and especially among the core Channel 4 audience of 16-34s. But topline viewing trends do not remotely paint the true picture. The current financial model appears very healthy in spite of the recent viewing decline and we at Enders Analysis think it will remain so over the next 5-10 years.

Only it is not enough to address financial sustainability on its own. We must also consider the sustainability of the Channel 4 remit and whether it can go hand in hand with financial sustainability. We get the impression at times that the Secretary of State thinks it is possible to have one or the other, but not both together. If so, this chapter seeks to dispel such thinking. We are confident that Channel 4 can both remain financially sustainable *and* deliver its remit to the full throughout its current ten-year licence ending in 2024.

Viewing trends: 2010-2015

The last five years have seen a significant 11% decline in daily Average Viewing Time (AVT) across all individuals aged 4+ (see Figure 1). The Channel 4 group decline is even greater at 17%. However, this is chiefly because much the heaviest decline has occurred among the under 35s, and Channel 4's core target audience is adults aged 16-34. But, as we shall see later, the critical metric for advertising sales is Share of Viewing, where the Channel 4 group has actually trended very close to the industry average.

We also note that Channel 4 is not just about delivering a large supply of 16-34 year-olds, but also a healthy ABC1 profile and various "harder to reach" minority groups (e.g. BAME), as specified by the Channel 4 remit. However, 16-34 defines the core commercial target audience, which has so far seen much the steepest decline in daily AVT, putting Channel 4 in the firing line; hence our focus on the 16-34s in this report.

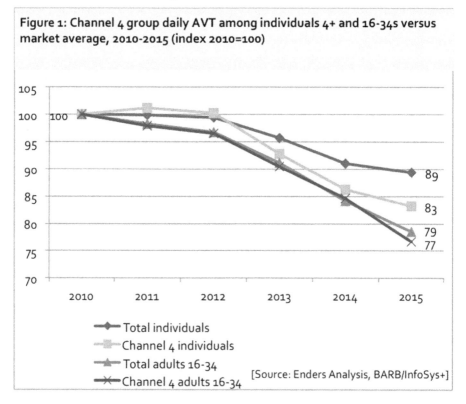

Figure 1: Channel 4 group daily AVT among individuals 4+ and 16-34s versus market average, 2010-2015 (index 2010=100)

[Source: Enders Analysis, BARB/InfoSys+]

The second point to make is that all four main public service broadcasters (PSB) were under severe pressure due to multichannel growth and digital switchover, which only reached completion in November 2012. In addition, Channel 4 experienced extra disruption over the course of 2010-2013 due to the discontinuation of *Big Brother* after its final season in 2010, followed by an intense period of creative renewal.

The pressures only started to ease from 2013, since when main Channel 4 has held its share. Indeed, its annual average share of total individual 4+ viewing notched up in 2015 for the first time since 2006. So, when John Whittingdale referred to the fall in Channel 4's market share over the last four years, he needed to be clear whether he meant the Channel 4 group or just main Channel 4. Lastly, although main Channel 4 saw a 20% decline in its share of total individual 4+ viewing between 2010 and 2015, two thirds was compensated by gains from its digital portfolio of E4, More 4 and Film4.

The importance of the 16-34 age-group is also plain for all to see if we compare Channel 4 group with the other PSBs and non-PSB average (see Figure 2). Most of the Channel 4 skew comes from its main channel and E4, which respectively stood out from other main PSB and leading PSB portfolio channels targeted towards younger adults.

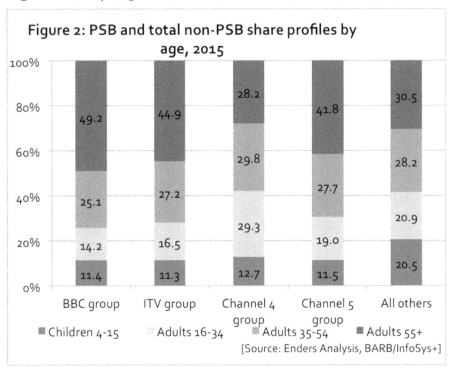

Figure 2: PSB and total non-PSB share profiles by age, 2015

[Source: Enders Analysis, BARB/InfoSys+]

That is not all. One other critical variable to consider when assessing the decline in viewing is its distribution by time of day, especially during peak (here defined as 6pm-11pm) versus off-peak viewing time. Peaktime, with its larger audiences, is important to Channel 4 not only for generating higher advertising yields, but also for delivering the programming remit with high quality content.

Inspection of trends confirms that Channel 4 group has achieved consistently higher viewing shares among both its core target of 16-34s and among the 35-54s. At the same time, Channel 4 group's loss of share has occurred pretty well entirely in off-peak and within the less important commercial demographic groups of children 4-15 and adults 55+.

Figure 3: Channel 4 group share of viewing by age group: 2010 vs 2015

	Peak (18:00-22:59)			Off-peak (23:00-17:59)		
	2010	2015	Change	2010	2015	Change
Individuals 4+	11.7	11.6	-1%	10.7	9.3	-13%
Children 4-15	12.7	11.6	-8%	7.5	6.9	-8%
Adults 16-34	18.5	18.4	-1%	13.9	13.3	-4%
Adults 35-54	12.5	13.5	8%	10.9	10.4	-4%
Adults 55+	7.6	7.8	3%	9.8	7.5	-23%

[Source: Enders Analysis, BARB/InfoSys+]

In short, Channel 4 group has certainly lost share of viewing during the last five years, but most importantly from a commercial perspective it has held firm among the 16-55s and in peak times. Meanwhile, the Channel 4 annual report for 2014 shows the broadcaster to be in very healthy financial condition and we expect 2015 to be even better.

The next ten years: 2015-2025
But how much further does the viewing decline have to run over the next ten years and what are the financial implications? To this end we have prepared long-term viewing forecasts of long-form and short-form video content by age group across all UK homes (i.e. both TV and non-TV) and screens. We have prepared our forecasts in the form of a 3x2 matrix:

- Axis 1: Three mutually exclusive and exhaustive measurement components:
  (1) BARB Gold Standard reported viewing of linear live and 7 day time-shift/catch-up to the TV set
  (2) All other viewing to the TV set
  (3) All viewing on other screens
- Axis 2: Two groups of content providers:
  (1) Live linear TV broadcasters, accounting for all viewing in category (1) and some in categories (2) and (3)
  (2) All other sources (including DVDs, SVOD, YouTube, etc.)

Figure 4 sets out our forecasts for category (1) reported viewing to the TV set, where we note a sharp slow-down in the rate of decline among younger adult age-groups during H2 2015. This probably reflects the fact that we have passed the peak phase with regard to smartphone/tablet adoption, explosion of apps and growth of social networks.

Figure 4: Reported broadcast linear daily AVT, 16-34s, 2010-2025f (minutes)

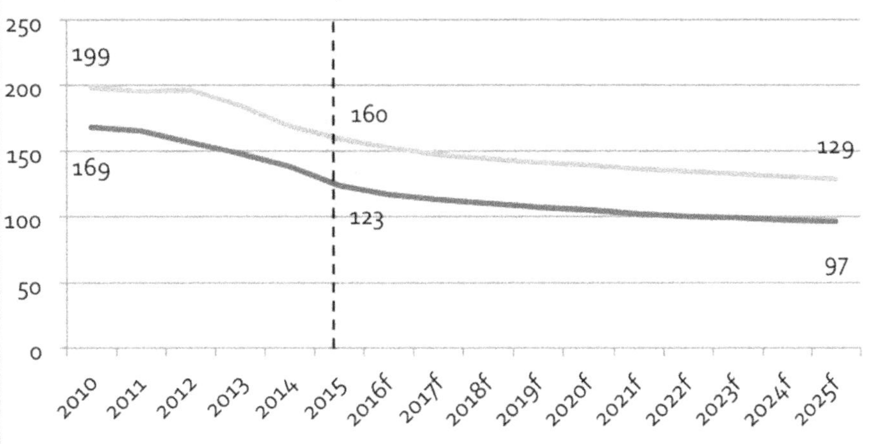

[Source: Enders Analysis, BARB/InfoSys+]

Of course, some of the decline seen by live linear TV broadcasters is made-up by increases in category (2) viewing to the TV set through 8+ day time-shift/catch-up, as well as category (3) viewing to other screens. Figure 5 summarises our latest projections of TV broadcast live linear and time-shift/catch-up share over the next ten years for the younger and older age groups. We project a big loss in overall share between 2010 and 2025 among younger adult age-groups, but at a substantially slower average pace from 2015-2025 than we have seen from 2010-2015.

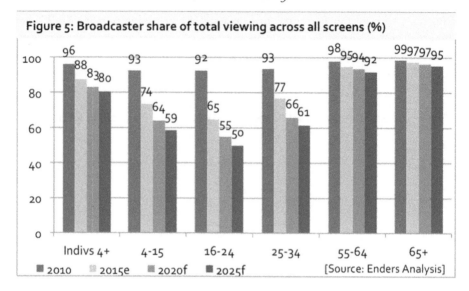

Figure 5: Broadcaster share of total viewing across all screens (%)

Indivs 4+   4-15   16-24   25-34   55-64   65+

■ 2010   ▨ 2015e   ▨ 2020f   ■ 2025f   [Source: Enders Analysis]

Impact of viewing decline on revenues

Channel 4 has undoubtedly seen a significant decline in viewing share across all individuals since the last year of *Big Brother* on Channel 4 in 2010. But the trends have stabilised since 2013 and in the case of John Whittingdale's concerns, we think that the overall 7% Channel 4 group decline in viewing share across all individuals 4+ is not significant when it comes to assessing the financial sustainability of the channel over the next ten years.

Two important points we made earlier are that the Channel 4 group has held its core audience profile of 16-34s steady throughout, and likewise its share of peak viewing. But this is far from all, as we list eight considerations that point to a very positive outlook over the next five to ten years:

1. Underlying positive growth trends in TV advertising
2. Trading dynamics of the UK advertising market
3. Location of Channel 4 viewing share decline
4. Closure of BBC3 broadcast channel
5. Growth opportunity in digital video
6. Personalised database of registered users
7. Portfolio share
8. Dynamics of Channel 4 business model

1. Underlying positive growth trends in TV advertising. Our advertising three-year forecasts published in February 2016 project 12% real growth in annual TV spot advertising spend across 2015-2018. This is based on favourable assessments of (a) the UK economic outlook and its impact on consumption trends, and (b) growth dynamics of television within total display.

Although the UK economic outlook looks favourable, we do not rule out a sharp downturn at some point during the next few years. Whatever transpires:

- All parties will be hit regardless of who the owners are
- The TV sector has experienced a severe recession in the relatively recent past of 2008-2009, which it saw its way through
- In Channel 4's specific case, its cash reserve of over £200 million will help to see it through hard times

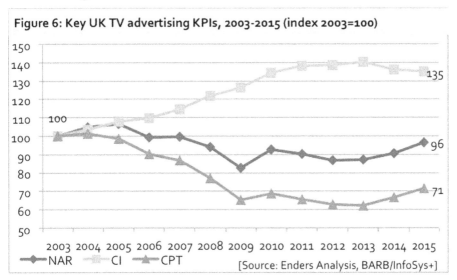

Figure 6: Key UK TV advertising KPIs, 2003-2015 (index 2003=100)

[Source: Enders Analysis, BARB/InfoSys+]

2. Trading dynamics of the UK advertising market. One major feature of the UK TV advertising market, which seems to be so often misunderstood due to its paradoxical nature, is that loss of total audience does not imply fall in total TV advertising revenues: in fact, quite the reverse it seems when we look at trends over past years (see Figure 6).

We make the following points:

- The total 30-second rate-card adjusted eyeball count for watching TV advertising spots, or 'commercial impacts' (CI), rose dramatically after the launch of Freeview on 30 October 2002, due to the transition from analogue to digital, which saw massive growth in the number of commercial channels with higher advertising quotas and steadily increasing share of audience at the expense of the analogue PSB establishment
- The rapid expansion in CI delivery and heavily discounted airtime prices for the long tail of commercial channels with small audiences led to steep

downward descent in both advertising costs per thousand and total TV advertising spend

- Only after the completion of digital switchover, when online growth has started to eat into linear broadcast TV audiences, have we seen a rebound and return to real growth.

- Though not depicted in Figure 6, even among adults 16-34, the total CI delivery in 2015 was still higher than in any previous year up to 2007. Despite appearances the 16-34 audience for commercials is still very substantial. We remain a long way from the often-mentioned cliff edge or 'death of television'.

Certainly, the viewing decline has not harmed TV Net Advertising Revenue (NAR), which grew at constant 2015 prices by 11% from £3,647 million in 2012, when the downward trend in younger audience gathered momentum, to an estimated £4,047 million in 2015. Quite the opposite.

3. Location of Channel 4 viewing share decline. As noted earlier, Channel 4 has throughout successively maintained share (a) with its core 16-34 target audience and (b) during peaktime daypart, both of which carry a price premium. If we follow the logic of supply and demand inelasticities in UK TV advertising as indicated above, the contraction of the 16-34 audience is not that harmful to Channel 4 and could be beneficial as long as Channel 4 holds share.

4. Closure of BBC3 broadcast channel. BBC3, with a circa 3% share of viewing among 16-34s, has been E4's closest PSB rival to E4 for reaching younger adults. The cessation of the BBC3 broadcast signal and BBC3's move to online in February only stand to benefit Channel 4 group during the rest of 2016.

5. Growth opportunity in digital video. So far we have focused on Channel 4's broadcast audience. But, online digital video represents a big revenue growth opportunity. We estimate that Channel 4 non-TV NAR income from advertising sales, including sponsorship, product placement, commission, receipts from third party sales and digital video, amounted to £132 million in 2014. But, with digital video as the main driver, we project this to double in real terms by 2025.

6. Personalised database of registered users. One important and distinctive feature of Channel 4 is its personalised database of registered users which now has 13.5 million individuals, including over half the 16-34s. We see this as a valuable commercial asset for maintaining live and 7-day time-shift/catch-up audiences and stimulating use of All 4. And the personalised database provides a useful and inclusive source of viewer feedback for purposes of commissioning original content.

7. Portfolio share. As shown in Figure 7, Channel 4 has gone further than any other PSB in spreading its audience across its portfolio. This has both an upside and downside.

Figure 7: PSB main channel and portfolio viewing profiles, indivs 4+, 2015

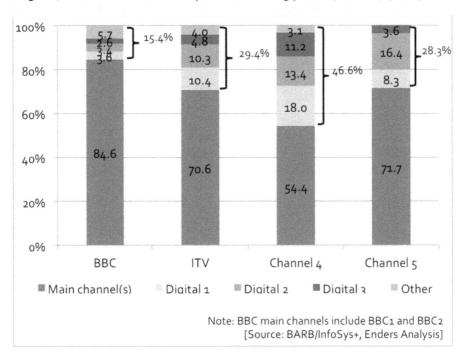

Note: BBC main channels include BBC1 and BBC2
[Source: BARB/InfoSys+, Enders Analysis]

On the one hand it has disadvantages in so far as the main channel carries a premium in airtime negotiations, where trend data show a diminishing share of NAR together with the decline in main channel viewing share up to 2013. In this respect, the year-on-year uplift in main Channel 4 audience share in 2015 should have brought much to be welcomed stability in airtime trading for 2016.

On the other hand, spreading audiences more evenly across the Channel 4 portfolio has presented a double benefit in terms of Channel 4's ability to sustain more highly prized peak time viewing share across the Channel 4 group and to reach a wider selection of target sub-groups with the main channel.

Overall, we think Channel 4 has ultimately more to gain than lose from spreading its audiences more evenly across its channel portfolio.

8. Dynamics of Channel 4 business model: As long as underlying revenue trends stay positive, which we are confident they will over the next five to ten years, this can only reinforce Channel 4's sustainability, as its business model dictates it feed back growth in operating margins into investment in content origination; good for maintaining audience share, good for the support it lends to the UK creative economy, and good for the remit.

Sustainability of the remit

As stated at the outset, financial sustainability of Channel 4 should not be looked at in isolation of the remit. Inevitably, there exists a tension between them as commissioning programmes that deliver bigger audiences and advertising revenues does not directly tie into a remit that places heavy emphasis on catering for minority audiences. There is no better example than *Big Brother*, where the decision to discontinue was strongly influenced by the fact that *Big Brother*, for all its advertising yield, no longer fulfilled any clear part of the Channel 4 remit.

However, this does not have to be the case, as it is perfectly possible for financial and remit sustainability to tie in together.

There is much evidence to draw from which shows Channel 4 to be sustaining its remit at a time when its financial outlook appears very positive; whether we looking at trends in remit delivery of leading programmes, successive Ofcom PSB reviews, industry awards, and so on. Yet, perhaps the measure that speaks loudest and clearest is Channel 4's quarterly remit tracking study, which it introduced in 2009. The remit tracker presents respondents with a series of ten statements which directly relate to the Channel 4 remit and asks the extent to which they agree for each of the PSBs. Figure 8 shows the scores in 2014 for Channel 4 alongside the 'next highest PSB' and 'average across other PSBs' as yardsticks for comparison. The results are impressive.

Figure 8: Audience perceptions against reputational statements, 2014 (%)

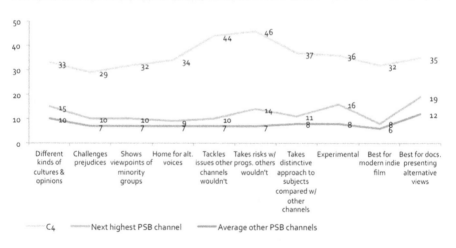

[Source: Ipsos MORI commissioned by Channel 4]

Of course, the other PSBs are not tied by the same remit. Still, the margins are wide and strongly testify to Channel 4's success in delivering all its particular remit objectives. Channel 4 has not yet released its audited figures for 2015, but we understand 2015 to have been another very good year, indeed the best to date.

Quite simply, financial sustainability and remit sustainability can go together, and Channel 4 is today performing strongly on both fronts.

Of course audiences matter, and of course it is reasonable for the Secretary of State to seek a review of the sustainability of the Channel 4 business model in light of the recent viewing decline.

Yet, as we have seen, the crucial BARB TV viewing metric is Share of Viewing, where Channel 4 has held its ground over the past four years both with its core age demo of 16-34s and the 35-54s, but also during peak times. Meanwhile, digital video audiences and advertising revenues are growing very nicely; plus the departure of broadcast BBC3 only stands to benefit Channel 4.

And so on. Nor is Channel 4 an exceptional case, as we need only to look as far as ITV to find another commercial broadcasting group that has seen a significant decline in viewing share since 2010, and arguably with less excuse. And yet ITV too is now seeing strong growth in TV NAR and other broadcasting and online revenues.

Odd, then, that John Whittingdale should show such concern over Channel 4, but not ITV, which reported excellent full year results for 2015.

This chapter is a condensed version of an Enders Analysis report Channel 4 viewing trends and sustainability, *published on 1 March 2016, to which the reader is referred for fuller background and references to other Enders Analysis reports on Channel 4.*

About the author
Toby Syfret covers television market developments in the UK and continental Europe for Enders Analysis. He has provided independent consultancy services on international TV broadcast and new media development issues and is a leading international authority on 'peoplemeter' measurement of television audiences. Toby previously managed the Ogilvy and Mather European media centre, and was head of new media at J. Walter Thompson. He holds a doctorate in philosophy (developmental psychology) from Oxford University.

References
Schofield, Kevin, 2016. 'John Whittingdale: I'm not some sort of Murdoch puppet sent in to take apart the BBC', Politics Home. Available online at https://www.politicshome.com/culture-and-sport/articles/house/john-whittingdale-i%E2%80%99m-not-some-sort-murdoch-puppet-sent-take-apart, accessed 17 March 2016

The £210m gamble

By Patrick Barwise and Gillian Brooks

Analysis of the consequences of privatising Channel 4 shows that it would almost certainly seriously damage the UK's independent production sector

Rational policy is based on the expected consequences of specific alternatives. At the time of writing, the government's plans for Channel 4 are unknown: we know that it is 'considering' privatisation but we have seen no concrete proposals. To evaluate its impact, we therefore have to make assumptions about what these proposals might be.

There is even some uncertainty about the government's aims. The obvious one is to raise revenue, but Culture Secretary John Whittingdale told the Commons Select Committee in January 2016 that the main reason why he was considering privatisation was not, as widely assumed, to raise money, but to 'ensure [C4] can continue to deliver the remit, in what is to become a very fast-changing and challenging environment'.[1] The implication is that he thinks the remit may be unsustainable as things stand but privatisation would somehow make it sustainable.

Privatisation would require primary legislation and a full parliamentary process, including a green paper with clear proposals and expected benefits. It will be easier to evaluate if and when we have these details. But, even without them, our analysis suggests that it would almost certainly seriously damage UK independent production, as well as being bad for consumers, advertisers, the economy, and many other aspects of public value (news and current affairs, diversity, etc)

The base case scenario: no privatisation

Figure 1, from Channel 4's 2014 Annual Report ('AR14'), shows its revenue and costs.

Figure 1: C4 Revenue and Costs: 2014[2]

	£m	% of revenue
Revenue	938	100
Content	661	70
Transmission and regulation	112	12
Sales	91	10
Marketing	39	4
Other costs	31	3

Our base case scenario takes these figures forward for a non-privatised Channel 4 using a recent revenue forecast by Enders Analysis. This projects a 48% increase in real advertising and sponsorship revenue by 2025.[3] We conservatively assume that Channel 4's other revenue (mostly secondary rights) remains flat in real terms; that the government continues to give it and the other commercial PSBs privileges (DTT spectrum at below market rates and EPG prominence) in return for their PSB commitments but introduces no new legislation or regulation to increase its or their revenue or profit, eg retransmission fees; and that Channel 4's transmission and regulation, sales, marketing, and other costs all grow at 1% per annum in real terms.[4]

On these assumptions content spend, treated as a 'balancing item', increases by 58% in real terms by 2025, assuming a small constant real annual surplus of £4m (Figure 2).

Figure 2: C4 Revenue and Costs: 2025
(Base case scenario: 2014 pounds)

	£m	% of revenue
Revenue	1355	100
Content	1045	77
Transmission and regulation	125	9
Sales	102	8
Marketing	44	3
Other costs	35	3

Obviously, if these projections are correct, Channel 4's current remit is easily sustainable over this period, as also expected by Channel 4 itself, Ofcom and Ernst & Young, as well as by Enders Analysis and ourselves.[5] In fact the 58% projected increase in real (inflation-adjusted) content spend by 2025 implies a big *increase* in C4's ability to deliver the remit.

We now turn to the privatisation scenario, starting with possible identities of buyers.

Who might the buyer be?

If C4 is privatised, it will most likely be bought by an existing media company seeking to move into – or, more likely, expand its existing operations in – the UK.[6] The main candidates are large US media companies such as 21st Century Fox, Comcast/NBC Universal, Disney, Discovery, Liberty Global, Scripps, Sony Pictures Television, Time Warner and Viacom.[7]

These companies have little if any experience of public service broadcasting except, to a limited extent, as a competitor.[8] Their US head offices are likely to lack understanding of, and empathy with, PSB and to see the UK as overregulated – perhaps admiring its very successful broadcasting ecology but with no intuitive sense of the PSBs' central role in this success. In other words, if any of these companies buys C4, the result will be a big change not only in the owner's *economic incentives* but also in its underlying *mission, governance, culture and values*, especially at a group leadership level.

However, they all base their main European media operations in or near London and – apart from a degree of bafflement about PSB and UK media regulation – are likely to regard Britain as a benign and congenial overseas market in which to do business, as well as being the only other big player in international broadcasting and popular culture, with many links to the US system.

The end of the 100% publisher-broadcaster model

One implication of the importance of potential synergies is that we think it will be hard to attract the right potential buyers without dropping, or significantly weakening, the requirement that C4 continues as a 100% publisher-broadcaster, with none of its own production. This change would clearly pose a threat to the indies, who benefit greatly from its publisher-broadcaster model.

Against this background, we now explore Channel 4 privatisation from the perspective of a generic potential buyer, 'MediaCorp', broadly representative of the US media companies listed above.

Three generic strategies for the buyer

MediaCorp would in principle have three possible strategies:

1. *Deep cuts in C4's content investment and other costs, accepting some reduction in its viewing share, share of commercial impacts (SOCI) and revenue.* This is the scenario explored in a recent investment bank presentation we have seen. It is likely to be the starting-point for most bankers, hedge funds and private equity investors. It assumes a 30% cut in content investment and a 10% cut in sales and

marketing costs, leading to a 5% reduction in revenue. To limit the revenue loss to only 5% with such a deep cut in programme investment (and with less sales and marketing support), MediaCorp would need to make aggressive changes in C4's programme and supplier mix along the lines we discuss later.

2. *Cutting costs as much as possible to increase margins while still broadly maintaining C4's viewing share, SOCI and revenue, by shifting to a more commercial mix of programmes and suppliers.* This is the most likely scenario in our view and the one we explore here.

3. *Seeking to increase C4's viewing, SOCI and revenue.* Like Options 1 and 2, this would involve a more commercial approach to programming, but the total content budget in this case might be slightly lower, about the same, or – in principle – even higher post-privatisation. MediaCorp would aim to capture revenue from other commercial broadcasters, while still increasing its profit margin from near zero to, say, 15-20%.

In our view, MediaCorp's most likely strategy is Option 2, or something close to it, i.e to reduce Channel 4's content and other costs as much as possible while broadly maintaining its revenue. Option 3 seems to us unlikely because generating a big enough revenue increase to provide a margin of 15-20% without a significant cut in programming costs would be challenging and risky, especially given the scope for retaliation by other commercial broadcasters[9]. Option 1 also seems unlikely because of the difficulty of limiting the revenue loss to only 5% with such deep cuts in the content budget and in sales and marketing support.

Potential sources of shareholder value

We now turn to the potential sources of shareholder value for MediaCorp post-acquisition: *efficiencies* (non-programming operating cost savings through better management); *synergies* with its existing businesses; and *getting more 'bang for the buck' from C4's content investment.* All are relevant to all three of the strategic options.

Non-programming operating cost savings

89% of C4's non-programming costs in 2014 comprised transmission and regulation, sales, and marketing (Figure 1). What is the scope for efficiency gains in these three areas?

- **Transmission and regulation**. The cost of regulation is non-negotiable but we assume that most of this heading (total cost £112m in 2014) is for transmission. We see no reason why private ownership would enable C4 to negotiate lower transmission costs. It is also likely to be committed to long-term contracts, so any reduction would take several years to come through. A 5% reduction in this heading would be worth £5.6m per annum.[10]

- **Sales**. Channel 4 Sales (cost £91m in 2014) now represents several other commercial broadcasters (UKTV, Box TV and BT TV) as well as the Channel

4 portfolio. It is a leader in the use of technology, including programmatic buying of online video inventory, and a strong number three behind ITV and Sky. We see no reason why these costs might be lower if C4 were privatised. If anything, the pressure on salesforce remuneration in the private sector would be upwards. Nevertheless, again optimistically, we assume a potential annual saving of 5% (£4.6m).

- **Marketing**. MediaCorp could of course cut Channel 4's marketing budget – £39m in 2014, 4.2% of revenue – as can every company, but only at the expense of losing some revenue (if the cuts were focused on publicity for its popular programmes) and/or reduced delivery of the remit (if they were focused on remit-related programmes). Again optimistically, the marketing budget could be cut by up to 10% (£3.9m/year) with no impact on revenue or remit delivery.

We estimated Channel 4's other non-programming costs at just £31m in 2014, 3.3% of revenue (Figure 1). Optimistically assuming that these other non-programming costs could be reduced by 20% with no reduction in performance, the resulting annual savings from this source would be £6.2m.[11]

Combining these four estimates of potential cuts in Channel 4's non-programming costs, we have a total annual saving of £20.3m (Figure 3): even with these optimistic assumptions about the potential for reducing Channel 4's non-programming costs, the annual savings would be very limited – just 2.2% of revenue.

Figure 3. Potential non-programming cost savings 2014 (£m)

	£m
Transmission and regulation (5% of £112m)	5.6
Sales (5% of £91m)	4.6
Marketing (10% of £39m)	3.9
Other (20% of £31m)	6.2
Total	20.3

Already a 'tight ship'

In reality, we would not expect even these savings to be achievable without impacting C4's commercial performance and/or remit delivery, because we believe it is already a 'tight ship':

- As a publisher-broadcaster with only 800 full-time equivalent employees,[12] C4 is a relatively small, simple and agile organisation. None of those proposing or analysing its possible privatisation has, to our knowledge, pointed to any evidence of significant inefficiency, unnecessary bureaucracy or excessive overheads.

- As some have noted, executive remuneration at C4 is generally higher than at the BBC, especially at the most senior levels. But it is much lower than for other commercial broadcasters. Total 2014 CEO remuneration was £855,000 for David Abraham (C4), £4.4m for Adam Crozier (ITV) and £4.9m for Jeremy Darroch (Sky). The previous year, 2013, Crozier's and Darroch's total remuneration was £8.4m and £17.0m, respectively.[13] We don't even know the equivalent figure for C5, nor would we, probably, for a privatised C4. But the idea that C4 executive remuneration would be *lower* if it were privatised is implausible.

- Another example is pensions. C4 closed its defined benefits scheme for new joiners in 2007 and for future accruals by existing members on 1 January 2015.[14]

C4's overall efficiency is reflected in its high revenue per employee: £1.16m – 17% higher than the equivalent figure of £0.99m for ITV Broadcast despite ITV's greater economies of scale.[15]

As with all organisations, Channel 4 has and always will have scope for greater efficiency. But we believe that the scope for *incremental* efficiency gains (i.e without weakening the business at a privatised Channel 4 relative to a C4 owned and managed as now) are minimal – significantly less than the £20m/year in Figure 3. A realistic, perhaps optimistic, estimate might be £10m/year.

Synergies

Given the minimal scope for incremental efficiency gains, the claim that Channel 4 can be privatised for a significant sum while maintaining the remit rests largely on the value of synergies with MediaCorp's existing businesses. Interestingly, the investment bank's analysis assumes no such synergies. Nevertheless, we believe that, depending on the buyer, there should be *some* scope for cost and/or revenue synergies with MediaCorp's existing businesses even without getting round the remit. These include:

1. Some small cost synergies from combining some of Channel 4's and MediaCorp's UK back office functions – finance, marketing, IT, HR, communications, etc. But, with *total* C4 employment costs of only £72m (7.7% of revenue),[16] the potential savings are small in absolute terms even under the most optimistic assumptions.

2. Some incremental revenue from increased viewing of C4's and/or MediaCorp's UK channels through cross-promotion, portfolio scheduling and collaborative marketing. This would have an opportunity cost (airtime that might have been sold or used to promote other programmes/services - eg, for Disney, its movies, theme parks and merchandise) but could still provide some net benefit across the combined portfolio.

3. 'Soft' synergies through access to Channel 4's talent, expertise, and commercial and informal networks

We see the value of 1 and 2 as broadly comparable to our 'realistic, perhaps optimistic' estimate of £10m/year incremental efficiencies discussed previously. The value of 3 is less clear, and would (in contrast to 1 and 2) be *higher* if MediaCorp has few or no TV assets in the UK.

Efficiencies and synergies: conclusion

Taken together, we see the value of efficiencies and synergies as limited. Our 'realistic, perhaps optimistic' estimate is £20m/year from cost savings/synergies and the benefits of cross-promotions, etc, plus whatever additional value MediaCorp attributes to the 'soft' synergies resulting from access to C4's talent, expertise and informal networks. MediaCorp might ignore these altogether, regard them as merely a small, unquantifiable bonus, or value them as much as the quantifiable benefits especially if MediaCorp has limited UK assets.

In combination, this would give a 'realistic, perhaps optimistic' range of £28-36m in potential annual benefits from the acquisition. Assuming a multiple of 11x,[17] this would justify a *maximum* realistic price of around £400-500m, including £200m or so from C4's 'spare' cash reserves and squeezing its suppliers by paying them later. Any value significantly above that approximate range can only come from MediaCorp's ability to get 'more bang for the buck' from C4's content budget, as we now discuss.

Getting more 'bang for the buck' from C4's content budget

In the words of the investment bank presentation, '*A [programming cost] cut of 30% alone would increase EBITDA margin by 20% assuming no associated losses in revenue*'. The big issue under all three strategic options is the extent to which MediaCorp thinks it can get more 'bang for the buck' (revenue per pound) from Channel 4's content investment. The only way to achieve this would be through some combination of the following changes in the percentage allocation of its content budget:

- From UK commissions to (mostly US) acquisitions
- From arms-length purchases from external suppliers to in-house purchases from its own production businesses
- From newer, riskier programmes and executions to safer, more mainstream ones, longer runs and more repeats
- From programmes focused on UK issues to programmes aimed at the US and global markets
- From working with a wide range of large and small indies to using fewer, mostly bigger, ones
- From finding and nurturing new talent to working with more established talent

- From loss-making or marginal genres to more profitable ones

Finally, as a PSB, C4 normally pays the full first-run production cost in return for only the primary broadcast rights and a share (15-50%) of some secondary rights revenues, eg from international sales and UK secondary transmissions. Other secondary rights (eg VoD) are subject to commercial negotiation and generally involve additional payment.

In contrast, the non-PSBs normally offer only deficit finance, ie they expect the producer to carry some of the first-run production cost and risk in the expectation of earning a long-term return from secondary rights. As part of its strategy to get 'more bang for the buck', MediaCorp would almost certainly seek to drive a harder bargain with producers than C4 currently does.

All of these ways of generating more 'bang for the buck' from C4's programme budget involve MediaCorp reducing its delivery of the remit.

The impact on UK independent production

To estimate the likely impact on UK independent production, we focus on MediaCorp's Option 2, which we see as its most likely strategy.[18] Specifically, we assume a 10% cut in C4's non-programming costs and a 20% cut in its content spend, with two changes in the supplier mix: (i) from 71% UK/29% overseas acquisitions to 50% UK/21% MediaCorp content/29% other overseas acquisitions and (ii) the size composition of UK programme suppliers is moved into line with the industry average, ie with fewer, larger suppliers.

We assume that these changes in the programme and supplier mix enable C4 to maintain its revenue post-privatisation despite cutting non-programming costs by 10% and programming costs by 20%. We see this as a realistic scenario, although there is clearly considerable uncertainty around it in terms of both MediaCorp's strategy and how successfully it would be executed. We certainly do not see it as pessimistic.

These assumptions are consistent with a **44% cut in C4's UK content investment**.[19] C4's *total* content investment was £661m in 2014 (Figure 1). In round terms, its UK content investment was 71% of this: £470m.[20] On this basis, C4 privatisation under Option 2 would lead to a **reduction of about £210m in C4's UK indie commissions in 2014** (44%), from around £470m to around £260m.

Projecting forward to 2025 and assuming constant percentage allocations, the equivalent impact would be from around £740m[21] to around £415m, **a loss of about £325m in 2025** (in 2014 pounds).

Proportionately, the cuts in *remit-related* content – public service genres, new, risky, innovative programmes, content aimed at minorities (BAME, disabled, etc) and commissions from small producers and those in the nations and regions – would be even greater than the 44% reduction in total UK commissions. These programmes and suppliers would all be cut by well over 50%.

About the authors

Patrick Barwise is emeritus professor of management and marketing, London Business School and visiting senior fellow in media and communications at the LSE. Gillian Brooks is post-doctoral research fellow, Oxford University Centre for Corporate Reputation, Saïd Business School and tutorial fellow in management studies, St Hugh's College, Oxford. This chapter is based on their report, *The Consequences of Privatising Channel 4*, commissioned by Channel 4, May 2016 (Barwise & Brooks 2016). This also analyses a range of other impacts and related issues.

Notes

[1] Kevin Rawlinson, 'Channel 4's public service remit will be protected, vows culture secretary', *The Guardian*, 21 January 2016. http://www.theguardian.com/media/2016/jan/21/channel-4s-public-service-remit-will-be-protected-vows-culture-secretary.

[2] C4 Annual Report 2014 ('AR14'), pp100, 149. Revenue comprises £869m advertising and sponsorship and £69m other revenue, mostly from secondary rights. Content cost includes £49m indirect programme costs. Other costs estimated by subtraction from the other figures, allowing for the £4m reported surplus.

[3] Toby Syfret and Claire Enders, *Channel 4: Sustainability and Privatisation*, Enders Analysis, 18 December 2015 [2015-118].

[4] This is a simple, broad brush assumption. In practice, we would expect some costs to go up by less than this (eg possibly sales) and others by more (eg distribution costs as online viewing puts increasing strain on broadband networks).

[5] Syfret and Enders, op cit, pp12-15; Ofcom, *Review of Channel Four*, July 2015, p4. Barwise and Brooks (2016) discusses in some detail the reasons for our, and the other experts', confidence that C4's remit is sustainable.

[6] Like David Elstein (Chapter 2), we see no credible case for an IPO or private equity sale to create a standalone business with no potential synergies.

[7] There are other possibilities including BT and Vodafone, discussed in Barwise and Brooks (2016), Section 4.8.

[8] The only exceptions we are aware of are marginal: Viacom now owns C5, the smallest and most commercial of the UK PSBs; Liberty has a stake in ITV and owns TV3 in Ireland; and Scripps owns 50% of UKTV in which the other partner is BBC Worldwide.

[9] However, a strategy between options 2 and 3 is possible. This would not affect our conclusions.

[10] Note that this assumes that, as part of the agreement to retain the remit, C4 retains its existing spectrum (and EPG prominence) without having to pay a market rate.

[11] 20% of £31m.

[12] 808 on average in 2014: AR14, p142, which also breaks this down by area.

[13] Abraham: AR14, p125; Crozier: ITV 2014 Annual Report, p85; Darroch: Sky 2014 Annual Report, p71.

[14] AR14, p5 and C4 internal documents.

[15] C4: £938m/808: AR14 pp100, 142; ITV Broadcast (ie excluding ITV Studios, which is more labour-intensive) £2023m/2042: ITV 2014 Annual Report, pp6, 120.

[16] AR14, p141.

[17] See Barwise and Brooks (2016), Section 1.1.

[18] Barwise and Brooks (2016) also analyses the impact under Options 1 (even worse) and 3 (less bad, but still almost certainly negative).

[19] 0.80x(50/71)=0.56. See Barwise and Brooks (2016) for the detailed calculations for all three of MediaCorp's strategic options.

[20] Based on AR14, p100: 'originated content spend' £430m out of £602m direct content costs. (This excludes 'indirect programme costs' – AR14, p140).

[21] 71% of £1045m.

Mutual advantage

By Terry Burns

Between the options of full privatisation and state ownership, there might be a third way that takes C4 off the government balance sheet and still protects its remit

This is an extract from the 'exit interview' in February 2016 for the Lords Communications Committee in which Lord Burns responded to questions about his time as chairman of the Channel Four board from 2010 to 2016.

The Chairman (Lord Best): *These last few years have been a creative and financial success for Channel 4. Your ratings and your share of viewing audiences are up, including among younger people, and you have achieved a financial surplus of some note. To what do you attribute the success that has certainly been achieved, particularly in this last year?*

Lord Burns: First of all, I would say the whole challenge of Channel 4 is to balance the creative side with the financial stability side. Channel 4 is not simply chasing after audiences and trying to do the best it can on the productive side. We care very much about the remit. We care very much about the quality of the programmes that are produced and that we are doing those things Parliament has asked us to do. The real challenge is keeping the two things in balance, because if they get out of balance problems can emerge. If the revenue side suffers, it means that less money is available for programming, which in turn means that the audience suffers, which means you lose your share of the advertising market, and it can become a cumulative process. We have very much concentrated upon keeping these two aspects in balance.

The main feature during the time I have been there is what we regarded as the process of creative renewal. Following a period when you will recall *Big Brother* took a very large number of hours on Channel 4, the decision had been made before I got there to bring it to an end, although it still had one more year to do, and of course subsequently it has been on Channel 5. It meant that there was a very big gap in programming and, indeed, on the financial side, because it had been effective financially. The whole programme has been to try to fill that

128

space, and to fill it with a greater mixture of programming that is very much focused on the remit but that would also work financially.

The second big decision taken was to embark upon a data strategy, which is really a programme for keeping in touch with viewers. We ended up, of course, as we have publicised, with a very large proportion of young people in particular who are registered with Channel 4, which has meant that we have been able to sell advertising much more effectively through the internet channels, because we know who is watching, and that has increased the value of what Channel 4 does.

I think Channel 4 has adjusted very well to the digital world, a world where people are watching on lots of different devices and platforms. It has put a lot of effort into that as well as into diversifying sales. We now do the advertising for UKTV and BT Sport, which provides additional income. It is a whole series of things that basically have taken some time to get established but which together have led to a very strong set of programmes on the creative side of things last year, aimed particularly at our key audiences of Channel 4 — the 16 to 34 year-old group and the ABC1 group — on the financial side of what we do, because that is where we sell most of the advertising.

Baroness (Floella) Benjamin: *There has been a document that says: 'Work should proceed to examine the options of extracting greater public value from the Channel 4 Corporation, focusing on privatisation options in particular'. Do you think that the sale of Channel 4, with its public service obligations, would be profitable for the Government? Are you concerned for those obligations should the Government seek to go ahead and privatise the channel?*

Lord Burns: My goodness, this subject has been on the agenda for the past few months, and we have been questioned a lot about it. My basic position is that if the Government are intent on keeping all the public service obligations for Channel 4, there is not a great deal in it financially from a sale. There are two objectives of privatisation. I can say in parenthesis that I was involved in an awful lot of privatisations when I was in the Treasury and it is something that I was quite close to. First, there is the objective of making money. Then there is a second objective, which in many cases is much more important, as to whether it would be better for the particular market with which one is dealing. The questions I have about the privatisation of Channel 4, if you were to do it, would be whether you were doing it for the money or because you really thought that the broadcasting industry in this country would be a better place if it were in private hands.

My view is if you keep the public service obligations that we have, there is not a huge amount of money in it for the Government, because at the moment we make it work by spending all our surpluses on other programming and investments in the future. If you want to create surpluses in order to make it commercially valuable to sell, some of the public service obligations would have to give; either the obligation would have to give whereby we commission all our programmes with independent producers, or we would have to reduce the number of loss-making programmes, which would mean news and current affairs. There would be less risk and less innovation. I characterise this as a situation where the more value you want to extract from it in a sale, the more you have to compromise the channel's public service obligations.

Baroness Bonham-Carter of Yarnbury: *I have a sense that maybe the penny has dropped about obligations versus value, but something else has come on to the page, which is part-privatisation, whatever that might mean exactly. Can you see any way in which that would work for Channel 4?*

Lord Burns: I cannot see how you can have part-privatisation of the holding company of Channel 4, because it would present the same set of problems as privatisation, which is that you introduce a share of ownership the objective of which would be increasing shareholder value rather than focused upon meeting the remit. The incentives then become very different and are very much those of audiences and of removing those loss-making programmes.

We have been very keen with Channel 4 to get into the world of joint ventures. In a way, we already do that on the advertising front, as I have already mentioned. We also do it with the making of some programmes. Indeed, with the way the whole broadcasting industry is working, I suspect there is a lot of joint-venture potential out there, and the freedom to do that is one of the advantages that one would have outside the public sector. Part-privatisation does not do much for the Government's balance sheet unless it is less than 50%, and, as I say, that does not change the basic story if it is at the holding company level. More freedom to do a lot more joint ventures and possibly borrowing money to invest in certain other activities makes more sense, but I am not sure that I would describe that as part privatisation or simply as greater freedom.

Baroness Bonham-Carter of Yarnbury: *From a slightly different angle, if there were to be privatisation, or indeed part-privatisation – and what you are really saying is that the effect on the remit would be the same – what effect would this have on the wider broadcasting industry in the UK?*

Lord Burns: As I say, the reality is that we run Channel 4 and we have run it on the basis that all surpluses are ploughed back into either programming or investment for the future. In order to build a dividend stream out of this, something would have to go, and one possibility that I have mentioned, and I am sure it is on a number of people's minds, would be doing its own programming rather than commissioning all the programmes from independent producers. Of course, if the end result was that Channel 4 ended up in the ownership of an American conglomerate, one of their greatest motives would be that of doing their own programming rather than doing it through the mass of small, independent companies that we use. I think that is a possibility.

The real pressure that comes from the fundamental Channel 4 model is that it is a model of inherent cross-subsidy. We make programmes that make money, which then gives us the ability to make programmes that lose money. The one that I always quote is *Channel 4 News*, which is the only hour-long news programme in peak time in this country, [and] loses money. You cannot gain as much advertising revenue during that one hour as it costs to make the programme. The same goes for quite a lot of the current affairs programming. That kind of programming is very difficult to sustain under privatisation. Over the years, the public service obligations that Channel 5, and indeed Channel 3 and ITV, had with regard to news and current affairs have been reduced because of the commercial pressures. They have gone back to the regulator and said: 'We cannot make these organisations work unless we are allowed to do less of them.' All those great programmes that I was brought up with – *Weekend World, World in Action, The South Bank Show* – slowly disappeared over time because of the commercial reality. I suspect that would be the consequence for Channel 4; we would move into more profit-making and populist programming that would command greater audiences relative to the cost of making them.

Lord Hart of Chilton: *Lord Burns, in 2015 you presented to the Government a structure whereby the broadcaster would become a not-for-profit company limited by guarantee, and then the entity would be off the books, the shareholders would derive no profit, and all money made would go back into the company. What would the benefits be for a not-for-profit company, and how would that improve Channel 4?*

Lord Burns: First of all, I have been fairly indifferent on the question of whether Channel 4 remains as it is, as a government company, essentially a not-for-profit company, or whether it is in the private sector on a not-for-profit basis. I put forward the option basically because if the Government were intent on seeing Channel 4 in the private sector, because it was thought that a broadcasting company should not be in the public sector, this structure would seem to me to best enable them to fulfil that objective and to continue to fulfil the objectives and the remit of Channel 4. I am not saying by any means that the Government could not get some money out of that process. It would be possible to put some debt on to the Channel 4 balance sheet where at present there is no debt, and the Government would probably be able to be paid something for it, but it would not be able to be paid as much as under what one thinks of as a normal privatisation, and it would remain a not-for-profit company rather than one that was motivated by shareholder value. That was the purpose of that. It was not that we see huge benefits in that – although there are some benefits such as resolving the issue of ownership indefinitely rather than having a periodic issue that comes every 10 or 15 years as to whether or not Channel 4 is going to be privatised. I think it would be easier to do deals and joint ventures with the private sector if we were actually in the private sector ourselves and not subject to government balance-sheet constraints. It may well improve the confidence of the people with whom we deal to think that the future had been settled.

There are some advantages. I think the executives who work in Channel 4 would quite like to be in a position of a safe harbour rather than having to refight this battle about the ownership of Channel 4 every 10 or 15 years. We have provided this alternative structure, because it is a structure that I am very familiar with. I did the same, with the co-operation of two or three other people, when we bought Welsh Water from a private sector company and turned it into a not-for-profit company. It has been very successful, but it was peculiar to the water industry. I am very familiar with the structure and with how it works and how it leaves you with a company that has a very different orientation from a normal shareholder company.

I would emphasise that for most activities in life I am a great believer in shareholder companies. It is not that I have a particular bee in my bonnet about not-for-profit companies; I just think that for most activities it is the best way of doing things. However, broadcasting is a very different type of landscape and requires different treatment. One of the great advantages of the UK broadcasting world is that it has a number of companies with very different financial structures, and I think people underestimate the extent to which these different players with different financial structures contribute to this extraordinary variety in the different types of programming that we get. I would regret it deeply if we took Channel 4 out of this and left the BBC as the only broadcaster doing public service broadcasting.

About the author

Lord (Terry) Burns has had a distinguished career in and out of Government. He was the Chief Economic Adviser to the Government 1980-1991 and Permanent Secretary to the Treasury 1991-98. Since he has chaired the boards of Marks and Spencer, Welsh Water and Santander. In broadcasting, he chaired the Review into the BBC Charter, which reported in 2006, and the Channel Four Board from 2010-2016.

Flourishing in Britain's creative greenhouse

By David Abraham

Channel 4 is winning awards, building revenues and allowing creativity to bloom across multiple programme genres. So plans to privatise it feel like a solution in search of a problem

This book examines the ownership model of Channel 4 – an issue that every chief executive of the corporation since 1982 has had to address. I've always been comfortable in engaging with it because Channel 4 is an organisation underpinned by a set of ideas. If we can't explain why these ideas still matter in a world that never stands still, we have no right to exist.

The challenge, of course, is that the hybrid mixture of ideas supporting Channel 4 is somewhat more varied and subtle than is the case with the BBC. But no less important for being so. Channel 4 remains a big investor (of some £700 million per year) in the UK creative economy, as well as being a small but perfectly formed cultural institution and defender of robust plurality in news and current affairs. It is part national talent accelerator and part defender of diverse audiences. It has been instrumental in developing more than 500 feature films since launch as well as introducing British audiences to extraordinary new creative breakthroughs like fixed-rig filming and Paralympic sport. Across multiple genres Channel 4 is a creative counterweight to the BBC because it competes directly and ambitiously against it – but with far smaller resources. In summary, we see ourselves as a highly efficient creative greenhouse – a place where ideas and people are incubated and nurtured for the nation.

This eclectic mix of outcomes is sometimes described by sceptics and competitors as a self-selecting and opaque licence to do what the hell we like – and to perpetuate ourselves institutionally. But that's not the way I see it. This special and unusual mix of objectives is what drew me to Channel 4 after 25 years in the private sector. I love the fact that Channel 4 is run as a business, hungry every day to earn its keep, lean in its use of resources, but set up to do what many talented people in the creative industries want to do first and foremost – good work. As one of my colleagues recently and memorably said to me: 'We don't do this to make money, we make money so we can do this'.

It has been six years since I arrived as Channel 4's sixth chief executive. From the outset I felt it was my responsibility to reinforce and build on 30 years of Channel 4 leading the way in creative innovation under a commercially-sustainable model. I'm proud of where we have got to today and confident that we can keep doing it. The tricky and lengthy process of creative renewal – to rebuild the schedule post *Big Brother* and *Friends* and introduce a mix of strong new returning hits alongside one-off, experimental and original titles — is now flourishing. That process was not easy and does not happen quickly and we worked hard with producers and viewers to get the mix right.

We built the pioneering Channel 4 data strategy – a huge technical undertaking that has transformed the way we interact with advertisers and viewers and which was initially greeted with a degree of scepticism. Our sales house was early to market with targeted on-line advertising, and we established important commercial partnerships with BT and UKTV.

These developments have put us on a sustainable footing to keep reinvesting back into the remit and into the UK's creative sector. That's a view endorsed by many – including Enders Analysis, Ernst & Young and Ofcom.

But in September of 2015, an unidentified civil servant was seen walking up Downing Street holding, but not quite concealing, a document that set out options for 'extracting greater public value from the Channel 4 Corporation (C4C), focusing on privatisation options in particular...'. Since then there has been a lot of information exchanged and commentary expended. And yet today we are not much the wiser as to the rationale for a privatisation of Channel 4. It doesn't appear to be about the relevance or importance of the remit or our creative performance, nor is it seemingly about the money. If there is any clarity at all, it is about some vague sense of Channel 4 becoming unsustainable amongst the hurly burly of new players about to undermine the existence, presumably not just of Channel 4, but every advertiser funded media business in the UK. Tellingly, those most ardent supporters of privatisation seem to have harboured those views for more years than such apparent threats have existed.

Continuing vitality

There was a time when hearing the words 'Channel 4, Catastrophe' might have sounded like a verdict on the channel's state of health. Yet not long ago we heard this announcement at the Broadcast Awards when Channel 4 won the comedy programme award for *Catastrophe*. We went on to also be named Channel of the Year. It was a moment and an evening that demonstrated the continuing vitality of Channel 4 and it was a triumph for the social enterprise model under which the station operates.

This is, ultimately, the point of Channel 4: to make television that draws in an audience for programmes of the highest quality. It is neither simply an art-house, nor simply a market place. Channel 4 at its best is both of those things, creatively fused. The prestige of the programmes and their commercial viability are part of the same package and it is a remit and a purpose that is working well, perhaps as well as it ever has during Channel 4's three decades of existence.

The model under which Channel 4 works embodies two virtues. Channel 4 fulfils its public service remit, which features both qualitative purposes and specific quota requirements set out in its Ofcom licence, while remaining self-sufficient in commercial terms. It is a marriage of commerce and public service; the former at the service of the latter. The purpose is to provide content of the highest quality that fulfils a specific, relevant and unique remit, while incurring no cost to the British taxpayer – by putting profits into programmes.

The social enterprise model of Channel 4 means that its surplus is not distributed. The accrued revenue all goes back into programme making and fulfilment of the remit. This, in turn, relies on a simple operating formula. Some programmes fulfil the public service remit but traditionally run at a loss. The obvious examples are news and current affairs, such as our recent *Escape from Isis* or *Unreported World* documentaries. These programmes are therefore cross-funded by others, on which a surplus can be generated. Others are more overtly and unashamedly commercial in focus, to make money to fund the loss-making, though even these – for example *Come Dine with Me*, acquisitions and even *Formula 1*, are not just cash cows but programmes that are commissioned or selected to sit within the overall mix. Indeed, even *Big Brother* which became that great commercial hit, began life as an interesting social experiment and was twice as diverse in its contributor make up than it is today on Channel 5.

Beyond this, and where we have placed a great deal of emphasis in the creative renewal process, are those programmes that hit the 'sweet spot' of delivering strong public value and commercial return: factual output such as *Hunted, Gogglebox, the Secret Life of 4 Year Olds*; dramas like *Humans* and *Fresh Meat*. Taken together the programmes that deliver a surplus are as much a part of a portfolio in which we take pride as *Channel Four News*. Because we don't see public service broadcasting as just a narrow set of boxes to tick, but as a framework to maximise genuine public value through programmes of all sorts of shapes and sizes that resonate and mean something to audiences about the society that is evolving around us. In contrast with some of our early forebears, we do not believe that in the 21st century, public service broadcasting is always about putting on obscure operas and avant-garde art films that might impress our friends. We think it's also about reflecting the society we are constantly in the process of becoming in ways that are engaging, innovative, popular and therefore financially sustainable.

The results are indisputable on both sides of the equation: the revenue and the quality of the programming. In 2014 (which as I write are the latest published figures) Channel 4 had revenues of £938 million, an increase of £30 million on the previous year. Revenues in 2015 and 2016 continue to grow. Digital revenues are rising rapidly. In 2016 we aim to exceed £1bn in revenues. Our balance sheet is solidly above £450m. As a consequence Channel 4 makes a consistent contribution to the UK's creative economy. A mere 800 employees support 19,000 jobs across the UK. In 2013 over a quarter of the British programme formats in the Top 100 were commissioned by Channel 4 and those formats grossed $0.5 billion (around £350m) in European broadcasting revenue.

In addition, Channel 4 has been described (by Simon Andrea when he was executive vice-president at Fox Broadcasting) as the single richest source of IP in the world in the television industry. These are proof points of an organisation that is fixed on the profit incentives baked into its model – to generate revenue and put its profits back into content and into the creative economy. If Channel 4's purpose were satisfied by financial viability then these numbers alone would certainly suffice. But, it must also be judged against the standard of world-class creativity.

In 2014 and 2015, Channel 4 won over 300 awards and this year has picked up 3 Oscars for *Room, Amy* and *Ex-Machina* to add up to a total of 19 Oscars won by Channel 4 since 2007. It won in multiple categories at the 2016 Broadcast Awards, and received 26 nominations at the Royal Television Society Awards – the most in a decade. All this recognition derives not in spite of the onerous demands placed on Channel 4 but *because* of those demands. The requirement for Channel 4 to be different is precisely what makes the Channel the particular success it is. It is by no means obvious that this range of requirements could be met if Channel 4 answered solely to shareholders on a shorter time horizon, subject to the demand for quarterly earnings reports.

Four elements at the heart of the remit
From the 12 major points of the remit (not including the further specific licence obligations we are subject to) there are four key points to expand on here.

First, Channel 4 is charged to stimulate public debate. This function is in part about public education, a responsibility discharged right across our output, whether series about mental health such as *Bedlam* or providing insights into lives around the World in *Tribe*. This is supported by online apps such as 'My Mind Checker' which allows users to test themselves on a range of mental health conditions. The app has been downloaded over 1 million times.

This requirement is also, though, about authoritative and trustworthy public information. Channel 4 provides more hours of long-form news and current affairs in peak-time than any other comparable channel, including BBC1. The reach of the news and current affairs coverage is global, exemplified by programmes such as *Sri Lanka's Killing Fields* (a film which was credited by the UN with helping to highlight the atrocities), or documentaries such as *Hunted* (about homosexuality in Russia) and *Unreported World: Jamaica's Underground Gays*.

Second, Channel 4 has to reflect the cultural diversity of the UK – and we do this in a variety of ways. Channel 4 has always championed the minorities who make up so much of our population – from the first televised lesbian kiss in *Brookside*, to championing BAME talent on and off screen, to putting disability centre stage in the Paralympics. A year after we published our 30-point 360

Diversity Charter, we have made 2016 our Year of Disability as we build up to the Paralympic Games in Rio.

Diversity is reflected in the way we work with the UK's production community rather than making our own programmes. It's about the 300 companies we partner with every year (more than ITV and Channel 5 combined); and it's also about representing and investing in the UK's nations and regions. Channel 4 spends more on first-run programmes made in the North of England than it does in the South and more than 50 per cent of programming hours are commissioned from outside the M25.

The great worry in television is that the viewing habits of the young are fundamentally different from their predecessor generation. It is not yet obvious what the full implications may be for the traditional broadcasters but we can already see that the only channel that is at all able to buck the trend is Channel 4, which attracts the highest share of the viewing done by people between the ages of 16 and 34. It is the only public service broadcaster in the world whose share of viewing by young people is higher than its share for all individuals.

E4 is the most popular digital channel with this audience as well. Twenty eight per cent of Channel 4's audience is between 16 and 34 compared to 15 per cent at ITV and 13 per cent at the BBC. The same holds true for the audience for news. Those who have registered with Channel 4 have done so because they trust our brand and can be confident about how Channel 4 will use the data we collect.

This relationship of trust that Channel 4 has established with young people is a great responsibility but also a great opportunity. We can, in the way no other broadcaster really can, reach young people on difficult subjects. *Cyber Bully* and *Don't Blame Facebook* talked to young people on how to stay safe in the digital world. Through programmes such as *My Big Fat Diary* and *Hollyoaks* Channel 4 has also talked directly to young people about mental health, eating disorders and drug abuse.

Third, Channel 4 has to champion alternative points of view which may not always be well-known, at least not at first, and, as a result, may not be immediately lucrative prospects for advertisers. But then, risk-taking is a character trait at Channel 4. When viewers were asked, they reported that Channel 4 took more risks and exhibited more points of view than any other broadcaster. It is surely likely that a model of shareholder finance would reduce the risk we take.. Private capital is likely to take less risk and hence reduce the diversity and support for SMEs by scheduling more 'bankable' programmes. Channel 4 had a clear lead in the public perception for its coverage of ethnic minorities, and issues around sexuality and disability. We strive to make sure that our most popular programmes feature a range of people from different walks of life – take *Gogglebox* as an example – and *Channel 4 News* features a particularly high proportion of stories from around the world. 83 per cent of people thought Channel 4 coverage of the Paralympics would improve the perception of disabled people. Indeed, it is hard to imagine the coverage of the Paralympics on any other channel. The same can be said of *Stand Up To Cancer* which will again be aired later in 2016.

Fourth, Channel 4 seeks to nurture new talent. The production model is designed to do just this. Channel 4 is a commissioner. It has no in-house production and the main channel works with more independent TV production companies than any other channel. In 2014 Channel 4 established a £20m Indie Growth Fund which provides 'smart' funding to help small independent companies to grow. The aim is that, on a horizon of five years, we can benefit from their success by exiting our investment. The success of Steve McQueen is just one example of Channel 4's creative commitment. We started with his first major film, *Hunger*, in 2008 and this culminated five years later when *12 Years A Slave* won an Oscar. Our Alpha fund is aimed at supporting SMEs around the UK. And then there is all the work we do off screen to support the work of Creative Skillset and the NFTS and through our pioneering youth schemes to bring a diversity of people into the sector.

Data pioneering

It is common in broadcasting that predictions about the pace of change should always move faster than the pace of change itself. Most viewing still takes place at the time of broadcast and most of it is taken up by the traditional providers of public service broadcasting. That is not to say, of course, that a vibrant company is not vigilantly watching the market, seeking to anticipate change rather than react to it. One vital business requirement for a modern broadcaster is a viable strategy for data collection. A broadcaster without a data strategy is like a submarine without sonar. Building on Channel 4's pioneering move into on-demand with the launch of 4oD (now All4) in 2006, Channel 4 further innovated with its own data strategy. It now has 13.5m registered viewers, which includes over half the 16-34 year olds in the UK. This asset is powering our digital revenues, which we expect to soon exceed £100m, a tenth of total revenues.

When Ofcom renewed Channel 4's licence for a further 10 years in 2015 it noted the difficult competitive situation that applies to all broadcasters, but specified that Channel 4 had adapted well. Respected, independent analysis from Ernst & Young and Enders Analysis reinforce this view. Every part of the model seems to be working well, perhaps better than at any point in living memory. Revenues are at record levels, the audience is telling us in our regular tracking that we're performing as strongly to the remit as we ever have. And programmes are winning audiences and awards. Channel 4 is stimulating public debate, nurturing new talent, giving a voice to the otherwise unheard and taking risks.

It is, in short, in a good state both commercially and creatively – and it continues to make an economic, social and cultural contribution of a kind I simply cannot imagine a company structured to maximise shareholder's financial returns being able to match. We have a strong balance sheet with strong reserves and are able to invest to grow our business. The idea of privatisation really does feel like a solution in search of a problem. Every management team that has had the privilege of leading this organisation has had to face challenges and adapt to change. Channel 4 has only ever existed at a time of market expansion and technological advancement – indeed it was itself a part of the early moves to move away from the old duopoly of British broadcasting. Tasked with the job of innovating and nurturing talent in our creative greenhouse, Channel 4 has always done that as much off screen as on.

And we are continuing to adapt and innovate in the way Channel 4 does things creatively and commercially. The job is never done and the challenges and opportunities shift and change. But one thing that my predecessors and I have in common is that we have all had one core priority in mind as we've held the baton – the unique remit. A remit to be innovative, distinctive, experimental and diverse. To be alternative and challenging; and to nurture talent, and to champion the entrepreneurs who make British TV production among the best in the world. For the sake of the next generation of audiences and creative talent, let's hope that never changes.

About the author

David Abraham became Channel 4's sixth chief executive when he took up the post in May 2010. Over the past five years the team he leads has creatively renewed the Channel 4 schedule post Big Brother; delivered the 2012 Paralympic Games; forged new ad sales partnerships with UKTV and BT Sport; launched 4seven, All 4 and Channel 4's Indie and Commercial Growth Funds; boosted Film4's output and attracted 13m viewers to register directly with Channel 4. David led Discovery Networks UK during a period of rapid growth between 2001-2004, led the revival of cable channel TLC in the US between 2005-2007, and repositioned UKTV's ten channels, including launching Dave, as CEO from 2007-2010.

David worked at the creative agencies CDP and Chiat/Day in the 1980s after earning a degree in Modern History from Oxford University. He was a founding partner of the influential 90s agency St Luke's. He is a member of the Creative Skillset Board

Put not your trust in remits

By Liz Forgan

Channel 4 was always a cultural, rather than a business, opportunity. But do today's Conservative leaders recognise that as well as their predecessors did?

That was then. This is now.

There is something unseemly about those of us who were at Channel 4 on November 2 1982 going on about the good old days. They were certainly good. Quite amazingly, incredibly good. And they have important lessons. But it was another country.

Three terrestrial television channels. No digits. No satellites. Television advertising sales an ITV monopoly. No pay TV. Virtually all UK television production made by the BBC or ITV in house.

Since then the world has changed completely and the Channel 4 licence has undergone many revisions including the scrapping of its original funding arrangement. But the brilliantly simple, infinitely flexible brief from Parliament – the remit – has remained essentially the same: be distinctive, innovate, cater for unrepresented tastes and interests, maintain a broad range and include programmes of an educational nature.

In this era of relentless focus on the economic value of the creative industries, the approach taken by the Conservative government of the 1980s seems visionary. This huge new opportunity, the first new television channel since BBC2 in 1964 nearly 20 years earlier, was seen as above all a cultural, not a business, one. The point was to broaden and enrich the range of programmes available to viewers. And to that end Home Secretary William Whitelaw was persuaded of the great truth that plural sources of funding is what gives you plural programme policies.

Channel 4 was not to compete with its peers for resources but for esteem and distinctiveness. It was to follow a remit to be different and given the funding freedom to take the risks that would deliver it.

That remit is seen as the channel's great bulwark but there is a real danger that it could become its greatest weakness in the forthcoming argument over privatisation.

That argument is now too simply focused on the issue of the remit as the sacred bellwether of Channel 4's future security. It is widely believed that the value of any transaction will be directly related to how much of the remit is written into the conditions of sale. The more the remit, the less revenue for the Chancellor: the more contribution to the exchequer, the less remit to be distinctive goes the argument. The channel's defenders are watching every word.

A handful of words

But there is a danger in sanctifying the remit in this way. It is only a handful of words. And their meaning is capable of quite elastic interpretation. Back in 1982 some of the ITV companies had fully expected that the injunction to cater for minority interests would mean badminton and macramé rather than football and variety shows and were not happy at finding indie movies and Irish politics on their screens. It all depends who is driving and what their destination is.

The power of the remit was and is only to *enable* courage and ambition on the part of those running the channel. It is a necessary – but by absolutely no means sufficient – condition of adventurous programming. And it is meaningless without two other things: a board and executive with creative courage and a funding context which gives it half a chance of realising its potential.

In the hands of its first chief executive, Jeremy Isaacs, the remit became a thing of wonder, scandal, creativity and exhilaration. He hired executives and commissioned programme makers who knew nothing about television as well as old masters. His peak time schedules ranged from Schoenberg Operas to Derek Jarman movies, from *Channel 4 News* to *Countdown*, from feminist comedy to the breakthrough feature film deal that became Film 4.

As with all genuine risk taking the results were sometimes appalling but full of new growth and creativity. The independent production sector was born. Dozens of new talents shot to national and international fame. The limits of the possible were broadened for a mass audience.

In the 34 years of the channel's life, successive bosses have squeezed and moulded the remit to their own creative ambitions and economic circumstances. More or less Golden Ages have come and gone. But each one in his way (women CEOs still being a risk too far) has felt the hand of history on his shoulder and pursued creative innovation and diversity as far as was consistent with generating the resources he needed to make programmes.

A brand with unrealised value

Privatisation – even with the remit word for word intact – would change that single-minded focus completely. It would put an end to the continuing financial protection that Channel Four enjoys today as a statutory corporation where all profits are returned to the business.

Shareholders would rightly demand a return on their investment. Profits would be distributed, not ploughed back, and the pressure to increase them by steering the remit towards the most popular forms of distinctiveness and the cheapest forms of innovation would become irresistible. The remit could appear in letters of gold at the top of the Memorandum and Articles and it would make no difference to a CEO bound to a different master.

Of course there is a perfectly good argument for privatising Channel Four. It is a brand with unrealised value which the market could release. It occupies valuable spectrum which could also yield more. It is a public asset which – some believe – could yield more public benefit if run on commercial lines. Furthermore the national debt is a good cause.

What it is not possible to believe is that a privatised channel would deliver as wide a range of programming or take as many risks with new talent and new ideas. The Whitelaw principle still prevails: different forms of funding produce different creative outcomes and profits distributed to shareholders means a pressure to play safe and rely on proven success.

It is widely assumed by the opponents of privatisation that it would lead to a plunge in programme quality. Possibly, but by no means necessarily. The media market can always produce quality. A privatised Channel Four could certainly pitch up-market with a high quality schedule catering – in faithful service of the remit – to tastes and interests not catered for elsewhere. What the free market in television always finds more difficult is range in programming – the very essence of Channel Four to date.

The question is whether this generation of Conservative leaders retain their predecessors' sense that television is a piece of the fabric of popular culture – where its ability to prioritise diversity and innovation makes a unique contribution – or an asset like any other to be grown to full value and then sold for cash.

Is the public benefit a criterion at all? If so does it reside in the particular form of wider choice that Channel Four in its present state can bring to the schedules or in the gains that would accrue elsewhere from realising its cash value to spend on other things?

Stability amid the turmoil
It may seem to some slightly absurd to worry so much about one old terrestrial channel when there are thousands more available at the end of a fibre optic cable or from a satellite dish. And yet the remarkable feature of the current market place is that, with all the choice available, viewing to the main broadcast channels remains extraordinarily stable.

Digital terrestrial TV remains the most popular way of watching television and the main five public service broadcasting PSB channels accounted for just over half of all viewing in 2014 even with 536 other UK channels to choose from. That share is dropping slowly, as is the number of minutes per day people spend watching live TV but the British public's loyalty to its traditional television outlets is remarkable.

The stable nature of public loyalty to the channels they know and love is borne out by the market. The vast majority of television advertising income is generated by traditional broadcast television and it is on the rise: from £3,143bn in 2009 to £3,838bn in 2014. Channel Four's share of that revenue was £483m in 2014 but, at only 12.5% of the total, could no doubt encourage prospective owners to contemplate growth with a slight tweak to the ever-accommodating remit.

The numbers show a healthy commercial market for traditional terrestrial television but they also show how wedded the audience is to the offering from the traditional PSB channels. Channel Four (including its digital family of channels) still has the third largest share of viewing in the UK with 10.5% of the audience, second only to BBC and ITV.

Television channels are not pork barrel futures or redundant government buildings. They are creators, patrons and purveyors of a highly popular (in both senses) variety of entertainment, information and culture to millions. In the days of spectrum scarcity the British broadcasting landscape was moulded with skill and deliberation to maximise sustainable choice for the viewer, with each broadcaster playing a distinctive role. That landscape has adapted to the arrival of the burgeoning digital marketplace and thrives alongside it to the benefit of both. Moving a major chunk of it to be something different and play a different part is a big step.

Channel Four was created by a visionary act of government and it became a special piece of the broadcasting offer, more bohemian than the BBC, more culturally ambitious than ITV, bigger and better resourced than most online channels. It is by no means the same animal as it was when it launched but creative ambition, not maximising revenue, remains its driving engine.

There will always be arguments about the Channel's success in delivering its remit. It no longer shows Sanskrit operas or Berlin Alexanderplatz in peak or any other time. But it remains a distinctive voice, an essential market for a wide range of quality UK production and a channel which dares to do things others can't or won't.

The abortive attempt to privatise the forests should perhaps have taught the government a more nuanced approach to valuing national assets. The BBC could reasonably claim that moving BBC3 to the web is simply moving the channel to its audience's natural home and thus serving it better. I have yet to hear anyone argue seriously that privatising Channel 4 would benefit its audience.

About the author

Dame Liz Forgan, who made her name in journalism editing *The Guardian* Women's pages, was a founding Commissioning Editor and then Director of Programmes at Channel 4. She is now Chairman of the Scott Trust, which owns the Guardian Newspaper Group. In a long and distinguished career of public service, she has also been Chair of the Arts Council of England and a Managing Director of BBC Radio.

Section 2:
The Charlotte Street years

Introduction by Fiona Chesterton

The founding of Channel 4 is an extraordinary and surprising story which, in the current Year Zero climate of much political and media debate, is well worth retelling.

Surprising because it was the Thatcher Government and a Conservative Home Secretary who gave it the go-ahead. Extraordinary because as the authors in this section describe, it was in some ways a happy accident, in others the result of a determined and passionate 20-year battle overcoming the power of vested interests, the inertia of so much of British life, and the sheer challenge of creating something without precedent in the broadcast world of the time, and where the odds of its survival – and flourishing – were stacked against it. The legendary TV producer Roger Graef calls it here a David versus Goliath battle.

It is a story rich in characters and some jaw-dropping episodes. Above all it is a story that reveals what sheer fun and adventure could be had in the making of television in the 1980s.

There are two men who can claim to be the founding geniuses of the channel: the one, Jeremy Isaacs, the first chief executive, the other, Anthony Smith. It was the latter who virtually single-handedly made the intellectual case for Channel 4 for getting on for two decades. The fourth channel was destined to be ITV2 but it was Tony Smith who indefatigably made the case for something much more ambitious, one which would give access to the then strictly-limited airwaves to a wider range of voices and interests, driven by what he calls 'neither competition, nor complementarity, but pluralism.'

In 1972, a decade before the Channel opened, he was advocating a radically new structure for a television company – one where there would be commissioning editors but outsourced programme making and studio facilities.

145

At a time when there were very few independent companies this was risk-taking indeed.

In his chapter he gives credit to the Conservative Home Secretary, William Whitelaw, for coming up with a new funding mechanism that would allow his vision to work. Tony summarises Channel 4's birth in 1982 as a key part of 'a national culture moving from an acceptance of closed hierarchies to a modern self-made pluralism'.

It was a culture where post-1960s spirits wished to see a breaking of the bounds in all sorts of ways, not least in concepts of taste and what could and could not be broadcast. The founding commissioning editor for comedy, Mike Bolland, reminds us of the key role Channel 4 had in saying and showing things that had not been seen on TV before, and just what creative comic genius flowed from that.

David Lloyd, who arrived at the channel a few years after its launch, paints an equally revealing picture of the unique culture at Charlotte Street, in the first of his series of sketches – which continues throughout the book – recounting key moments he witnessed. Broadcasting House it was not.

From the other side of the glass doors, the first wave of independent producers were carving out another revolution. One of their number, Bernard Clark, describes how the channel gave people like himself a 'crash course in how to set up and run a company'. He also describes how in those pre-regional-quota days, he cannily set up his offices (with a well-filled drinks cabinet) just a few hundred metres from Charlotte Street, to attract commissioning editors on their way home. From those less-than-ideal (from a diversity point of view) beginnings, sprang first a 'cottage industry (which) became a confident indie sector and then a major global industry'.

Clark is sure that one of the key reasons that Channel 4 worked so well was that producers were allowed to get on with making their programmes, and complains at current micromanagement. He calls for producers to be set free again in a new-model channel.

The overall message of this section is well-summarised by Peter Preston, editor of *The Guardian* at the founding of the Channel and now a wise commentator on the media. Channel 4 was an 'institution that you couldn't invent', a 'hodge podge that works'. But his is far from a rose-tinted spectacled view; he describes it now as a bit of a ragbag with much that is formulaic and a million miles in some ways from the vision he heard Jeremy Isaacs describe in 1982 with high art galore. But at its heart still remains something very precious – and for cherishing.

1986: Separate tables

By David Lloyd

'Now, I have to warn you – this is not like the BBC at all; this is the Animal House programme review!'

My cautionary guide was Paul Bonner, as we descended the lift to the ground floor boardroom for the weekly lunchtime meeting of commissioning staff to review the past week's channel output. Paul was the founding director of programmes and one of the few people at the channel's original base in Soho's Charlotte Street whom I had known back at the corporation. What sort of process was I about to witness? Could I ever fit in? This really mattered to a husband and father who had crossed London for nothing more secure than a three-year contract. Jeremy Issacs had decreed that no commissioning editor should stay longer for fear of becoming stale in the job, and as a patron, rely only on his cronies.

At the BBC's programme review, heads of department sat around an enormous, gargantuan table and lobbed sophisticated verbal missiles at their peers and rivals, while defending their own programmes against all-comers in return; the only creative talents that were likely to survive this gruelling process were those whose reputations were judged un-trashable.

At Channel 4, by comparison, word was out that the previous week the commissioning editor for Science and Religion (sic – thus were Dawkins and Darwin combined) had jumped upon the table and recited from the Book of Revelations at some length, before being argued out of his unconventional stance.

Sadly, on this occasion, I was not to be treated to any such display, but the differences between W1 and W12 still amounted to far more than the size of the table.

Looking across that reduced woodwork, I took the opportunity to identify and assess my new colleagues: most refreshing about them was that they did not all hail from television backgrounds, nor were they all careerists, in the strictest sense; the effect on the resulting quality and range of conversation was dynamic indeed, not least because – incredible to relate by today's standards – reference to the audience achieved, at least as a defence of the programme, was ruled out of bounds.

Television culture is, and has always been, inherently solipsistic, having regard only to itself, and comparing itself for reference points likewise. But around this table were film-makers with little experience of television itself, former members of the Institute of Contemporary Arts, a team of two to look after animation, who had already scored the channel's first big coup with *The Snowman*, academics with a sociology pedigree put to audience research use, and only the occasional former member of the Open University's production arm. The most professional corps was assembled under the Entertainment banner, who had already gained notice for *The Comic Strip Presents...*, and for discovering lasting new talents such as Jennifer Saunders, Ben Elton and Harry Enfield; Jonathan Ross was soon to follow.

The most significant broadcaster with a BBC history was Paul himself, but he was sidelined in his office, the reason for which was something of a puzzle, even though a quick peak through the porthole in the door to his sofa-lined office confirmed little sign of activity. In the absence of hard fact, it was generally believed among the commissioning team that he had mounted a coup to displace Jeremy Isaacs as chief executive and there were even dark rumours that the founding chairman, Edmund Dell, had put him up to it. Those rumours were, as it turned out, false. The most comforting thing about these shenanigans was that, for a young company, barely transmitting for three years, Channel 4 was already showing its media mettle by taking its place as the epicentre of gossip and rumour both dark and opaque, imaginative and outlandish, normally the province of more veteran broadcasters. So yes, I *COULD* learn to fit in here, after all! But my attention was already wandering from programme review. The mantra that bonded this disparate assembly of talent could have been, though was not so described at the time, 'courageous and outrageous' – a talisman that was to survive to this very day. And if one were looking for a single intellectual attitude that defined this gathering, one could do no better than 'iconoclastic' – in whatever programme genre. This helped to define a particular 'spirit' that I have experienced only within commissioning, rather than production, cultures. (While the BBC came, after some while, to catch up with it, and is now predicating its entire future upon it, across both genres and media, Channel 4 remains, quite simply, the better, more professional and more experienced commissioning operation, understanding the methods and obligations of a publisher/broadcaster, because that is its founding mission).

But there was one other refugee from the corporation, whose presence was already proving to be even more significant: Channel 4 head of drama David Rose, the originator of major BBC hits including *Z-Cars*, was charged with the extraordinarily bold ambition to bolster and 're-boot' the British film industry, under the banner of Film 4 – long, long before BBC Films had even thought of pinching the idea. And the portfolios of other colleagues reflected similarly unconventional strategies: there was, for instance, a commissioning team for

Independent Film and Video, which, in effect, catered for 'all those polemicist film-makers who couldn't be house-trained to believe in fairness and regulation' and, more important, who proselytized for lesbian and gay rights. Recognising now how LGBT issues have become mainstream – indeed part of orthodox reportage – and same-sex marriage legalised under a Conservative administration, one can only marvel at the sheer boldness of this initiative a full thirty years ago.

No less prescient was the founding of a multi-cultural department, long before 'multi-culture' was in the everyday lexicon. Indeed, not solely identified with hunting down racial inequality or justice, the multicultural department was responsible for one of the channel's biggest, and funniest, audience successes – the sitcom *Desmond's*, about a British-Caribbean barber shop starring Norman Beaton. Thus had Jeremy Isaacs translated parliament's statute to 'cater for minorities' and – in public service terms – this original commissioning structure has always placed it several leagues in the vanguard of contemporary culture, diversity and tolerance – so much in its DNA that it has survived, even prospered under, the many boards and chief executives that have followed.

One final – some might say delicious – irony from my first programme review meeting: while Channel 4 can be described, and has proved itself, as one of the great triumphs of Mrs Thatcher's founding administration, I numbered around the table no fewer than two self-confessed, and very proud, Marxists.

1987: A table for the producer, please
By David Lloyd

'Stop! Stop! Whatever you do, don't let Jeremy take that train to Glasgow!'

The outburst, delivered to no one in particular, was from Liz Forgan at her most matronly. It was also, however, unsuccessful, since the chief executive's chauffeured limo was now showing a clean exhaust as it turned the corner into Tottenham Court Road and sped Jeremy Isaacs towards Euston.

'It's a disaster,' she explained to me on the stairs. 'Tom's an independent producer, a Scot, one of his oldest chums, and has manoeuvered to sit next to him all the way to Scotland. In that time Jeremy could easily hand him the entire programme budget!'

Now, as it happens, evidence never emerged of such a raid on programme finances but the point was that it *could* have occurred. As the first publisher/broadcaster, Channel 4 was a small company and its administration had been designed by the first managing director, Justin Dukes, to *enable* rather than obstruct – as was notoriously the case at other public service broadcasters. Internal heads of department – of programme finance, programme presentation and scheduling, or legal services – were heads of 'yes' rather than the many heads of 'no' that I had learnt to navigate around at the BBC. While there were necessary checks and balances, particularly in the scrutiny of budgets, this culture always allowed C4 to be fast on its feet, and could enable it to pip dear old Auntie to any post with distinctive, timely programming.

Certainly, there were the occasional inefficiencies at the channel, but they were not endemic or revered – as in W12, or even W1A. Equally the budget scrutiny, while paternalistic towards a fledging production economy, was extremely meticulous yet brisk, and budgets were bespoke rather than driven by slot price – all of which assisted the distinctive originality of each project on screen. (In an era when slot price and its resultant conformity tend to rule supreme, this is one founding principle of Channel 4 practice which could happily be rediscovered, albeit in an updated form).

More important still, while the advent of Channel 4 had unleashed opportunity to a massive reservoir of creative talent hitherto closed out of organised broadcasting, and ultimately leading to one of the great financial success stories of post-war Britain, the first independent producers were independent only in name; in effect, they were *dependent*, and Channel 4's early monopoly of the market it had created was reflected in the Soho-centric collection of small offices that attached to the channel's Charlotte Street base.

This market place was visible at its most vivid around lunchtime; throngs of producers crowded the small, Charlotte Street foyer, aiming to ambush a commissioning editor or deputy to press their case for a commission or follow up on unanswered correspondence. The atmosphere resembled an Arab souk, but of ideas rather than goods. After a while the commissioning team had to realise that there was simply no escape since there was no back exit from the building (as was to be carefully designed at Horseferry Road, the channel's later premises); the only way to avoid the lunchtime bazar was to eschew lunch entirely, or ask your PA to bring in sarnies.

A walk along the Charlotte Street 'strip' between 1.30pm and 2pm needed careful anthropology to assess the business being conducted, and could be summarised as follows:

L'Etoile: long lunches only, with access to the wine list for additional stamina; suitable for discussions on returning series or major feature film projects only. The restaurant for BIG COMMISSIONS.

Villa Carlotta: good for anybody you simply want to catch up with. The closest thing to a surrogate canteen. Situated immediately opposite C4, useful bolt-hole, if making a run for it, when dodging the gauntlet to avoid a particular producer pest. No gastronomic regrets likely after lunch, as standard fare of prawn cocktail and lasagne easily enlivened by monster pepper mill. Upstairs, particularly good for launch parties, as one October Friday in 1987 to inaugurate *Dispatches*.

White Tower: 'Greek fusion' (as would now be described); refreshes palate. Very suitable for first conversation with Liz Forgan, where she offered me a portfolio of current affairs and natural history. Like an idiot I turned it down and thus became synonymous with low audience-share programming. My argument that I knew nothing about 'furry beasties', as Liz described them, unfortunately prevailed.

Chez Gerard: good, honest 'chain-French'; my preference for no-nonsense meetings with presenters or producers.

Gianni's: two entire floors slot-booked by commissioning staff for rest and recuperation after Thursday programme review. Canny, independent producers sussed this out and could waylay stragglers at their tiramisu.

So all-encompassing was the lunchtime congress that even the Channel 4 chairman, Edmund Dell, was also seen to travel the strip – even if only to the sandwich bar and the upmarket bookshop. Dell reminded me, in looks if not in manner, of no one so much as my old school headmaster. So much so that when I happened upon him one lunchtime I immediately whipped my hands out of my pockets. God knows what impression he formed of his new signing. In fairness though, the morose, sometimes misanthropic, Dell took his responsibilities very seriously, perhaps rather too seriously for a non-executive. A growing disappointment with this London-centric commissioning culture developed particularly in Scotland, where there was much untapped talent, particularly in feature film production. In answer, a commissioning *caravanserai* threaded its way to Edinburgh and Dell demanded to be present. As it turned out, this was an unwise request, as at the 'get-to-know-you-all' dinner at one of Scotland's most baronial restaurants some producers became seriously overtired and demonstrated their disappointment with the chairman by chucking bread rolls at him. An inauspicious beginning to a very important widening of the commissioning horizon, but to its credit, and in answer to unrelenting pressure from the producers' lobby PACT, Channel 4 mended its ways with great alacrity and a nations and regions commissioning strategy was quickly brought to bear – long before Media City or Salford was a gleam in anyone's eye.

However when Jeremy Isaacs departed Channel 4 for the Royal Opera House, it has to be admitted that he left with much 'work in progress'. *Channel 4 News* had been founded on a number of rigid, even unworldly, principles: it must differentiate itself from the dominant press culture and avoid at all costs too great an interest in the royal family, sport and crime. Thus, when the Hungerford massacre[1] occurred, shortly after I took over responsibility for the programme and asked the interim editor David Mannion to take me through any coverage difficulties he had had, he explained that he had found it extremely difficult to persuade some of the team to include this enormous event in the running order at all.

Note
[1] http://news.bbc.co.uk/onthisday/hi/dates/stories/august/19/newsid_2534000/2534669.

A twenty year gestation

By Anthony Smith

When Channel 4 was finally born in 1982, it owed its conception to creative visionaries who had been lobbying, briefing and cajoling for nigh on two decades

There are many ways to recite the history of Channel 4 and many people whose actions and arguments provide the pivotal points in its coming to pass. That it came into existence at all is amazing, given how vested interests operate in the UK and given the forces stacked against innovation and against pluralism within the reigning institutions. And yet, one day in 1982, a national television channel went on the air fed by some 200 new enterprises that had sprung into existence seemingly overnight. The struggle for Channel 4 – and it was a struggle – had lasted for twelve years, and the debate between politicians, unions, television companies and programme-makers for twenty. Each way of reciting the narrative gives precedence to different protagonists, different issues. This is how one protagonist (me) looks back on the rivalries that culminated in the founding of a channel dedicated to being different.

The origins of Channel 4 lie in a public debate or, rather, a widespread discontent, which arose during the later 1960s of which the key word was 'access'. With the establishment of BBC2 in 1964, television moved to the centre of cultural life in the UK. The medium was no longer just a source of popular entertainment and daily news. It had come to provide opportunities for serious new drama and serious debate. It fed hungrily off the new movements in politics, music, literature, not to speak of the new 'underground' youth culture. Commercial television too was firmly established and was starting to slough off the bad habits which the Pilkington Report (1962, Cmnd 1753), greatly under the influence of the late Richard Hoggart, had castigated as 'triviality'. ITV, too, was starting to play a more determined part in reflecting the ideas and controversies of that era of global rebellion.

But though television tried to reflect all that was happening it did not present itself as a medium which people could use for themselves, as they could the world of print. And now that the moving image dominated as print had formerly, there existed no way of entering the seemingly locked worlds of BBC and ITV. Television was simply what these organisations did. The new youth culture of the 1960s was finding its way into all of the media of communication, including television, but from it were flowing people who had things they wanted to express for themselves, ways they wanted to entertain as well as causes they wanted to support. The rules of formal balance inhibited the flow. The duopoly of BBC and ITV was itself at the centre of the stage. To have a career in television you had to excel in their terms. Many of the new cohort of programme makers – not to speak of the writers, directors, artists and performers they worked with – felt somehow dispossessed. The frustration was summed up in the word 'access'. Some saw the economic potential in making television programmes and selling them but there was no-one to buy them. Some just wanted to make television without enjoying an institutional career. An alternative to the duopoly was what was required.

There were some opportunities available. From the late 1960s the BFI was encouraging the setting up of video workshops around the country. Its Production Board provided a few grants for experimental films. The film schools were producing a steady stream of trained directors and technicians. In some cities there were places where independent and 'underground' filmmakers could show their works. There was a well established film society movement. But in television itself it was a case of Access Denied. And this was the theme of many public discussions. One influential regular discussion was the annual Manchester University television convention where the late Stuart Hall, one of the pioneers of the study of popular culture, inspired participating television producers and executives.

In 1970 the Government opened up a debate on the use of the fourth channel, the last available set of wavelengths which covered the entire kingdom and the Minister of Posts and Telecommunications (at that time all broadcasting came within his remit) announced a preference for an ITV-2, for giving the vacant channel to the network of regional companies which between them provided the country's single commercial channel with its monopoly of advertising; to be fair, the Pilkington Committee, a decade before, had said that if ITV reformed it should one day be granted the fourth channel. It had reformed. Its executives believed they were owed a channel in which they could provide a service of programmes complementary to ITV, just like the BBC. Some, however, believed that a second commercial channel should compete with the existing one rather than complement it. The BBC's second channel had been demonstrating the benefits of complementarity. (A Broadcasting Act back in 1963 had planted the idea that – one day – a second commercial Channel might be run in competition).

While the idea of an ITV-2 still struck some as 'fair' it struck others as outrageous. These companies were making fortunes from their monopoly of television advertising and here was a government inviting them to double their money. The opponents were many but the substitute policies were few. A new

Minister took office in 1972, Sir John Eden, and provided a White Paper formally advocating ITV-2. The Government imposed a special levy on ITV profits and thus was not overly tempted to take steps which might de-stabilise the UK's commercial channel. One would have looked to the ACTT, the left-wing union which organised ITV and film industry staff, to galvanise the opposition to a Tory plan but from this quarter there came mixed and muffled messages. Their members produced the ITV programmes and were extremely well paid. The masters of commercial television were supine in their dealings with the ACTT, happy to put up with over-staffing and high pay, so long as nothing interfered with the flow of ad revenue. The notion of a third force in television left them cold.

To many, television technology itself demanded that the making of programmes be locked up inside large companies and regulated authorities. All the people in the country who knew how to make television programmes had learned how to do so in one of these regulated monopolies. Videotape itself was only just starting up, with wide tapes and heavy spools. It was hard to imagine how the various tasks of television could take place away from the teams of technicians and their benevolent regulatory bureaucracies. There hung over ITV-2 the sense of inevitability and over all rival plans a sense of insecurity.

One other idea was on the table, that the Open University should run the channel, but that did not generate much enthusiasm, It was in fact the other broadcasting union, the Association of Broadcasting Staff, often thought of as a BBC company union, which promoted more radical thinking on the matter. It set up a committee to react to the 1972 White Paper and in the course of its discussions the idea emerged for a different kind of channel, quite unlike any of those that existed in the UK – or elsewhere. The doctrine behind it was neither competition, nor complementarity, but pluralism. Part of the inspiration for the idea came from the Netherlands, which had developed a system whereby different political parties and religious groups formed their own radio and now television companies and shared out the time in their national radio and television channels. The programme makers all aimed at the same national audience but were able to offer programmes which reflected a more complete range of the public's attitudes and beliefs.

Then Peter Fiddick, features editor of *The Guardian*, asked me to write a piece developing further this idea of a more open kind of channel. In April 1972 I sent him a piece which tried to put flesh on the idea, by advocating a National Television Foundation (NTF) run like one of the great charitable Foundations, in which a group of editors would select and commission projects from people who sent in suggestions: a channel essentially without any of the paraphernalia of a television authority as we knew it, without a programme-making staff, even without its own studios. It would be an outsourced channel, its funds coming from a diversity of sources: commercial, academic, charitable, industrial. It would not try to compete, but to add, experiment, inspire.

Fiddick managed to squeeze 4,000 words into a single Guardian page and let me have hundreds of offprints which I sent out around the broadcasting and political world for months afterwards. A few months later Sir Hugh Greene, a retired and very great BBC Director General, gave the annual Granada Lecture in which he said that the NTF should be given part of the channel, with the rest given to ITV. *Late Night Line-up* on BBC2 did a programme about it, in which Greene said this again. He, like most others, thought that it would be impossible to conjure up, out of the air, a whole independent freelance industry of programme makers. Two years later Peter Fiddick asked me to do another, longer, article pulling together the ideas which had emerged from public discussion (and three years after that he asked for a third version).

The basic idea did not change. The channel was to be run by people who were trustees rather than governors and their job was to supplement rather than to compete, to stimulate and spread rather than to balance, to represent the changing interests of the audience and programme-makers. Above all – in the cultural ferment of the times – they were also to listen to interest groups and offer them time to say what they wanted. It seems rather obvious in 2016 but the bill of fare was novel in the 1970s. The trustees could be elected or selected as representative but would still be within the ultimate regulatory purview of the Minister of Posts and Telecommunications. What we hoped was that this editorial formula would end the 'segmented slotting of time' into which television had degenerated, the endless competition, hour by hour between channels fighting for the same audience. In those days there was no iPlayer, no 4-on-demand, no home video, no cable, no dvd, (and no prospect of any of these) only three dawn till dusk television channels with a few regional opt-outs.

Harold Wilson had set up the Annan Committee in 1970, a month or two before losing the election and going out of office. It was to have examined the whole question of the fourth channel in addition to various other broadcasting matters. It remained in suspense for the years of Edward Heath's government (1970-74), but talk about a fourth channel continued in the press and in politics. Wilson was back in power in 1974 and this time Noel Annan was summoned again and his committee sat for four years, and a very lively debate ensued. By this time it was clear there were many people able and eager to make programmes and there were new technologies on the way which made feasible production by small groups (ACTT permitting).

But Annan added something of importance to the debate. His report in 1977 emphasised the value of the Broadcasting 'Authority' as a way of guaranteeing that editorial power was held at arms' length from government, but could be reviewed publicly by Parliament from time to time. Annan recommended a form of the NTF which he called an Open Broadcasting Authority. This made all the other cultural arguments for a different kind of editorial approach to programming much easier to stomach, though the supporters of ITV-2, together with their regulators at the IBA, continued to demand the additional channel for ITV but they had became willing, keen even, for part of its airtime to be used by independent programme-makers; the IBA too had been mollified but remained very cautious about the financial practicability of large scale freelance production outside the main commercial companies of the ITV system.

In the consultations which followed the publication of the Annan Report a number of fresh voices were heard, prominent among them the lively Free Communications Group which advocated many reforms and an opening up of the management of UK television but had not been wholly convinced of the need, in cultural terms for a new fourth channel. The Independent Filmmakers Association argued for an altogether different approach to the running of a new national channel, demanding opportunities to bring to the screen the controversial, and the unfamiliar. The Channel 4 Group supported the OBA idea but wanted it placed within the IBA because they feared that the existing commercial companies would gradually take over the airtime of the OBA through sheer influence, cash and political heft. They felt a powerful regulatory authority was needed. The Incorporated Society of British Advertisers pressed for a separation of the two commercial channels in order to break the price control exerted by the ITV monopoly over advertising. And this support of an OBA-within-IBA was now joined by the ACTT, under pressure from a growing membership of hopeful freelance programme-makers. Post Annan the debate had indeed moved onwards. One remaining fear was how the new channel, however regulated, could be built to retain its cultural independence without its own robust financial resources.

The vision of the channel moved on again when Jeremy Isaacs, later to become the first CEO of Channel 4 for seven rather glorious years, gave the MacTaggart Lecture at Edinburgh in 1979. As the programming chief of Thames Television he had leant towards an ITV-2, but now tried to describe the necessary ingredients of a new channel: he emphasised the vital catholicity of the programme content, which should not incessantly fight for major audiences against its three rival channels. He spoke of 'a fourth channel that everyone will watch some of the time and no one will watch all of the time'. That echoed the feelings of pretty well everyone who wanted to see a change in television which would both reflect and encourage new needs within the public.

The Labour Party was still in government when the report was published and seemed to give its assent to Annan's several plans, but failed to get on with the task of turning them into legislation. It accepted the basic tenet of Annan, that a four-channel system could degenerate into a permanent ratings war and must be avoided. But it let the debate run on. When one lobbied members of the government they said they liked the OBA plan but as weeks passed and a General Election drew near one could feel any passion for it slipping away.

The 1979 Election was won by Margaret Thatcher. She was not yet, however, a Thatcherite. Her 'ism' would not take full shape for another couple of years. In the meantime the thinking of her government was still somewhat open on a number of policy fronts. Sir Keith Joseph was her guru. I contrived an invitation to go to see him and argue the case for the OBA. After all, though it had been supported by the cultural left it would result in a new industry of small companies. They would compete. They would employ. They might even export. He nodded and agreed, with what appeared to be enthusiasm. He called in an assistant and asked him to take up the idea and have it discussed within a wider circle of colleagues. He would talk to William Whitelaw, the new Home Secretary who was now in charge of broadcasting policy. I handed over a pile of material and departed.

It was in September of 1979 that Whitelaw addressed the subject of Channel 4 and laid down the framework of what ultimately came to pass. In a speech at Cambridge he made clear his support of the cultural plan for a non-ITV-2 which could take programmes from the existing commercial companies and regional companies but in great part from the new independent producers; editorially it was to be distinct from ITV even though it was to be placed under the umbrella of the IBA who should not, he adjured, permit the ITV companies to dominate it. Indeed, it was to provide opportunities for the smaller interest groups and have a distinctive approach to many different topics. The fourth channel was to constitute a third force in UK broadcasting.

It is to Whitelaw that the unique funding formula of Channel 4 is ascribed. The Annan Committee had declared that channels competing for the same audience should not compete for the same revenue. So how to build a fourth channel funded by advertising without commercial competition? The answer was that the advertising would be sold by the existing commercial companies, i.e non-competitively, but the companies would hand over to Channel 4 a sum of between 14% and 17% of their entire revenue, drawn from two channels (this would take precedence over the government's advertising levy). Editorially the channel would be in separate and independent hands, reporting to its own board. This unique and ingenious formula was to survive until the Channel was made into a separate Trust selling its own advertising, but still subject to the IBA, some years later.

It was decided that Channel 4 would start to broadcast in 1982 and a board of directors was appointed. In choosing us, the IBA went to great lengths to guarantee the necessary cultural diversity: a Tory lady and a former Labour Cabinet Minister, a local councillor, a trade unionist, a very famous actor, a successful television filmmaker, an academic, a representative of the BFI (me), three figures from ITV, and others – all utterly different but all committed to diversity, all inspired by the cause of pluralism. Now, around that time the 'Gang of Four' who had walked out of the Labour Party announced the formation of a new Social Democratic Party. At the next meeting of the Channel 4 board, one of the members looked around and drily observed 'Look at us. We've been chosen from every corner of the country but this morning I think we are all SDP!' It was almost right and identified a cultural shift in the UK of the 1980s, which was given expression by Channel 4. Later the *Daily Mail* was to castigate Channel 4 as 'an Islington cooperative of Guardian-reading-feminist-single-parent-social-workers wearing Guatemalan sandals'. The caricature stuck for a while as the Channel reached for its many audiences.

But look back from the channel's programme schedule of 1982 over two decades and you can see, through the fog of argument, a national culture moving from an acceptance of closed hierarchies to a modern self-made pluralism, invading every corner of the society, following the directions to which economics and technology were pointing.

Channel 4 has not been just the register of that change. It has also been an engine.

About the author

Anthony Smith was a founding board director of Channel 4, having worked for the Annan Committee on the Future of Broadcasting. Between 1979 and 1988 he was Director of the British Film Institute and was involved in the conception and establishment of the Museum of the Moving Image on London's South Bank. He was appointed President of Magdalen College, Oxford University, from 1988 until 2005. He was made CBE in 1987. He is Chairman of the Oxford/Russia Fund and a Board Member of the Choir of the Sixteen.

Some earlier accounts of the founding of C4

Lambert, Stephen (1982) Channel Four: Television with a Difference, London: BFI

Blanchard, Simon and Morley, David (eds)(1982) What's This Channel Four? an alternative report, [with illustrations by Will Hill] London: Comedia Publishing Group

Kustow, Michael (1987) One in Four: A Year in the life of a Channel Four Commissioning Editor, London: Chatto & Windus

Docherty, David et al, (1988) Keeping Faith? Channel 4 and its Audience, BRU Monograph, London: John Libbey

Isaacs, Jeremy (1989) Storm Over Four: A Personal Account, London: Weidenfeld and Nicolson

Potter, Jeremy (1989) Independent Television in Britain vol.3: Politics and Control 1968-80, London: Macmillan

Bonner, Paul and Adams, Lesley (2002) Independent TV in Britain: New Developments in Indepednent Television 1981-92: Channel Four; TV-am; Cable, London: Palgrave Macmillan

Hobhouse, Dorothy (2007) Channel Four: the early years and the Jeremy Isaacs Legacy. London: I B Tauris

Boycott, Rosie and Etherington-Smith, Meredith (2008) 25 x 4 Channel Four at 25, London: cultureshock media

Brown, Maggie (2007) A Licence to the Different – the story of Channel Four. London: BFI

Caterall. Peter (2013) The Making of Channel Four, London: Routledge

How David beat Goliath

By Roger Graef

The long battle to create Channel 4 was an unequal one that pitted the public interest against giant corporate and political forces. Remarkably, the little guys won

People rarely have their dreams come true. Especially when they involve a major new enterprise in a well-established landscape, a huge cultural expansion of taste and propriety, and the creation of an innovative political and financial structure to make it work as intended. Yet that is what happened to launch Channel 4. In such a conservative country, with a Conservative government, and two long-established broadcasters occupying almost all of the available space, it was extraordinary. It was even more improbable given the two-decades-long insistence by ITV to claim the fourth channel as ITV2. Television sets built in the seventies had a button listed as ITV2. It looked like a done deal. Even in the late 1960s the Minister Chris Chataway said ITV should be given the extra channel. It was only the protests of Anthony Smith and others that saw it differently. Smith became the architect of the fourth channel in various iterations, expressed at length in a series of articles in *The Guardian*, and then on the Annan Committee. He made the dream into a proposition that could win support.

The support was to grow across the 1970s. A number of filmmakers, producers and journalists were increasingly dissatisfied with the status quo, both in newspapers and television. Too many stories were spiked at the big newspapers, and television suffered from tight editorial control at the duopoly of ITV and the BBC. Moreover, strange as it may seem today with the proliferation of channels, with only three TV channels to air programmes, there was not enough space for other ideas outside the mainstream to be shown. That was the reason ITV had long planned to establish its own second channel.

I had worked as a freelance for both the BBC and then for seven years at Granada during that period. There was a lot of frustration in both places. There was even an underground newspaper in my department at the BBC called *Urinal* (a takeoff of *Ariel*, the BBC internal paper) which published management horror stories. Although personally I had quite a lot of freedom to pursue my own projects, I felt strongly that there needed to be more space and diversity of programming and of suppliers on television. And more risk taking. In those days, the fledgling independent sector scrambled to get a handful of commissions, and the vast majority of filmmakers had to work for the two broadcasters or do corporates to make a living. Indeed, I had broken that barrier in the 1960s with a series of arts documentaries for the BBC, but was one of the very few independent filmmakers to do so.

I also did not like the editorial caution in all media that was often killing important stories. I was involved in a collection of independently-minded journos known as the Free Communications Group. The FCG published a monthly mag of stories and issues that had been squashed. As early as 1971 the television critic of *Time Out*, John Howkins, staged a conference at the Polytechnic of Central London in Oxford Circus. It was co-sponsored with the Free Communications Group, and packed with journos, programme makers, teachers, Bow Group Tories, Labour people, and other folk. The conference called for a fourth channel to be created independent of ITV.

In ensuing years, the FGC and the aftermath of the conference led to the creation of the TV4 Campaign and Channel Four Group. Frustration mounted with each new tale of blockage or strong ideas and stories going unrecognised. But with ITV lobbying hard, we felt our chances of success were limited. (1)

Then came the Association of Cinematograph Television and Allied Technicians (ACTT) strike against ITV, in which it was exposed that while Granada and other ITV companies and their shareholders were coining it, they were not sharing the benefits with their staff. I still recall the picket line outside Golden Square having three executive producers and a commissioning editor on it. We then went to the ACTT office in Soho Square and were so appalled by their timidity and ignorance of the ITV finances, a number of us took a leading role in guiding what happened. The Tories were especially hostile to the power of unions at ITV, which was a significant factor in their approval of the C4 model.

So I was among the many independent minded television folk – most notably Michael Darlow, a young Michael Jackson, and producer Sophie Balhatchet – who took on ITV's confident claim to that fourth channel space. But at the time it felt like we were David v Goliath.

That made it all the more astonishing when Willie Whitelaw gave a speech at the Royal Television Society Conference and followed it with the Broadcasting Act of 1980 that created Channel 4. It seemed to adopt almost all of our objectives. Moreover, it created a brilliant funding mechanism that freed it from selling its own advertising. That was the brake on creativity that hindered ITV. Remarkably, in an unequal political battle against vested interests, the good guys backing the public interest had won!

That's what made the original Channel 4 so precious and rare in the broadcasting world. It was not a state institution, nor was it a for-profit commercial one. Its remit was to be original, educational and innovative and to make programmes for audiences not already served by ITV. It also called for a significant amount of programmes by regional itv companies and independents. This was a wonderful and inspiring challenge. But the question was, could we rise to it? Were there enough indie filmmakers and producers to deliver this?

ITV bosses felt confident that there would not be. They presumed that the lion's share of the new channel's programming would be made by them, even though the Act discouraged that. Jeremy Isaacs gave the MacTaggart Lecture at the Edinburgh TV Festival that year and while welcoming the channel and the challenge, he made clear he too shared the view that independents would be minority players (15% was the going rate, and in a post speech session he mentioned 10%), while ITV would make most of the programmes. That was disturbing but not surprising. Jeremy was a highly respected director of programmes at Thames Television until falling out with the new MD Bryan Cowgill. He would say that, wouldn't he? But it was later to be held against him by the newly-appointed Channel 4 board when looking for its CEO.

I was surprised to be invited to join that C4 board by the director general of the Independent Broadcasting Authority Sir Brian Young, a former headmaster of Charterhouse. I like being on boards, having served on the board of London Transport, the DOE Review of Planning Law, Bafta, the BFI, and I spent thirteen years on the board of the Institute of Contemporary Arts.1

I soon found there was a special culture of deference to the executive and to the chair that inhibited British board members from speaking out. Because I was an American, and a New Yorker to boot, I had no such inhibitions. My outspokenness did not always endear me to fellow board members nor to the chair, nor to the executives when I criticised or disagreed with them. But many staff members in all those institutions used me as a channel for their concerns. Over time, my fellow board members gave me space to say the unsayable.

But the invitation to join the Channel 4 board came at an awkward time. I was intensely busy making the *Police* series for the BBC.2 So I reluctantly declined. But Brian Young did not give up. He called me in to his office on a Saturday. Alone in the IBA headquarters in Knightsbridge, this kindly patrician ur-Englishman looked at me from across his desk and said: 'I asked you here on a Saturday because I wanted to speak frankly, and hope you will reconsider.' I was touched he was so keen. He then delivered the *coup de grace*. 'If you don't accept, it will have to be Michael Peacock or Gus Macdonald. How would you feel about that?'

These men were both heavy hitters in television, and good acquaintances of mine too. Peacock had run BBC2 and Gus had moved from being a radical politically, and a member of the FCG, to a top executive post at Granada. Despite their obvious qualifications, neither seemed ideally suited to represent the independents who now faced a major opportunity, but still had to overcome strong ITV pressure to claim most of the airtime. Because of that I feared that if I did accept, I told Young that I might well be bullied into silence, or at least outvoted regularly by the number of ITV executives on the board. 'We've thought of that,' he said. 'And we've appointed thoughtful and flexible people to those posts. Brian Tesler of LWT, Bill Brown from STV, and David McCall from Anglia.' These names, plus the presence on the board of Tony Smith, the original thinker behind the fourth channel, and the energetic presence of Richard 'Dicky' Attenborough, was reassurance enough. So I agreed.

We were a motley crew, with only Tony Smith and I having recent first-hand knowledge of programme making, (and he had left the BBC a decade earlier to write about broadcasting). The chairman was Edmund Dell, an irascible ex-Labour minister turned banker, with a huge set of opinions and prejudices, but no experience of broadcasting except as an occasional consumer or interviewee. Dell turned most board meetings into lectures, and was not disposed to listen to anyone else. Having left his bank and politics, he filled his time interfering with the channel. Not ideal chairman material.

When we set about choosing a director of progammes, a number of names came up. Jeremy Isaacs was deemed by many board members too confident he would get it, because of his Edinburgh speech setting out his plans to run the channel and his caution about independents. So to make it a real contest, others were being considered. I was asked to approach Brian Wenham, then running BBC2, to ask him to apply. He told me he wouldn't. Wenham said he would take the job only if he was offered it without competition. No dice.

Charles Denton, then running Central Television and a supporter of adventurous programming, was also approached to apply. But he had just renewed his contract and honourably felt it would be disloyal to consider it. John Birt, then Director of Programmes at LWT, did apply. With a strong track record and a brilliant, incisive mind and manner, he was a serious alternative to Jeremy Isaacs. And he had the backing of his boss, Brian Tesler. But he came for his interview with a surprise that took us all aback: several years of programming hour by hour (prepared for him by Sue Stoessl at LWT). Given the channel was intended to be flexible, responsive and innovative, the board all felt his presentation seemed singularly inappropriate.

By contrast, Jeremy's approach was the most flexible and adventurous. He had thought a great deal about ways of meeting the remit, and by now had expanded his expectations of the independent sector. Tony Smith and I were especially keen he should get the job

But the chairman had never heard of him, despite Isaacs' high esteem in the industry, especially for the major historical achievement of *The World at War*. As a historian as well as a banker and Labour grandee, Dell should have welcomed Isaacs, whose respect for history was also shown after he left Thames in his impressive BBC series on Ireland with Robert Kee. But Dell was not happy with him. And in what was to prove a series of confrontations with the board during his chairmanship, Tony Smith and I had to rally support to stand up to him. And we won.

Jeremy was a real visionary. The board's role was to support his vision in ways that protected the channel. Brian Tesler wanted a cap on staff, roughly equivalent to the Forces Broadcasting system. No more than several hundred. (That didn't last.) I had proposed we support Jeremy by creating a deputy director of programmes (the job went to Paul Bonner). Jeremy wanted to be CEO and director of programmes but over his objections, we devised an managing director role to handle admin. I had met Justin Dukes who was MD of the *Financial Times*, and persuaded him to apply. He got the job.

So the good ship Channel 4 set out in due course, with a characteristic Jeremy gesture. He had been interviewed by the editor of *The Guardian*'s Women's page, Liz Forgan and was impressed. So despite her total lack of TV experience, he put her in charge of almost everything: news, current affairs, documentaries and more. It almost didn't happen. I knew Liz from playing tennis. And I rated her journalism. But just as we arrived at the board meeting which was to approve her appointment without knowing her, I was called away to Reading on police business. So I missed it, and missed hearing Jeremy propose her. Much as I have approved of her achievements at the channel, I would have to admit I would have tried to persuade the board she had too little experience. Jeremy was proved right, and I am mightily relieved I did not have the chance to intervene.

The following years saw the channel grow in confidence, and the board generally supported the risks which came to us. Given the current ecology of broadcasting, and its preoccupations with ratings, it is worth recalling that the original slate included programmes which are hard to imagine being commissioned now by anyone. *Whatever You Want*, with the mercurial Keith Allen, pushed the boundaries of taste on each outing. An all-day full-length showing of *The Orestaia*, in masks. Pina Bausch being given a whole evening for her hypnotic dance from Sadlers Wells. A regular programme on Ireland, another on trade unions, and a series on black issues, and the Third World. There were many others on the borders of what was known as 'taste and decency'. Many programmes did not draw viewers, but met savage criticism from the *Daily Mail*. Film 4 soon became the source of funding for a wide range of filmsfrom all over Europe that would otherwise not have been made.

My biggest defeat was about the new building. I wanted a converted warehouse in Kings Cross, that could change as the channel changed.. Dell wanted a glossy architectural signature flagship. He won. I still regret the edifice complex that hovered up many millions and led to tower of open plan and conventional offices looming over Horseferry Road much like any other corporate enterprise. But it was a heady time, and I am extremely proud to have been a part of it.

Thank you Brian Young.

About the author

As a director, producer and executive producer, Roger Graef has been responsible for more than 160 documentaries to date, spanning current affairs, criminal justice, communication, business, city planning and architecture, science, comedy and the arts.

His other credits include *In the Name of Allah* – the first full-length film on Islam for Western television, and the first observational films inside major institutions *The Space Between Words*, as well as the first three Amnesty International comedies, *including The Secret Policeman's Ball*, and with Brian Hill, the BAFTA-winning experimental prison musical *Feltham Sings*. In 2004, he was the first documentary maker to be awarded a Bafta Fellowship for lifetime achievement. In 2006, he was awarded an OBE for services to broadcasting. In 2014, BAFTA hosted a tribute evening to celebrate his fifty years of groundbreaking work. Last year he directed *Monty Python: the Meaning of Live*, and *Brett: A Life with No Arms*, a sequel to his very first film, the award winning *One of Them is Brett*, about a Thalidomide child.

Notes

[1] I even made films about decision making at the board of British Steel and Occidental Petroleum

[2] I quit Granada after the strike because of their lack of support for Inside Europe. The next job I was offered was to make a series on Anti-Semitism for the German partner of that series. I didn't fancy chasing ex-Nazis around South America so when the BBC rang up and said 'we don't suppose you'd like to make an obdoc series about the Police,' I readily agreed. But it was just as intense and time consuming, if not more so.

Set the indies free. Again.
By Bernard Clark

Somewhere between childhood and early middle age, the channel lost sight of the importance of giving its indie producers free rein. But it's not too late to go back

It is easy for me to remember when Channel 4 went on air, because it was the very night our first son, Sam, was born. So instead of being underwhelmed by the first night schedule of *Book 4*, *Walter* and *In the Pink*, I was at the Royal Berks Hospital in Reading being overwhelmed by a very different kind of birth.

That odd coincidence has meant I have always known exactly how old Channel 4 is. Right now, thirty-three and half; and if Sam's experience of life is anything to go by, it's well-adjusted, happily settled down in multicultural Britain, financially stable, ambitious, liberal with a small 'l' – and always having to protect its independence, especially from the perpetual nonsense of outside interference. (Sam works in Ofsted-dominated education so, yes, like Channel 4, like son.)

From the early 1980s, my journey as an independent producer reflects Sam's journey of growing into an adult, as my fledgling company has built from the tiniest baby into a large and complex global entity, with a turnover of nearly £10 million, and more than a hundred staff handling thousands of hours of programming. Although being an indy has a precarious harshness that superannuated corporate staff would not abide, it has been an exhilarating, hugely creative, if perilous, 30-year expedition through every high and low that a life in television can offer, with some wonderful, crazy characters, and great programmes to boot – most of which would never have happened without Channel 4.

I first heard about Channel 4 after a BBC cricket match next to Anthony Smith's house near Minster Lovell in the late 1970s. I was a young reporter at Lime Grove and until that evening my expectation was that the impending fourth channel would be ITV2; but as the wine flowed, we were joined by some of the radical thinkers actually working at ITV, who didn't have that view at all. Indeed, perhaps because of their time at Granada or LWT or Thames, they were fiercely opposed to ITV having anything to do with any new channel. 'A thousand flowers will bloom', they said, 'if it could be a truly new, properly independent channel – a commissioner broadcaster, with the programmes made by companies that would be personally owned by the producers'.

I could hardly sleep that night, so exciting was that vision.

Until then, there were few, if any, real opportunities for independent producers. The 'Duopoly' as they were known – a self interested and self perpetuating alliance of the BBC and ITV – treated third party interlopers, especially producers, with a we-know-better, patronising disdain; and worse, if an outsider had the temerity to set up a company, they would be frozen out as if carrying an infectious disease.

So across the whole of television few people understood how companies worked, let alone had actually been in business. The great and good had a sniffy word for such grubby folk – 'traders', people who are 'not us'. Therefore, it was all the more surprising to find that the greatest enthusiasm for a Channel 4 came from cerebral people whose radical left-wing credentials seem to have marked them out as anti-business, most of whom had embraced the existing highly-politicised TV unions. Confused? Yes, we all were.

But none of that mattered, because the vision that Channel 4 began to expound was quite remarkably positive – that not only would a savvy producer with a good idea get a contract after perhaps just one chat with a commissioning editor, but the channel would help you set up a company, sort out the budget and provide the necessary cash-flow financing upfront, then leave you alone. It seemed too good to be true, but my very first experience put it to the test.

Crash course in running a company

By then I was working as an executive producer in the BBC's Music and Arts Department. The writer and journalist Bernard Levin, a good friend, had the idea to follow the route of Hannibal from the South of France to Italy, which had been commissioned by BBC2 controller, Graeme McDonald. However, a couple of days before the final green light, Levin's column in *The Times* deeply angered McDonald, and he cancelled the programme. When I called Levin he cursed: 'Damn it, damn it; that was my summer fun. Isn't there somewhere else?' Of course, in the past there was not, but now there was Channel 4. I had one meeting with the commissioning editor for documentaries, John Ranelagh; Jeremy Isaacs talked to Levin, and we had a commission, literally, the next day. It really was that direct.

But better was to follow. The lawyer at C4, Don Christopher, and the cost controller, Peter Flood, then sat down to give me a crash course on how to set up and run a company – something I knew virtually nothing about. The simple contract was about twenty pages long, but 'the only bit that matters,' Don said frankly, 'is the one-page cover sheet that has all the dates, figures and names on it; the rest is just guff'. He was completely right.

The Channel 4 budget form was even more revealing. Again, about twenty pages long, each page was an itemised list of possible costs across any conceivable kind of production – from drama, through entertainment and sport, to current affairs and documentary. So all we had to do was go through it line by line, filling in the boxes with resources we would need, then totalling them all up, to provide a final budget figure. Like shopping in a virtual supermarket, going aisle by aisle, picking '32-days camera crew', or '20-nights hotel' off the shelf, all added up at checkout. At one point, Peter and I couldn't agree on how many days of hire-car we would need shooting in the Alps. He thought fifteen, I thought twenty, but we both agreed there was no way actually to *know*.

'Toss you for it,' Peter suggested, to break the impasse. 'Done', I agreed. I won, so we got twenty. Subsequently, we used only fifteen; a small agreed windfall that stayed with my new company.

Now I must share a guilty secret. Fifteen years earlier, I began my career at the BBC as a television cost clerk, in an office of hundreds, essentially budgeting and then costing programmes. But for all our efforts everyone knew that, at best, the BBC had only a vague idea of what any programme cost, and were often out by hundreds of percent. In my view that is still largely the case today. However, as I began to work with Channel 4, I discovered that is certainly not the case in independent production. For all its seeming amateurishness, both Channel 4 and especially the independent companies know *exactly* what everything costs, down to the nearest pound, and with very little effort – because all indie production is based on cash.

Yet again I was astonished. That simple concept, that there is a finite and agreed pile of cash, makes all the difference; with a glance at the bank statement along with costs-to-completion, a production knew exactly where it was, financially. Given that no one at the BBC or ITV ever knew, or cared, it was a revolution, and made the nervy step of starting my own company less worrying.

Creative liberation
It was also liberating from a creative view point. Questions like: 'will we have an extra day's filming/editing, or hire an extra researcher?' were now entirely in the hands of the production crew, along with decisions on personnel, timetabling and accommodation. For instance, I decided that, instead of booking hotel rooms for eight times forty days en route, we'd rent a huge mansion in the Rhone Valley. Apart from saving a small fortune on hotels, the crew's families could visit from the UK, so the whole shoot became a wonderful six-week party, all paid out of the company budget – and not a whisper of overtime on the many long days, and even longer nights. The almost-Trotskyist TV Unions wouldn't have approved, but no one told them and, in any case, they were fast becoming irrelevant.

Certainly, the ACTT, a breathtakingly cynical trade union that had mercilessly fleeced ITV for decades, had it coming, but as the independent movement flourished, now many of the most rampant transgressors of union diktats, were exactly the people who had previously been the most fervent enforcers of union strictures. My theory is that their previous unrestrained activism had been driven by a sense of disenchanted disentitlement. Now that they had their own companies, and owned their own means of production, in both the Marxist and enterprising sense, their creative instincts were able to take charge. There are many ironies to the advent by Channel 4 of independent production, but the destruction of the radical media unions by politically radical producers, who went on to build highly profitable companies, is among the greatest.

My original plan had been to make *Hannibal's Footsteps* for Channel 4, and then return to the BBC. But such was the joy of this form of production, the liberated exhilaration, and sheer fun, that I never returned to Auntie. Until then, I had been working from the small back bedroom of our house near Henley, with only a very early portable photocopier (a £500 Panasonic – by far my best ever capital purchase) and occasional typist, but now C4 wanted to discuss a second Levin series, a 180 minute current affairs programme and a season of material from Japan, so I had to take the plunge, and rent a London office.

54 Tottenham Street was a semi-derelict terraced house, a hundred yards from Channel 4's front door on Charlotte Street, chosen partly because I felt daunted to be embarking on such a long term responsibility, and being next to C4 would somehow be reassuring – but mainly because it was cheap. Half-a-dozen of us had to spend a whole weekend clearing rubbish, scrubbing floors, painting walls and rewiring before it was even vaguely habitable. After which, it was our very own production office, with eight desks, a U-matic edit suite, a phone system, fax machine and Clark Productions on the door. Another plus to being so close to *The Channel* (as C4 had become known) was the number of commissioning editors who discovered on their way home that we had a well stocked fridge, so we often knew more gossip than Charlotte Street.

To me, that's how Channel 4 started, pulling hundreds of Britain's most enterprising producers, and then their companies, along in its wake. A thousand flowers did, indeed, bloom, and many are still blooming as our cottage industry became a confident indie sector and then a major global industry. And there I was, in at the beginning – what a privilege.

Jeremy's visions

There are many people to thank and several are in this book. Anthony Smith, the channel's intellectual father, canny and patient and, what is more, a natural born optimist. While many around him had doubts, Anthony never quavered or wavered; I often think he never considered the possibility of failure, the true quality of the institutional innovator. Willie Whitelaw, the movement's political leader, with a very large 'P', a man who conducted competing parties like an orchestra leader, so that everyone thought it was their own tune.

And then, of course, more even than them – Jeremy Isaacs.

Even in the early days of the channel no one used his full name, he was just 'Jeremy'. His ideas – 'visions' they were nicknamed, and there were many of them – went beyond the schedule or the programmes, but to the core of how a wholly different, but complementary, channel might function, from the doorman to the director of finance. Nothing was 'a given', every aspect was subject to looking anew, finding a different way. Over the years I'd heard pronouncements like this many times before: the difference with Jeremy was – he really actually did them.

Like… commissioning editors didn't necessarily need experience of working in TV. (Jeremy appointed several such 'rookies', including head of news and current affairs Liz Forgan, who was rumoured, perhaps unfairly, not even to have had a TV).

Like… Channel 4 should remain lean and mean. During Jeremy's tenure, there were never more than three hundred people to run the whole channel.

Like… No commissioning editors should be in post for more than four years. This was to engender freshness, and continual innovation, a splendid idea, but one which inevitably did not survive Jeremy's own leaving.

And, overwhelmingly the most important: Jeremy genuinely believed, to the depths of his soul, that C4 should be a publisher broadcaster. i.e, the channel was primarily there to publish/broadcast other companies/producers programmes. And this went beyond not making the programmes, it included not interfering with the process of production. After a simple commissioning process, the Channel would schedule and broadcast what they were given by programme-makers, with maybe (but not always) a quick viewing to check for legal compliance. There was a recognition that it was the producer's programme all the way along the chain to the viewer. A long-running *series* would be 'owned' by the production company; the commissioning editor didn't decide what was in each programme; they often weren't even consulted.

Ultimately, that was the concept, more than anything, that gave the channel its distinctive originality and, to me even more importantly, built the hugely successful UK independent sector, with a capital 'I'. However, Jeremy's brave, unprecedented vision was being watered down even while he was still chief executive – and then almost fell of the proverbial cliff after he left. Sadly, the channel controllers, the finance holders, the marketing maestros, and – absolutely and unforgivably – the schedulers took over, and the producers were banished well below the salt by the bosses who controlled all the money and owned all the airtime. And, boy, did they let us know who was in charge of our next project.

Micro-management on an industrial scale
After a very long period of meetings with an assistant commissioning editor, a commissioning editor, a head of genre, an assistant head of department, indeed, almost everyone who wasn't actually making the decision, a small development might be agreed, which down the line might lead to a commission, albeit with a detailed and onerous contract. Next, pre-research outlines, pre-filming scripts, interview questions, sign off by the channel of all the talent, and much of the production team, after which came post-filming reports, pre-edit scripts, music and graphics approval, oversight of contracts, viewing of rough cuts (there may

be many), narrative notes, the fine cut, and finally, after several further edits – delivery. Except, the finished (well, almost) programme would then be viewed upstairs and a whole new batch of scripting/editing/narrative notes would float down, with re-re-re-re-cuts right up until an hour before transmission. Think I'm kidding? Sadly, no.

This was micro-management on an industrial scale, and Channel 4 did it because it could. And is still doing it, but more self-consciously these days. Caught in a vortex of too many commissioning staff and over centralisation of decisions, us producers can see in their eyes that their hearts are elsewhere, away from the bureaucratic tyranny of upwards referral, hankering back to the past for a creative future. Oh how desperately do they need Jeremy, or a 2016 equivalent, to bark, 'for God's sake, set them free to make their programmes, or otherwise we should make them ourselves.'

Channel 4, conceived in the intellectual and creative high ground of British inventiveness, moved from extraordinary promise, to being yet another channel, but – and here's the lifelong optimistic programme maker in me – with a fantastic inheritance and, crucially, a wonderful remit still intact.

Now, when I look back on those gorgeous, heady, all-too-few years from conception to age seven or eight, I am not only grateful to have been there, but have a sense of optimism for what might yet be achieved, because the basic building blocks are still there: Channel 4 has no significant borrowing, no shareholders, no overbearing charter, surprisingly few enemies and no commercial competition within its niche. So if it positioned more towards its original purpose, of being experimental, catering to different audiences and complementary to the rest of the TV business, it will not only be more financially stable, the Channel will be left alone and not privatised.

There are signs this is happening again, with a realistion that the remit is not only a creative boon, it's good for business too – but not so good that the suits and hedge funders will want to take the train set away. 'Leave us alone,' the bosses at Channel 4 seem be saying to the Government at last, 'and we will enrich the landscape with different kinds of programmes, and behave in a different kind of way', which, if true, underlines the genius of its founders four decades ago.

I would also echo that back to the present managers. On behalf of the independent producers, the people who are really behind the Channel's success – yes, the people who actually make the programmes: 'Leave us alone. Don't micro-manage us. Don't interfere with our creative passions. Trust us. Be a commissioner/publisher broadcaster again, as the channel was designed to be. Otherwise, what really is the point of indistinctive middle aged you – why not pack you off to privatisation?'

After all, because of all that work forty something years ago, Channel 4 has an unrivalled freedom to be what it wants to be, and to do what it wants to do. That's part of its magic, and the recipe for its success. But it's now time that it allowed, as it did in its early years, the most important ingredient of its success – the producers – to have part of that freedom, too.

About the author

Bernard Clark has done most jobs in radio and television, as a cost clerk, technician, studio manager, DJ, reporter, TV news reader, director, producer, executive producer. At the BBC he helped start BBC Radio Bristol in 1970, *Newsbeat* (1973), originated *Watchdog* (1980), *Timewatch/Bookmark* (1984), and for the last thirty years CEO/Chairman of Clark Productions/TVT.

You'll laugh about this. One day.
By Mike Bolland

Blowjobs at teatime, 'fuck' counts, sacriligeous cigar commercials and scandal-hit ministers (nearly) unmasked: no wonder Mary Whitehouse wasn't a fan

I arrived at Channel 4 in October 1981 with a brief to commission programmes for a young adult audience. In the first weeks we created weekly evening sessions where young people met up with sympathetic producers in order to thrash out what this television should be. After several meetings it was clear that music and comedy were top of the agenda. There was a strong feeling that young adults couldn't see people like themselves or any of their interests reflected on television. We had a strategy.

The first pitch came from 'alternative' comedian Peter Richardson. He proposed a series of films featuring the cream of the new wave comics. The satirical films would be parodies of different genres. He got particularly animated when describing *The Comic Strip Presents...Five Go Mad In Dorset*. The wicked lampoon of Enid Blyton's Famous Five adventures was already well formed in his mind. It challenged class, racism and sexism from an entirely different angle. It was a no-brainer. The new comedians had been hard to televise. They didn't lend themselves to conventional coverage. Peter offered an accessible way of getting those radical performers on air.

Then came Andrea Wonfor from Tyne-Tees Television. She offered *Jamming* – six half hours of music. I really liked Andrea and her producer Malcolm Gerrie. I greatly admired the shows they made for ITV but *Jamming* didn't excite me. I had this huge tranche of airtime to fill on Friday and I was quietly concerned that live television didn't seem to be on anyone else's shopping list. I put the idea of a six-month run of a live music show with attitude to Andrea and Malcolm.

At first I don't think they believed that I was serious but when the penny dropped they went for it with incredible enthusiasm and inspirational creativity. *The Tube* was to be energetic, irreverent and funny. The music was live and relevant and the comedians ranged from weird local Foffo Spearjig The Hard through French and Saunders to Dame Edna Everage. The early slot was problematic, and at times brought us many slapped wrists from Ofcom's ancestor, The Independent Broadcasting Authority (IBA). We regularly appeared on *Right to Reply*. Apparently any mention of blowjobs at teatime is taboo. Who knew? Nowadays French & Saunders are national treasures! Who'd have thought?

In the summer of 1982 we filmed *Five Go Mad In Dorset*. News that Channel 4 had commissioned the show reached the BBC and – surprise surprise – they exercised the option they had taken on The Young Ones. With the bulk of the cast gone to the BBC we had to postpone filming after *Five Go Mad*. We only had one episode of *The Comic Strip Presents...* available and Jeremy Isaacs scheduled it for the opening night. The day before the launch my phone rang.

'Oh Timmy, you're so licky'

The call was from solicitors representing Enid Blyton's estate. They had read about our show and were threatening an injunction. It was agreed that lawyers for both the estate and the publishers could view the film later that day. The viewing took place in my tiny office at Charlotte Street. We squeezed two barristers, two solicitors, Enid Blyton's niece and the man from Hodder & Stoughton into the room and switched on the VCR. With C4 colleagues I stood outside watching through the glass wall. One by one the lawyers were covering their faces with their papers in order to hide unseemly mirth.

We got to the night scene of a tent into which Timmy the dog had his head and front quarters. His rear end was sticking out and his tail was wagging vigorously. The immortal line from Dawn French, 'Oh Timmy you're so licky,' heralded the end of any composure. One of the solicitors couldn't hold it in any more and she loudly guffawed. The tears were running down her face and that relaxed the others. Soon my wee room was full of laughing lawyers. The man from H&S also laughed. The lady from the Blyton estate didn't. Mr H&S gently chided me as they left. He thought that we had pushed our luck but that it was really funny. The show went out to a mixed reception seriously splitting the audience down the middle. That felt to me like a result – as did the fact that I didn't get fired on Channel 4's first day of transmission.

For some reason the IBA had a stricter code on language for comedy and entertainment than it had for documentary or drama. There was constant dialogue between us about whether or not certain sweary words were funny and/or acceptable. It was like a war of attrition, an amiable war but a long war nonetheless. We'd argue the 'fuck' count for *Comic Strip* on a regular basis and slowly but surely the barriers came down. Part of the problem was that the style and rhythm of the comedy was alien to many (older) people who viewed it. Often we were arguing from completely different standpoints with little or no common cultural reference points.

Jeremy Isaacs persuaded the watchdog to allow a screening of *Richard Pryor: Live in Concert*. Technically it was a documentary but in essence it was a record of a performance – a comedy performance. The 'fuck' count was high and the Channel 4 audience was introduced to those words and much worse. It was a big psychological leg-up for my side of the argument. Sadly the battle to screen *Life of Brian* hadn't at this point been won. Crucifixions were not yet the stuff of comedy.

An eternity of brutal bestial torture

Who Dares Wins was made by the team that later morphed into Hat Trick Productions. The comedy was in part satirical, at times observational and always bitingly funny. The offending sketch was a dig at the advertising industry. It had no dialogue and satirised the old cigar advertisements in which any desperate situation could be fixed by puffing on a Hamlet. The crucifixion scene was beautifully shot. It resembled a religious renaissance painting. Choral music played as a cigar was given to Jesus. He was unable to get a light from a flame which was on a long stick tantalisingly just out of reach. He wrenched his hands away from the cross in order to bring it nearer. He lit his cigar. The music changed to Air on a G string. He fell out of frame. Sacrilegious but funny.

There followed, unsurprisingly, many difficult exchanges with the IBA, Mary Whitehouse muttering about criminal blasphemy, and a toe-curling appearance on *Right to Reply*. Many viewers wrote in support of our standing up to previously unassailable institutional taboos. Many were less supportive. My favourite letter vividly described in detail the horrors of an eternity of brutal bestial torture in Hell. It came from a church minister in Scotland.

We were now no longer permitted to transmit live. We recorded on Friday night for a Saturday evening transmission. After each recording a VHS copy of the show was sent to Channel 4 controller Paul Bonner. The producers and I met on Saturday mornings to edit the show taking into account Paul's notes. What could possibly go wrong?

The new system worked for a while until the production team got a tipoff that news and current affairs bosses were being warned off any mention of alleged sexual shenanigans involving a very senior member of Margaret Thatcher's Cabinet. This was the era of the D-notice. But we were lowly entertainment beings therefore not party to any news briefings. A sketch was performed in which Jimmy Mulville interrupted an interview in front of the audience. Something bad had happened, he said and, in a handheld camera shot, we all left the studio and tracked through the reception area into the gents' lavatory. Above the urinals there was graffiti. It read: 'The Cabinet Minister involved in the sex scandal is…' and then the first two letters of his name, with the rest scribbled out. Who on earth could it be?

Next morning we started the edit fully expecting a phone call with instructions to remove the offending item. It never came. The sketch was transmitted. There were understandably demands for heads to roll. As ever, Jeremy Isaacs was a pillar of strength throughout and, although he was unhappy with our actions, gave us his full support. There was to be no *Right to Reply* appearance this time. There was no public outcry. It all went very quiet. With hindsight it's easy to see why.

The channel then installed an experienced current affairs executive producer, John Gau. He was a lovely man who was never quite sure why he was there but seemed to enjoy every minute of it. We continued to upset people – only now with John's blessing. Importantly *Who Dares Wins* was a very funny show that stretched boundaries and found a hitherto unengaged audience.

Breeding the new national treasures
Who Dares Wins was my last commission as youth editor before moving to look after entertainment overall. My change of role was scheduled to happen the week after the crucifixion debacle so it felt good to be employed, let alone promoted.

My new job was to give me the opportunity to realise a major ambition.

Saturday entertainment has always been a challenge for television channels. *The Tube* started the weekend in fine style for the young audience but where were the shows for the slightly older viewers – the young at heart? The plan was to create a variety show for the eighties. Producer Paul Jackson and I had discussed this for a long time and our starting point was a sort of *Tube* in reverse – a live show driven by new comedy. There would be music but on *Saturday Live* comedy was king. With the weight and experience of London Weekend Television (LWT) production behind us we went on air in 1985. The first series had a different guest presenter each week and introduced all sorts of new faces to television. It made stars of Ben Elton and Harry Enfield. It introduced us to Stephen Fry and Hugh Laurie. Channel 4 favourites Rik Mayall and Ade Edmondson brought us the Dangerous Brothers, a genuinely funny take on slapstick – with added genuine danger.

The second series was fronted by Ben Elton and Harry Enfield who created Stavros and Loadsamoney. By the time we moved to Friday Ben and Harry were well established and Loadsamoney had become the iconic symbol of Thatcher's Britain. Amongst the new faces in those series were Paul Merton, Julian Clary, Jo Brand and Lee Evans as well as Bing Hitler AKA Craig Ferguson.

Saturday/Friday Live had a pre-watershed transmission. This meant that it had to be tightly scripted and LWT had lawyers all over it. In many ways it epitomised the tension that sometimes arose between the big ITV companies and Channel 4. Editorial responsibility rested with Channel 4 as publisher. In truth, the companies didn't really get that, and always had one eye on their own franchise renewal. By the third series I was conscious of LWT regarding the show as their property. Paul Jackson was no longer there so the team had changed, as had the dynamic. It didn't have any effect on the show. It was in the creative hands of the Geoffreys Perkins and Posner so all was well but by now it had done its job. It was time to call it a day. Quit while you are ahead.

In 1986 two young researchers came up with the next big thing. They were working on the music show *Soul Train*, produced by (my wife) Katie Lander. One of them was Alan Marke, who had been one of the young people on the 1981 'think tank', and had given up working in local government to pursue a career in television. The other was Jonathan Ross. Together they proposed making a British version of *The David Letterman Show*. It was a great idea. The only problem was that in order to make the David Letterman Show you need a David Letterman.

We were going to make a pilot so we would have to find a host. Alan, Jonathan and I spent a lot of time searching for the elusive talent. We auditioned in London and at the Edinburgh Festival. We drew a blank. Over the course of this search Jonathan would brief the candidates and demonstrate what style was required. It soon became obvious that he was far better suited to the role than any of the hopefuls we had seen. I asked him if he would do it. He said yes.

We made the pilot. I thought that Jonathan was great but the show didn't work. We had to find a new producer. I showed the tape to several noted names. None of them got it, nor could they see what I saw in Jonathan. The words 'speech impediment' came up more than once. The one person who shared my confidence was Colin Callender. Colin had produced the acclaimed *Nicholas Nickelby* early in Channel 4's life. The Callender Company would make the show. Colin brought Katie in to produce it as she had experience both of studio shows and of working with Jonathan Ross. The first show went out very late on the 6th February 1987. We prerecorded it at five o'clock and from the minute we finished that first recording we all knew that we had something very special. It felt different to any other chat show. It felt fresh. It felt right. The pre-recording and the transmission time felt wrong. It should be live and it should be earlier.

In those days at Channel 4, new challenges could be met with brave resolve. Jeremy Isaacs listened to my case for a live show and asked what my preferred slot would be. I said that the show would play well at ten thirty. From day one this slot had been a sort of 'disease of the week' slot. Putting an irreverent chat show in there would fundamentally change Channel 4 on a Friday night. Quite. We got the green light to go live as soon as possible allowing for print TV listings to be in sync. It took less than four weeks until *The Last Resort* settled into its new live slot. It proved to be a huge hit for Channel 4.

Not letting it lie

The next big challenge was improvised comedy. Improv had been tried on earlier shows but had failed. Hat Trick pointed out that there was a great new show on Radio 4 that would work really well on television. *Whose Line is it Anyway?* was made by a bright young producer named Dan Patterson, who had devised a format which enabled improv to work, to be believable and funny. When the BBC found out that we were interested Dan ended up in the middle of a bidding war. Controller of BBC2 Alan Yentob personally took on the job of winning the show so poor old Dan was getting frantic phone calls yanking him in every direction. I'm sure that Hat Trick's involvement helped win the day for Channel 4 and I honestly believe he made the correct choice. It was the right home for the show. It proved to be another huge hit and ran for ten years on the channel. Dan's company still makes the show in America.

At the end of the eighties there were many changes at Channel 4, not least the departure of Jeremy Isaacs and the arrival of Michael Grade. I ended up as controller of arts and entertainment and deputy director of programmes. It wasn't as grand as it sounds. I didn't do much deputising and I didn't have a programme budget. Jonathan Ross and Alan Marke had found an exciting new act and were seeking a commission. The problem was that none of the commissioning editors wanted to spend any of their budgets on the idea. There was, however, a contingency budget to be won and Michael Grade was the man to convince. Vic Reeves and Bob Mortimer were performing their show live at the Albany theatre in Deptford. We took Michael to see the show or rather he took us in his chauffeur driven car - lots of us all squashed in. He got it right away. *Vic Reeves Big Night Out* owed much to the Goons and Monty Python but it also had its roots in music hall. The surreal comedians had excellent catchphrases. Michael could be heard proclaiming, "He wouldn't let it lie" for many weeks after the performance. The show was commissioned and *Big Night Out* launched the career of those unique performers whilst pioneering a type of comedy that has inspired many new acts since.

I left Channel 4 in 1990, just as *Drop the Dead Donkey* was starting. Damien, a character in *Who Dares Wins*, inspired the series. It was a narrative comedy whose only home could be Channel 4. Its directorial style, its subject matter, its topicality and great characters gave it a distinctive feel. Following this success entertainment commissioning editor Seamus Cassidy went on to have the biggest hit of all – *Father Ted* – one of the great British sit-coms of all time. Both shows were produced by Hat Trick.

Over the years Channel 4 has continued to offer fresh takes on comedy. Titles like *Peep Show, Black Books, The IT Crowd, Smack the Pony* and *The Inbetweeners* have kept the comedy flag flying. Many new comedy writers and performers have made their debuts on Channel 4. BBC3 has inexplicably been 'demoted' to an online presence making it vitally important that Channel 4 carries on with the innovative work. *Peep Show* and *Fresh Meat* are coming to an end but shows like *Catastrophe* and *Raised by Wolves* are still being commissioned.

Comedy has flourished on 4. *Brass Eye*, Ali G, *Green Wing*, Peter Kay, *Armstrong and Miller, Absolutely*, Paul Merton, *Friday Night Dinner*, Mark Thomas, *Bo' Selecta*, Adam Hills, Paul Calf/Steve Coogan, *Spaced*, Jack Dee, *So Graham Norton*, Clive Anderson, *Desmond's*, Keith Allen and *Black Books*. A list spanning more than three decades and, inevitably, I've left out lots of great names. The point is that Channel 4 takes the initiative to air new talent. The angry young things from the channel's early days are now amongst the good and great of broadcasting across all networks. Indeed they probably now represent the very generation that they railed against in the past. Is it time for a new wave of performers to challenge them? I think it is and I believe that Channel 4 should encourage and support them. Its current constitution certainly makes it the natural home for new voices. Nobody else is going do it.

About the author

Mike Bolland joined BBC Scotland as an office boy in 1963 before going on to become a film editor. In the early seventies he moved to the BBC's Community Programme Unit as a producer/director. In 1981 Mike became the commissioning editor for youth programmes at Channel 4. He went on to be senior commissioning editor, entertainment before becoming responsible for arts and entertainment overall. Following the C4 years Mike was an independent producer with Channel X, Head of Arts and Entertainment at BBC Scotland and Creative Director at the NFTS.

If it didn't exist, you couldn't invent it

By Peter Preston

Nothing about the channel has ever been quite as expected. But we must understand its value as that uniquely British thing: a hodge podge that works

Long ago and very far away, Jeremy Isaacs, launch CEO for Channel Four, came to a Guardian morning conference and talked about the high art and high ambition his new strand of public service would deliver. There'd be inspiring drama in King Lear's top class. There'd be fine music and deep debate, plus mirrors held up to everyday life untainted by the stain of Hollywood. There would also – and I winced a little even then – be no sport. This seemed television nonpareil. And Jeremy had one still better surprise up his sleeve.

I'd sent Liz Forgan, our dynamic Woman's Editor, along to interview the emerging Isaacs. They'd got on so well that she came away with a good, informative article - and, rather to my chagrin, a job offer to boot. Liz, who'd arrived via the *Tehran Journal*, the *Hampstead and Highgate Express* and the *Evening Standard* leader writing room, thereupon departed to become a founding commissioning editor and then Director of Programmes at Four. That interview chance offer opened a whole new career. She went on to be head of network radio at the BBC, creating Five and making it live. She had the great good sense not to agree with John Birt when he shifted the *Today* show and much else to White City, and could smile when – years later – the caravan trooped back to Portland Place. She became Dame Liz, chair of English Heritage then chair of the Arts Council; she was also chair of the Scott Trust which benignly superintends the Guardian.

Why so much Forgan back history here, you wonder? Because, for me, amid all the twists, turns and altered trajectories, it mirrors what happened to Channel Four itself. Nothing, from those first founding days, was quite delivered as expected. 'No sport!' turned out to mean many afternoons spent racing from Wincanton, supplemented by the Grand National – and the Paralympic Games as well. We may talk about sacred missions and excellence, about artistic creativity and intellectual adventure: but the story of Four is far more of an exploration along a winding, rutted track.

It isn't the vision sketched out in that Guardian editor's office as the eighties began (with Mrs T ruling a baleful roost). It is *Gogglebox* and *Alan Carr*; it is *Embarrassing Bodies* and *Come Dine With Me*; it is *Kirstie and Phil*, conservatory makeovers and *Grand Designs*; it's a ragbag collection of good things, different things, formulaic things - but in no real sense things like they used to be or things as intended. But it's also that uniquely British thing: a hodge podge that works, an institution you couldn't invent because, somehow, it's just grown. Topsy TV. Which, in a curious way, is why it's so important and so threatened as another Conservative government seeks to tear up the roots of governance, structure and opportunity that first gave it life.

Nothing about C4 and its burgeoning offspring – the Mores, the Es, the Films, the plus and minus 4 rest – quite makes sense. But then, the choice of chief executives and chairmen doesn't make much sense either. Michael Grade succeeded Jeremy Isaacs: the bouncing, cheerful jack of all trades at the BBC and ITV served his time and saw the once-narrow vision broaden. Michael Jackson, the most feted TV executive of his generation, came next, before somehow disappearing amid canyons of American media. Then there was Mark Thompson, who came and went back to lead the BBC after a short exploratory while; followed by Andy Duncan, who marketed stuff for the corporation and wasn't really a much of a creative hand at all. So to David Abraham, the smart ex ad man who whipped up Dave and other reheated channels (and doesn't mind taking an £800,000-plus salary if that's what public service provides).

A passing parade of TV wizards

Is there any binding link along this passing parade of TV wizards, marketing magicians and simple ad blokes? For a while you might have sensed a BBC testing academy, a chance to show what you could do and explore new ideas before you went on to claim corporation acclaim. Maybe, too, the likes of Lord Attenborough as chairman staked out a patch of elevated influence. But then came right-wing entrepreneurs and former Treasury mandarins, succeeded today by a onetime travel trade boss who specialises in selling things (like C4). The government of the day, through Ofcom nomination, finds it easy to set the mood and the direction whilst crying "Look, no hands". Independence for Four is a four-syllable word without great meaning: and, meanwhile, the route back to the BBC appears to have lapsed. Jay Hunt arrived as the creative brain after a very distinguished time at BBC One. In other eras, you'd have expected her to return once the big jobs at Broadcasting House fell vacant. But no: Channel Four, in a way, is more isolated than ever before.

It depends on the commissioning structure that defines it. C4 buys what it needs from the indie sector. There's no single button a director of programmes or departmental supremo can push. You're dishing up a smorgasbord of this and that. You're constructing a menu from what's seasonally available, not deciding what must be done. That automatically makes channel identity difficult going on diffuse. King Lear turned out to have a *Big Brother*. The once and continuing *Countdown* sits oddly alongside Noel Edmonds opening boxes that may or may not make you rich. Can anyone coming to E4 or More4 afresh truly tell where their target audiences lie?

Of course the crown jewels of C4, liberally feted in polite liberal society, trail prestige and branding in their wake. An hour of news at seven with Jon Snow and Co is a good deed in a bad world. *Dispatches* at its often-formidable best recalls the dear, dead, shit-stirring days of *World in Action*. The channel can seem more serious about news in depth than any of its British competitors. It can also, on occasion, show *Panorama* a clean pair of heels. There's a Guardian feel to the best of *Channel 4 News*, an open-minded fairness of mind that doesn't always take balance too seriously. There's an almost tabloid challenge to documentary film-makers: come in, and kick over a few tables. But look at the ad breaks amid so much really good stuff. *Channel 4 News* often barely seems to take a break – and certainly raises scant reward. The money men want to flog their wares elsewhere. Branding is one thing: commerce, in this case, rather another.

The danger now, a danger inherent in semi-demi privatisation with Channel Four sold to some professional private company bent on turning consistent profits whilst – an HMG condition of sale – agreeing to keep the totems of public service in place, is not that Snow, Frei and Newman will be out of a job: they'll be a protected species, the symbol of continuing devotion to the founding precepts. No: the threat is very different. It's that the ragbag will be turned upside down; that the channel will become much more ruthlessly targeted, far keener on defining audience segments, far more anxious to hone an identity. Think ITV1 or Channel Five. The backroom boys there know what works. They rarely take a chance. If Morse is dead, call Lewis: when Lewis grows too old, summon young Endeavour. What goes around *Downton Abbey* or *Mr Selfridge* comes around. What fills the waking and dozing hours of Five – NCIS meets CSI – means proven, predictable trips to the LA studio well. I'm a Big Brother Celebrity, Keep Me Warm in Here. No imagination or undue risks required.

Channel 4, to be sure, grinds out similar fodder year after year. Buying houses; choosing exotic villas in the sun; renovating either of the above, or going to Cornwall after all: you know which channel you're watching the moment you hit the remote. The long, long Saturdays of nothing happening and nobody trying – except, perhaps, to win some bargain basement cookery competition – seem bent on audience repulsion. And yet somewhere amongst the rags at the bottom of the bag you'll find something unexpected: *The Inbetweeners*, *Peep Show*, *The Good Wife*, *Shameless*, *Father Ted*, *Time Team*, a Friday night documentary that makes your heart stop. Nobody says that films or bought-in series can't have subtitles: the iron rule that hobbled BBC2 for decades. Nobody seems to pencil out the gags on late game shows as too steamy for comfort. Who's really going lose their wick over C4 freewheeling? Even the *Daily Mail* can't raise much wrath these days.

A human institution in a digitally-drowned age

Of course C4 could raise more ad money if it really concentrated. Of course the slightly haphazard feeling, the schedule of the good-natured shrug, could be polished into more concentrated life. Of course the actual amount of time and effort spent on political thought and political discussion is pretty derisory: one stream of public service nobody seems to get right. And of course – see the breakthrough that Richard Klein in his time as controller of BBC4 made when he started buying Scandi thrillers and opened up the rich cupboard of European TV drama – C4 can be a bit slow off the mark as well, launching its own European drama season a little on the late side.

We're not talking crown jewels here. We're often shambling around in search of a cutting edge. The most irritating experience on TV is stumbling on an old *Grand Designs* or Kirstie Allsopp and trying to puzzle out whether it was made in 2015 or 2005. Independent producers? You can have too much of a good thing, a mesh of formulas tying you down. Incisive schedule-making? Talk to some of those indie producers about the time it takes to get a commissioning decision. Nothing in TV, as in life, is perfect. Channel 4 often falls very far short of perfection.

But it's absolutely not nurse, with something worse round the corner. It's a human institution in a digitally-drowned age. It is always likely to stumble on something wonderful. You couldn't invent it because, in a sense, nobody did invent it. It is a training school for upwardly mobile TV executives and a refresher course for the jaded. It is a brilliant achievement and a continually missed opportunity. It could be in the vanguard of television's move to conquer the web – or it may not notice anything's happened until far too late.

The thesis in the trade is that not even Messrs Osborne or Whittingdale will privatise C4 successfully because the public service requirements to sale will carve away at profit forecasts and desirability. In fact I don't think that's such a problem. Public service can be a few ticks in boxes – Snow and Frei at 40 minutes not 55 – with much else seeping in around. The real test of survival is more important, and nebulous, than that.

Look, perversely perhaps, at the programme wealth of the Sky Arts channel. It's almost what Jeremy Isaacs promised for 4 so long, long ago. Not surprising, perhaps: the chairman of Sky Arts is a fantastic old chap called Jeremy Isaacs, and he's an indefatigable champion of the good and the great. But what do you – an ordinary Joe not extraordinary Jeremy – want to watch over supper on an average evening? A good bit of this and a great bit of that, a game with a laugh, a crude shock or two, and a shrewd slice of human experience: the kind of odd mix no Secretary of State shuffling his papers would prescribe. Only Four would have been imaginative enough, and free enough, to hire Liz Forgan on first acquaintance. Only Four would have piled different talents and visions together with such insouciant abandon. Only Four is shamblingly able to raise two fingers when an oppressive Government comes to call. An alternative definition of public service we all need.

So ask the question you'll never find in one of Noel Edmonds' boxes: who or what is Channel Four for?

Answer: it's not for burning.

About the author

Peter Preston edited *The Guardian* for 20 years between 1975 and 1995 and continued to write widely on broadcasting and the media. He was co-director of the Guardian Foundation. Peter died in January 2018.

1989-92: The age of the Antonines and how all good things come to an end

By David Lloyd

'Oi!'

True, my tread had quietened as I passed Michael Grade's open door, so in the circumstances some sort of summons was inevitable. Nevertheless, the tone was one of banter rather than barracking – and certainly not the administering of a bollocking, which in any other channel might have been judged appropriate. That bollocking had just been dished out to Michael himself on the phone by Lord Hanson, at that time a revered captain of industry who seldom attracted bad copy. As per normal procedure, Michael's PA, the estimable Ros Sloboda, had listened in and was able to report the full contents of Hanson's fulmination:

'Michael, that man Lloyd you employ is a total $@!ehole! Do you hear me, Michael? An $@!ehole!'

Untypically, Michael was still reeling from the call, and I made haste to admit the cause. We had recently transmitted a particularly pokey *Dispatches* about his lordship which effectively argued that he was an asset-stripper. When he wrote to complain, I confess I had a certain amount of fun with the response, resorting to a facetiousness and irony certainly unknown to complainants to today's BBC Trust: 'In the absence of full transparency at the recent AGM I believe it falls to television and the media to assert the public interest on behalf of shareholders and the City alike!' Perhaps the wonder is that he didn't have to be carted off to the cardiology ward.

But the reason that I felt emboldened to write in such terms was that I could fairly guess that Michael would broadly support me, as he was stalwart and robust for all his commissioners and programme-makers when properly and accurately carrying the channel's banner. Not for him the cut-and-run of the supposedly bold executive, fearless until the heat arrives. No doubt it is a function of his own family background that leads him to understand, instinctively, the psychology and needs of those who bare themselves in the interest of entertaining or engaging an audience. That understanding certainly bonded the commissioning team to and around him, through thick and thin and many a run-in with the courts and the *Daily Mail*, who poisonously branded him 'the pornographer in chief'.

Not that his reign began so auspiciously; he arrived at the very moment that ITV was about to embark on a bidding round for new franchises and the board were concerned that bidding consortia might tap up the talent at Channel 4. A conventional response to such a danger would be to pay for their loyalty and thus was born the 'golden handcuffs' row when the payments were leaked to *The Independent*. But the handcuffs were to be placed only on Jeremy Isaacs' Praetorian guard of administrators, not to any of the commissioning team. For several days, the phones were red hot from the channel's founding fathers and independent producers alike, who had thought that the channel lived by other rules than orthodox commerce. Michael was summoned to attend a meeting with the commissioning team and I had the invidious task of presenting our case, ending up in *Private Eye* for my pains. To this day, I regret not having rebutted the suggestion strongly enough that I had leaked an account of this meeting; I hadn't and it's not my style (Michael, please note).

When the board appointed Michael to succeed Jeremy, it was Sir Richard Attenborough (known as 'Dickie Darling' throughout the channel), who had stepped into Edmund Dell's shoes as chairman, and who had led the way in judging that 'cometh the hour, cometh the man'. Given that Michael was at that time known only as an unfettered populist, it was an appropriately bold choice and led to Jeremy's infamous threat to throttle his successor if 'he ruined my channel!'[1]

But, in truth, it was unlikely that Michael would see any reputational advantage in doing any such thing. And besides, the 1990 Broadcasting Act was about to change the terms of the whole debate.

Under Jeremy's tutelage, the channel's income was delivered by the ITV companies each selling its advertising airtime, as well as their own; under the Act the channel must now raise its own income by recruiting a dedicated advertising sales staff, while its programme purpose and credentials remained unaltered – as a non-profit-making public service broadcaster, with a defining remit to innovate and cater for minorities otherwise unserved. To soften any hard landings a 'funding formula' was devised whereby ITV would bail out its smaller competitor, and vice versa if ITV hit danger (which at that time didn't seem very likely). Though Michael was later to rail at the funding formula to anyone who would listen, I actually witnessed his first reaction, which was one of unqualified joy and relief. At that time, many in the advertising industry believed that the channel was a 'goner', with or without the formula, but the plot was to thicken in the most surprising of ways.

Many advertising and space-buying luminaries coveted the job of the first C4 director of advertising sales. Tess Alps was rumoured in the press to be the favourite, but in the event Michael and the board made an inspired choice in Stewart Butterfield – 'an intellectual among barrow boys'. He it was who spotted that the freedom that Jeremy had possessed to invent a channel, outside of commercial pressures, that could be identified with 'the courageous and outrageous', playing to the demographics of the young male rarely reached by advertisers, could be a selling proposition. And indeed, that in the midst of the Thatcher hegemony of Britain, the channel that her government had created might come to be seen as the people's only friend. (In the film *Mona Lisa* the Bob Hoskins character enters frame at one point as a television screen plays in the corner; on the screen a couple are enjoying vigorous, near-bestial sex. Hoskins remarks: 'Oh Channel 4?') Many years on from *Mona Lisa* or any such cavortings Stewart remains, in my view, the unsung, forgotten hero of Channel 4 because he – with Michael's creative support – put us on the commercial, mainstream map, with a robustness that prevails to this day.

Not that this proposition was an overnight, commercial success: legend has it that the channel went on air in its new status without a single advert sold.

While today's television management, across all channels, is notoriously unaware of history – even careless of it and dismissive of its continuum – Channel 4 only survives today, albeit in a very different, multi-channel, Internet-dominated world, because the founding heroes – commissioners and producers alike – delivered such a strong, identifiable, intelligent brand to their successors. Today's leaders owe their paychecks, if not their bonuses to them. And a decent number of viewers still press 'select' on 4 not because of the extraordinary ability of the current management but because of the legacy of their predecessors.

Losing It – In Retrospect (1991-1992)

Two first-hand experiences summarise the necessarily mixed legacy of Michael Grade to the channel: near the start of his tenure I commissioned a controversial *Dispatches* from Sean McPhilemy entitled 'The Committee', documenting collusion between the then Ulster police force (the Royal Ulster Constabulary) and loyalist paramilitaries. The programme's allegations were founded on an interview with an anonymised, Loyalist 'insider', and the Attorney General demanded to be better acquainted with his identity. The channel resolutely refused to break its journalistic promise to this insider, and we found ourselves shortly in the Royal Courts of Justice[2]. Our continued refusal could have closed down Channel 4, and we all knew what we were up against.

At any other broadcaster of my acquaintance, the board and chief executive would have folded, but Michael was made of very different stuff. When I told him that, as a result of the controversy, poisonously fomented by Andrew Neil's *Sunday Times*, Sean was losing commissions from other broadcasters and was in danger of losing his house, Michael declared: 'That's appalling. I won't have anybody lose their family home for honest journalism.' He invited his chairman Richard 'Dickie Darling' Attenborough to attend court to show solidarity and impress the judge with his celebrity status.

Indeed, that the enlightened Mr Justice Woolf was hearing the case at all was no accident. When the issue first loomed, Jan Tomalin, the head of legal services – and a 'head of yes', par excellence arranged to research the upcoming lists, and the identity of the judge originally slated for the case. 'Oh God,' declared our advising solicitors. 'A total neanderthal!' What to do, with the channel's very future at stake? Simple: feed a story to *The Observer* that the channel will fight tooth and nail for its journalistic credentials of free speech – and next thing Mr Justice Woolf is to preside. Our QC declares in court: 'We will bend the knee but we cannot bow the head'; the judge establishes the legal precedent of 'qualified anonymity'; and the channel survives to fight many more illustrious days. Michael is, and always has been, utterly robust in his support of journalists. Particularly by comparison with John Birt's BBC, the channel was a great place to do good journalism. The longevity, reputation and robustness of today's *Dispatches* and Channel 4 News owes an enormous amount to Michael's unfailing support, and interest.

As for the channel's own growing status, creatively and commercially, one is reminded of Edward Gibbon's description of the Roman Empire in the age of the Antonines.

> *If a man were called to fix the period in the history of the world, during which the condition of the human race was most happy and prosperous, he would, without hesitation, name that which elapsed from the death of Domitian to the accession of Commodus. The vast extent of the Roman empire was governed by absolute power, under the guidance of virtue and wisdom. The armies were restrained by the firm but gentle hand of four successive emperors, whose characters and authority commanded involuntary respect. The forms of the civil administration were carefully preserved by Nerva, Trajan, Hadrian, and the Antonines...* **Edward Gibbon, The History of the Decline and Fall of the Roman Empire, Vol 1, Chapter 3.**

In 1992, Michael is giving the MacTaggart Lecture at the annual Edinburgh Television Festival[2]; backed by ourselves, his channel cohorts, he enjoys himself hugely as he lams into John Birt and his 'internal market' prescriptions for the BBC, and we are all rolling in the aisles. Michael's sense of timing a joke is always faultless in delivery, and here he is perfectly catching the mood of the industry as a whole, both outside and inside the BBC.

But all of us at the channel at that time must now share the blame of living in the present, rather than the future, which many a newspaper editor was already obsessing about. We at Horseferry Road – at every level – have grown too comfortable and smug at our own success. With the benefit of hindsight we should have detected that our core, young audience would be prey, beyond all others, to the attraction of digital – and beyond that, peripatetic digital, via i-phone or tablet. Yet Michael stayed almost to the Millennium, essentially bullying the board to keep him. And strategic planning was there none, which was disastrous for a channel which had lived and prospered in the vanguard of youth taste and habits. When I analysed this to an ITV Elder recently, he remarked, 'Ah, Michael. Great tactician; no strategist.'

Another industry friend advised: 'Never forget Scott Fitzgerald's famous dictum, that the rich are different from us; rare amongst senior broadcast management, Michael believes it is his birthright to be wealthy; Michael stayed that long at the channel because he had nowhere more lucrative to go to.' While this assessment may seem attractive, particularly in the light of Michael's changed attitude to privatisation now laboured across the red benches in the House of Lords, it can not serve as the last word as I have since been directed to his autobiography, in which he speaks of the offers he did receive – and lucrative ones at that. Why didn't he take them, when his foot was clearly off the gas to the channel's future? The enigma remains. (The identities of both these confidants are available on request, but of course, only on condition of qualified anonymity.)

Notes

[1] See: Lebrecht, N. (2000) Covent Garden: The Untold Story: Dispatches from the English Culture War 1945-2000. London: Simon & Schuster.

[2] See: Durham, M. (1992). Channel 4 faces ruin for protecting sources: Sequestration of television company's assets may be the only way to ensure that the law is enforced, the High Court was told, The Independent. Available at:
http://www.independent.co.uk/news/uk/channel-4-faces-ruin-for-protecting-sources-sequestration-of-television-companys-assets-may-be-the-1536142.html

Section 3:
Where's the remit now?

Introduction by John Mair

It is three miles from Charlotte Street in London's Noho to Horseferry Road in Pimlico, yet the distance that Channel 4 has travelled in programme terms from one to the other is immense. From *LGBT Basket Weavers* and *Walter* in 1982 to wall-to-wall *Come Dine with Me*, *Countdown* (with and without *Cats*) and a plethora of fixed-rig documentaries like *24 Hours in A&E* today. Would Anthony Smith and Jeremy Isaacs recognise the 2016 Channel 4 output as distinctive or near the remit they set out? The jury is out on that.

In this section we put the remit to a stress test with faces old and new, young and old. Their verdicts are not universally positive.

First, old Channel 4 hand David Lloyd continues his series of sketches by recalling the move to SW1 and the joy of a back entrance to escape wannabe producers pitching for projects, as had been the bane of many an executive's life in the Charlotte Street lobby.

One programme has been fixed in the schedule since Day One: *Channel 4 News* at 7pm. It may be a guaranteed money loser for the channel (just look at the threadbare 'ad breaks'), but it is a totem. Move or destroy *Channel 4 News* and you have put a dagger in the heart of the channel, say the defenders. Professor Steven Barnett is a long-time champion of public service broadcasting, and he is crystal clear: 'It is difficult to envisage any restructuring… which would sustain a journalistic legacy that has survived and thrived for nearly 35 years'. Professor Richard Tait was a very distinguished editor of the programme for eight years, then editor-in-chief of ITN and later a BBC governor. He knows about broadcast regulation. In his chapter 'One false move and the puppy gets it' he looks to a private C4 future with Ofcom regulating and keeping the new owners honest. He is not that hopeful: 'However well Ofcom policed the arrangements, history suggests that privatisation would put the incoming owners, not the regulators, in the driving seat.'

One of the liberating effects of Channel 4 was that it freed up documentary makers who felt constrained in the BBC and ITV. A thousand flowers did bloom through strands like *Cutting Edge* and series including *The Sixties*. Channel 4 was the 'go-to' channel for serious programme makers for several decades. But now in 2016, have Mitsubishi and Channel 4 altered the way we see documentaries? Is it all fixed rig and fluff with little left of the cutting edge?

We took the format of one of the channel's current big hits, *GoggleBox,* and applied it to a week of its documentaries in February 2016. The twist was that our 'viewers' were five very distinguished documentary makers: Molly Dineen, Roger Graef, David Pearson, Sue Bourne and Kim Longinitto. Their verdict on the channel's output (in our chapter 'Googledocs') is, at best, mixed.

Farrukh Dhondy was one of the cornerstones of the Isaacs and post-Isaacs Channel 4. He commissioned for thirteen years. He all but invented multi-cultural programmes through strands like *The Bandung File*, comedy hits like *Desmonds* and big films like *Bhaji on the Beach*. As he puts it in his chapter 'Remit, Schmemit' he interpreted his job as venturing into the parts of the new communities that other programmes and channels had not reached: This entailed the 'recruitment of people to the manner rather than the manor born'. But in his long hard look at the channel's 'diverse 'output today, Farrukh is less than impressed: 'A few weeks of watching Channel 4 as it is now in 2016 leads inexorably to the conclusion that the remit doesn't exist. I must have missed the Act of Parliament that changed or relaxed it.'

Also there on the first night and still here today was Film Four (in various incarnations according to CEO preference and profit/losses). The channel always saw it as part of its remit to provide seed money (or more) for British feature films. Its trophy cabinet is overflowing, following notable successes from *Four Weddings and a Funeral* to *Slumdog Millionaire* and *12 years a Slave*. But with putative privatisation, could this part of the family be one of the first to be cut loose? Paul Moody's chapter 'For Those in Peril' examines the likely effects and concludes that it could harm the 'British' film industry.

Karen Brown helped re-invent the genre of 'education programmes' as commissioning editor, then deputy director of programmes, at Channel 4. Fiona Chesterton did much the same when she took on the mantle of the first head of daytime at the channel. Both aimed then at growing a young audience for the channel. It was a challenge two decades ago; it is an even bigger one now with broadcasting fragmentation and platform plethora. They are not convinced it is a challenge to which the current management is rising: 'As we write, with the refugee crisis raging and the British people deciding whether to remain or leave the European Union, where on Channel 4 (let alone anywhere else on British television) will you see that from the perspective of the young; say a documentary through the eyes of a 14-year-old Syrian or a young Polish worker...?

The young get their voice in this book too. Emily Jennings, an early career broadcast journalist recalls: 'Channel 4's programmes have provided a backdrop to my childhood and adolescence and still does to this day'. Melanie Downing, now a junior doctor, spent much of her youth too watching Channel 4 and believes that its current affairs output had a big influence on her ultimate choice of career.

Channel 4 set out in 1982 to try to feed a sea full of production minnows dependent on them for the odd small (and not-so-small) commission. Some fell by the wayside quickly. As is the way of media capitalism, oligopoly ruled in the end. The minnows were swallowed by bigger fish who were swallowed by even bigger fish to become whales (or even sharks!). Torin Douglas was a journalist observer (first for the BBC) at the beginning. He has followed the 'consolidation' of companies from a 'thousand flowers' blooming to a 'few flowers' of super indies since with some professional interest. Torin's chapter traces the career of Peter 'Baz' Bazalgette from a two-room office in Kensal Rise making one series for the BBC to his huge multi-national company – Endemol – partly through the success of *Big Brother* on Channel 4. He is now <u>Sir</u> Peter Bazalgette, retiring chair of the Arts Council and incoming chairman of ITV Plc. Sir Peter is grateful, as he thinks the UK should be, for indie freedom: 'One of the reasons the UK does so well internationally is that we have more competing channels trying out new programme ideas than anywhere else in the world.'

Minnows, whales, sharks. This is exactly the territory that Lorraine Heggessey now occupies as adviser to the Channel 4 Growth Fund – a fertiliser reservoir to help little indies grow big. Lorraine herself has climbed the summits of British broadcasting as Controller BBC One and CEO of Talkback Thames. Earlier, she had a starring role in a Channel 4 *Dispatches,* door-stepping the master door-stepper himself Roger Cook in an hilarious encounter over his breakfast. Lorraine's chapter looks at how the channel has carefully nurtured on screen talent – a sentiment firmly echoed by Jamie Oliver in his preface to this book. For example, Lorraine shows how Channel 4 nurtured Nick Curwin and his Garden Productions with some development money for *One Born every minute.* Out of that begat fixed rig-documentary filming and modern hits like *24 hours in A&E* and *Educating Yorkshire*. Heggessey concludes: 'Channel 4 feeds ideas and talent into the airwaves that has an impact on all our broadcasters as well as on the production sector. We meddle with that ecosystem at our peril'.

Over the past three decades, Channel 4 has tried to be a style-setter both in content and on air. Martin Lambie Nairn created the iconic multi-coloured '4' logo – a truly distinctive piece of modern British design – for the launch. It served well until last year. Then, for reasons best known to itself, the channel decided to change its image by sloughing off the Lambie Nairn logo and breaking it up into its parts. Dean Stockton, a former Channel 4 designer and one of the sharper minds in TV style, deconstructs this move in not an entirely positive way. He concludes of the new channel idents: 'Without any obvious narrative, they just merge into the content that surrounds them, appearing so indistinguishable that they are drowning in their own pretence.'

As in the previous section of this book, it remains for David Lloyd to continue his own individual 'journey' through the Channel (and his history there) with remembrances of times past. Now, 1997 and the arrival as chief executive of a TV wunderkind from the BBC whose nickname said it all: '...while Michael Jackson was often dubbed 'Whacko Jacko' (at least outside the channel), his behaviour could be eccentric and skittish, and he had the attention span of Charles the Second, he also had his occasional instinctive brilliance. For those in his confidence, he had the most commendably open and creative management style.'

On balance then, is the famed 'remit' crafted by Tony Smith, Willie Whitelaw and Jeremy Isaacs alive and well? Only just; the 'distinctive' and 'different' Channel 4 has become the Paralympic Channel with plenty of fluff around it... convoluted or what?

As for the audience view: well, you decide.

1994: Going up in the world

By David Lloyd

The white van men had lugged the last gear into the building, the pantechnicon had disgorged the mixing and transmission desks, the taxis had sped their fares to investigate their new offices, and we stood marveling at the Machu Pichu steps that would confront any new arrival to the Horseferry Road building. Beyond the awesome, self-confident, corporate statement that Richard Rogers had delivered us, with glass lift 'bubbles' speeding us to the upper floors, what of the unique starting culture of channel would be likely to survive this transplant to modernist steel and glass?

Certainly, advantages immediately presented themselves: a garden and patio at the back wherein thoughts could be thought, and the southern sun enjoyed on a good day; and an underground car park reached by basement lift whence escape could be attempted from even the most importunate independent producers gathering in the lobby. But the true heroes of this move were Frank McGettigan, the general manager and director of personnel who had organised it (and, it was rumoured, personally overseen the import of the Carrara Marble 'risers' to the building's entrance), and David Scott, the managing director, who had sagely advised that the channel had to own, rather than rent, any new headquarters to bolster its asset base, and give it the option of 'sale and leaseback' if hard times truly visited. (Scott Trust, please note)

In fact, Victoria was the final, rather than first, choice of location; the commissioning body was given some access to the discussion, assisted by artists' impressions of the competing sites. Clerkenwell was in the mix, a location which I personally favoured for its proximity to ITN and the *Channel 4 News* team, and could imagine the area being revived with small offices for independents and edit suites in properties with no obvious defining purpose. There was also a vile canard doing the rounds that Michael's preference was Hammersmith, just near the bridge, given credibility by the fact that, uniquely, the artists' impressions had dignified this site with a private jetty, and a yacht.

In the event, SW1, Victoria, won the board's approval – for its proximity to SW1, Westminster.

The need to move at all was not a function of a 'grown-up' institution needing to assert its permanency, still less driven by corporate grandiloquence, but by the simple need to accommodate the adverting sales and marketing team, which had been housed, unsatisfactorily, in rented colonies up and down Charlotte Street, as far as Fitzroy Square. Unlike the BBC's disastrous dabbling in property extension in White City, in the 1990s, (with so-called 'media centres' and the like), this new headquarters was brought in on budget, with business-like efficiency and purpose, and was not abandoned, as some white elephant, thereafter.

But would the spirit of Channel 4 survive this relocation? Not in every sense, for the foyer was too cavernous and echoey to have presented the same welcoming aspect as had greeted visitors to Charlotte Street. Thus for the sake of comfort and branding, two emissaries were dispatched: commissioning editor of arts Waldemar Januszczak to acquire or rent some artworks that could consolidate our purpose to all-comers; and Peter Ansorge, commissioning editor for drama series, to investigate the quality of the surrounding restaurants. When he reported that the food was fine but the clientele dominated by oil men, a petition was launched to Frank McGettigan for a canteen (which he preferred to think of as a restaurant) and a gym. We got the former. And, thanks to Waldemar, a load of Damien Hirsts in formaldehyde.

But there was one more touch to add to reaffirm our remit. The personnel department made sure to include amongst the receptionists a disabled meeter and greeter – a move which did not convince all-comers. As Kelvin MacKenzie confided in my office: 'I must have a word with Michael; this gives quite the wrong impression!'

An endangered species

By Steven Barnett

Channel 4 News's editorial agenda has remained remarkably stable and its ratings have held up well in the face of audience fragmentation. Private ownership could kill it

> We did not want stories of individual crime, or of minor natural disaster. We did not want coverage of the daily diaries of the Royal Family. _Channel 4 News_ would deal with politics and with the economy. It would bring coverage of the City, and of industry. It was to report on developments in science and technology, and in the arts. It was to cover the politics of other countries and to supplement that reporting with the output and insights of foreign television news programmes. (Isaacs 1989, p126)

This was the vision that Jeremy Isaacs, writing a few years after the fact, outlined for _Channel 4 News_ when he sat down as its first chief executive to interpret the statutory framework that the government had bequeathed him.

That framework was itself the result of a remarkable fusion – some might argue a collision – of left and right wing values which found its apotheosis in an entirely new approach to television. Its vision derived partly from a centre-left ideological perspective inherited from the previous Labour administration in opposition to a perceived establishment, male, metropolitan, middle-class culture. This provided some of the intellectual background for the Annan Committee's report of 1977 which advocated an interventionist approach to the new channel: it would foster diversity rather than a liberal market solution which would (as ITV had fiercely argued) simply give the commercial incumbents the second channel they craved. Annan therefore favoured a new organisation with a mandate for cultural diversity, operating as a publisher rather than a fully integrated broadcaster, and therefore facilitating more access to this powerful medium for the growing number of journalists, producers and creatives outside the existing duopoly.

Allied to this was the growing clamour from the right to provide more opportunities for those entrepreneurs and small businesses who had equally felt excluded by the corporatist, bureaucratic and monolithic BBC, as well as by a monopolistic, indulgent and anti-competitive ITV in hock to militant trade unions. A new channel unfettered by internal restrictive practices and freed from bureaucratic constraints, went the argument, would be nimble enough to break the duopoly and give the buccaneering free spirit programme makers an opportunity to thrive.

As a result the 1981 Broadcasting Act mandated a fourth channel with a statutory obligation to provide 'innovation and experiment in the form and content' of programmes and to ensure 'generally that Channel 4 is given a distinctive character of its own'.[1] The key rationale behind Annan was that while the channel would be funded commercially through advertising and sponsorship, competition for commercial revenue could risk compromising its carefully crafted public service remit. Thus, its airtime was to be sold by ITV which – much to the frustration of advertisers as well as devotees of free market liberalism – was allowed to keep its advertising monopoly. Freed from the imperative of competing for commercial revenue, Channel 4 was able to concentrate on interpreting and building its unique public service obligation to break the mould. This remit provided a firm statutory foundation which was to define Channel 4's approach to news for the next 30 years.

From statute to *Channel 4 News*

While Parliament established the guiding principles and structure, it was left to Channel 4's founders to interpret how the slippery notion of 'distinctiveness' would be applied to each genre of programming. In news and current affairs, explicit ambitions were set from the very beginning by its founding chief executive Jeremy Isaacs, whose blueprint was a serious one-hour news bulletin at 7pm. While accepting that television was essentially a visual medium, as a distinguished and experienced factual programme maker himself, Isaacs did not hold to the Postmanite view that this made television inevitably a trivializing medium. Why not, he asked, 'provide a framework in which different choices were possible, and promulgate a brief for a programme instructing that different choices would be made'? (*ibid*, p126). In other words, the editorial agenda for the channel's news would follow the spirit of the channel's statutory remit, and would take an explicitly 'broadsheet' approach that privileged thoughtful analysis and eschewed trivia and sensationalism.

It was a vision of news which broke every rule in the commercial television rule-book: the early peak-time slot is where audiences start to build, and any programme which is certain to give competitors a ratings advantage would be unceremoniously dumped at the design stage. Even in the digital age of catch-up and online viewing, the linear models of audience inheritance still apply, and in purely commercial terms Channel 4 hobbled itself from the beginning. Moreover, the Isaacs vision of one hour devoted to serious stories and long-form analysis was a guaranteed recipe for diminished audiences and therefore diminished revenue. For television journalism, it was a living example of how structural protection could facilitate a very different kind of news bulletin unburdened by traditional constraints of either money or medium.

The next question was how to make this grand vision operational while ensuring that audiences were not so minuscule as to render the experiment a critical as well as ratings failure. As a publisher-broadcaster, Channel 4 could not generate its own news team, nor – given the huge cost of launching a TV newsgathering operation from scratch – would it have the resources. Who would be its news supplier? Independent Television News, which had been supplying ITV with its news for over 25 years, was the obvious choice, with the track record and expertise to provide a credible and authoritative service. But would it be able to adapt its journalistic practices from a populist, mainstream approach demanded by a mass audience commercial channel to the kind of philosophy demanded by Isaacs? In her book on the history of Channel 4, Maggie Brown records ITN's initial response when C4's first commissioner of news and current affairs, Liz Forgan, outlined its news agenda of 'no sport, no royal stories, no plane crashes and lashings of foreign news'. Back came the reply, an era-defining combination of sexism and condescension: 'Well, my dear, there's just one thing you have to understand: the news is the news is the news' (Brown 2007, p24).

In practice, however, there were no other options and the contract went to ITN whose first *Channel 4 News* bulletin went out on the fledgling channel's opening day in November 1982. Within a year, despite protection from the remit and a clear journalistic vision, the bulletin had failed to achieve that delicate balance between a modest but acceptable audience and a serious, distinctive bulletin. Projected audiences of 1.5 million were never achieved, and had fallen below 250,000. Whatever the insulation from commercial pressures – which would inevitably have driven editorial content towards crime, royalty and showbiz – audiences mattered because no producer or journalist likes to invest time and money in making programmes for empty chairs.

The bulletin was turned round partly through the appointment of a new editor from within ITN, Stewart Purvis, who combined journalistic flair with managerial acumen; and partly through its coverage of the bitter and divisive 1984 miners' strike, during which the main Coal Board and miners' union protagonists were brought together for an explosive Channel 4 debate (securing 2 million viewers). Journalist Jane Corbin produced a lengthy and moving report from one of the divided mining villages which even drew the admiration of miners' arch-enemy Prime Minister Margaret Thatcher (Lindley 2005, p269). Gradually, audiences climbed to a million which, while still a fraction of the 10-12 million routinely generated by the main BBC and ITV news bulletins, justified continuation of its place in the schedules of a channel dedicated to doing television differently. Within ten years, it became an established part of the channel's DNA, able to maintain both a stable audience and a highly distinctive, broadsheet approach to news. But from the early 1990s onwards, it was forced to confront two very difficult challenges.

The challenge of competition

First, the 1990 Broadcasting Act represented a deliberate liberal market assault on Britain's broadcasting ecology, ironically being signed into law in the very week that its architect Margaret Thatcher fell from power. Amongst many destructive elements, the Act decoupled Channel 4 from ITV, obliging it from 1993 to sell its own advertising airtime in direct competition to ITV. Given the proliferation of cable, satellite and digital terrestrial channels to come, it may only have been a matter of time. But this systematic attack on a painstakingly constructed framework inevitably meant that Channel 4 had to assess carefully the commercial damage – and commercial potential – of its programmes and scheduling. The bean-counting process – which programmes were profitable and which were subsidised – were bound to affect its thinking about news just as any other programme whose ratings and revenue did not cover programme costs.

That bean-counting exercise was quantified just a few years later by an internal report which concluded that *Channel 4 News* earned about half its costs in advertising revenue; it acknowledged that commercial imperatives might dictate a scheduling shift to 7.30 (and probably a half hour rather than hour long bulletin), but that such a move would be potentially 'extremely damaging' to the channel's reputation (Brown, *op cit*, p225). This was confirmed when Channel 4's head of news and current Affairs, Dorothy Byrne, informed a 2007 House of Lords select committee enquiry during oral evidence that costs of around £20 million were met by revenues of around £10 million, leaving a funding gap of £10 million. While raising a few eyebrows when she told committee members 'I am proud to say that *Channel 4 News* loses more money for Channel 4 than any other programme that we make', she was explicit about the public service commitment to both the nature and length of that daily bulletin:

> If we continue, as we must, with our one-hour, serious news programme in which 40–50 per cent of its content is foreign, that programme is not going to make money. But we should not cut back on its seriousness, its quality or its length – I am absolutely sure of that… not just for Channel 4 but also for British democracy. I think the existence of *Channel 4 News* is vital as a very serious competitor to the BBC. (House of Lords 2008, Q73).

Channel 4's second challenge, exacerbated by the first, was of course the fragmentation of audiences and advertising faced by all the mainstream channels as first cable and satellite and subsequently online and mobile began to transform the television landscape. How would the terrestrial minnow fare? During the course of Ofcom's 2008–9 public service broadcasting review, questions were raised not just about programme sustainability but channel survival. Ofcom concluded that audiences wanted a public service alternative to the BBC and that 'a second institution with clear public purpose goals and a sustainable economic model will help to ensure wide availability of public service content' (Ofcom 2009, p63). The public policy objectives of pluralism, quality and distinctiveness were enshrined in the 2010 Digital Economy Act which extended Channel 4's remit, but essentially left the channel to continue to fend for itself in an increasingly competitive television advertising market. Concerns have been raised over whether these public service objectives have been compromised by the drive for economic sustainability, in particular whether long-standing programming commitments have become diluted. As far as *Channel 4 News* is concerned, a systematic study of news content carried out at University of Westminster provides an unambiguous answer.

Channel 4 News content – the evidence

This study, the most comprehensive longitudinal content analysis of British television news to date, analysed over a thousand evening news bulletins on the main terrestrial channels spanning 35 years from 1975 to 2009 (Barnett et al, 2012). It therefore covered the period from Channel 4's launch through its protection from advertising competition to the modern era of outright competition.[2]

Overall, the research demonstrated a healthy stability in the volume of serious news across all the main evening bulletins, but the figures for *Channel 4 News* are particularly remarkable. Over 30 years, its editorial agenda has barely moved, with around half its bulletins devoted to domestic broadsheet issues (Table 1). There appears to be a slight shift of around 10 per cent away from coverage of foreign issues towards lighter or more 'tabloid' stories, but Table 2 puts this shift in perspective by comparing the channel's 2009 figures with its four terrestrial rivals. The level of tabloid content on *Channel 4 News* remains the lowest of all the main evening bulletins, and the volume of foreign coverage is exceeded only by the BBC's *10 O'Clock News*.

Table 1 Channel 4 News: % of broadsheet versus tabloid in bulletins 1985-2009

	1985	1990	1995	1999	2004	2009
Broadsheet Domestic	49.0	54.8	54.8	51.9	50.0	50.5
Broadsheet Foreign	39.4	40.7	39.3	37.5	33.1	30.6
Tabloid	11.1	5.1	4.8	10.6	16.9	18.8

Table 2 Main evening bulletins in 2009: % of broadsheet versus tabloid news

	BBC6	BBC9/10	ITV early	ITV late	C4 News	C5 News
Broadsheet Domestic	55.1	46.4	44.3	40.8	50.5	31.6
Broadsheet Foreign	21.8	34.4	21.4	26.2	30.6	17.2
Tabloid	23.2	19.2	34.4	34.1	18.8	51.2

These broad-brush data were reinforced by more detailed analysis at the secondary level, which showed how *Channel 4 News* has consistently led the way on coverage of political affairs and social policy (Tables 3 and 4). Thus, it appears that the legacy of Jeremy Isaacs' vision of the programme survived the competitive onslaught and continued into the 21st century.

Table 3: Political Affairs coverage in main evening news bulletins 1975-2009

(% of bulletins in each year)

	1975	1980	1985	1990	1995	1999	2004	2009
BBC6	25.6	15.2	14.1	32.6	20.8	14.6	30.0	26.0
BBC9/10	31.6	22.1	19.0	32.8	22.1	15.3	35.6	30.6
ITV Eve	22.2	17.9	16.2	31.3	19.7	12.6	30.0	19.3
ITV Night	30.2	24.7	18.9	30.0	19.9	10.1	28.1	20.0
C4			17.6	33.3	25.4	15.8	35.4	30.0
C5						5.8	35.5	10.5

Table 4: Social Policy coverage in main evening news bulletins 1975-2009
(% of bulletins in each year)

	1975	1980	1985	1990	1995	1999	2004	2009
BBC6	5.3	13.8	11.7	7.9	17.2	15.1	13.6	18.1
BBC9/10	5.4	12.3	7.2	3.3	10.8	9.9	10.8	14.7
ITV Eve	2.4	9.4	6.7	8.4	10.1	10.8	10.5	16.6
ITV Night	2.1	10.0	8.3	10.6	8.3	5.4	4.4	11.4
C4						15.5	13.1	20.2
C5						13.5	8.6	11.7

Anomaly in need of protection

Those figures tell a clear story of how regulatory structures can protect a commercially funded channel not only from inevitable peak-time scheduling pressure but also from an inevitable ratings pressure on the nature and length of story selection. While the most recent research data are now over six years old, anecdotal evidence (including some of the detail provided by Richard Tait in the fillowing chapter) suggests that nothing has changed: if anything the volume of tabloid news recorded in 2009 has receded to earlier levels. That kind of editorial consistency would be highly unlikely to survive Channel 4's privatisation as new commercial owners looked for areas to maximise revenue. As the channel's outgoing chairman Lord Burns told the House of Lords select committee during his exit interview in 2016: 'The more value you want to extract from it, the more you have to compromise its public service obligations.'

While the bulletin's ratings have held up very well against audience fragmentation – running at around 650,000, or two thirds of its 1980s average while BBC and ITV audiences have more than halved – those figures could not survive scrutiny by shareholders seeking to maximise their return. A regulator might succeed – at least in the short term – in holding new owners to the timing and length of *Channel 4 News*, but it could not possibly dictate the editorial output nor instruct it to pursue awkward investigations which hold governments and corporations to account. As David Abraham, Channel 4's current chief executive with a long history of running commercial TV operations, told a meeting in Parliament to discuss the channel's future in March 2016: 'When you're running commercially funded channels, there are places you do not go.'

Channel 4 remains an international anomaly: a free-standing public body, funded entirely from advertising, and committed to editorial priorities in journalism that it has championed since 1982. It is difficult to envisage any restructuring beyond its current publicly owned, protected status which would sustain a journalistic legacy that has survived and thrived for nearly 35 years.

About the author

Steven Barnett is Professor of Communications at the University of Westminster and an established writer, author and commentator who specialises in media policy, broadcasting, regulation, and journalism ethics. He has acted several times as specialist adviser to the House of Lords select committee on communications, and over the last 30 years has directed numerous research projects on the structure, funding, and regulation of communications. He is on the management and editorial boards of the *British Journalism Review*, has authored a number of books, and writes frequently for the national and specialist press. He is author of *The Rise and Fall of Television Journalism*, published by Bloomsbury Academic in 2011, and co-edited *Media Power and Plurality*, published by Palgrave Macmillan in 2015.

References

Barnett, Steven, Gordon Ramsay and Ivor Gaber, *From Callaghan to Credit Credit Crunch: Changing Trends in British Television News 1975-2009*, London: University of Westminster.

Online access: http://westminsterresearch.wmin.ac.uk/15450/1/From-Callaghan-To-Credit-Crunch-Final-Report.pdf

Brown, Maggie (2007), *A Licence to Be Different: The Story of Channel 4*, London: British Film Institute.

House of Lords Select Committee on Communications (2008), *The Ownership of the News, Volume 2: Evidence*, HL Paper 122-II, London: The Stationery Office

Isaacs, Jeremy (1989), *Storm Over 4: A Personal Account*, London: Weidenfeld and Nicolson.

Lindley, Richard (2005), *And Finally.....? The News From ITN*, London: Politico

Ofcom (2009), *Second Public Service Broadcasting Review: Putting Viewers First*, London: Ofcom.

Notes

[1] 1990 Broadcasting Act, s. 25(1). The 2003 Communications Act updated this to demonstrating 'innovation, experiment and creativity in the form and content of programmes', appealing to 'the tastes and interests of a culturally diverse society' and exhibiting 'a distinctive character.'

[2] A full explanation of the methodology employed is contained in the report, but the sampling process ensured an even spread of days and years over the measurement period. Each story was classified into one of 31 story categories, and then consolidated into broad categories of broadsheet, tabloid and foreign. There was also a more finely tuned analysis which grouped categories into five headings.

One false move and the puppy gets it

By Richard Tait

Concern for the future of Channel 4 News has helped the channel dodge the bullet of privatisation before. But will it do so this time?

For the last quarter of a century, Britain's broadcasters have been masters of a political stratagem known in the trade as 'one false move and the puppy/kid gets it'. Like villains of the B-movie Westerns, brandishing their pistols and threatening to use them on a defenceless hostage (whether canine or human) if they don't get their way, the bosses of UK television have been skilled at identifying the programmes which really matter to politicians and regulators and warning of terrible consequences for them unless they get the concessions they want.

For years, ITV argued successfully that it needed to be allowed to merge into a single company and simultaneously cut back, progressively, its public service obligations as the price for maintaining some part of its commitment to network and, particularly, regional news (Tait, 2006). In the 2015 licence fee negotiations, the BBC threatened to dispatch a whole kennel of puppies – closing BBC2, BBC 4, local radio stations and radio news in the nations – if it was not given some mitigations to help offset the cost of free licences for the over 75s. They were cuts which would have outraged a number of very influential sections of the public and caused maximum embarrassment to the government on or just after Budget Day. Although initially the Treasury thought the BBC was bluffing – it had, after all, absorbed a big budget hit at the time of the 2010 licence fee negotiation – the threat worked and the government gave ground (Snoddy, 2015).

Channel 4 has always known which part of its remit most appeals to the politicians and regulators. Once it recovered from its initial catastrophic launch (Lindley, 2005, p260-272), *Channel 4 News* has been the one programme in the schedule guaranteed to have an appreciative audience at the regulator – first the Independent Television Commission (ITC) and now Ofcom – and at Westminster. One senior ITC figure once told me that the only Channel 4 schedule changes the regulator would probably not countenance would be to cut

Channel 4 News to half an hour and/or to shift its start time from 7pm; Denis Thatcher, denouncing the broadcast media as far too left-wing over a glass or two at a Conservative conference event, once spotted the *Channel 4 News team* and pronounced: 'now YOU are communists – but you're very good'.

It could be argued that *Channel 4 News* is not, actually, a typical Channel 4 programme. Whereas much of the channel is about change, its news has been about continuity: the programme has been produced since the launch date not by a series of hipster indies but by Independent Television News (ITN), one of the last survivors of the golden age of ITV; it has had, over a quarter of a century, just two commissioning editors at Channel 4 (first David Lloyd, one of the editors of this book, and now Dorothy Byrne); its main presenter over the same period has been the brilliant Jon Snow who has now overtaken even Jeremy Paxman in terms of longevity as a news anchor.

But even the most sceptical regulator or politician could see (or be persuaded) that *Channel 4 News* was uniquely vulnerable to any significant change in Channel 4's ownership or structure. The programme's audience and revenue has never justified its budget or its slot. Channel 4's director of programmes, Tim Gardam, was reflecting the received wisdom at Channel 4's Horseferry Road headquarters when he wrote in an internal strategy document in 2000 that running nearly an hour of news at 7pm meant the slot lost the channel money; the programme's revenues covered only half its costs; the news got far fewer viewers than more popular programming would have. However, he continued, changing it (or cutting it down to a half hour) would be a reputational disaster, and not least because Jon Snow was the face of the channel (Brown, 2007 p223).

Saving the nice man in the stripy tie

The sense that, as one Channel 4 senior executive once said to me, with one false move the nice man in the stripy tie would be no more, was a recurring theme in the struggles over privatisation. The 1988 White Paper, *Broadcasting in the 90s*, proposed a number of possible new structures for Channel 4. The first option on the list was privatisation (Goodwin, 1998). In the battle with the Thatcher government that followed, Michael Grade, the new Channel 4 chief executive, saw off privatisation with the clear warning: 'The choice facing the government was simple. They could have a privatised channel or one with a public service remit, but not both. No amount of regulation would preserve public service broadcasting intact in the face of an economic downturn, lower revenues and a load of unhappy shareholders' (Grade, 1999). He persuaded first the Home Affairs Committee and then the government that Channel 4 should sell its own airtime but not have shareholders. The privatisation option went away (Bonner and Aston, 2003).

When privatisation was again on the agenda near the end of the Major government in 1996, similar arguments were deployed. Michael Grade had a meeting with the Financial Secretary to the Treasury, Michael Jack, and told him that the easiest way for a privatised Channel 4 to boost profits by £12 million would be to remove *Channel 4 News* ands replace it with American films. Combined with the skilful political lobbying of the chairman, Sir Michael Bishop, a prominent Conservative supporter but a resolute opponent of this particular privatisation, the idea went away, and as a bonus the campaign got Labour to commit itself not to privatise Channel 4 in the future (Brown, *op cit* p200-201).

Now, twenty years on, the first Conservative majority government since then is once again considering the privatisation of Channel 4 and again the role of *Channel 4 News* is at the centre of the debate. Lord Burns, Channel 4's outgoing chairman, made the point in one of his first public comments on the prospect of privatisation: 'It is no secret that as an economic proposition *Channel 4 News* doesn't really do terribly well. You can see this by the absence of adverts in the breaks. I struggle to see any alternative ownership that would be able to put on an hour-long news programme at that point in the day and of the quality it is.' (Jackson, 2015).

His chief executive David Abraham took the same view, arguing that news and current affairs would be the first genres to suffer under a new commercial owner: 'Would we do as much news and current affairs in primetime? No, we would find ways of shaving that. Promises can be made by a buyer in the short term. What you would do is try and minimise the number of *Dispatches* drastically, [then] try and see what you could do to cut the news hour down or shunt it out of that [primetime] slot.' (Sweney, 2015a).

So will the case for the defence work this time as it did so successfully in the past? *Channel 4 News* is still a very good programme, but operating in a more crowded market place. Many of the techniques it pioneered have been successfully copied by its competitors – the main bulletins on ITV and BBC1 at 10, for example, are full of expert analysis, live interviews with correspondents and high production values in graphics and video editing. And the broadcast news universe has expanded way beyond the bulletins of the public service broadcasters – there is a plethora of British and international news channels providing 24 hour coverage and a wide range of perspectives.

Above all, perhaps, the new digital players like *Buzzfeed* and *Vice News* and the new platforms – such as Facebook and Twitter – are redefining what video news can be and how it is consumed, particularly by younger audiences. *Channel 4 News* now has a pretty good presence on social media but like the rest of British commercial broadcasting has been running hard to catch up after wasting much of its first mover advantage. In this apparent glut of news, does a single weekday bulletin of 50 minutes still really matter? I think it does, both in terms of what the programme brings to British journalism and in its role in the complex and quite fragile network of programmes and relationships which currently make British broadcast news respected worldwide.

Investigative emphasis
First, the programme itself remains unique – 50 minutes of high quality news reporting and analysis, with a welcome emphasis on investigations. As the recent

disasters at *Newsnight* have shown, doing investigative journalism in the context of a daily programme is very difficult and potentially risky (Tait 2014, p15). *Channel 4 News* has always had the budget and the encouragement from Channel 4 to do it successfully – from Bob Parker's series on Colin Wallace and MI5 in the 1980s to its most recent award for an investigation into people smuggling in Macedonia. It is not at all clear if *Channel 4 News* were to disappear in its present form that other programmes would fill the gap – BBC News was recently criticised for not even having an investigations unit despite employing 4,000 journalists (Jones, 2016). The nearest equivalent, BBC 2's *Newsnight*, has still not fully recovered from the horrors of Savile and MacAlpine and is facing potentially terminal competition in house from the newly extended BBC1 *10 O'Clock News* (Pauley, 2016).

Having 50 minutes of space to fill encourages the programme to widen the news agenda to under-reported but important stories – from war crimes in Sri Lanka to human rights abuses and oil in Equatorial Guinea. In broadcast news the proliferation of platforms does not necessarily mean a wider agenda – indeed, more and more news seems to focus on a limited number of stories. News editors keep a very close eye on what their competitors do – and the existence of a programme which often goes beyond the obvious agenda and comes back with great journalism helps encourage every newsroom to do the same.

Channel 4 News also has a role in helping maintain the complex structure which has protected quality in British television news over the last thirty years. The £25 million *Channel 4 News* contract is vitally important to the continued health of my old employer ITN, a unique company providing bespoke news programmes to three competing commercial public service broadcasters: ITV, Channel 4 and Channel 5. It represents more than a quarter of the company's £80 million a year revenue from news production. The loss or diminution of the Channel 4 contract, whether because a new owner wanted a different news supplier (or already had a news service of its own) or was free to dispense with the current programme and its comparatively generous budget, would be a serious financial blow to a company which in 2014 reported an after tax profit of £4.2 million on revenues of £112million.

Whereas once the value of the ITV contract was five or six times the size of the Channel 4 contract, now the ratio is about two to one. ITN is a well-run company and has survived enough near-death experiences in its 60 year history for no one to underestimate its resilience and powers of survival, but the loss or diminution of its Channel 4 business would not only be a financial blow. It would undermine the complex network of relationships between the services for different broadcasters – pooling core coverage, sharing overheads – which have enabled ITN, despite Channel 4 and ITV from time to time inviting competing proposals from Sky News, to see off attempts to take over its two key contracts.

And it would be an unwelcome element of instability at a time when the long-term future of broadcast news in the UK looks under serious pressure. So far all the speculation over a US company bidding for ITV has proved to be hot air

(Williams, 2015) but it is not inconceivable that ITV and a newly-privatised Channel 4 could follow Channel 5 into US ownership with unknowable consequences for ITN. The BBC is facing another round of substantial cuts in its news operations with the future of its news channels and 5 Live service under review (Conlan and Sweney, 2016). Sky News is in good shape but has always been Rupert Murdoch's personal project. The success of British television news has come from having three strong organisations – the BBC funded by the licence fee, ITN funded by its customers' advertising revenues and Sky News funded by subscription. All three organisations face some big challenges over the next few years – destabilising *Channel 4 News* would make an already shaky situation even worse.

Focus on the regulators

If the privatisation does go ahead, the focus will be on whether regulation can preserve all or part of the remit. Michael Grade has argued that any new owner would want to 'preserve the brand and work out what the brand was about. My supposition would be that *Channel 4 News* is a big piece of what makes Channel 4 different. These things are controlled by licences, you are licensed to broadcast and we have a very strict regulator.' (Sweney, 2016b). Elsewhere in this book David Elstein (see Chapter 2) takes a similar view, believing that Ofcom could ensure that the current commitment to news and current affairs could be maintained if it adopted a tough and rigorous approach to quality control and measuring the Channel's output against clear criteria.

They are of course, right in theory: good regulation should protect quality journalism. But in practice, as David Elstein himself points out, the track record of the commercial television regulators, first the ITC and later Ofcom, has been a patchy one. While Channel 4's remit remains virtually unchanged, there has been a fairly drastic reduction in ITV's public service obligations in areas such as education, arts and children's programmes (Fitzwalter, 2008 p252). The regulators may have tried harder to protect ITV's news heritage but they have not been particularly successful.

The ITV companies, when bidding for their 1992 licences, promised they would spend on average £60m a year on the network news (*ibid* p318). By 2002, they had cut that budget to £35.5m – halving it in a decade in real terms (*ibid* p237). In 1992 many of the companies promised to keep the *News at Ten* in their new schedules. Halfway through the first year of their new licences in 1993 they announced they had changed their minds and were going to move the prime time news from 10pm. It is hard to find anyone who thinks the decade-long fiasco over the scheduling of *News at Ten* which ensued was anything other than a terrible mess which the regulator was unable to resolve (Lindley *op cit* p326-349).

The regulators also wanted to protect regional news on ITV since their own research suggested it was the most unaffordable of ITV's public service broadcasting obligations. They allowed ITV to cut back its other regional programming and reduce its licence payments to try to encourage ITV to meet its regional news commitments (Tait, 2006 p30-31) But in less than a decade, ITV's position as the dominant player in regional television news in the UK had disappeared – its audience share had halved (Newspaper Society, 2005) and for the first time in its history, it was being outspent by the BBC (Ofcom, 2004a p57-62))

Patricia Hodgson, the shrewd last chief executive of the ITC (and now the chair of Ofcom), who did her best to sort out the *News at Ten* debacle, told the Royal Television Society's Cambridge Convention in 2001 that the moral of the story was not to over-estimate what any regulator could do when faced with a determined commercial management. Ironically the past ten years have demonstrated this in a positive way – if the ITV News is now back at 10pm with an increased budget and if ITV's regional news has survived and is now thriving, it is less because of regulation and more because ITV's bosses over the last decade or so – Michael Grade and then Adam Crozier – have taken a different and more positive view of the importance of news.

The main lesson to be drawn from this story is, as Patricia Hodgson explained, that broadcast regulation is always in part a negotiation (Lindley, *op cit* p347-8). The current Channel 4 licence only commits the channel to 208 hours of news somewhere in peak viewing in a year: no indicative budget; no statement of resources, bureaux, crews, specialist correspondents; no definition of quality in terms of approach and editorial remit beyond the channel's general remit. It would be very easy, for example, for a new owner to turn the current programme into a low-cost interview show with perhaps just a headline news service and claim it was still producing news analysis.

A new role for Ofcom?

This is not to say that much tighter regulation could not protect the programme, at least in the medium term. It would need a very different approach from Ofcom's current light touch. But Ofcom is likely to take over the regulation of the BBC in 2017 (Clementi, 2016) and that will need an equally radical change of approach on its part. Ofcom could add a much tighter regulation of Channel 4 to its enhanced BBC responsibilities and become much more involved in the quality of the output of both broadcasters. Protecting *Channel 4 News* would need a very much clearer definition of what the programme was and how it would be delivered in terms of scheduling, resources, budgets and staff, but it could be done and would probably be easier to police than many other genres. The key would be to get acceptance from any new owner of Channel 4 that it was committed both to the cost of producing the service and to accepting the opportunity costs of having a loss-making slot of an hour in peak time each weekday. And the regulator would have to hope the new owners do not start complaining about the lack of similar rigour in the regulation of, say, ITV and Channel 5.

However well Ofcom policed the arrangements, history suggests that privatisation would put the incoming owners, not the regulators, in the driving seat. If they like the nice man in the stripy tie and see *Channel 4 News* as a key part of the brand of their new acquisition, all could be well. If not, it would be the first and most important test of Ofcom's determination to hold the line and protect the channel's single most important programme.

About the author

Richard Tait is Professor of Journalism at the School of Journalism, Media and Cultural Studies, Cardiff. From 2003 to 2012 he was Director of the School's Centre for Journalism. He was editor of *Newsnight* from 1985 to 1987, editor of *Channel 4 News* from 1987 to 1995 and editor-in-chief of ITN from 1995 to 2002. He was a BBC Governor and chair of the Governors' Programme Complaints Committee from 2004 to 2006, and a BBC Trustee and chair of the Trust's Editorial Standards Committee from 2006 to 2010. He is a fellow of the Society of Editors and the Royal Television Society and Treasurer of the International News Safety Institute.

References

Bonner, Paul and Aston, Lesley (2003) *Independent Television in Britain, Vol 6*, p242-4. Basingstoke: Palgrave Macmillan

Brown, Maggie (2007) *A Licence to be Different: The Story of Channel 4*, London: BFI

Clementi, David (2016) *A Review of the Governance and Regulation of the BBC*. Available online at https://www.gov.uk/government/publications/a-review-of-the-governance-and-regulation-of-the-bbc, accessed 7 March 2016

Conlan, Tara and Sweney, Mark (2016), 'BBC Radio 5 Live could go online-only in radical cost cuts' *The Guardian*, 24 February. Available online at http://www.theguardian.com/media/2016/feb/24/bbc-radio-5-live-online-only-bbc3, accessed 6 March 2016

Fitzwalter, Ray (2008) *The Dream That Died: The Rise and Fall of ITV*. Leicester: Matador

Goodwin, Peter (1998) *Television under the Tories: Broadcasting Policy 1979-1997*, p98-104. London: BFI,

Grade, Michael (1999) *It seemed Like a Good Idea at the Time*, p308 London: Macmillan

Independent Television News (2015), *ITN Annual Report 2014*, London: ITN. Available online at http://www.itn.co.uk/wp-content/uploads/2015/06/1430410475-itn_annual_report_-_2014_ipages.pdf

accessed on 7 March 2016

Jackson, Jasper (2015) Channel 4 News in current form 'unlikely to survive privatisation' *The Guardian*, 1 December. Available online at http://www.theguardian.com/media/2015/dec/01/channel-4-news-unlikely-survive-privaisation-chair-terry-burns accessed on 6 March 2016

Jones, Meirion (2016) The BBC Savile and Investigations *Open Democracy* 22 January. Available online at https://www.opendemocracy.net/ourbeeb/meirion-jones/bbc-savile-and-investigations,

accessed on 3 March 2016

Lindley, Richard (2005) *And Finally…? The News from ITN*, London: Politico's

Newspaper Society (2005) *Review of the BBC's Charter: Newspaper Society Submission*, London: Newspaper Society

Ofcom (2004a) *The Communications Market – Television*, London: Ofcom

Ofcom (2004b) *Channel 4 Licence*. Available online at

http://licensing.ofcom.org.uk/binaries/tv/c4/c4drl.pdf, accessed on 3 March 2016

Pauley, Nigel BBC Bosses at war over changes to 10 pm news show which could kill Newsnight, *Mirror* 9 January 2016 http://www.mirror.co.uk/tv/tv-news/bbc-bosses-war-over-changes-7148731 accessed on 23 March 2016

Snoddy, Raymond (2015) How BBC Warnings of Financial Meltdown brought Government to Negotiating Table, in *The BBC Today: Future Uncertain*, Mair, John , Tait, Richard, Keeble, Richard (eds) Abramis: Bury St Edmunds, pp 19-27

Sweney, Mark (2015a) Channel 4 sale would jeopardise news output, says chief executive, *The Guardian*. Available online at

http://www.theguardian.com/media/2015/nov/16/channel-4-sale-jeopardise-news-output-chief-executive-david-abraham, accessed on 2 March 2016

Sweney, Mark (2015b) Michael Grade: Channel 4 sell-off would create media powerhouse *The Guardian* 7 December 2015
http://www.theguardian.com/media/2015/dec/07/michael-grade-channel-4-sell-off-would-create-media-powerhouse accessed on 1 March 2016

Tait, Richard (2006) What future for regional television news, in Franklin, Bob (ed) *Local Journalism and Local Media; making the local news*, Abingdon: Routledge pp 27-36

Tait, Richard (2014) History repeating itself? Hutton, Savile and the future of the BBC, Mair, John, Tait, Richard and Keeble, Richard *Is the BBC in Crisis?* Bury St Edmunds: Abramis pp 12-26

Williams, Christopher (2015) ITV investors disappointed as Comcast denies bid claim, *The Telegraph*, 22 December 2015. Available online at

http://www.telegraph.co.uk/finance/newsbysector/mediatechnologyandtelecoms/media/12064149/ITV-investors-disappointed-as-Comcast-denies-bid-claim.html, accessed on 3 March 2016

Goggledocs

By Molly Dineen, Roger Graef, Sue Bourne, Kim Longinotto and David Pearson

The format of Channel 4's most-watched current factual programme is simple: we watch viewers watching television from the previous week. For this special edition John Mair asked five very distinguished British television documentary-makers to watch the factual output of the channel for the first week of February 2016 and keep notes

Tuesday, 2 February, 8pm: *The Secret Life Of The Zoo*
The channel bills this as: 'An observational documentary series capturing, in incredible detail, the remarkable behaviour of the animals at Chester Zoo, and their relationships with their keepers. Grumpy elephant Thi is expecting a baby. The chimps battle for dominance. Red panda Nima gives her partner Jung the cold shoulder. And the meerkats prove they're not as loveable as they first seem.'

In Holloway, London, Kim Longinotto, distinguished maker of social documentaries including Dreamcatcher and Hold Me Tight, Let Me Go, is positive.

Kim: This is entertaining and fun. The keepers are interesting.

In Stroud Gloucestershire, David Pearson, who directed Channel 4's first documentary series The Sixties back in 1982 and has gone on to make much more since including Baglady and Mugabe and the White African is less upbeat.

David: Cheesy opening – Blue Peter-esque. Is this aimed at 5-year-olds?
  … 3 mins in there is nothing secret about this. It is just anthropomorphizing animals. Yuk.

In Dorset, Roger Graef OBE, fifty years a TV film-maker whose work includes The Police and The Secret Policeman's Ball, is also watching.

Roger: Best when straight and factual. But full of judgements like calling the meerkats 'The dirt of the zoo world'… We jump into labour after eight hours. But amazing to watch. Hope they won't interrupt such an amazing sight. Far and away best scene, including the family stuff.

The series claims to use fixed rig filming – a Channel 4 speciality – to get to the secret life of the institution. Do they succeed?

David: Finally something 'secret' – the elephant at night. Could have been at 2 mins in.

Roger: The trouble with chimps had potential but we are told what to think all the time.

David: Ah! something I haven't seen before. Steve the vet gets crapped on by a chimp. Right. So why do chimps dislike vets so much? What is the secret behind that? We won't find out.

Roger: At last, the vet scene is real but again interrupted by interviews. The otter stuff is good, but again we are told what is going on before we watch them interacting. No trust of viewers.

So, in general what did our documentary Goggleboxers make of the Zoo programme and series?

Kim: A very enjoyable programme.

Roger: Nice about porcupines and meerkats Good pics. But a slightly annoying anthropomorphic tone by everyone, not just commentary. I liked the concept, and casting was good, but not very secret apart from elephant giving birth.

David: I found it very patronising, infantile and cloying. Come back Molly Dineen's *The Ark*, or the best Attenborough series! Described as 'observational' but not much true observation here, rather loads of interviews that dish up what we already know from better programmes. It would have lost me as a viewer after 5 mins.

I'm struck by how the form of Channel 4 docs as well as the content itself has become so much more narrow in the past 10 years. Where's the risk taking, pushing of boundaries, and sense of adventure?

A lot of factual TV, not just on C4, takes the tone of yesteryear's children's TV, treating the audience as dumb, when it isn't. Nor is it taken in, as is so clear from the reactions to TV of the characters in the excellent *Gogglebox* series.

Tuesday 2 Feb, 11pm: *First Dates*
This is simply reality or, better titled 'Embarrassment TV'. People sent on a first date with a complete stranger in a rigged restaurant under the watchful eye of a Maître D.

Just one film-maker, Sue Bourne in South West Scotland, plucks up the courage to watch it and squirm … at least initially.

Sue: First up are Lauren, 29 and Danny, 38. I feel myself preparing to be bored but you do sort of get sucked in, cringing when they say something stupid or sniggering when you see an adverse reaction. You sit there passing judgement on everyone that passes in front of you so reckon that must be part of the programme's appeal – saying how nice/not nice people are.

She finds herself slowly but surely drawn into the created narrative of the format.

Sue: Back with Danny and Lauren I am having to reappraise him. He lives with his nan 'cos it seems half his family got cancer so he stepped into the breach to be a good son and help out his sick mum. Would never have guessed he'd have that sort of back story… its funny that even though it's not my cup of tea the programme flies by at a good old lick and my attention is not really waning.

The result of this liaison not what the programme makers or Danny wanted.

Sue: Lauren says Danny would be good for her best friend but not for her. Think he is a bit gutted because I think he thought he had made a hit … but he hides it well. They say goodbye at the taxi. This turns out to be a critical turning point in all the different stories – whether they do/ do not share the cab.

Overall Sue ends up not unimpressed with the programme and format

Sue: Part Three – by now am into it. There are no pretensions as to what this programme is about, and it does what it set out to do. The hour spins by quickly and engagingly. Not my cup of tea but can definitely see the attraction. We need programmes of all sorts so this is definitely one of a type. A very successful type of entertainment, using real people who are willing to go along with it.

Wednesday, 3 Feb, 9pm: *24 hours in A & E*
This is the flagship modern Channel Four fixed-rig doc. The billing says 'Forever Young. Cameras film around the clock in some of Britain's busiest A&E departments. An 81-year-old cyclist is brought into A and E after being hit by a car.' It is part of the genre invented by C4 production companies – fixed rigged filming in which locations are turned into studios with (usually hidden) cameras everywhere.

In Scotland Sue Bourne, maker of Fabulous Fashionistas for C4, is a fan before it starts.

Sue: Great format incredibly well executed and sure-footed. There was always something wonderfully life enhancing, gentle and positive about it when I last saw it so hope it has remained the same. Great opening sequence – laid its wares on the table – about the unpredictability of life, about the fact any of us could be in A&E any day…

In Dorset, Roger Graef comes from an era well before fixed rig filming was invented.

Roger: Charming start of two young people waiting to be seen fancying nurses. Observed, overheard. Best use of rig.

Sue: 81-year-old Bill – on his bike and run down. Not in good shape. Lovely gentle humour as we then hear from Betty, his wife. It's about love.

Roger: Better storytelling than *Secret Zoo*, but still too much redundant commentary. e.g. 'Bill's wife was in hospital and told about accident by her son'. Cut to Bill's wife saying 'I was told by my son.' … Everyone tells us their life story, relevant or not. The doctor tells his love of his mother just when we want to know what happens to Bill.

Sue: What *24 Hours* does so well is tell people's stories: their back stories, their love stories, their lives… it's a delight. The episode is called *Forever Young* and the film does indeed become a lovely portrait of the different ways people deal with being old … with gentle humour and stoicism.

In West London Molly Dineen, the doyenne of British documentary-making with films like The Ark and Home from the Hill on her stellar CV, is pondering the rig.

Molly: The rig is an interesting evolution in our documenting of real life. There's no doubt it's gripping. We all slow down on the motorways to watch the remnants of the crash, so with ambulances dashing about, thriller suspense music and a voice over telling us an old man who's been knocked down is going to A and E and WE RE GOING TO GET TO SEE HIM SUFFER. YAHOO!!

It's a no brainer it's so watchable. It's behind the curtain, it's seeing glimpses into people's bodies, wounds and life, and is totally mesmerising. On-going soaps with real life turned into the stage set.

Roger: The physics of story-telling are carried by the interviews, and helped by warm casting.

In Scotland Sue has had her hopes met. But Molly remains a sceptic.

Sue: I really enjoyed this episode. This is rig programming at its best. Beautifully executed. Gentle and humorous. Not exploiting people or their situations but looking for the humanity in it all. Lovely!

Molly: It made me LOVE the medical profession. My god they are magnificent and that's a HUGE plus of the series, but after 'injured old person number 3' though, I began to feel this was more voyeruism disguised as documentary. Who knows?

Wednesday, 3 February, 11.10pm: *The Undateables: Wedding Bells*
Channel 4 re-inventing its remit? After the Paralympic Channel, the 'Channel for social outcasts'? Last of series. People featured on this show are making plans to get married.

Kim: I always find introductory trailers very annoying. This one has spoilers and it tells you what you are about to watch. It doesn't seem at all necessary as the film is very accessible anyway.

In Stroud , David Pearson is viewing this with an open mind.

David*:* Commendably gives rarely-heard voices a hearing – but the risk is of sensationalising the vulnerable. Will this avoid patronising the subjects and the audience?

In Dumfries Scotland, Sue is less sure of the ethics of this type of film.

Sue: I know Channel 4 say they are doing a huge public service by making these films, showing people the human face of disability in the same way they claimed that *Benefits Street* was about showing the rest of the country what life on the dole was really like. I am just not sure I buy that line. I really object to being invited to either dislike / hate / condemn other people without being offered insight or greater understanding of them and their situation. The opening sequence was designed to shock. Matthew has a terrible debilitating stammer, but the opening sequence shows him taking his kit off to pose for a women's hen night drawing class. My hackles were already up a bit. Were the production company taking advantage of Matthew's naivety by persuading him that being filmed naked in front of a group of women was a good thing? Not sure that anyone without learning difficulties would have agreed so eagerly.

Kim: There were a couple of good conversations that made me smile: "What will the future bring?" "We might go to Eastbourne..." The scene of Matthew's art class was great. The women going red and joking about doctor's appointments.

David: Daniel saying 'We might go to Eastbourne' made me laugh. Such simple and charming pleasures.

Sue: This really is a film about the fact that people with learning difficulties are capable of love... of finding it ... of giving it and of receiving it. It's a wonderful thing to witness.

But the great and good of the British film-makers believe there is too much talking in all the films.

David: Like most docs today there is relentless commentary which still leaves obvious questions unanswered.

Kim: Some of the commentary was ok but it becomes intrusive at times when it tells the audience what the people we are watching are feeling ('Matthew is feeling nervous'). At times it's silly ('It's important not to be deterred by heart-ache').

David: How I dislike pointless spoon-feeding commentary that treats the audience as stupid. "While Mathew sums up courage to propose, Jessica has a surprise of her own." You think we couldn't work that out? Then the commentary goes and does that again!

The Undateables pulls at the heartstrings, especially at series end.
Sue: Stammering Matthew is practising asking his girlfriend to marry him. Then the cameras follow him to the Thames where he gets down on one knee and pops the question. On camera. In front of lots of smiling clapping people. Again, I feel uncomfortable. It all feels orchestrated for the sake of the camera. I am not sure that is right... Whose interests were at the fore-front? The production company's or Matthew and his girlfriend's?

Kim: The programme was sensitively filmed and fun to watch. Matthew's proposal on the bridge was lovely.

And what else to end the film with but an Undateable who has found a partner for life? We drop in on their wedding.

Sue: Steve's wedding. What is really really moving is discovering that Steve had three brothers all with the same disease... all of them now dead. His mother has the disease too. She is still alive and still happily married to her husband, Steve's dad. The amount of suffering that family must have gone through is impossible to imagine. But we are getting jolly music and not much time for thought or reflection.

Even hard-nosed David is now hooked on Steve's story

David:*(On Steve's parents talking about how to handle the wedding day).* Moving. Foregrounding the great dignity and wisdom of everyday people is one of the wonderful benefits of having documentaries. Although I did wonder how they felt about the possibility of having grandchildren who might share the same fate as Steve's brothers.

So, in general from the comfort of their sofas, what did our jury make of the Undateables? Opinion was, shall we say, divided.

Kim: I found this programme very charming and, at times, quite moving. Daniel and Matthew were both engaging people and they spoke openly to the camera. I felt that the filmmakers had a really good relationship with the characters.

Sue: Viewing figures are not the most important thing. I love films that make us better understand and empathise with people with learning difficulties. I just question whether this style of programme making – with its jaunty music and simplistic approach – really is the best we can do.

David: Impossible not to be moved by these characters, their hopes and aspirations and their determination to search for love and happiness, despite the makers sometimes unnecessarily obvious or needless commentary, and a sense of some heavy handed manipulation of the audience's sympathy.

Sue: Given that the title of the series is *Undateables,* I now rather fear the whole thing is about a dating agency for people with learning difficulties. Agree this would be a truly great initiative to help people with learning difficulties find a partner and happiness. Just not so sure I agree with it being turned into a programme to entertain people. Sounds a rather dangerous thing to be doing for my money.

David: It's striking that so many documentaries on C4, as well as other channels, adopt such similar forms, whatever the subject, and that the sense of being able to make things in different forms has largely disappeared or been pushed to the very outer margins. It's partly a function of declining budgets and the rise of formats, I suppose, and fewer documentary auteurs being given prominent slots. And a lack of courage.

Thursday, 4 February, 9pm: *Keeping up with the Khans*
This was Channel Four's big factual offering of the week: *Keeping Up with the Khans* explores the lives and aspirations of new migrants to Britain, and the impact that immigration has on one community: Page Hall in Sheffield was once home to a predominantly white working-class community. This series explores the impact of immigration on Page Hall, and meets the people coming here to make a new life. Haider, Ehab, Pride and Omar are fleeing wars and trying to start new lives in Britain. They live together in a house rented by the Home Office, but can't work or study unless they are granted asylum'.

Our film-makers sitting on their living room sofas in Stroud, Dorset and Dumfries were confused from the start .

David: Weird title for this.

Roger: What is the title for? Not at all what the film is about. Very jolly, if frantic, opening

Sue: The opening montage went on forever. There were so many things happening it was rather head spinning. Did not bode well… you felt the kitchen sink was being thrown at this to keep it as high octane as possible.

Kim: The programme is good straightaway – but the intro feels a bit long. I like the tone of this film: it's not sneering or patronising and it promises stories with characters.

Sue: My heart sank at an early scene – a man from Lebanon showing where his country was on map – then when asked where the UK was he did not have a clue – pointing over to USA and Canada. It rather felt like we were being invited to despise him for his ignorance… made us feel uneasy. Immediately you could sense a *Benefits Street* approach was the order of the day here.

Good films are all about characters and soon enter a big one: Steve the Landlord

Roger: Steve is a good character - because he's more sympathetic than you expect.

Sue: Steve – great character. He could prove to be one of the stars of the show. Very funny and good observations born of experience rather than blind prejudice. He is a landlord and lots of immigrant/ asylum seeker tenants. Dealt with it with humour and wit.

David: The landlord may disapprove of the refugees but is still happy to take the Home Office money for the rent.

And another character: Julie, a Muslim convert returned home to the UK, who then finds foreign bugs in her bed.

Roger: Foreign bugs, great scene. 'Bombing the house not like bombing in Gaza'. Charming. Pakistani lady wants to stay despite bugs foreigners and riots. But asylum seekers want to go back, interestingly.

David: Mercifully it's free of the idiotic commentary in so many other C4 docs.

Molly: Really interesting subject matter, important subject matter in fact, trying to put a human face to what has predominantly been a news issue, that of immigration and asylum seekers. What an incredible character Omar was and how very moving Steve's conclusion at the end of the film when he turns to us and says 'Wouldn't you do the same?' Brilliant stuff. BUT – and it's a massive BUT – how tragic that these fantastic insights and views into people's lives should be compressed into this format that is now so common in factual entertainment.

All the tricks of their film-making trade are there, like the older asylum seeker Haider acting as a tourist guide for the newbie Omar.

David: I Liked Haider showing Omar 'his' city. Nice scene of Omar's reactions and fantasy to UK. He sees a nice life, with his selfies. Sheffield's fine buildings and fountains are admired and appreciated by the migrants in a way I doubt that many locals do.

Kim: I'm now engaged with the Home Office story and hearing how long it takes for them to get an answer about their asylum.

David: Why does it take the authorities so many years to process these claims? Meantime these people, who want to work, are a cost to the state and give the locals the impression that they won't contribute. Stupid system.

Roger: Story starts to evolve but repetitious theme of better life, and sceptical white neighbours. Love it that Omar wants to move if he gets visa to a city 'that is 80% English'. Steve suggests Benidorm. Great!

Sue: Omar and Steve proved to be a great double act. Omar may only have just arrived in the UK but his story was lovely. He got a visa, he became a UK citizen, he found a job, his work mates were welcoming, he was happy and you could see – you hoped – that he would make a go of it.

David: The simple things in docs can be the most powerful. Omar wants to make friends and a workmate invites him to join them.

Kim: All the scenes of Omar – on his date and at work –– are lovely and really make the film come to life. I want to stay with him and find out what happens next.

Roger: Nice Omar visa story. Overall sympathetic and rather revealing, especially Haider and those left in limbo. Good casting.

But in Scotland, Sue has lost the plot, and in London, Molly is losing patience.

Sue: My attention is starting to wander a bit now. I sense it really does not know what it is.

Molly: But the omnipresent music, telling us how to feel about every scene, the characters often intercut to a line at a time, the patronising voice-over that honestly reminded me of those Johnny Morris 1970s *Animal Magic* programmes where he would imagine what the chimp might be thinking made me sob with frustration.

Sue: *Keeping up with the Khans* was made by Love Productions, the same people who made *Benefits Street*. I think they were wanting to whip up a big audience any way they could rather than say something intelligent and thoughtful about the phenomenon they were purporting to be reporting on.

Molly: TV should be the vehicle, not create the format. If the woman filming Omar had been allowed to make a proper film about him, what a wonderful film she could probably have made.

David: Insightful and revealing series about migrants living in Page Hall in Sheffield. Good characters, with a revealing and timely account that chimes with the national concerns over migration – reflecting both the benefits and problems of migration. A shame that the British people who were set up as being 'against' the migrants are reduced to a series of soundbites and without more context that would have made it a richer mix, but still a good and relevant commission of the sort C4 used to do more of.

Molly: I'm not talking about long self-indulgent, obscure documentaries, I'm talking about giving individual film makers a voice, a viewpoint, to go out and find these stories and people from whom we could learn so much (and enjoy). Somewhere in the frenetic muddle of this programme was access of a brilliant sort to people in very difficult circumstances, and some wonderful material but they were drowned in this factual romp. Every single 'show' is the same. These are not documentaries made by individuals this is product and what's so sad is that this was precisely what Channel 4 was not supposed to be.

So, our *Goggleboxers* found that Channel 4's factual output a bit of a curate's egg; good in parts, amusing in others but too often formatted and formulaic. But, like *Gogglebox* itself, that seems to work for their audience. Remit anyone?

About our Goggleboxers

Sue Bourne has just finished *The Age of Loneliness* for BBC1 which was transmitted in January 2016 . She is now discussing a new film for BBC and also in development for a feature doc with funding from BFI and Creative Scotland. The last film she made for Channel 4 was *Fabulous Fashionistas* in 2013 which had an extraordinary international impact.

Molly Dineen is the doyenne of British documentary makers. She has been garlanded with awards from Bafta, the RTS, the Prix Europa. Among her best known films are *Home from the Hill* (1987), *Heart of the Angel* (1989), *The Ark* (1993) and *The Lie of the Land* (2007).

Roger Graef OBE is a filmmaker, writer and criminologist who has spent 50 years making documentaries for British and American television. He was a founding board member of Channel 4 in 1982. His oeuvre, mainly for the BBC, includes *Police* (1982) on The Thames Valley Police *The Secret Policeman's Ball* (1979) on an Amnesty international concert and more recently *Great Ormond Street*. He runs Films of Record and has been given a lifetime achievement award from the Sheffield Documentary festival and a BAFTA Fellowship.

Kim Longinotto's first film *Pride of Place* (1976) was a critical look at her boarding school. She has made many others since including *Divorce Iranian Style* about a Family Court in Tehran, *Love is all*, an archive film about love in 20th and 21st century UK films and *Dreamcatcher* in 2015 about young Chicago prostitutes.

David Pearson is an award-winning executive producer, series editor. producer and director with many years of experience at the BBC (including running and commissioning *Under The Sun* and directing *Baglady* 1992), he has also worked for ITV (*Fisherman's Friends* 2011), C4 (*The Sixties,* 1982) . He produced the Oscar-shortlisted and BAFTA-nominated 2010 cinema film *Mugabe and The White African* (2009), also shown on C4. He is lecturer in Screen Industries and Practice at Reading University.

Remit, schmemit

By Farrukh Dhondy

Multiculturalism was an essential part of the channel's unique formula. But has creatively diverse programming given way to simple headcount checks?

I didn't read it myself, but when Liz Forgan, controller of programmes at Channel 4 in the nineties left to be the BBC Radio Supremo (not the job title under which the post was advertised) she told an interviewer that being at Channel 4 was 'the best job in the world.' She went on to qualify her enthusiasm: 'Where else would you get a commissioning editor for religion who is an atheist, a commissioning editor for arts who doesn't believe in art and a commissioning editor for multicultural programming who is a racist?'

The quote may be apocryphal or distorted, but it points, in Liz's inimitable summarising style, to a positive truth about Channel 4's raison d'etre. It was born to defy, to swim against the current, to disbelieve. It was a purpose determined by parliament; a mission to bring to the small screen what other channels didn't and to represent the voice of 'minorities'.

The remit was formulated through the social and political experience of the 70s and early 80s. There were new if nebulous conglomerations whose lives, opinions and even presence seemed unrepresented and locked out of mainstream BBC and ITV. There was the feminist voice, the presence and lives of the gay community. There were the new communities of Britain who appeared on TV either as stereotyped outsiders or as rabble rousers with a mission to complain which TV occasionally patronised. There were potential converts to sports other than soccer and cricket. There was the need to integrate the disabled into the fabric of the premier socialising, entertaining and conversational medium of the country.

Of course the 'remit' was open to interpretation and Channel 4's first chief executive Jeremy Isaacs, and consequently the team he chose as 'commissioning editors', a job title he conceived and introduced into British TV, did precisely that. There were checks on this freedom of interpretation. The Tory government of Margaret Thatcher, with William Whitelaw as the moving force, set up the channel. They insisted, through the appointed board, that the channel take on a commissioning editor for Northern Ireland, a person through whom reports on the insurgency and 'Troubles' could be filtered. A trusted Conservative who had served the government was appointed to the post and given the added remit of being the editor for Ireland and chess! Perhaps the latter included all board and carpet games, though I can't recall a series devoted to tiddlywinks.

Liz's probably-apocryphal remark points to the freedom the commissioning editors had in the first decade-and-a-half of the channel's existence. It was to do something unexpected and yet representative. As the second commissioning editor to be appointed to the multicultural remit, a year after the channel was set up, I interpreted my job as venturing into the parts of the new communities that other programmes and channels had not reached. This entailed the recruitment of people to the manner rather than the manor born. It was not a complexion-counting exercise. I recruited Tariq Ali and Darcus Howe, both journalists with vast experience outside the mainstream, both with firm connections in the Asian and West Indian communities and with a commitment to international perspectives, to edit a socio-political programme. They had formed a production company with others, non-ethnics, experienced in TV reportage. The aim wasn't jobs for black boys. It was getting a probing programme with a radical agenda that fitted the remit.

So also commissioning the situation comedy *Desmond's* from the team of Trix Worrell (black) and Humphrey Barclay (very white), wasn't an attempt to boost the headcount of what has hideously come to be called 'diversity'. It was an attempt to present the comic dimensions of a Black British community. It worked.

That was twenty and more years ago. Since then, the whole scape and scope of TV, with the multiplication of commercial channels and the superposition of computer media, have changed. In Channel 4's early days we would screen a season or two of Bollywood films and, very early on weekday mornings, we would show the dawn-risers of the Asian community episodes of Pakistani and Indian serials. With the availability of a dozen or more Indo-Pakistani channels specialising in films and serials, that programming necessity no longer exists.

Whatever you do, don't' call it diversity
What Channel 4 also did in the past was give debut opportunities to feature film directors of ethnic origin such as Mira Nair, Gurinder Chadha, Deepa Mehta, Shekhar Kapur, Jamil Dehlavi, Horace Ové, Faris Kermani and Ahmad Jamal to mention those who come immediately to mind. They brought to the screen alternative visions from Britain's new communities. They also proposed alternative ways of interpreting Bollywood's dancing, singing conventions into serious drama. No such commitment can be seen on Channel 4 today.

There are reasonable arguments on both sides for reviving such a multicultural remit or for redefining it and calling it something else (but please not DIVERSITY!). The necessity for investigative, observational, dramatic and comic formats penetrating the diverse minority communities of Britain is as acute as it ever was.

Regardless of the fact that a growing number of 'ethnic' Britons work their way through education and enterprise into the meritocracies of the country, including jobs in TV, the communities from which they come remain increasingly ignored, isolated and sealed off from televisual scrutiny.

Much more frequently than in the mainstream communities, the tragedy, criminality and developments within the ethnic communities arrive on our screens as scandals that have escaped notice. Rochdale, Rotherham, young jihadi girls heading for Raqqa, the machinations within the Tower Hamlets Council, even the transformation into an international sensation of a Pakistani illegal immigrant who sold fish on the pavement by singing fish-mongering slogans – all remain unnoticed, undetected, unexplored or uncelebrated. Come back *Bandung File* in any other avatar – all is forgiven!

A few weeks of watching Channel 4 as it is now in 2016 leads inexorably to the conclusion that the 'remit' doesn't exist. I must have missed the Act of Parliament that changed or relaxed it, though I haven't missed the fact that women's programmes have completely absorbed feminist ideology, that gays find representation of sorts on TV and that perhaps the imperatives that governed early Channel 4 are deemed by those who run it to have melted away.

The 'remit' seems to confine itself to a diluted 'diversity'. Channel 4's responsibility is to get some 'diverse' faces on screen and to enjoin the companies that produce programmes for it to include some 'diverse people' in the production process. The headcount is all – apart from the pursuit of audience figures with which it should be compatible.

There was a deputy editor with a distinctly diverse name on the Channel 4 evening news. The weather reporter was also a diversity-wallah. In the Jamie and Jimmy cookery show, Usain Bolt turned up and introduced the café and the viewing world to jerk pork. The same programme featured Tandoori chicken in a real garden-constructed tandoor. Diversity with celebrity on a cookery programme. I can bet the present commissioning editor for cookery is not a vegan or anorexic. The advertisement that interrupted the programme featured 'pulled pork'. A jerk is as good as a pull?

Multiculturism by numbers

A programme called *Gogglebox* had some diverse people amongst others saying inane things about the programmes they were watching. This is a Borgesian invention and lends itself to making a programme about people watching *Gogglebox* and then a further series about people watching the programme about people watching *Gogglebox*.... and so on to infinity or until a Black Hole (Diverse Hole?) with a hefty gravitational pull sucks it all up.

On the same night BBC2 had a programme called *Artsnight* in which 'diverse' people, some male gay, some lesbians, some transgender people and some people of colour went around an art gallery and commented on the paintings. So, full marks for head-counting diverseness, some for insight into the parallels the diverse people saw between their own existences and the paintings and very few marks for furthering my knowledge or appreciation of the art works. In my Indian school in the Pune of the 1950s, this programme would have won the BBC class prize for 'Progress' – most probably the reward of a paperback called 'Biggles Hits the Trail' – multiculture by any definition!

Again, indulging the numbers game I counted diverse faces popping up in a programme called *Tattoo Fixers* and some in a comic series from America called *Brooklyn Nine-Nine*. There were too many characters for me to make a percentage estimate of black:white ratios. *Come Dine with Me* had some diverse characters and featured their interactions with food. The programme made me wonder if it was brought to the screen by the same vegan or anorexic commissioning editor for food who gave us Jamie and Jimmy's celebrity diversities.

Any time spent in an Accident and Emergency department in Britain would have an ample contribution to diversity and the programme dedicated to observing the department for 24 hours, called *24 Hours in A&E*, must have been intended as a counter to the anti-immigrant current of opinion and should have worked that way. *Super Shoppers* had a black presenter and again counts towards the on-screen-presence tally.

One can't consider today's Channel 4 programming without commenting on their series entitled *Keeping up with the Khans*. It's dedicated to examining a part of Sheffield called Page Hall which was, until recently, almost entirely inhabited by Pakistani immigrants of the third or even fourth generation.

The series concentrates for a few episodes on the newcomers to the area, the Syrian and African refugees and the East European Roma who are happy to settle there. It examines, if only cursorily, the tensions that these newcomers face in attempting to integrate into British life. The series, in true dedicated fashion to cultural multiplicity, has an episode featuring a relatively fat Muslim wedding.

Since this is not a straight review of the series, allow me dear reader, to come at one of its episodes obliquely. Here's a story from Indian history: In the 14th Century Muhammad Tughlaq, a Sultan of Delhi, decreed, somewhat in imitation of Emperor Nero, of whom he may not have heard, that the entire population of the city relocate itself to a new Capital he was building and naming after himself. The move was to be enforced by his army and the terrified if reluctant population deserted the city. The only two people left within the walls of Delhi were a blind man and a lame man, the first not being able to see his way out and the other unable to move even if he wanted to. Nevertheless, the Sultan determined to make an example of them for supposed defiance and one was hurled to his death from a human catapult and the other trampled to death by elephants.

One of the episodes of *Keeping up with the Khans* featured the whites (part of diversity?) who remain behind in Page Hall. All of those featured in this episode were in one sense or other on the fringes of society. The main character Joanne was a pregnant homeless woman partnered with an alcoholic and drug-addict called 'Monkey'. Among others who were featured was a gentleman in a mobility chair whose knee had got irreparably infected by his pet dog licking a wound in it. There were others featured in the episode and all of them, like the lame and blind man of my allegorical story above, were marooned in Page Hall which the whites of Sheffield had long since abandoned. They said they were isolated in an alienating sea. The pregnant, homeless girl Joanne gave birth to a boy which her boyfriend, who soon succumbed to his alcohol addiction, disowned. Joanne said she wasn't abusing the Pakistanis through racism, she was 'just jealous.'

Laudable and very watchable though I think the series was, its purpose was unclear. I don't mean to imply that observational narratives ever have or ought to have a single purpose. One could take from the series, without anything in it pointing to this conclusion, that the immigration policies of the 1960s and 1970s had allowed Page Hall to grow into an exclusive, enclosed Pakistani community which can now be seen as a failure of social or assimilative policy.

The series could also lead a perverse viewer like myself to conclude that the present government's immigration policy is a repeat of that failure, as it directs Eastern Europeans who have a right to enter Britain and asylum seekers who have been afforded that right, to settle in places with privations such as Page Hall suffers. They end up unemployed or washing cars for a living.

The only glimpse we were given into the already settled Pakistani community was the wedding episode. Introduced by a pretty little Pakistani infant girl it was a twee insight for the rest of Britain into what Muslim weddings are like. To some it will have proved that multiculturalism is in the main exclusive. None of the episodes went any way towards penetrating the negativities of multiculture – the breeding within jihadi madrasas, the Trojan Horse infiltration of Muslim schools, or even the attitudes and opinions that generate the racism that made some Pakistani characters in the series resent the new immigrants. Perhaps that's a function of there not being a hefty proportion of diverse folks in the production team (I can only tell from the credits that there didn't appear to be many Khans etc.). Or perhaps that sort of exploration is left for other series

To be fair there have been other series. Channel 4 ran a series – *4Ramadan* – from within the Muslim community of preparations for Ramadan. There was also a series, *Pakistan's Hidden Shame*, on the sexual abuse of Pakistani children – – not in British-Pakistani communities but in North Western Pakistan. And then, closer to home, there was a series called *Men with Many Wives* exploring polygamy in the British Muslim community.

All brave initiatives – albeit from 2013 and 2014 – in keeping with the vanishing remit.

Channel 4 seemed to redeem itself with a survey into the opinions of Muslims transmitted in April 2016. It gave the nation a long-neglected insight into the attitudes of British Muslims. Eight out of ten said they were happy to be British. A significant percentage said homosexuality should be illegal. Approximately a third were in favour of introducing Sharia law in their enclosed communities and a third were in favour of polygamy and said that it was the duty of wives to obey husbands unquestioningly.

The statistics demonstrate how isolated from 'mainstream' British opinions and value systems the Muslim communities are. I have no doubt that a survey of Jehovah's Witnesses or indeed of British Catholics would produce controversial results or opinions contrary to those of the majority. Of course these would be seen as opinions emanating from the faiths of British minorities but will in no way be assessed as threatening.

Not so the results of Channel 4's Muslim survey. This book goes to print before the nation's reactions or the response of the Government to the survey are evident. That there will be comment and debate and even possibly some form of 'backlash' is certain.

The Channel 4 initiative in providing these statistics is to be applauded as it is the penetration of a wall of silence. What statistics cannot do, however, is inform the national conversation about the genesis of these attitudes, the tensions within the Muslim communities that may or may not be generated by them, the possible gestation and developments from them or the prospects for challenging or changing them.

That, one would have thought (and as someone who has worked as a commissioning editor at Channel 4, I do think), is the job of observation, investigation, drama, comedy, soap and all the other forms and genres known and to be invented for the small screen. Surely that's what the channel's remit is about?

About the author

Farrukh Dhondy is a screenwriter, playwright and best-selling novelist whose vast output includes the films *Red Mercury* and *American Daylight*, novels including *Bombay Duck* and *Come to Mecca*, and TV shows including *King of the Ghetto* and *Annie's Bar*. He was commissioning editor for multicultural programming at Channel 4 from 1984-97, where he commissioned, amongst many others, the Oscar nominated *Salaam Bombay*, Shekhar Kapoor's *Bandit Queen*, and award-winning TV shows like *Desmond's* and *Family Pride*. He also wrote the series *Tandoori Nights* for the channel. His latest books are *London Company* and *Words – My Private Babel*.

For those in peril

By Paul Moody

Film4's importance to British film has never been clearer. So what consideration should be given to the cultural value of maintaining its non-profit status?

Channel 4 started producing films as part of its 'Film on Four' strand in the early 1980s, releasing *Walter,* directed by Stephen Frears and broadcast as the highlight of the channel's opening night, in 1982. By 1987, the channel claimed to be financing over half of all the films produced in Britain (Smith & Mayne, 2013), and its projects remained closely embedded within the channel's overall drama output. By 1998, its film operations had been rebranded as Film Four, and disengaged from the main channel's activities under the leadership of Paul Webster, who set himself the mantra 'make good films, make money' (Smith & Mayne, 2014, p533). But by 2002, after recording losses of over £5.4m in the previous financial year, film production was brought back 'in house' under the control of Tessa Ross, as head of drama at Channel 4, and the department's budget was reduced from just under £30m to £10m per year.

Despite the modest financial support, Ross was able to exert greater control over content, after asking the then chief executive of Channel 4, Mark Thompson, to write off the initial investment, arguing: 'Let me call it making great work rather than making money, and then we might get somewhere' (*ibid,* p550). Rechristened as Film4 in 2004, Ross oversaw a number of critical and commercial successes, including *The Last King of Scotland* (Kevin Macdonald, 2006), *This is England* (Shane Meadows, 2007), *Slumdog Millionaire* (Danny Boyle, 2008), *Four Lions* (Chris Morris, 2010), *The Inbetweeners Movie* (Ben Palmer, 2011) and *12 Years a Slave* (Steve McQueen, 2013), and by 2010 the Digital Economy Act had enshrined in law Channel 4's commitment to investing in, distributing and broadcasting films (Digital Economy Act, 2010). Since Ross's departure in 2014, Film4 is once again independent from Channel 4's drama department, although it appears that her legacy has placed it in high regard within the channel's senior management.

Nevertheless, Film4's semi-independence from the Channel 4 hierarchy, coupled with the nature of its output, places it in a perilous position if the mooted privatisation of the broadcaster was to go ahead. In his final public appearance as Channel 4 chairman, Lord Burns noted that for the television operation, a for-profit model would only become commercially viable if some of its public service obligations were removed (Burns, 2016), a view echoed by David Abraham, Channel 4's chief executive, who believes that if the channel was privatised, it would have to cut its programming budget by up to a third in order to deliver the profit margins expected by shareholders (Williams, 2015). In this scenario, much of the riskier, more expensive shows that it is identified with, predominantly in drama and comedy, would have to be shelved. As this is Film4's primary output, by implication most of its films would also be under threat, and if the department is able to survive that, it would be reborn as a cosier, more commercially-driven film company – a strategy that has had mixed success in the history of the British film industry.

The Inbetweeners: Film4's role in the British film industry

Abraham distils the challenge to the pro-privatisation argument into one simple question: 'Does Britain want another Channel 5?' (*ibid*). While not intended as a criticism of the broadcaster, Abraham draws attention to what makes Channel 4 distinctive, and what it can offer that is different to its similarly-sized commercial rival. While working as a keen reminder of the important aspects of Channel 4's remit, the 'Channel 5' argument poses several dangers for Film4. Placing this question within the context of the British film industry, the most readily available commercial comparison would be Working Title. Yet whereas Channel 5 has a relatively small audience share, with few mainstream breakout successes and even fewer critically acclaimed productions, Working Title has for decades been producing big-budget commercially successful British films, and has had notable critical success along the way. Ironically, a number of its films in the eighties and nineties were co-productions with Channel 4, but this only serves to highlight how a commercial film company has grown out of similar origins, and if the question posed for Film4 is 'does Britain want another Working Title'? box office returns suggest a resounding 'yes' from the British (and international) cinema audience.

Conversely, Abraham's question can also be recast with BBC Films in mind, asking, 'does Britain want another public service film company?'. BBC Films, with its licence fee funding, robust remit and a number of critical and commercial successes to its name, arguably provides the culturally important productions that a company like Working Title does not invest in, along with the numerous training and development opportunities that its support provides for British cast and crew. This, coupled with the new production drive of the British Film Institute (BFI) in the wake of the UK Film Council's demise, provides a wide range of artistically significant British cinema and leaves Film4 in the no man's land of, on the one hand, not quite being a commercial film operation and, on the other, not quite being a purely non-commercial one either. However, the argument that Film4 would, in a profit-driven culture, produce more commercial films and appeal to a wider audience, is dismissed by its former head David Aukin as being based on 'a fallacy that we know what is commercial…*Four Weddings and a Funeral* (Mike Newell, 1994)…*The Crying Game* (Neil Jordan, 1992), no one had any idea [how successful they would be]…we would all like to make commercial films – you tell me how' (Aukin, 2016, interview with author).

Film4 has certainly carved a niche in the British cinematic landscape by producing smaller-budgeted, riskier films that appeal to non-mainstream audiences, but while this works in the television world, it inevitably raises questions about public value in a cinematic context. Television, which is broadcast into every household across the country, providing numerous opportunities for viewers to stumble upon interesting, challenging drama or documentary, has a much clearer claim to be delivering a mass public service, matching quality with reach. But there has always been the underlying suspicion that Film4's audience was more rarefied, the urban middle class elite that would watch these films at their local arthouse cinema. Of course, many of these venues might have struggled to survive without screening some of the more commercially-successful Film4 productions, and as such, its importance in supporting Britain's non-mainstream cinema networks cannot be underestimated. However, by making the case for Film4's economic impact, one also implies that a profit-driven Film4, with a greater incentive to generate financial returns, may be of even greater significance to the British exhibition sector. Aukin states that 'I've never met a filmmaker who doesn't want the biggest possible audience to see their films' but accepts that the distinction at Film4 is that while 'this can be translated into a commercial imperative…it wasn't the overriding imperative', and the question of audience reach or financial return was rarely, if ever, discussed during his tenure.

This is partly due to the types of productions greenlit by the company (itself due in part to its unique remit), but also attests to the lack of control that it has over cinema distribution and exhibition. Outside of the major conurbations, the opportunity to view a Film4-funded production in the cinema is rare indeed, whereas British moviegoers will have been much more readily exposed to Working Title's *Shaun of the Dead* (Edgar Wright, 2004) or *The Theory of Everything* (James Marsh, 2015). In an environment where Abraham has to deflect criticism from Ofcom of Channel 4's audience share decline from 7% to 5.9% during his tenure (Williams, 2015), Film4 faces the even tougher task of explaining how it is meeting public value when its productions rarely venture beyond London and the major British cities.

This criticism, which was also often levelled at the UK Film Council and earlier incarnations of the BFI Production Fund, further emphasises the importance of the link with Channel 4, and the exhibition platform it provides (now both on its dedicated Film4 channel and Channel 4 itself). As Aukin argues, 'it is extremely important that the remit is attached to an entity that not only produces films but has an end use for them… it changes the nature of the process, because you are not just developing in a vacuum'. The link with Channel 4 provides the reach that is not available to any other British film production company, with the exception of BBC Films – although whereas Film4 has positioned itself as a distinctive film brand, as Ross identifies, 'when you call something BBC Films you sound like you are talking about television' (Smith & Mayne, 2014, p548).

This is England: cultural diversity

Film4's strongest argument against criticism of audience reach is found in its remit's specific commitment to culturally diverse British cinema. While Film4's biggest commercial successes have come from comedy and drama fronted by white men, like *The Inbetweeners Movie*, it has a long tradition of producing commercially and critically successful non-white British cinema, from *Ping Pong* (Po-Chih Leong, 1986) through to *East is East* (Damien O'Donnell, 1999). Arguably the most successful black British filmmaker of the last decade, Steve McQueen, has worked exclusively for Film4, and Richard Ayoade, who directed *Submarine* (2010) and *The Double* (2013), can also be regarded as a homegrown success story. Likewise, the channel was instrumental in the carers of notable female filmmakers, such as Gurinder Chadha and Carol Morley.

However, with the BFI's new diversity standards, which commit filmmakers to a certain number of minimum requirements for inclusion in order to receive public funding, much of Film4's remit has been overshadowed. Whereas in the 1980s, Channel 4 was the only British film producer that would develop these 'minority-interest' projects, in recent years challenging work by artists of the calibre of Andrea Arnold and Amma Asante has been nurtured by the BBC and the BFI. In this context, it is clear that the notion of what 'diverse' production actually means needs to be expanded, and returned to its roots in content and story, rather than in the BFI's more quota-driven approach. To maintain its distinctiveness, Film4 has to embrace stories that other funders will not consider, ensuring a range of voices that would otherwise go unheard, summed up by Aukin's commissioning philosophy that 'if you wanted to know what it was like to be alive in Britain during the 1990s, you would learn more from our films than from any history book'.

As Aukin identifies, these cultural questions are inseparable from the notion of 'Britishness', and what Film4 can offer to British culture in general. With the ownership of Channel 5 by Viacom and the rumoured takeover of ITV by American investors, a non-privatised Channel 4 would remain, along with the BBC, as one of the two solely British-owned television broadcasters. Within the context of British cinema, the BBC and the BFI are the only British-owned film producers that are capable of raising enough money independently to fund a feature, with Working Title now part of the American-owned Universal Media Group. The sale of Film4 would therefore potentially have implications for the production of authentically 'British' cinema, at least as defined by industrial or economic criteria. Of course, as the case of Working Title demonstrates, a foreign ownership structure does not necessarily mean the dilution of 'British' stories, but whereas Working Title has for decades been producing mainstream content that follows the Hollywood model and traverses national boundaries, Film4's content may not be as easy a proposition to maintain under non-British owners.

If the threats to Film4's in house commissions in a post-privatised world would be formidable, then the risks posed to the many smaller production companies that rely on it for co-funding are potentially catastrophic. Since 2000, it was instrumental in a number of UK Film Council successes, such as *This is England* (Shane Meadows, 2006) and *Touching the Void* (Kevin MacDonald, 2002), and has supported what is arguably Britain's most successful independent film company of recent years, Warp Films. As Aukin notes: 'If Film4 committed money to a project…it drew other people in'. Equally as important, the infrastructure provided by its links with Channel 4 enabled it to invest in a number of innovative and award-winning short films by first time writers and directors. While the Hollywood studios are often held up as exemplars of privatisation, none of them provide regular funding for short films, so it can be reasonably assumed that this aspect of Film4's activities would be among the first to be dissolved once placed within a profit-making environment. This would leave British short film production entirely reliant on investment from the BFI, with no obvious link to television broadcast or development within an established production company.

How I Live Now: A future in the Netflix age

It has been noted that Charles Gurassa, the former EasyJet deputy chairman and newly installed Chairman of Channel 4, has previously overseen two high-profile stock market flotations; Virgin Mobile in 2004 and Merlin in 2013 (Jackson & Conlan, 2016). But the most interesting aspect of his CV as far as Film4 is concerned is his former chairmanship of LoveFilm, which, while it has been subsumed into Amazon's operations, has relevance for the new Netflix-dominated film landscape, where streaming and on-demand are the new bywords of success. With its special remit to appeal to younger audiences, Film4 can be expected to thrive in this area, especially in light of demographic changes which have resulted in young people spending less time pursuing traditional media for online alternatives. One example may be seen in the recent release of Ben Wheatley's *A Field in England* (2013), which was simultaneously streamed online, broadcast on Film4 and Channel 4 and shown in cinemas.

These challenges are exacerbated by the distinction in filmmaking between a cinema release and all other forms of exhibition. Whereas a television writer/director will receive the same value from a traditional terrestrial broadcast or a series commission from Netflix, online does not yet possess the same status in the filmmaking community, where a cinema release is still regarded as the defining feature of a 'quality' film. The dreaded 'direct-to-Video/DVD' branding still carries the stigma of a substandard product, and while Netflix has established streaming as a viable alternative for 'television' series, it is still unclear how a film business can be developed and sustained via a streaming first or exclusively online policy. In addition, film directors and writers will be wary of this as a way of developing a career, especially with companies that do not have any requirement to cultivate artists. As Aukin argues, Film4's remit 'enables it to develop talent and ideas that [companies like Netflix] cannot do…it is difficult to think of another financier in the film industry anywhere who would have taken [*Room* (Lenny Abrahamson, 2015)] on and nurtured and promoted it in the way Film4 has'. That particular example culminated in four Academy Award nominations and a Best Actress Oscar for Brie Larson.

Film4 faces many challenges to maintain its position in a rapidly changing digital landscape, while emphasising its unique qualities in relation to Channel 4 and British cinema. However, in all aspects, its importance to the British film industry has never been clearer, and the impact that privatisation would have on it boils down to the following fundamental question that David Aukin poses:

> What becomes the imperative in the commissioner's mind when they commission a film? Is it, "this is the film we should make because it will be commercial", or is it "this is the film we should make because I love it and because it fulfils [the remit]"? Clearly there is a shift. It may only be marginal, but there is a shift, and the shift over years will increase, and the pressure will increase as the search for commercial success increases.

The recent announcement that Film4's budget will grow this year from £15m to £25m (*Televisual*, 2016) suggests that, if Paul Webster's previous experience of managing significant resources at the Channel is indicative, these commercial pressures may come to bear sooner rather than later. The challenge is to navigate them in a way that produces financial returns for the channel, yet retains the distinctive contribution to British culture that its non-profit structure enables it to provide – in other words, to reaffirm Film4's purpose in the contemporary British film industry.

About the author

Paul Moody is a Lecturer in Film Practice at Brunel University London. His research interests encompass early British cinema, national identity, and contemporary international film policy. He is currently working on a history of the British production and distribution company, EMI Films.

References

Burns, Lord Terence (2 February 2016), *House of Commons Communications Committee.* Available online at http://www.parliament.uk/business/committees/committees-a-z/lords-select/communications-committee/news-parliament-2015/lord-burns-evidence-session/, accessed on 5 February 2016.

Digital Economy Act 2010, Chapter 24, London: The Stationery Office.

Jackson, Jasper and Conlan, Tara (2016), 'EasyJet's Charles Gurassa appointed as Channel 4 chairman', *The Guardian*, 26 January. Available online at http://www.theguardian.com/media/2016/jan/26/easyjet-charles-gurassa-channel-4-chairman-lord-burns, accessed on 10 February 2016.

Martinson, Jane (2015), 'Lord Burns: "They seem to believe you can keep Channel 4's remit while privatising it"', *The Guardian*, 8 November. Available online at http://www.theguardian.com/media/2015/nov/08/lord-burns-channel-4-privatisation, accessed on 5 February 2016.

Smith, Justin and Mayne, Laura (2013), 'A Film4 Timeline', *British Universities Film & Video Council*. Available online at http://bufvc.ac.uk/tvandradio/c4pp/the-project/film-on-four-timeline, accessed on 24 February 2016.

Smith, Justin and Mayne, Laura (2014), 'The Four Heads of Film4', *Journal of British Cinema and Television*, Vol. 11, No. 4, pp. 517-551.

Televisual, 2016, 'C4 to boost spend on film productions in 2016', 10 February. Available online at http://www.televisual.com/news-detail/C4-to-boost-spend-on-film-production-in-2016_nid-5811.html, accessed on 24 February 2016.

Williams, Christopher (2015), 'Channel 4 Chief prepares for privatisation battle', *The Sunday Telegraph*, 13 June. Available online at http://www.telegraph.co.uk/finance/newsbysector/mediatechnologyandtelecoms/media/11671049/SUNDAY-INTERVIEW-Channel-4-chief-David-Abraham-prepares-for-privatisation-battlechannel-4-humans-david-abraham.html, accessed on 5 February 2016.

The Big Fat Teenage Challenge

By Fiona Chesterton with Karen Brown

The channel's special alchemy in making programmes for older children and younger adults is one of its most valuable attributes – and must remain so for future generations

When considering Channel 4, especially as two former commissioning editors, it might be tempting for us to look backwards. But in this chapter we are resolutely aiming to focus our gaze on future generations of their audience. Think November 2022 , when we hope that Channel 4 will be celebrating its 40th birthday. We equally hope that it is still engaging tomorrow's teenagers: those children who are as we write entering primary school. Think about those charmers in *Secret Life of 4, 5 and 6 Year Olds*, the first generation who have grown up with screens in their hands from toddlerhood. Can Channel 4's remit to entertain them but also to support their education – to help them understand themselves, their relationships, and help make sense of and take their place in the wider world – survive?

While it is generally known that Channel 4 targets the under 35s, it is much less appreciated that its portfolio of channels, especially E4, also has a remit regulated by Ofcom to provide content, including educational material, for older children and teenagers as well. Until relatively recently, this was fulfilled – certainly in terms of volume – by formal schools programming. The educational world has now moved on, and there is a wealth of formal learning materials online, little of it provided by the traditional broadcasters. What we are talking about here is informal educational content.

It is easy to confuse the commercial mission to reach younger adults – this cohort has long been much prized by advertisers and so is a key revenue driver for Channel 4 – with that more 'public service' objective. We will argue that there is still a role for C4 (including E4) to fulfil that part of the remit – with innovative and stimulating programming for teenagers, including the younger end of that 10- to 20-year-old spectrum.

As argued previously in the context of the BBC Charter Review (Chesterton, 2015) there may be a wealth of entertainment content available to British children, but there is relatively little factual, educational and informative material designed for them on TV (Ofcom, 2014). The BBC has become the sole commissioner in these genres for children, but they struggle to reach the over 10s (BBC Trust, 2013). That must in part be attributable to the BBC brand, which has always had characteristics less attractive to teenagers. Unlike C4.

Why has Channel 4 carved a place in the heart of succeeding generations of older children and young adults? What is the special alchemy in the commissioning and production of programmes over the years that has special appeal to them – some aimed squarely at them, some more mainstream – from *Skins* to *Big Breakfast?* We will argue in this piece that it is as much to do with the Channel 4 intent as the formal remit; that that intent needs to be reinforced and emboldened, that creative risk – including risk with young talent – is central to the realisation of that intent, and that privatisation would imperil that. What is special about the current funding and remit of the Channel as a public corporation that has delivered – and could still deliver programming – that the market will not readily supply?

The primary motivation for commissioning in a purely commercial environment – to state the obvious, but it is too easily forgotten – is to deliver an audience for advertisers and/or to increase profitability for shareholders. This tends to drive towards reduction in commissioning and production costs and the reduction of risk.

The motivation for commissioning in a public service context is also to get an audience but is more complex; it can take account of a remit (though not be slavishly driven by it), can be driven by passion and excitement for an idea and its realisation, and can afford to take creative risks.

At its best Channel 4 has inspired the producers it works with to push those creative boundaries and has had more freedom than the BBC to brave public opprobrium – especially in some sections of the press – with programmes that go beyond the conventional and the comfortable. Young people throughout the channel's history have warmed to that, have often seen their own lives and dilemmas better reflected in those programmes, and love testing those boundaries themselves.

Bolder and braver

Of course, there is a welter of content of all shapes and sizes out there in the internet universe. Young adults, usually defined by advertisers more broadly as the 16 to 34 year olds, will be served – some would say super-served – in this environment, but the iron laws of the bottom line push steadily against risk, towards already proven ideas and talent, and the huge dominance of sheer entertainment in all its forms, and to marginalising, in particular, programming with a more serious intent, especially for those not yet adult. We already have much evidence that the dominance of images of idealised, beautiful, sexually confident, and yes thin, thin, thin young people is having a huge effect on the self-image, confidence and mental health of an increasing number. Hence it is

Channel 4 and its sister channel E4 – and not the rest of this huge maelstrom of internet content – that stands out with *The Undateables* and *My Big Fat Teenage Diary*.

We still, though, want Channel 4 to be even bolder and braver in its commissioning for young people. Let's look at its stated intentions and current output.

It starts from a confident position. Channel 4 has a significantly higher proportion of the 16- to 34-year-old audience compared to any other public service broadcaster and – arguably a more significant pointer for the future – boasts half of this younger adult audience signed up to the online platform All4. In 2015 E4 was the most watched digital TV channel for young adults, and that position should be consolidated in 2016 with the migration online of BBC3. E4 majors on entertainment, but it should also be noted that *Channel 4 News* attracts a higher audience share among young viewers relative to news programmes on the other PSB channels (and no coincidence surely, it also attracts relatively larger audiences from ethnic minority backgrounds as well).

So a great springboard – and a great creative challenge surely – to take risks on challenging content for the younger end of that young adult spectrum plus older children desperate to reach adulthood.

It is disappointing, then, that although there is a dedicated education budget, none of it is now directed at the 10- to 15-year-olds. We will return to that but let's look first at their strategy for the 14- to 19-year-olds where the channel does focus its thinking and spend its budget. That budget is not huge (a minimum commitment of £3.5m in 2016 on TV and online) and is a tiny proportion of its total commissioning spend – but still enough to do some interesting and exciting things especially if the mainstream of the channel is also alert to the younger audience and committing some of its spend to satisfying them.

Channel 4 can certainly claim to know that audience very well and does an impressive amount of research into their attitudes and lifestyle - they actively sign up subscribers to All 4 as well as investing effort in reaching them through social media. The Tribes project which has been ongoing for a decade now (www.uktribes.com) puts some of this insight into the public domain. This places young people into an extraordinary number of subset groups like 'alternative, young alts' and 'mainstream, fan girl'. The project also enables frank conversations with them about all sorts of subjects, including their views on their formal education. So Izzy, (leading edge, indie scenester) says: 'I can honestly say I've never received any life advice of any use at school.' Tribes concluded from the research that PHSE (Personal, Social, Health and Economic) lessons at school were 'significantly outdated'. Young people wanted more real and relevant issues, like how to enjoy social media safely and deal with online abuse.

Addressing their mental health at school also featured in the list of priorities with Josh (alternative real gamer) quoted as saying: 'Teaching kids about stress, depression and anxiety is extremely important.' Not surprisingly, issues around sex and sexual identity also feature highly.

Lowest-hanging fruit?

Such insights give the channel a lot to think about in terms of its commissioning and the results last year on television included the *Born in the Wrong Body* season, dramas like *Cyber Bully* and factual programmes like *Revenge Porn*. Online a home for all content relevant to teenage audiences has been created under the umbrella *Am I Normal?* Some excellent content, of course, and we don't want to appear carping – but have they chosen the low-hanging fruit here and, in time-honoured Channel 4 fashion, the more lurid titles? It has been the BBC rather than Channel 4 that has put mental health centre stage this year. Commissioning priorities for 2016 too are stated to be more of what worked for them in 2015, i.e. 'online behaviour, relationships and sex, and family and friendships'.

Is this now safe, rather than creatively challenging, ground? While they may not come to the top of young people's minds, there are surely other issues that concern them: money worries, getting a job, debt, housing, and surely issues in the wider world too. Young people's lives may start in their bedrooms and revolve around their school or street but it is a disservice to end there and to offer little bespoke content beyond what seems fashionably to be described as their 'precinct'. BBC 3 (now online only) with its *Life and Death Row* series is a pointer to what might be looked for as well.

As we write with the refugee crisis raging and the British people deciding whether to remain in or leave the European Union, where on Channel 4 (let alone anywhere else on British television) will you see these stories from the perspective of the young? How about a documentary through the eyes of a 14-year-old Syrian or a young Polish worker? Or giving impassioned 16-year-olds a voice (as they won't have a vote) on Europe. Surely it is not enough to give the whole burden of that to the *Channel 4 News* team?

At its best Channel 4 rises to the challenge of taking tough subjects and making them accessible and engaging. The will to do this weakens the more insecure the channel's commercial base becomes, as in the recent years of recession. How much more difficult would it be to sustain this commitment – even the desire to go there at all – if there are shareholders to account to?

Do not hold out too much faith either in the ability of a regulator like Ofcom to help. Under its aegis, public service broadcasting commitments generally to children's television have been steadily diluted over the years (Chesterton, 2015). One wonders how long they could hold any channel, particularly a privatised Channel 4, to a commitment to challenging programming for young people, especially the 10- to 15-year-olds who are of limited value to advertisers as an audience. Although she was referring to the regulation of the BBC's Charter content requirements rather than Channel 4's, Ofcom's chief executive Sharon White said this was not an area where 'naturally we have the deep degree of comfort in'. (RTS 2015)

Channel 4 under its current regime seems happy to continue to nurture the over 14s – and still makes some brilliant programmes for them – but has walked away from dedicated commissioning for the 10s to 14s, persuading Ofcom of its argument of what it calls a mainstream programming policy.

Ofcom noted of this aspect of Channel 4's Media Content Policy(June 2015): 'C4C plans to move away from commissioning any bespoke content for 10-14 year olds, and instead seeks to serve this audience with general commissions on the main channel in pre-watershed, peak-time slots, which you consider will resonate with both older children and a broader audience. In the light of the concerns raised in the 2014 Digital Economy Act Review consultation about the limited volume of content provision for older children it is particularly important to ensure that the new strategy is demonstrably measurable against C4C's statutory duty. As part of further discussions, you have provided us with examples of three 2015 commissions which C4C expects will appeal to the tastes and interests of older children. These were: *The ABC*; *Educating Cardiff*; and *Naval Cadets.*'

Naval Cadets became *Royal Naval School* which, like *Educating Cardiff* were high-profile fixed rig documentaries produced by Two Four and featuring teenagers as prime characters. One might note that both were broadcast at 9pm rather than in Ofcom's seemingly preferred pre-watershed slots. *The ABC (working title)*, an ambitious drama series also set in a school, (and not yet broadcast at the time of writing) was commissioned for 8pm although one wonders how much of a creative constraint that will be to the programme-makers. In any event, it is a moot point how valid the distinction is between pre- and post-watershed output in a world where increasingly young people access what they want to watch on demand.

Aim higher

Clearly the Channel 4 board is committed to the 'mainstream' strategy too. Lord Burns in his 'exit interview' session with the House of Lords Media Committee (See chapter 5) confirmed this during questioning by that doughty champion of children's television, Lady (formerly Floella) Benjamin.

It is going to be some while before the outcome of this strategy can be evaluated but the risks are clear – that the line can be very easily blurred between what used to be called 'family entertainment' and programmes that may offer something of especial value to 10- to 15-year-olds.

The channel's research suggests the most popular programmes currently on the main channel with this cohort are 'light in tone and feature some sense of excitement or challenge': programmes like *Bear Goes Wild with Barack Obama* and *The Jump*. Programmes featuring children naturally do well, like *Gogglesprogs* a spin-off from the hugely successful *Gogglebox*, the *Educating...* series and *The Secret Life of 4, 5 and 6 Year Olds*. With care and good intent these programmes can offer a lot more than simple entertainment, and can offer supporting educational content online and via social media.

Why if Channel 4 were privatised would they bother?

When Channel 4 is bold and committed as it can be under its current constitution, spotting and nurturing young talent, identifying the issues that young people care about and the means by which they want to view it, Channel 4 thrives. The best of each new generation of commissioners knows that they succeed in Channel 4 terms only if they aim higher. Each new generation of producers knows that Channel 4 commissioners will sometimes listen – but not always – to a fresh and special idea. And, so far, each generation of young people has found Channel 4 for itself and known it was there for them. Here's to that being as true for those coming of the age in the 2020s as it is now.

About the authors

Fiona Chesterton was controller of adult learning at the BBC and the first Channel 4 commissioning editor for daytime programmes. She was also deputy commissioning editor for news and current affairs at the channel. She now writes about television issues, contributing to the books *BBC: Future Uncertain* and *Is the BBC in crisis?*

Karen Brown is a former deputy director of programmes at Channel 4 and before that commissioning editor for education and controller of factual programmes at the Channel. As chair of BookTrust and governor of Ravensbourne (university sector college in the field of digital media and design) her interest in education spans different stages of learning, informal and formal. She is also chair of Oxfam and writes here in a personal capacity.

Thanks to Daniel Cohen and Emily Jones of Channel 4 with their assistance in supplying research and background.

References

Chesterton, F, (2015), 'Who's Looking after the Children': chapter , in *The BBC Today: Future Uncertain* ed Mair, Tait and Lance Keeble, Abramis: London

Ofcom, (2014), Public Service Broadcasting Review Annexes; Children's PSB Summary, Available online at: http://stakeholders.ofcom.org.uk/binaries/broadcast/reviews-investigations/psb-review/psb3/Annex_6.i_PSB_Review_Childrens_summary.pdf Accessed 21 March 2016

BBC Trust, (2013) *Review of the BBC's Children's Services*, Available online at: http://www.bbc.co.uk/bbctrust/our_work/services/television/service_reviews/childrens_services.html Accessed 21 March 2016

RTS, 2015, Sharon White interviewed by Stewart Purvis, RTS Cambridge Convention, Available online at rts.org.uk/article/rts-cambridge-watch-session-ten-keynote-sharon-white-ofcom. Accessed 21 March 2016

Ofcom Letter to Channel 4 Corporation on its Statement of Media Content Policy 2014-15. Available online at http://stakeholders.ofcom.org.uk/binaries/broadcast/tv-ops/c4

4ever young

By Emily Jennings and Melanie Dowling

Two viewers from the middle of the channel's core demographic explain why C4 has played such a key part of their cultural upbringing – and influenced their life choices

In researching and thinking about the previous chapter, *writes Fiona Chesterton*, I was very conscious of the dangers of pontificating about the interests and needs of a much younger generation than mine. Indeed these sorts of debates about television invariably run the risk of majoring on the views of the middle-aged, however wise, expert and experienced they may be. So I set out to court contributions from those who are in their twenties, the core target audience for 4. I was expecting in today's crowded media landscape, I might find a lukewarm view of the role and relevance to them of Channel 4. I was wrong: while I realise I was speaking to a self-selected and so unrepresentative sample, I was surprised at the very positive feedback.

Shanade James, for example, said: 'It's always been part of my life... open to fresh ideas and fresh content.' Of *Channel 4 News* compared to other news she felt it was 'more outward looking, with more international news and in depth'. She perceived other broadcasters being targeted at mainstream demographics while Channel 4 gave a platform to minorities. She did not think that anything online offered what C4 and its news did.

Rebecca Hartmann agreed: she thought that the internet narrowed rather than broadened people's perspective on the world. The algorithms tended to offer more of what you had previously selected to watch and read about. So you could get the 'same stories about the same people doing different things... you need a platform that offers a range of things... things you've not thought about before.' She identified Channel 4 as providing that.

As well as *Channel 4 News*, programmes these two appreciated on Channel 4 now – usually accessed via All 4 rather than live – included *Food Unwrapped*, *Deutschland 93*, *Indian Summers* and *Utopia*.

I invited two young women to write at greater length and here are their contributions.

Emily Jennings: It shaped my social awareness

Before the internet provided a peek into the lives of others, Channel 4 offered snapshots into different groups within British society – often those that were overlooked or suffered prejudice. It always felt as though the channel's purpose was to shine a spotlight on minorities and advocate for diversity. For any impressionable teenager that type of undetected education is invaluable in shaping their tolerance levels. It rode the wave of changing attitude in the 1990s towards a more inclusive, multicultural British society.

Setting itself apart from the BBC, ITV and Channel 5, its content was risky without seeming crass and it presented obscure niche programming to a wider audience. With a direct line to young people that no other channel can boast, it has brought up a generation of British youth with attitudes that differ from their parents. Off the top of my head I can't think of a single group that hasn't been represented on Channel 4 television – LGBTs, IT nerds, Irish priests, sexually eager teenage boys, wannabe chefs. On a more personal note Channel 4's programmes have provided a backdrop to my childhood and adolescence and still does to this day.

Father Ted was a show both my parents and I could watch together. They'd slope in from a night out, snacking on crisps, while I'd curl up beside them slightly perplexed at their lingering laughter but delighted all the same. And when the actor who played Father Jack, Frank Kelly, died recently I heard how it was Channel 4 that gave the show its break. Those revelling in this factual titbit were incredulous that Ireland's national broadcaster deemed the series too risky and offensive for the Irish viewer. At a time when the Church still had a stronghold over the Irish people it was a small stand for a generation who grew up stifled by religion. It was refreshing satire about an institution long considered untouchable. A tiny Irish comedic rebellion supported by a British broadcaster.

A stand-out memory of mine is the launch of *Big Brother* in 2000. This was the start of an entirely new genre of TV and it was Channel 4 that showed the way. I remember so vividly spending that summer fascinated by these everyday people in that house. While my parents watched on fascinated by my fascination, it was the start of a new millennium and the cultural theme of the year, cutting edge and futuristic —which *Big Brother* embodied. The night of the final my sisters and I watched on our old-style portable TV set crammed into my bedroom buzzing with anticipation. And as Craig was declared the winner it truly felt like it was the start of a new era. This one programme would essentially change the format of television entertainment and the notion of celebrity for the next decade.

All my dreary afternoons spent home sick from school were brightened up by *Countdown*. And my teenage years were played out alongside episodes of *Friends*, *The O.C* and *Skins*. All of which meant I developed a typical adolescent viewpoint of the young adult world; a hilarious mistaken expectation that life would be one long coffee date interspersed with boozy nights out and lazy afternoons lounging about on California beaches.

I wiled away too many Uni afternoons watching *Come Dine With Me* marathons. And I wasn't alone in this obsession. This alternative angle to a cooking show sparked something of a cultural revolution. Soon there were groups of friends up and down the country picking up mixing bowls and forks proposing four-way cooking duels. The glory of being crowned ultimate chef of their social circle deemed a worthy prize. Not to mention the privilege of rubbing said title in their friends' faces down the pub forevermore. My chicken korma lost out to a mean beef casserole and I still feel the sting of it. With that the program embedded itself firmly in the history of British popular culture.

Then there was *Deal or No Deal* – what utter simplistic genius. Looking back it's incredible how the basic set-up of the show could mesmerise a group of twentysomethings after a day of mundane office work. We were glued to it. And if we were lucky enough to pick the right afternoon to witness the unexpected £250,000 box selection – well it went down in legend; the time that Wednesday in February where Sheila from Bromley beat the banker.

As I grew up shaking off the selfish shackles of adolescence and taking a proper look at the real world a sense of social awareness began to settle in. Obsessions with *Dispatches* and *Unreported World* ensued. Exposing injustices and tackling niche elements of societal crises here at home and across the world - they opened my eyes to obscure corners of society I was previously blind to. They ignited my interest in journalism more than any news bulletin could.

Over the past decade the way we watch television has shifted with online streaming services the biggest game changer, of which 4OD led the pack. Whether you watch everything online or the traditional way, programme viewing is cemented as a popular British pastime. And for me these days I'm hooked on old episodes of *Location, Location, Location* where for an hour I can live vicariously at a time when the housing market was fairer and Phil Spencer's hair-line more prominent.

When considering the influence of a TV channel it's staggering just how far-reaching and powerful broadcasters truly are. As a viewer you essentially surrender yourself to whichever programme you choose to watch. Television contributes to your social perspective and the narrative by which you view the world. I believe that Channel 4, above other entertainment broadcasters, is attuned to this responsibility: broadcasting considered programming, pushing boundaries, educating viewers and asking us to look outside our own social standing and consider other lives.

Melanie Dowling: It made me want to help the world

These days I am a hard-pressed junior doctor with little time to watch TV. Channel 4 still means a lot to me though and I wanted to write this article to show the value it has for me and how in a significant way it helped me become what I am.

I am a member of the last generation to remember life before the internet, being a teenager without a mobile phone and a world with only four terrestrial television channels. I was, however, still a teenager during the explosion of social media and feel I straddle the divide between being a digital native and digital immigrant. Whilst the boom of social media hit as I became a young adult, it was television that has influenced my outlook of the world and for the most part met my entertainment needs. My favourite channel since my teenage years has been Channel 4.

Coming from a middle class family in the south of England my day-to-day upbringing did not provide me with much insight into the wider more diverse society. Over the past two decades I have gone from a child to adult and have 'grown up' watching Channel 4. Before I was interested in mainstream news or politics, documentaries on this channel would catch my attention and teach me about the world around me in a way that was understandable. One of my favourite shows was *Faking It*. In the age of reality TV there have been many shows aiming to entertain with negative behaviour but this had a more positive tone and there were some great friendships created here. I remember a history of art student and stereotypical country boy who 'faked it' as a graffiti artist. This program grabbed and entertained because of the relationship between him and his mentor, a graffiti artist in London. They were such different people but became great friends and it was a lesson in the advantages of acceptance and embracing people from different backgrounds. This show exemplifies one aspect of Channel 4 at its best providing humorous and touching entertainment by taking different people and challenging them in a completely foreign environment.

Do you remember *Smack the Pony*? – hilarious and all the more unusually from a female team. I loved this show. I have always enjoyed live and televised comedy but so often it is male dominated. The team behind *Smack the Pony* also went on to write *Green Wing*, an amusing and often bizarre sitcom set in a hospital. Possibly the most surreal of all the episodes was when the crazy staff liaison officer gave birth to a lion after stealing sperm from a doctor in a coma. It really happened. I still enjoy comedy shows mainly on C4, either witty stand up or farcical sitcoms, but this show still stands out for me and makes me smile.

My favourite Channel 4 programme is *Unreported World*, covering foreign affairs that go unnoticed by the majority of the media. From sex trafficking in India to murder and the selling of body parts for 'traditional medicine' in South Africa this programme is eye opening at the least and deeply shocking on a regular basis. After watching *Channel 4 News* and programmes such as *Unreported World* I knew I wanted a career that revolved around helping people and eventually I decided to apply to Medical School. As a medical student, motivated to 'make a difference' I travelled to Zambia to volunteer with homeless children and to India to teach health care workers in a slum. My presence on these trips might have made a small difference to the people I met and worked with but definitely opened my naïve eyes to the true extent of inequality and the limitations of small charitable interventions. Thank you Channel 4 for that inspiration.

Since qualifying as a doctor I rarely watch television. When I do it is mostly for escapism. I enjoy comedy programmes such as *Eight out of Ten Cats* (plus or minus the '*does Count down*') and *The Last Leg*. Aside from comedy, Channel 4 has excellent shows on property and architecture. I also love watching *Location, Location, Location* for the amazing Kirsty and Phil, and *Grand Designs* for the innovation and creativity. I now rarely watch documentaries. Maybe this is because of the long hours that I work, and the serious nature of the work that I do, that leave me wanting to detach and be entertained by more superficial ideas.

I look back at my idealistic sixteen year old self watching documentaries about inequality and hoping to change the world and sometimes wonder where she went. I still hope to take the skills I am developing and use them for the greater good when I am a fully-qualified surgeon but I now have a heavy dose of realism.

Whilst I have changed Channel 4 has remained the same diverse and entertaining friend of my teenage years but has expanded (More 4 and E4) and become more accessible with online access and on demand viewing. Looking forward, I hope in ten years it will still be there in the form we know it now and maybe I will have combined experience, knowledge, realism and becoming a Consultant Surgeon with helping other people in the UK and around the world (as C4 first inspired me). Who knows I might even have a better work-life balance – and might claw back more time for watching television.

About the author

Emily Jennings is a journalist, working for Sky News.

Melanie Dowling is a junior doctor and surgeon working in the NHS.

Thanks also to Shanade James and Rebecca Hartmann, both postgraduate students at City University.

Let a few flowers bloom

By Torin Douglas

Major consolidation in the programme-making industry means that a small number of 'super indies' now dominate the field. But will that ultimately stifle creativity?

Thirty years ago, the world of independent TV production in the UK was widely seen as a cottage industry, made up of hundreds of freelance producers, eager to make programmes and be their own bosses but not so keen on the business side. There was a belief that independent production was 'not so much a business, more a way of life'. (Bonner and Aston, 1998)

Programme-makers in the 1970s who felt shackled by the duopoly of the BBC and ITV embraced the idea that 'a thousand flowers should bloom'. They were galvanised by the prospect of the new Channel 4 and the Thatcher Government's support for independent producers as a new force in broadcasting.

In a speech setting out his plans for Channel 4 – calculated to stir things up – Home Secretary Willie Whitelaw told broadcasters 'there must be assured and adequate finance for the purchase and commissioning of programmes for the channel from independent producers.' (Brown, 2007, p26)

Speaking at the Royal Television Society's 1979 Cambridge Convention, he insisted that independents should supply 'the largest practicable proportion of programmes on the fourth channel' (Isaacs, 1989, p21) and it 'should not be dominated by the ITV network companies.' (Brown, *op cit*, p26)

Almost eighteen months later, when Channel 4's founding chief executive Jeremy Isaacs held an open meeting for would-be programme-makers at the Royal Institution, 'some 600 independents turned up, spilling out of the hall into the lobby outside the lecture theatre.' (*ibid*, p 43)

Isaacs himself had not envisaged the independents playing such a major role in the new channel, even though he acknowledged they had had 'a raw deal' until then. Questioned after his 1979 MacTaggart Memorial Lecture at the Edinburgh Television Festival, he suggested that their initial contribution would be modest, perhaps only 10 per cent of the programmes. The Independent Broadcasting

Authority thought 15 per cent would be realistic, with the rest coming from the ITV companies and their production offshoots. (*ibid*, p 22)

Yet when Channel 4 went on the air in November 1982, after its first commissioning round, it emerged that 61 per cent of the commissions had gone to independent producers. (*ibid*, p 51)

Isaacs wrote later: 'Channel 4 entered into thousands of contracts each year with hundreds of suppliers to make hundreds of individual programmes... Producers have to make a living but, in the case of most of our suppliers, the purpose was not merely to make money; it was to say something that mattered, describe something that might move us or might give pause for thought or just make us laugh.' (Isaacs, *op cit*, p109-110)

By the time Isaacs stepped down at the end of 1987, independent producers had made another significant advance, successfully lobbying for the right to make programmes for the other channels. Isaacs wrote: 'BBC and ITV are required to take 25 per cent of their output from the independents. There is now a guaranteed and expanding market for them. Channel 4 can justly claim to have shown the way to that.' But, he also observed, 'independent production is still at the cottage-industry stage. Few companies are viable and secure.' (*ibid*, p108-109)

A global powerhouse – but foreign-owned

Almost three decades later, the cottage industry has turned into a powerhouse of global TV production, with UK companies among the world's leaders in programme exports and entertainment formats. But most of them are now foreign-owned, after a series of takeovers that bundled up the most successful independent producers into so-called 'super indies' and then saw them bought by some of the world's media giants – NBC Universal, Warner Bros, Sony, Rupert Murdoch's 21st Century Fox and Discovery.

How did it happen? Sir Peter Bazalgette played a significant part in the changes. His story – from one-man-band to media millionaire and cultural leader – exemplifies the growth and impact of the independent producers over the decades.

Appointed in 2016 to be chairman of ITV, he has had a long and distinguished career in broadcasting and the arts, having served as chairman of the Arts Council and English National Opera, president of the Royal Television Society and senior non-executive director of the Department of Culture Media & Sport.

Bazalgette set up his first independent production company in 1987 as a young freelance producer for the BBC. Through creative drive and financial acumen, he helped turn the entertainment producer Endemol into a global giant, best known as the creator of *Big Brother* and now part of one of the world's biggest production houses, Endemol Shine.

Bazalgette's business grew from a canalside studio office in North Kensington, with three full-time employees (including him), ten freelances and a first-year profit of £70,000, to more than 5,000 employees in the Endemol group worldwide, generating turnover of £1 billion and profits of around £220 million when he left in 2007.

He began his career as a BBC news trainee, later becoming one of Esther Rantzen's bright young researchers on *That's Life*. His breakthrough came as the producer of *Food and Drink*, where he devised a popular new format, centring on the 'Crafty Cook' Michael Barry and wine buffs Jilly Goolden and Oz Clarke.

'I set up Bazal Productions in 1987,' he told me. 'By 1988 we all knew that the 25 per cent quota was coming to the BBC, ITV and Channel 4. It was a typically Thatcherite move to modernise broadcasting and introduce a competitive content market with more varied sources of programming. Until then the BBC and ITV had maintained a vertical production model, making and broadcasting the programmes, and it was very hard for anyone else to break in.' (Bazalgette, 2016, interview with author)

Bazalgette was in the right place at the right time. 'If the BBC was going to meet its quota, it needed to out-source some major series,' he said. 'I was a freelance producer and I had created a successful programme formula for the BBC. I was also making corporate videos and I had a turnover of a million pounds, so they gave me the commission for *Food and Drink*.'

Bazalgette was an admirer of the UK advertising business, which led the world in strategy and creativity in the 1980s. He thought broadcasters could learn a thing or two about audiences, research, creativity and how to pitch ideas (Coates, 2013). Borrowing those techniques, he created a wave of popular lifestyle programmes for the BBC. *Ready Steady Cook*, *Changing Rooms* and *Ground Force* attracted audiences of over 10 million and had a huge impact on national life, encouraging people to take pleasure in cooking, DIY, interior design and gardening.

But it was another change in broadcasting policy that gave him and other independents a chance to spread their wings. The Thatcher Government decided that ITV licences should be awarded by competitive tender, a decision that also opened the way for would-be publisher-licensees, such as Carlton, to commission all their programmes from independent producers.

'In 1990, it was known that bids would be coming in for the ITV licences – and they needed production expertise' Bazalgette told me. 'We sold our company to Broadcast Communications, which was owned by the Guardian. We also became part of the Sunrise consortium (later re-named GMTV) and won a share of the breakfast TV licence.'

A box full of glowing tulips

By 1998, Bazalgette was restless again. 'We had made some hugely successful programmes and became fed up with being owned by a newspaper that wasn't doing much in the TV business, so we told the Guardian they should sell us to Endemol' he said. 'I had met them at the MIP programme market in Cannes, and saw they were interested in entertainment programmes. On the day the deal went through, a box full of plastic tulips arrived at our offices in Bedford Square – and they lit up!'

There was more excitement to come. Endemol made *Big Brother*, the ground-breaking show which throws ten contestants together in a house for several weeks, cut off from the outside world and the media, and constantly monitored by TV cameras and microphones.

The programme was already a success in its native Holland – gaining notoriety after one couple had sex live on TV, albeit discreetly under a duvet. The format spread quickly to Germany, Spain and the USA, where it aroused controversy and complaints.

Inheriting the UK rights, Bazalgette had the task of selling the show here, first to a broadcaster - Channel 4 – and then to the viewers. A few days before the first series began, I interviewed him for Radio 4's *Today* programme. As we walked round the *Big Brother* house, he pointed out the cameras hidden behind one-way mirrors in every room. 'Even the shower room?' I asked naively.

On the eve of the first show, Channel 4 executives were nervous, unconvinced it would attract an audience. But the tabloid newspapers loved it and within weeks it was also making headlines in the broadsheets and on TV news. 'Do you remember the huge fuss over Nasty Nick?' Bazalgette later recalled to me. 'That got on to the *One O'Clock News* - the news! It was crazy.'

When Nick Bateman was evicted, the audience reached 6.9 million – huge for Channel 4 - and the programme website crashed. In the final poll to decide the winner, 7.4 million people voted.

Bazalgette is widely credited with making the changes that turned *Big Brother* into a huge international hit. He denies this, though he is proud of the show's success. 'It was a good show before it came to the UK but our team at Endemol UK, working with Channel 4, made it better.'

He said it was Channel 4 that decided that evictions should happen weekly, rather than fortnightly, to create an 'event' on Friday nights. Other new elements suggested by Endemol UK were the theme music and the look of the programme – the 'eye' logo and a warmer, more stylish set.

A spin-off series was to create even more headlines a few years later, when *Celebrity Big Brother* sparked global ructions, after a housemate's remarks about the Bollywood actress Shilpa Shetty were widely construed as racist.

Yet it had all started so innocently. 'People forget that the first time we made *Celebrity Big Brother* was with the BBC. It was for *Comic Relief* and we showed it on both BBC One and Channel 4!' said Bazalgette.

Big Brother was one of several TV formats made popular around the world by UK independent producers, making several of them rich in the process. They included the appropriately named *Who Wants To Be A Millionaire?* hosted by Chris Tarrant, *The Weakest Link* with Anne Robinson, *Survivor,* and the talent shows *Pop Idol* and *Britain's Got Talent* (which spawned huge American hit shows) and *The X Factor*.

The digital holy grail

Bazalgette and Endemol were particularly successful financially.

'At Endemol, we benefitted from the dot com boom,' he said. 'Because we'd been using interactivity and the web in our programmes, we were seen by investors to be linking the TV to the telephone and the Internet – the digital Holy Grail. In March 2000, we were bought by the Spanish telecoms company Telefonica at the very height of the market – the day that Lastminute.com floated – for 5 billion Euros, a multiple of 100 times earnings.'

In 2005, Endemol's founder John de Mol departed and the Spanish owners asked Bazalgette and his longtime colleague Tom Barnicoat to step up and run the group internationally. Bazalgette became chairman of Endemol UK and chief creative officer of the global Endemol group.

Meanwhile, the fortunes of UK independent producers had been transformed by another decision of the regulators and politicians. 'The 2003 Communications Act played a huge part because it gave independent producers the rights to sell their programmes overseas and without that the companies could have no real value,' Bazalgette said.

The change didn't come without a fight. PACT – the Producers Alliance for Cinema and Television – had been campaigning to persuade the Independent Television Commission and the Department of Culture Media & Sport that the UK would sell far more programmes and TV formats abroad if the producers, rather than the broadcasters, held most of the rights. They said it would also encourage the growth of fewer, stronger production companies. (Brown, *op cit*, p280)

The broadcasters were strongly resistant. Greg Dyke, director general of the BBC, famously told MPs on the Culture Media & Sport Committee in 2003 that the BBC was not there to make independents rich. 'That was a catastrophic remark,' said Mark Thompson, then the chief executive of Channel 4. 'The BBC then missed its quota and that was appalling… and PACT was able to drive a hard deal.' (*ibid*, p 281)

Brown observed: 'The independents won the opportunity to build up real assets, instead of being the cost-plus producers they had been since the start of Channel 4. A number built up sizeable businesses and either amalgamated, accepted takeover offers or floated on the stock exchange.' (*ibid*, p 280)

Endemol was a big beneficiary, as Bazalgette recalled: 'In 2005 we did an IPO on the Dutch stock exchange for 9 Euros a share. Eighteen months later, in the summer of 2007, we sold the company for almost three times as much – 24 a half Euros a share – just before the credit crunch. The buyers were a consortium of Goldman Sachs, John de Mol and Silvio Berlusconi's Mediaset. I left a few months later and became a boulevardier!'

Under its new owners, Endemol continued to grow, before merging in a $2 billion venture with 21st Century Fox's Shine and Core Media Group, the owner of *American Idol*. As well as *Big Brother*, the group's productions include *Deal Or*

No Deal, *Peaky Blinders*, *The Bridge*, *The Island with Bear Grylls*, *MasterChef*, *Grantchester*, *Broadchurch* and *Humans*.

Other independent producers took similar advantage of the 2003 terms of trade to grow into super indies.

Shine was set up by Elisabeth Murdoch (daughter of Rupert), after leaving Sky where she had been managing director of programming. It grew as a programme-maker from 2002 to 2005, when it took over two of the most highly regarded producers, Kudos – maker of *Spooks*, *Life on Mars* and other ground-breaking dramas – and the factual producer Princess Productions. After further acquisitions, it was bought in 2011 by Rupert Murdoch's 21st Century Fox and was merged into Endemol Shine in 2015.

Shed Productions was another independent producer that grew organically to start with. Co-founded in 1998 by the former Granada producer and LWT managing director Eileen Gallagher, it made its name with the popular ITV dramas *Bad Girls* and *Footballers' Wives*. In the indie 'gold rush' following the 2003 Communications Act, it took over three highly-regarded factual producers – Ricochet (*Supernanny*), Wall to Wall (*Who Do You Think You Are?*, *Back in Time for Dinner*) and the current affairs producer Twenty Twenty Television. Other hit productions include *Waterloo Road*, *The Voice*, Gareth Malone's *The Choir* franchise, *Don't Tell The Bride* and the Oscar-winning film *Man on a Wire*. In 2010, Shed Media sold a majority stake to Warner Bros and in 2014 it became a wholly-owned subsidiary, changing its name to Warner Bros Television Production UK.

All3Media took a different route, setting out to buy up production companies, merge their back office functions and gain economies of scale. It began as the management buyout of Chrysalis Group's TV division, led by the former ITV executives Steve Morrison, David Liddiment, Jules Burn and John Pfeil. Between 2003 and 2014 they swallowed up Bentley Productions, North One, Cactus TV, Company Pictures, Lion Television, Lime Pictures, Maverick, Objective Productions, Zoo Productions, Studio Lambert, One Potato Two Potato, Optomen, John Stanley Productions, Little dot studios and Apollo 20. Its best-known productions include *Midsomer Murders*, *Hollyoaks*, *The Only Way Is Essex*, *Skins*, *Shameless*, *The Village*, *The White Queen*, *Undercover Boss*, *Gogglebox*, *Horrible Histories* and Gordon Ramsey's cooking and lifestyle shows. In 2014 the company was taken over by the US Discovery group and Liberty Global, owner of Virgin Media.

Victims of their own success?

In August 2014, a headline in *The Guardian* read: 'British indie TV producers a victim of own success as foreign owners swoop' (Sweney 2014). The story began: 'In a world where media giants are trying to woo viewers with high-class programming, the UK's flourishing independent TV production companies have become prime bid targets…. The most recent to succumb was the UK's largest "super indie" All3Media, maker of shows including *Skins* and *Midsomer Murders*, which accepted a £550m offer from John Malone's Liberty Global, which owns Virgin Media, and US entertainment group Discovery.'

Chris Graves, a director of the corporate finance firm Ingenious, who helped sell Shed Media to Warner Bros, said: 'The UK has a hugely creative production sector: it is the biggest net exporter of TV formats worldwide and English language shows travel well. And the UK has the strongest regulatory framework to protect production companies: they own the intellectual property of the content, which is critical in terms of making money from a show.' (*ibid*).

Later that month, giving the 2014 MacTaggart Lecture at the Edinburgh Television Festival, the chief executive of Channel 4 David Abraham sounded a warning. 'Our independent sector, built up and nurtured over decades, is being snapped up almost wholesale and acquired by global networks and sold by private equity investors. It is estimated that soon the proportion of turnover of UK production that will qualify as "independent" will drop from 76 per cent to around 50 per cent. The term "super indie" has, in effect, become redundant.

'And while UK production is an undoubted commercial success story, I wonder if it will continue to be a creative one. Scale demands an increased focus on cost-cutting and margins. Reformatting ideas is more efficient than the messy business of finding new ones.' (Abraham, 2014).

Perhaps not surprisingly, Sir Peter Bazalgette is less concerned.

'You can't have an open-border, free-trade market and also have protectionism' he said. 'Where there are public service obligations, laid down by a regulator, an overseas company has to abide by them. And the evidence is that most US companies now want to keep strong local companies who provide strong local content – not just American content as they sometimes did in the past.'

Bazalgette is proud of the super-indies phenomenon. 'The change in the terms of trade has been a great success' he said. 'Exports of finished UK TV programmes have more than trebled and we now have half the world market in entertainment formats. I think that consolidation is absolutely fine provided you still have lots of new companies and new ideas coming through. After all, people don't have to sell up!'

But is it as easy for new companies to get established these days? Mark Sweney's Guardian report stated in August 2014: 'Channel 4 admitted that the number of production companies it used last year fell dramatically, from 460 to 367, partly due to consolidation in the sector.' (Sweney, *op cit*)

Bazalgette said: 'I think Channel 4 has played – and still plays – a critical role in commissioning small and medium companies and encouraging new ones. It still commissions almost 350 independent producers. But the BBC is also very important. In my early days, *Changing Rooms* and *Ground Force* sold all over the world. One of the reasons the UK does so well internationally is that we have more competing channels trying out new programme ideas than anywhere else in the world.'

But would that survive any change in status at Channel 4 or the BBC? Only time will tell.

About the author

Torin Douglas was the BBC's media correspondent for 24 years and has reported on media issues for over 40 years. He was one of the founding editors of Marketing Week and the launch editor of Creative Review. He now speaks, writes and chairs events for a range of media, arts and academic organisations and is a trustee of the Sandford St Martin Trust, which promotes excellence in religious broadcasting. Torin is visiting professor in media at the University of Bedfordshire. He was awarded the MBE in 2013 for services to the community in Chiswick, where he has organised a range of cultural events. He is director of the Chiswick Book Festival.

References

Abraham, D. (2014) James MacTaggart Memorial Lecture. Available at http://www.campaignlive.co.uk/article/david-abraham-mactaggart-lecture-full-text/1308919 [Accessed 4 March 2016]

Bonner, P. and Aston, L. (1998), *Independent Television in Britain, Vol 5*. London: Macmillan, p183

Brown, M. (2007). *A Licence to Be Different: The Story of Channel 4*. London: British Film Institute

Coates, A. (2013). *How Did They Do It?* London: The Prince's Trust

Isaacs, J. (1989). *Storm Over 4, A Personal Account*. London: Weidenfeld & Nicolson

Sweney, M. (2014). British indie TV producers a victim of own success as foreign owners swoop, *The Observer*. Available at http://www.theguardian.com/media/2014/aug/10/british-indies-tv-production-companies-americans-coming [Accessed 4 March 2016]

The incubator

By Lorraine Heggessey

Channel 4's unique culture of innovation – it launches on average more than 350 new programmes every year – would be unlikely to survive privatisation

Since the debate about the possible privatisation of Channel 4 became a live issue, many television professionals have spoken about the unique creative ecology that we have in Britain, with each of the main broadcasters and the multi-channel companies playing very different roles. It is hard for people outside broadcasting to understand this, but because each network was set up in different ways, they have different cultures and different approaches to the ideas they commission. It is this breadth that has made the UK such a fertile ground for ideas. For such a small country, we punch way above our weight in terms of the number of original formats we create and export. Channel 4 plays a particular role in this landscape. From the outset its remit gave it the licence to do be different, to be bold and daring. This difference has spawned many new stars, launched many breakthrough programmes and helped many independent production companies build thriving businesses, which I would argue simply wouldn't have come into existence without it.

Channel 4's brief is very different to those of the BBC or ITV. It is to be 'innovative and distinctive', to 'champion alternative points of view', to 'nurture new and existing talent' and to 'reflect the cultural diversity of the UK' (Channel 4 2015, p6) The BBC is still underpinned by the Reithian trilogy of 'inform, educate and entertain', so the commissioners who work at the corporation strive to find programmes that do all three things simultaneously. From its launch, Channel 4 was defined as being many of the things the BBC was not and could never be. It was noisy, provocative, flamboyant and it courted controversy. A culture of risk-taking was established that pervades the Horseferry Road headquarters to this day. Andrew Newman was head of entertainment and comedy at Channel 4 until 2009: 'The BBC sets the tone for all of television in this country and does it brilliantly well, but having C4 there as a slightly disrespectful impish kid brother makes the whole of TV a little bit more quirky and interesting. The BBC is less risk taking partly because of its size and partly because of its visibility. The fact that it gets money from everybody is both a brilliant thing and a burden, as the BBC has to worry about not offending people in a way that Channel 4 doesn't. Channel 4 has to worry about not being too derivative and boring.'

ITV's focus is on popular mainstream programming. Its commissioners are seeking hit shows with broad appeal to bring in the large audiences that will keep advertisers and shareholders happy. Although Channel 4 is primarily funded by advertising revenue, its structure is very different to ITV. It is publicly owned and not for profit, so it doesn't have to generate money for shareholders. The nuances of approach taken by the different networks is inextricably linked to their culture, which stems from the way they are funded. Newman believes this inevitably affects commissioning decisions: 'When the worst type of failure is that something you do is low rating, it limits the kind of things you do. Channel 4 is much more free. You didn't want to fail, but it was better do something interesting that didn't work than something bland that was just ok.'

Risky decisions
Channel 4 has always felt part of its mission is to back new ideas and to support fresh talent both behind and in front of the camera. The statistics show it doesn't just pay lip service to this mission. It tries out far more new programme ideas than any other UK channel, with 354 titles launched on average each year. That's way ahead of the licence fee-funded BBC Two, which comes in second place with 281 launches and considerably better than Channel 4's commercially funded PSB competitors. Five launches a mere 93 new titles whilst ITV has an average of 190 new programmes in its schedules annually. (Channel 4 2015, p21) Many producers believe that this record of innovation would change if Channel 4 were to be privatised. Charlie Pattinson, co-founder of Company Pictures, produced the ground-breaking drama *Skins*: 'Privatisation would be a disaster because it is precisely the ability to back the difficult programme that makes Channel 4 on the one hand potentially incredibly commercial, and on the other hand a potentially risky commercial proposition. *Skins* was a perfect example. We'd taken the idea to everybody and nobody wanted it. Teen drama that was written by teens and starred teens, that didn't have any stars in it, and that was badly behaved, was an incredibly risky proposition. The Channel 4 drama commissioner said it wasn't right for him but that they were going to launch drama on their new digital channel, E4. I don't think anyone else would have done that at that point and left us alone. Then, critically, they did what Channel 4 at various points in its history has done brilliantly, which was to market *Skins* in a way that in effect defined the show.'

The risk paid off. *Skins* was critically acclaimed and a ratings success, largely because many of the creative team involved came from the young demographic they were targeting. It was to run for seven series and 61 episodes, but the risk taking didn't stop with the commissioning. After the second series, the team announced that they wanted to start again with a completely new cast. Charlie Pattinson says Channel 4 were very supportive: 'If you think about it from an entirely commercial perspective where you've invested around £20 million in the production and marketing budget building a drama brand promoting Nicholas Hoult as your star, it was a brave decision to agree to dispense with that after two years. We were never called to task on that and it became the culture of the show.'

Company Pictures produced drama for ITV and the BBC, but Charlie Pattinson is adamant that only Channel 4 would have commissioned one of its most significant shows, *Shameless*. Co-founder George Faber remembered a Paul Abbott script that the BBC had never green-lit. He called Abbott who said he had always wanted it to be a soap but nobody would do it. Channel 4 snapped it up. 'No other broadcaster would have done that. To allow a drama to be quite so scabrous and the central character to be on the surface so degenerate and potentially unlikeable, it was impossible for any other channel to do it. It was obvious C4 was the home.' Pattinson says: 'The risk was in the tone and the attitude and in the world. Paul was at the height of his powers and one of the most successful TV dramatists at that time, but what Channel 4 were able to do in a way that no other channel was able to do, was to allow that voice space in an unadulterated fashion. They were able to do that partly because that was the remit of the channel. What was unique was that Paul Abbott's voice could be unfiltered and that was what made it a great drama.'

It's not just producers that see Channel 4 as a risk-taking innovator. Viewers also see it as something that differentiates the channel with 46% of them saying it's a risk taker compared to 14% for its closest competitor. (Channel 4, 2015, p20)

Growing new stars
It is incredibly difficult for new talent to break through on big mainstream channels like BBC One and ITV. More edgy or unusual presenters often need time to develop and find their audience in a place where the ratings expectations are lower. Channel 4 has played a key role in establishing many of the UK's most successful entertainment hosts who moved on to primetime on ITV and BBC One. It is able to take an artist with little or no television experience and give them the space to grow and experiment. Chris Evans through *Big Breakfast* and *Don't Forget Your Toothbrush*, Jonathan Ross through *The Last Resort*, Harry Hill through his eponymous show before he moved with it to ITV. Graham Norton is a case in point. His agent Melanie Rockliffe says Channel 4 approached Graham after they saw him stand in for Jack Doherty on Five: 'They said they wanted to build a show around him and we did a pilot in which he was allowed to be himself and do what he wanted, even though he wasn't very well known at that time. It very quickly became apparent that C4 was a very good home for him. I don't think it could have been done anywhere else because a lot

of the stuff he did was also extremely rude as well as incredibly funny. I can't remember Channel 4 ever saying to him "No you can't do that".'

Again the risk taking paid off for Channel 4. *So Graham Norton* ran for five series and 76 episodes, followed by *Very Graham Norton*, the nightly chat show that ran for 65 episodes. Rockliffe says it was the creative freedom that led Norton to stay at the channel: 'Graham felt he was very well looked after there. He felt master of his own domain, forging his own show and taking the chat show into a different era. The channel didn't insist he had A list celebrities and Hollywood stars on the sofa, he chose his (sometimes quite quirky) guests himself. His sensibilities drove the feeling of what this show was and the excitement and fun and camp-ness of it, and C4 were happy to go along with it.'

Andrew Newman sees Channel 4 as uniquely placed to grow talent: 'Graham is now seen as a mainstream BBC One star but he wouldn't have been able to go to BBC One without having first built up a profile. He had only done a couple of things when C4 gave him his chat show and the BBC at the time would not have been able to have such a camp person who was so rude.'

As the person who eventually persuaded Graham Norton to jump ship when I was Controller of BBC 1, I totally agree with Andrew Newman's point. Even with Graham as a well-established performer, the press were very critical of me for taking him to the BBC!

Channel 4's experimental culture ultimately makes it possible for all of British television to be more adventurous and to keep evolving. Even the most unlikely talent can eventually break through. Keith Lemon, played by Leigh Francis, is an ITV favourite in shows like *Celebrity Juice* and *Through the Keyhole*, but this outrageous character came from Francis's Channel 4 show *Bo Selecta*. The way this programme came into being is a quintessentially Channel 4 story, as Andrew Newman recalls: 'Leigh used to turn up in reception, dressed in character as Avid Merion and say "I've got a pizza for you", and the pizza would be made of cut out photos of his face. It's good that Channel 4 can have this special position where we can say that we think it's really funny, it might break out and become the most rated thing, but if it doesn't it doesn't matter because we've given an unusual maverick a voice. Channel 4 can be a bit more gung-ho because it doesn't get money from every single household in the way the BBC does, and if people complain we'll roll up our sleeves and defend it.'

Crucial backing for indies

The history, growth and success of the flourishing independent production sector is inextricably linked with Channel 4, which still has no in-house production department and commissions all its programmes from external suppliers. As Charlie Pattinson, founder first of Company Pictures and then of New Pictures says: 'The rise of the producer entrepreneur would not have happened without the support of Channel 4. They are entirely responsible for the way the landscape is now.' Channel 4 has supported many indies through their early days with development deals, or more latterly through the Alpha

Fund, which was established to help start ups, regionally-based companies and projects involving diverse talent. In 2014 CEO David Abraham set up the Growth Fund, which invests in start-ups as well as small to medium sized indies looking to take their business to the next level.

Pattinson and Faber had both been star BBC producers, but by 1998 both felt that they were in a creative strait jacket which spurred them into branching out on their own: 'At the BBC as a producer I could only go to BBC One or BBC Two and that began to feel very restrictive as I sat on developments I loved. I wanted to be a creative producer and so I needed the widest possible range of buyers.' At that time there were only a handful of production companies that did drama, partly because it was difficult to be economically viable with the long lead times that drama entails. 'Part of the reason we survived was that Channel 4 did a first-look deal with us right at the beginning.' That deal provided Company Pictures with the cash to keep them afloat whilst they focused on the lengthy process of developing new dramas and securing their first commissions.

Nick Curwin, who with fellow producer Magnus Temple set up two factual indies, Firefly and The Garden, found Channel 4's support crucial in both cases. 'We started Firefly in 2004 without any commissions or even any paid development. We only had a three-month window with which to get cash flow or we'd have to fold. We didn't have any savings and we both had babies and mortgages. Channel 4 approached us and asked if we wanted a development deal of £20,000 in return for pitching them a couple of ideas a month. It was just a fantastic thing to do, because apart from having a little bit of cash to help with our development, it was something that we could announce that Channel 4 was doing and it showed faith in us because we weren't at all well known at the time.'

That faith was well founded as the company went on to deliver one of its biggest hits, *One Born Every Minute*, and was the main driver behind the 'fixed rig' show which revolutionised the way observational documentaries were made because you no longer had to have a film crew in the room. Having sold Firefly to Shine, part of a pattern of consolidation that was growing in the indie sector, Curwin and Temple left after three years to set up The Garden. Curwin says: 'The breakthrough for us was *24 Hours in A & E*. It was a commission of scale that changed everything – 14 episodes! We had intended The Garden to be boutique and tiny but obviously nobody in their right mind would turn down a commission like that.' That was clearly the right decision, as they are up to 134 episodes, and partly as a result of this success The Garden was bought by ITV Studios in 2013.

The story of the genesis of *24 Hours in A & E* is a good illustration of the way Channel 4 incubates ideas. Nick Curwin: 'It's part of a line which starts with *Going Cold Turkey*, which nobody's ever heard of, which we made for C4 about heroin addicts trying to give up. We had to find a way to film it without anyone being in the room so we borrowed the tricks of *Big Brother* and used remote cameras. We realised this was an interesting way of filming. You could be in private spaces that you otherwise wouldn't get access to and it felt very unmediated but was also very emotional. So we brainstormed what else we could do with it and we ended up making *The Family*. That was the first proper rig show and then we did *One Born Every Minute*.'

Curwin insists that what made that evolution possible was the way in which Channel 4 commissioners worked with producers: 'There was a particular way of working at the channel, which was one of the reasons those things came off. It was very intimate and you sort of buddied up with somebody you got on with, (in our case that was commissioning editor, Simon Dickson), and you talked and talked and had meetings and lunches. There was a mutual desire to come up with something clever and new and interesting. We were very hungry to do something original so we were constantly trying to cook something up. I passionately believe that the whole evolution of the rig show is an absolutely direct consequence of C4's behaviour and its very particular way of working with producers.'

Channel 4 is not just an incubator of ideas and talent; it remains an incubator of production businesses and believes it is important to back new and emerging companies to keep the sector vibrant. In the current era of large consolidated groups such as All3 Media and Endemol Shine, the channel could take the easy option of commissioning from tried and tested suppliers. But it doesn't. It provides many companies with their first commissions, working with around fifty new suppliers every year and proactively supporting companies in the nations and regions. This is demonstrated by the way it has increased the proportion of its spend on indies with a turnover of £25million or less from 8% in 2011 to 28% in 2013. (Channel 4, 2015, p14)

Jess Fowle is creative director and co-founder of Leeds-based True North. Landing a 25 episode commission for *Building the Dream* was a game-changer for the company: 'Channel 4 were really good from a business point of view. It was a risky commission because people were building their own houses so they weren't going to see anything for 18 months after we'd started shooting it, but the commissioners were brilliantly trusting and collaborative. They were also quick to come back and order more as they really understood the dynamics of being an indie and needing to know whether you had a commission, particularly with something like this where you need to get on to start shooting for the next 18 month cycle.'

Channel 4 subsequently invested in True North through the Growth Fund, the initiative established to support small and medium sized companies. (I am an advisor to the fund). Jess Fowle believes this helped them to have their best year ever: 'It felt like a really good fit for us. It's not that we get any special treatment, but particularly as an out-of-London company it gives you a connection to the heart of the industry that we wouldn't otherwise have. We've been able to beef up our development department significantly and go from something that was rather ad hoc to something that is proactive and significant. We've also put money into trying to promote our formats in the States in a way we wouldn't have been able to before. We're in a much more ambitious place than we were prior to the investment.'

We meddle at our peril

I am in no doubt that the British broadcasting landscape would change dramatically if Channel 4 were to be privatised. It's hard for the kind of experimentation I have been talking about to sit hand in hand with the drive for profits that shareholders would expect. Channel 4 feeds ideas and talent into the airwaves that has an impact on all our broadcasters as well as on the production sector. We meddle with that ecosystem at our peril. I'll give the final word to The Garden's Nick Curwin: 'Channel 4 is an absolute gem. The way it's set up and its remit, structure and governance just work. It produces innovative and creative programming and has helped produce a flourishing production sector that's a very valuable part of the creative economy. I feel to experiment with unpicking that model is really risky and not in a good way. It does an extraordinary job in all sorts of ways all at once and if you add into the equation that it has to deliver profits to shareholders rather than putting them back into programmes then I think you're loading up a gem with too much of a burden. I say leave it alone.'

About the author

Lorraine Heggessey is Chair of The Grierson Trust and the independent external advisor to Channel 4's Growth Fund. As the first female Controller of BBC 1, she oversaw a major revamp of the channel introducing many new programmes including *Strictly Come Dancing*, *Spooks* and the reinvented *Dr Who*. She was CEO of one of the UK's largest independent production companies, talkbackTHAMES, producing 600 hours of programming a year, including *Britain's Got Talent*, *Grand Designs* and *QI*. In 2012, she founded a new production group, Boom Pictures and built it to become the seventh largest indie in the UK.

References

Channel 4, 2015, *Britain's Creative Greenhouse: A summary of the 2014 Channel 4 Annual Report and other key facts*. Available at:
http://www.channel4.com/media/documents/corporate/annual-reports/C4_Brochure_Single_Pages_2ndJune15.pdf [Accessed 4 Mar 2016]

Identity crisis

By Dean Stockton

Channel 4's iconic logo has stood the test of time for three decades, and will continue to do so long after its current arthouse curio idents are long forgotten

I've heard it said so many times that it was a defining moment for British Television. Thatcherism, the miners' strike, cruise missiles, Mary Whitehouse... not a time you'd expect a revolutionary new TV channel to be launched. But launch it did. And as a designer in the art department during this time, it also became a defining moment in my career.

In retrospect, everything about the period comes across as surprisingly conservative; similar to Punk Rock, so shocking in the seventies, now looking and sounding so tame. But looks can be deceptive. The broadcast media landscape was far different in the early 1980s: only 3 main TV channels to choose from, no internet, no mobile devices. It was a time when branding was still something you did to a cow, and anything and everything was possible; when Levi 501's were the only things to be seen in and a copy of *The Face* magazine was the only thing to be seen with. Pop video production was at its peak, British advertising at the height of its creative powers and as a consequence of Channel 4's birth there was a re-invigorated British Film Industry and growing independent television production sector. More significantly for everyone involved, it coincided with the advent of digital video post-production and computer generated 3D graphics, resulting in a flourishing creative services sector and the opportunity to create concepts never attempted before. And with the old work practices disappearing, there now an opportunity for young talent to be let off the leash.

The focal point of all this change was Soho, a hotbed of creative energy and excitement. Everything revolved around this historically-renowned red light district, home to many film-related businesses. Nearly every building appeared to house a film and television related business. Digital post production companies were springing up everywhere and Channel 4 was just a stone's throw away from Soho Square. There was a hedonistic culture and a new philosophy of work hard, earn lots and play hard. The pubs, bars, restaurants and private clubs were packed with arrivistes and creative media types, full of idealistic apparitions. We imagined we were the avant-garde – ultra-radical, ultra-outrageous – but we never lost sight of the fact we were in a privileged position, and with that position went a responsibility to the audience, to the TV Licence payer.

It was this creative energy, the idea that anything and everything was possible, that was our inspiration; we weren't just an art department, we were The Art Department. We were valued as artists, given a blank canvas and allowed the freedom to be brilliant, to take risks, to break the rules, to learn by our failures. We were smack bang in the middle of a creative revolution. We were encouraged to shake everything up, be innovative, imaginative and most of all, ground breaking. And as luck would have it, we possessed the most powerful of all communication tools and with it, a sizeable captive audience at our disposal.

However, arriving at Channel 4 was initially quite a surprise. I'd been working at the BBC's state-of-the-art Topical Production Centre in Lime Grove, where I had a foretaste of the digital future to come, but I needed to escape the one-dimensional nature of BBC Current Affairs. I expected my new home to be state of the art plus. I was wrong; it was more state of the art minus. Their Quantel Paintbox was languishing in the basement, tucked away in the corner of an electricians' storage room, wired up to a ridiculously out-of-date black and white rostrum camera used to capture paper weather maps that were delivered every day by motor-bike messenger (these were the days before couriers). I set about making promotion slides with the crayons and Letraset.

I spent little time dragging the art department kicking and screaming into the present. I must have been a right pain in the arse – but within 6 months, I'd persuaded the powers that be that by utilising the technology at our disposal we could dramatically improve output. So, out went the peg bars, cow gum, crayons and Letraset and in came the Quantel Paintbox and digital post-production.

Responsible revolutionaries

Although we were all aware of the strict rules surrounding the use of the 4 logo, we never lost focus that our role was to promote our brand and content as imaginatively as possible, to increase audience share. We may have been revolutionaries but we were responsible revolutionaries. We understood the language of television. How it was structured, the narrative of a break pattern and how we could manipulate this space to our advantage. I would analyse the break patterns of commercial TV, examine ways I could reconstruct them to create dramatic effect.

We were allowed to be imaginative and playful with the 4 when producing seasonal campaigns and other, more specific, genre-driven on-air creative; an example being the legendary snorting American Footballer, created for Channel 4's NFL coverage. There was even a Hamlet cigar commercial spoof of the logo, proof we were in the public consciousness. Would any present-day on air identities inspire a commercial product to spoof them in 2016?

Another instance was *The Friday Zone*, where the Channel 4 logo animation mutated into a piece of anarchic scratch audio-video grunge that morphed into two hours of alternative television. At the time this was seen as revolutionary, surprising and unexpected. Mr L-N must have spilled his cocoa.

And so, we cross fade neatly through to Mr L-N and his iconic Channel 4 logo. Martin Lambie-Nairn is arguably the most important person in the creative narrative of the channel. He created the original logo with its vivid, almost Lego-like, coloured blocks representing the diverse elements that made up Channel 4's output. The ground breaking 3D animation and graceful round and back swooping movement that combined with all the other many design elements, was probably the first time a TV company had ever created itself a true brand identity in the modern sense.

The Channel 4 logo became one of the key factors in the early success of the channel. It was cool, it was new, it was different and it was popular; the perfect icon to represent the channel. But would it, could it stand the test of time? Could it truly become a lasting design icon?

Over the intervening years the 4, like Dr Who, has had many re-incarnations. The 1990s was its nadir – people tapping on your TV screen, celebrity endorsements, white circles, one dimensional After Effects animations – all derivative, all devoid of any real originality or inspiration. There was, however, always one constant: the 4. Over 20 years later, those nine blocks were still there, even though all those glossy, bright colours had worn away over time.

Thankfully, in 2004, Brett Foraker was appointed as Channel 4's youngest ever creative director and the guiding force behind 4Creative, creating the multi-award winning Channel 4 idents – Tokyo, Diner, Container Terminal, Council Estate, Yellow Cab, etc – where the camera steers the viewer through an everyday scene and the 4 appears for a single fleeting moment, fashioned from elements contained within the scene. These were still, after ten years, truly ground breaking and a pleasure to watch every time they appeared. Beautifully produced, they never became familiar, there was always something new you could discover and appreciate.

Explaining the kryptonite

So why did Channel 4 feel the need for change? Was it change for change's sake? Maybe we can gain a little more insight from the main protagonists? James Walker, head of marketing, said: 'Channel 4's main channel identity has been running for ten years and has been hugely successful. This ground breaking brand refresh pushes it forward once more, reflecting our public service remit to be diverse, challenging and innovative.' Nothing new there, then?

'Most TV branding these days is like watching wallpaper. It's pleasant but gets boring very quickly.' So said 4Creative heads Chris Bovill and John Allison. 'We started with the original, iconic Lambie-Nairn 4 logo and broke it down into its constituent parts; the nine blocks. The blocks are free to demonstrate our remit;

to be irreverent, innovative, alternative and challenging. They are free to flow through everything on the channel.'

It's those famous words 'innovative' and 'challenging' again.

Grant Gilbert, creative director of DBLG, the agency that worked on the new branding, cut straight to the chase when he added: 'We decided early on that we didn't want to mess with the logo but instead find different ways to present it on air. However, Channel 4 is much more than just a big shiny number and some nice vibes. These elements that play out dozens of times every day are now free to be playful, surprising, dynamic and ever changing. We have created an identity for Channel 4 that has longevity and will evolve and express itself in different ways. The idents present the blocks as kryptonite-like. They tell the story of their origin and how they have a powerful impact on the world around them. Just as Channel 4 does. It is a story that we shall build on.'

Wow, it sounds so exciting, even playful?

Even internationally-famous typographic designer Neville Brody was hired to 'cut two exclusive new typefaces, Horseferry for display and Chadwick for information.' That's original. And why they need two typefaces to essentially do the same job, only Mr. Brody knows.

So, enough of the PR nonsense; the only way you can ever judge the quality of something is after experiencing it for real. Here goes…

> *Ident 1.* We open on some monkeys. Boom! A quarry is dynamited. Cut to men in white forensics suits. What can they be searching for? For what's left of the monkeys? Or scouring a major crime scene? No, they're just searching for blue quartz? Sorry, blue 'kryptonite-like' stuff.

> *Ident 2.* A bloke crosses a stream. It's autumn. There's a waterfall, more 'kryptonite-like' stuff (red, this time), falling water, falling rocks, Splash! Bloke runs away.

> *Ident 3.* Somebody dressed in a feather skirt, shaking feather boas whilst bopping. He's wearing what looks decidedly like a thatched roof and a fly's head, with gold 'kryptonite-like' stuff stuck to his face.

> *Ident 4.* Entirely different in style to the others, we see what looks distinctly like the hob from an electric cooker? Is that a gold bar baking in the oven and are they oven ready microchips? No, just more 'kryptonite-like' stuff again. Hang on a second, did I just spot Jabba the Hut lurking at the end?

Where on earth did they source such large quantities of that 'kryptonite-like' stuff?

Now I'm not denying these new on air idents are well-made curios that would feel perfectly at home, constantly looping on a minor gallery wall somewhere. But in my home, when viewed in context, what are they? Do they actually work? Are they really suitable as on-air idents? The answer is, not really. Without any obvious narrative, they just merge into the content that surrounds them, appearing so indistinguishable that they are drowning in their own pretence.

The 4Creatives can explain away their concepts by dressing them up as high art but what they can't hide is poor execution. Here's Grant Gilbert, Creative Director, DBLG again: 'We didn't want to tell people what channel they're watching. We wanted to tell them why they're watching it in the first place. They watch because Channel 4 stands for something important. We wanted the new branding to reflect this'.

Right, yeah…

Actually, I'm sure they are there to be a visual reminder of which channel they are watching, the brand you want to encourage the audience to associate with so they hopefully make repeat visits? A deserved breather in the crash-bang assault on our senses that are today's TV break patterns. Or are they just a collection of Art House films, someone's private fantasy, something a few well-heeled media darlings can discuss at London dinner parties? A form of intellectual elitism – if you don't understand them you must be stupid? I was always under the impression that Channel 4's remit was to be inclusive.

You can discover everything you need to know about a channel's personality by its on-air ident. So what do these new idents say about the channel in 2016? Is Channel 4 claiming to be a high brow 'uber' arts channel? I can't remember the last time I watched a programme about the arts on Channel 4, or any of its sibling channels for that matter. Are they trying to articulate that this is a playground for the artistic elite and not for riff-raff? Or is it just a blatant case of navel-gazing? Having to explain away weak ideas like these by dressing them up as high art is pathetic. Do these little curios really 'flow through everything on the channel', as Chris Bovill and John Allison promise? Do they really reflect *Gogglebox* or *Hollyoaks*, *Countdown* or *Come Dine with Me*? I very much doubt it.

Brand police around every corner
Everything in the media is about telling stories, whether it's print, radio, photography or the moving image. If it's 3 seconds or 3 hours, we are telling stories. When you have only seconds to tell that story you have to cut through all the clutter. In a book, newspaper, film or on a supermarket shelf, the audience has ample time to look closely and digest the information. But in a few seconds of a channel ident, your message has to be simple, clear and to the point. It has to speak to the audience and be original enough to withstand repeat performances. Something the audience appreciate seeing time and time again. Channel 4's new curios embody none of the above. It seems the idents have become like everything else: designed and created in isolation and with no thought to context. Inserted into a mish-mash of stings, promos, adverts and end credits that no one can read.

I recognise the need to create more engagement, be more interactive. I see every day the fashion for adding some kind of social media or response mechanism in break patterns, in a futile attempt to appear hip and contemporary and stem the inevitable migration by young audiences to the ever-growing landscape of competing non-linear viewing experiences. But does this improve the experience? Is it true engagement? Is there an emotional response, a reaction? It may be clever but that doesn't mean it's good. As more and more audiences migrate to non-linear viewing habits, the requirements on us all are changing.

In 2016 BBC3 and *The Independent* newspaper both closed their traditional media outlets and became online only. Is this the writing on the wall or a giant billboard with flashing lights? Is the concept of the TV channel as we know it doomed? We've heard this all before and the jury's still out – but this time I have a feeling it's inevitable.

Even in today's crowded media landscape, television is still a powerful medium, but for how long? The concept of a TV channel will always remain linear. In 2016 things are now far more sophisticated and complex. The Brand Police are around every corner. Whole teams of people are now involved in the creation and decision "process". But decisions are risk averse, everything is consensus driven, mediocrity is rewarded. There's a lack of courage that permeates the media, for individuals to stand up and make a difference. Revolution is now transformation. The ordinary has become invisible, dressed up as pretentious jargon. 'New', 'clothes' and 'Emperor' are the words that come to mind.

Just take a look at the credit list for bringing Channel 4's new on air branding to our screens: They needed two executive creative directors, a head of production, five creative directors, a creative, an executive producer, a business director, a senior producer, two producers, a production manager, eight animators, a writer/director, a director of photography, a production designer, an editor, a lead post supervisor, a post producer, a team of FX designers, two costume designers, two designers, three typographers, three strategists, a fixer, a head of marketing, a group marketing manager, a musician and an artist in residence at London's Southbank Centre… and these are just the important people! Overkill?

I ask myself: did they really need so many opinions? Did all these people improve things? But there's my issue. All the effort, focus and PR, has been spent on the little curios and nothing on the execution or the context.

Awards? Or bums on seats?

Thirty years ago, break patterns were crafted by people. They had time to breathe. Programmes were viewed to find the perfect point for a commercial break. There was a thoughtful narrative structure to everything – television presentation and promotions were used as a dramatic device. Today it's all crash in and out of programmes and cram everything in. It's difficult to be heard, to tell your story. There is now too much visual noise to cut through nothing really speaks to the audience. Everyone one talked about Channel 4 back then, as they now chat about Netflix. Some of it was praise, some of it was vitriol but people talked about it. It was in the public consciousness.

I remember Jeremy Isaacs' response to criticism that our risqué output was a little too avant-garde for the British public. His solution was to ask me to create the Red Triangle (Special Discretion Required), to be used in and around a season of films that the viewer may find too distasteful. These were mostly cult films that would usually have rated a zero audience. Not once the red triangle appeared. Viewing figures rocketed, with viewers tuning into such gems as Derek Jarman's 1976 film, *Sebastiane*, Claude Faraldo's 1973 cult-classic, *Themroc* and Dusan Makavejev's 1981 film, *Montenegro*. An unintended strategy in helping to fulfil Channel 4's remits.

On another occasion I had to contend with angry young mothers complaining on the *Right to Reply Video Box* that a Channel 4 Winter Season animation I'd created was scaring their children. Looking back, maybe it was a little unsettling (twilight, a television at night, white noise on the screen… suddenly a hand appears out of the noise, and out of the hand spins a Venetian mask). The intention had been to surprise the audience. Grab their attention. And this it certainly did.

What makes both of these instances memorable wasn't any level of creative magnificence on show, or any pretentious PR. They simply fulfilled their purpose; they worked. In context, both had a profound effect on the audience and surpassed their intended brief, which at end of the day is what it's all about.

I remember once asking a young promotion producer if he thought his on-air trailer to promote a TV series was a good trailer or a bad trailer. He replied that he thought it was a brilliant trailer, even award winning. When I pointed out that it had failed because the viewing figures for the TV series it was promoting went down, he told me that in his opinion, that was irrelevant. Winning awards was his most important consideration.… not bums on seats. Why does this ring true?

I've always believed that, wherever I worked, I was just a caretaker, a guardian until the next generation took over. I just hope and pray the present generation don't break it. The Channel 4 logo has so far survived thirty years of abuse; will its voice now be lost in the car crash that is present-day automated on-air presentation scheduling and by too much intellectualising? I hope not. Only time will tell if the current offering lasts another ten years. I know the 4 itself will survive for another thirty. And when all those names on the credit list above have vanished into obscurity, I'm sure that the justly talented Martin Lambie-Nairn will not be forgotten, or his baby.

Footnote

There is one footnote I'd like to add before closing. Martin Lambie-Nairn is an RDI (Royal Designer for Industry), a Fellow of the Royal Television Society and an ex-President of D&AD. He received the D&AD President's Award, won a D&AD Gold Pencil for his work on Channel 4, multiple D&AD Silver Pencils and a BAFTA for his BBC re-branding. He was awarded the Prince Philip Design Prize, Promax Lifetime Achievement Award and is in the Promax Hall of Fame, in the US. In this country, architects, product designers, advertising executives, fashion designers, artists, actors, TV personalities and sex offenders, have all been awarded gongs over the years. So why hasn't the designer who created a British Cultural Icon, that's lasted over thirty years, ever received one?

Maybe Spitting Image had something to do with it....

About the author

Dean Stockton is senior director, creative, at Liberty Global. Before that he was senior director of creative at Chellomedia (Now AMC International) for 10 years where he won an NMA award (Best use of Interactive TV) and a World Promax Gold (Best B2B Marketing Campaign). In 2007 he was nominated for an Emmy Award, for outstanding achievement in interactive television. Dean has previously worked as a successful independent producer director in both advertising and broadcast television and in senior roles for some of the world's most prominent media organisations (ITV, BBC, Channel Four, Disney, BSkyB, Canal Plus...), winning several accolades, including D&AD and RTS awards. He studied at Camberwell School of Arts and Crafts, in London.

Note

All quotes contained in this chapter are from one source: *The Channel Four Press Office (2015)*. Available at: http://www.channel4.com/info/press/news/channel-4-refreshes-iconic-main-channel-brand

1997: Between two controllers

By David Lloyd

It was an otherwise ordinary afternoon and this workaholic had – as so often – eaten lunch in his office with a take-away in a polystyrene tray from the canteen (sorry, restaurant) when the rumour started taking hold. I have seldom witnessed such panic, as the gossip ran like wildfire through the commissioning floor. Had Richard Rogers not designed an air-conditioned building, people would have been checking the window locks in preparation for self-defenestration... There had been a 'leak' from the board, sitting in a huddle upstairs to choose Michael Grade's successor – and they had selected Alan Yentob as the next chief executive.

If anything other than the result of an early round of discussion (and it was never even checked out whether he had even applied or was part of the conversation), it might not have been an unreasonable choice to have selected the then-controller of BBC 2, as what we needed was a forward-looking 'creative' of some distinction, and the panic was at least prompted by a credible cause. What was at issue was the credential of detailed, decisive organisation, and it was argued that not even the excellent David Scott, as managing director, might have kept the train on the rails. (It was only while preparing this chapter that I was able to confirm that Yentob was in the running and interviewed.)

What this rumour did demonstrate, however, was that the character of the channel was unreasonably dominated by the choice of chief executive and that a wrong choice could even bring it to its knees. More immediately it served to clear the way for the actual winner, Yentob's twin BBC controller, Michael Jackson, to be welcomed with unusual relief, delight, and support. Certainly, as a founding independent producer, his pedigree was perfect, but in his researches for the post he had taken much poison to his ear from former BBC colleagues – which to his credit, he quickly jettisoned in favour of his own experience, and more objective advice at the channel. Certainly, I had my work cut out to persuade him that Jon Snow did demonstrate the values of the channel, and wasn't some tedious 'pinko hothead' He later evolved into one of Jon's most dedicated admirers.

On the wider front, he quickly set to work with great, liberated, energy to play 'catch-up' on all the future planning that had been neglected; consultants and flip-charts were back IN, and he was hugely assisted in his search for new sources of investment by New Labour's repeal of the funding formula, which had in practice obliged the channel financially to assist ITV out of its travails – rather than, as had been intended, the very reverse. Thus, he inherited no more than draft thinking for an entertainment 'offshoot' (later E4) and a fledgling plan to establish a subscription film channel, but with an inadequate stock of films. Soon David Scott was to be seen scuttling off to Sky to beg access to the Fox feature film library.

Indeed, while Michael Jackson was often dubbed 'Whacko Jacko' (at least outside the channel), his behaviour could be eccentric and skittish, and he had the attention span of Charles the Second, he also had his occasional instinctive brilliance. For those in his confidence, he had the most commendably open and creative management style, and under him the channel DID – largely – catch up, rather against the odds, at least on screen, as is now evidenced by the successful 'family' of C4 channels. More immediately, he brought a new buzz to drama and entertainment via Gub Neal and Kevin Lygo respectively. Writers like Russell T Davies and performers like Sacha Baron Cohen (aka Ali G) gave the channel a second wind, which prolonged its active life markedly. Further, while his industry star may now be in something of a limbo – particularly after his sudden departure to a phantom job in the USA – he it was that came to the (correct) decision that the commissioning team was significantly underpaid – so can, without qualification, be numbered as an all-round 'Good Guy' in this role of honour.

More seriously, he was the last chief executive to possess a true instinct for programming, which – at the top – had always differentiated C4's purpose and culture from the herd, and to him is owed the later longevity of the Channel 4 idea, surviving the changed federal structure of ITV, and the resulting 'heft' of its advertising house, together with the new, digital, habits of the channel's intended demographic.

Section 4:
Imagine...

Introduction by Ian Reeves

I posted a press release back through time.

It was published by a company called Amazon in 2016[1], and I sent it to the founding architects of Channel 4, so that they could open it just as they were about to launch in 1982.

It read as follows:

'Channel 4 [has] developed a Big Data control panel (BDCP), a web-based interface to allow analysts to spin up and spin down Amazon EMR clusters, submit queries through Apache Hive and Pig, monitor job status, and extract sample or actual data to run in modeling applications.'

Unsurprisingly, its recipients were puzzled: 'Who or what is Amazon?' they wondered. 'What is this thing called a web?' 'Why is there a Pig involved?'

'And anyway, what has any of it got to do with our new television company?'

Fair questions.

It's easy to forget quite how dramatically the technological, commercial and cultural landscape has changed in those three-and-a-bit decades since the 4 logo first whirled into view. The world wide web was barely a glimmer in Tim Berners-Lee's eye; it would be another dozen years before Amazon set out on its mission to transform the way we buy (and now watch) stuff, largely based on the capture of data about our preferences and recommendations; and whichever whizzkid invented the computer platform Pig was probably not even born.

As for what it all has to do with their television company... well, by 2016, kind of everything.

That press release, once you have parsed the baffling technical guff, illustrates the seismic changes that the industry is undergoing as the old analogue businesses do battle in a digital age. It is about Channel 4 using Amazon-built

273

web technology to understand more about the huge audience that watches its video-on-demand service. This is something the channel does very well. As John Newbigin, Chair of Creative England, points out in his chapter in this section of the book, C4 is proud to boast that more 16-34 year olds are registered on All4 than are on the electoral register.

And he makes the eloquent case that while Netflix, Youtube, Instagram and all the rest of the new media players (including Amazon Prime) have important roles to play, they are 'no substitute for an organisation whose stated purpose is to promote diversity, nurture new talent, bring new ideas from the margins into the mainstream, broaden people's horizons, provide news and analysis that holds public institutions and government to account, and give a voice to the unheard.'

Yet it is concern about the channel's viability within this increasingly fractured landscape that has, in part, driven Culture Secretary John Whittingdale to wonder whether the ownership model of the channel needs reassessing.

He should be careful what he wishes for, says Roy Ackerman, creator of many great documentary and arts programmes and now managing director of non-scripted television at Pulse Films. While it's true that the commercial pressures on Channel 4 are greater than ever, and that its imperfections can drive you mad as both a viewer and an independent producer, nonetheless its vital public service remit cannot be compatible with private ownership. And the knock-on effects could be disastrous: 'my gravest concern would be the effect privatisation would have on the independent production sector and the wider creative economy,' Ackerman writes.

David Graham, chief executive of Attentional, is no stranger to innovation. He was dabbling with idea of 'Personal TV' on his first Apple Mac computer decades before YouTube's founders had their famous 'dinner party' moment of revelation.

Here he puts forward a fascinating four-point reform agenda for public service broadcasting – not just Channel 4 – which includes significant ideas about the funding of it, including a 'joint subscription pack' for PSBs. A lack of properly strategic thinking on such matters, he argues, has already cost the country dear: 'The chance to play a dominant role in Europe has not so much been spurned as simply shrouded in a mist of ignorance'.

In her wide-ranging chapter, Professor Sylvia Harvey provides a broad analysis of why Channel 4 still works – and how it has adapted so successfully to the changing media world from when it was one of four in an analogue world to today's global media landscape. Ultimately, she says, it's the capacity to take risks – both commercially and creatively – that have made it what it is: 'Without such risk there is little serious innovation and few unexpected pleasures for audiences.'

Colin Browne and Sophie Chalk represent VLV, the Voice of the Listener and Viewer, and examine the channel's track record from the perspective of the people watching it – whichever device they happen to be using. Crucially, they say, the uncertainty over its future is likely to hamper the channel's ability to produce new, innovative content from which many other broadcasters shy away. 'The best way to ensure the healthy survival of Channel 4 is for its existing licence, which is due to expire on 31 December 2024, to be considered as set in stone. The Government should respect the agreement which it signed up to in 2014.'

Alex Connock, managing director at Shine North, looks at the major contribution that Channel 4's model makes to the creative economy outside London – and specifically the North. The conversation about the much-vaunted Northern Powerhouse, he notes, should be about a lot more than just trains and airports. He poses the question: 'Is it possible for the state to own assets that function commercially, incubate startup businesses, trade with profitable global corporations, create powerful export numbers and enrich creative value across the full spectrum of the nation, both geographic and cultural?' The answer is emphatically in the affirmative.

Our book's final two contributions take us on a journey into the future. John Mair imagines the broadcasting landscape in 2022, following a part-privatisation of Channel 4 in 2017. Unless your surname is Murdoch, it ain't particularly pretty. Finally, David Lloyd completes the journey he has been making throughout this book, imagining a Channel 4 schedule in which creativity, editorial credibility and any nods to diversity have been sacrificed on the altar of the High Priests of shareholder value.

It is, he describes, a 'dark vision' in which its new owners have 'given up trying to reconcile remit with return and [sold] out to one of the truly predatory US multinationals who do a deal to forget the remit entirely in order to bolster the channel's capital base.'

Perhaps it won't come to that. Perhaps. But the events of 2016 will certainly shape its likelihood. If somebody from 2046 could send me a press release to let me know how it turns out, I'd be most grateful.

Notes

[1] Amazon Web Service press release: https://aws.amazon.com/solutions/case-studies/channel-4/

No success like failure

By David Graham

Channel 4 still has a key task in supporting innovation and the creation of new creative companies. But some early hopes and aims have been surrendered

I am going to write about some specific things that drove me to be part of a campaign for a 'publisher channel' 35 years ago and what has happened to those aims and ambitions. Reviewing that story has made me hope there are still some open minds out there, ready to think again about some of the fundamentals of our broadcasting system.

Support for innovation was a key part of the original plan and it has worked. From this perspective, C4's role is basically a functional one. It has a job to do. That job is to help the emergence of new production companies. Channel 4 is therefore a component or element in a strategy for growing and maintaining a successful entertainment industry.

As one entertainment economist puts it, every new creative start is a new piece of research and development (Vogel 2004). It has a high risk of failure. There are still no viable models for investment in new TV content outside the broadcasters: the slates of new start-ups are built on founders' time and funded only when commissioned by a broadcaster. We may be seeing the emergence of new models, such as VICE News, but they are nowhere near ready to play an equivalent role. Creative industries need start-ups to power innovation.

A TV or film production company also differs from a tech company in another significant way. The economic life of one successful innovation, say a successful TV series, is limited. It does not 'scale'. The nearest you get to a successful tech launch in entertainment is a long running soap or a franchise like the Star Wars or Bond franchises. They are rare.

It's true that one success may build a company that can then become an engine of new development and carry a degree of risk, but a project only goes forward with carriage on a broadcast platform. As I have suggested above, this may change. It hasn't yet.

I therefore see C4 as a part of a plan or economic strategy which, though proposed long ago, still holds. But let's not stop there.

History of a point of view

This short biographical part that follows is just a way of delineating a point of view or position that I know is not widely shared. All significant change is driven by many people – I can't think of a single thing I have done that was not stimulated by someone else. But, at the risk of being over-specific, a story can sometimes say more than an argument.

I didn't know my country well until I was in my late twenties. We lived abroad for most of my youth. I went to university in the UK, then to the US as a postgraduate and subsequently emigrated to Canada.

I knew I was aiming for a creative career but was not quite sure where and how. Toronto, where I lived in my middle and late twenties, was a lively place. My apartment was near the university and we used to see Marshall McLuhan walking to work. The initial idea of being a writer – I had a first novel in draft – shifted towards 'multimedia'. I made radio documentaries and worked in advertising.

But on a return visit I was offered a job by the BBC. The sheer novelty of the idea appealed and I joined the staff of BBC Radio Derby in 1971.

A week before we went to air, Rolls Royce went bankrupt and had to be rescued. I was out on the street interviewing the shop stewards and reporting mass meetings. Thus my journalistic career started with a sudden and unexpected perception: I was going to have to get to know about a failing economy. I had come from a place that was prosperous and buzzing with new ideas. This was a shock. 'My country' was in a mess.

I needed to know something about economics, read through Samuelson, found it interesting and enjoyable and have continued to buy later editions.[1]

By 1977 I was a producer working for *Panorama* under Roger Bolton. I was able to explore our society: I saw the depths of poverty in places where an economy had failed. (Bolton 1990). There I also learned how the political process worked and how, if one felt passionately about something, it might be possible to influence an outcome.

For those needing help with the chronology, the Labour government led by James Callaghan ground to a halt in the so-called Winter of Discontent in 1978/79 when the 'social contract' with the major labour unions broke down. Another motivating crisis!

That was just two years before the launch of Channel 4.

A few years before this I had bought an Apple computer and learned BASIC programming and was exploring an idea that some combination of the computer and video cassette technology would enable you to make and distribute your own content. TV regulation would be irrelevant. I even created a little promotional video for what I called Personal TV.

That of course never happened, but during this time I became aware of the movement to create a new kind of channel. Anthony Smith,[2] a key influence, put me in contact with some of the significant players in the movement for a publisher broadcaster, as against the ITV2 that had originally been proposed.

The campaign was successful and Channel 4 was defined as a publisher broadcaster, with content to be supplied by third parties. Jeremy Isaacs was appointed. I submitted some proposals about which Jeremy was very enthusiastic and very quickly I was offered a proposition. While ITN would produce a daily one-hour news, on Friday it would be abbreviated to half an hour and the other half would be called *The Friday Alternative*. The programme was inspired by the work of the Glasgow Media Group led by Greg Philo and the work of cultural critic Stuart Hall, both of whom I knew by then. It was to be a 'critique' of mainstream news.

I guess you could say that by this time my thinking had solidified into a 'position'. First, 'entertainment' was an important economic activity which, like any other, would make a greater contribution to public welfare if it was functioning optimally, i.e. it would contribute more jobs and tax revenues. This connected with another passion. Freedom of expression was curtailed by a nexus of rules falling under the general rubric of 'public service broadcasting'. The two issues were closely connected. The latter issue was both very important in its own right and was inhibiting the first.

So I was excited by the opportunity I was being offered to challenge the status quo.

No Success Like Failure
Since the news critique was driven by the left and I felt we should aim young, the available style models were magazines like *City Limits* or *Time Out*, so we worked on a TV format close to those. I also added in ways of getting at grassroots opinion via a series of representative groups attached to the programme. We called them contributing groups and we tried to recruit something like a national sample of the population.

We had a stormy launch and the programme did quite well in the ratings winter in which Channel 4 launched. But sometime in the first season I was called in to the IBA (as it then was) and told by David Glencross that the programme was in breach of the Broadcasting Act because of its lack of impartiality.

At the end of its first season, *The Friday Alternative* was cancelled at a frenetic board meeting.[3] I still feel a disappointment when the first half hour of *Channel 4 News* ends. It was a historic opportunity. Later on I was disappointed too by the demise of a programme called *Europe Express*, which used English-speaking journalists from around Europe reporting on European stories. Though I was successful in getting *The New Enlightenment* made, which looked at the revival of classical liberalism[4], I gradually came to feel I might already have done my best work as a producer.

Jeremy Isaacs and Liz Forgan fought very hard for *The Friday Alternative*. Its replacement, *Diverse Reports*, based on the idea of 'balance' across a series and aiming at an 'Op-ed' approach, did good things but it proved hard to build a strong brand around that concept.

The opportunity to get rid of, even moderate, the constraints imposed by the 'due impartiality' rules and inject new vitality and energy into political reporting went away. I am not saying C4 has not done some good and challenging journalism. I watch *Channel 4 News* whenever I can. But it failed to change the rules of the game in the way some of us had hoped.[5]

New Terms

I had got to know Professor Brian Griffiths, Mrs Thatcher's advisor. He became an ally. Could we make the British entertainment industry a better contributor to the British economy? What reforms or changes might drive this? He believed the independent production sector could be a driver. Some of us formed a group to campaign for a 'quota' for independent production on BBC and ITV. The Conservative government asked Professor Alan Peacock to report on the industry. He supported an independent production quota and it was put into legislation.

The new company I formed in 1990, now called Attentional, became a kind of engine of the change process. We were commissioned by the Office of Fair Trading to monitor the BBC quota compliance through most of the 1990s. During that time John Woodward, then head of PACT, the producers' association, was thinking about the next step and there emerged the first outline of what are now called the 'Terms of Trade' in the industry. The paper was called *The Courage to Compete*.

The paper argued that the broadcasters were a 'monopsony', extracting all industry profit to the broadcasting function, leaving production to live on cost-plus with no rights in its originations. The broadcasters were 'warehousing' content, that is, starving the new digital channels. They were no good at exports because they had other priorities. Independent producers were proving be more innovative. And the broadcasters were inefficient.

The document argued that producers should retain all other rights than the 'primary' right which would be retained by broadcasters. There were secondary issues but this was the most important and it became the key element in the so-called Terms of Trade which became operational in 2002.[6] My policy role ceased and I moved on to other things and places.

In the mid-1990s, Chris Smith, then Culture Minister, had bought into the concept, still novel, of the Creative Industries. As a result, stats on revenue, employment and exports are now updated on a regular basis. In 1999, my company was also commissioned to write a report called *Building a Global Audience*[7], which established a reporting trend that has been kept going since then and highlighted some of the obstacles which our content puts before overseas buyers.

So I was part, along with many others, of a process that defined a new policy framework for broadcasting, that recognised the need for innovation, and that had stimulated growth.

The status quo, as defined in the last paragraph, is broadly supported by Channel 4 and the production industry. Its achievements could be seen to provide a good argument for doing little or nothing.

But the structure of which C4 is part feels more and more tired and obsolete. 'There's no success like failure,' Bob Dylan said, 'and failure's no success at all.'

Old Thinking

I referred to Channel 4's 'functional' role. It is there to support the emergence of creative companies. That role has been a useful one, now supplemented by terms of trade that impose a similar role on other public broadcasters. Privatising C4 would not be a smart move unless we could be sure it would not dilute that obligation. I doubt if that assurance is possible.

But this perspective, as above, positions C4 as an organisation with a particular role in a larger system – the UK creative economy – which I think is still significantly under-performing. I hope that in considering the future of C4, government and regulators pay some attention to the bigger picture too.

Here are some items for a provisional reform agenda:

(1) The definition of Public Service Broadcasting. The current rules for PSB impose a requirement for domestic production in a range of genres – entertainment, documentary – that are essentially part of the commercial entertainment spectrum. In return, the PSBs get benefits – like guide prominence. This is partly based on a view that our culture, that is, the culture of the UK, needs to be protected, which is illusory. We are a robust culture, which would be stronger, more dynamic and more interesting without bureaucratic interference. The concept of Public Service content needs to be redefined to cover just those basics, such as educational content, in which there is a public interest in good, available information free-to-air or unencoded on pay platforms.

(2) The Impartiality Rule. This rule still requires 'due impartiality' in matters of public policy. 'Public Policy' means in practice any issue on which a recognised political party has a position, which in turn requires that representatives of each relevant party are heard on the topic. This absorbs a massive amount of time and has turned the news and current affairs reporting staff of the main broadcasters into kinds of courtiers at Westminster. This kind of reporting can be enjoyable and lively but the fact remains that a programme like *Any Questions* is, in effect, a shared party political broadcast. How refreshing it would have been to see 'Europe' discussed on TV outside this framework![8] As for news bulletins, I am sure that the leading channels would wish to maintain 'impartial' news programmes after the abolition of the rule.

(3) The BBC. In my view the BBC has fumbled its future. Its main problem – and the country's also – is its addiction to the Licence Fee as the entertainment world moves to various modes of Pay Television. This addiction can be easily explained in corporate terms: most senior managers are risk avoiders and the licence is an effective revenue guarantee. Its addiction has meant that the BBC missed the chance to move towards a 'studio' status and convert its licence fee to subscription at a time when it would have offered terrific value for money.[9]

(4) The other PSBs. In my view it will eventually become clear that the PSBs have hung onto their traditional sources of revenue for too long. TV advertising is still a viable business model but runs the risk of obsolescence as broadband speeds up. This poses a tremendous challenge to those who have relied on advertising as their predominant revenue source. ITV has indeed moved towards a 'studio' mode, that is a business reliant on the ownership and control of a large catalogue of rights. C4 can't do that if it is to retain the key function of supporting UK creative companies, so it faces an even bigger challenge. A default solution might have to be a joint subscription pack with other former PSBs.

The combined effect of these unreformed constraints has made our TV industry provincial and inward looking. Yes, the Terms of Trade for independent producers drove a surge of exports. But the chance to play a dominant role in Europe has not so much been spurned as simply shrouded in a mist of ignorance. All European channels play English language content in primetime, dubbed or subtitled. The UK and Eire are the only exceptions. Has no one spotted that this offers a huge competitive advantage?

In fact, our export performance has been hugely over-rated by apologists. USA film and TV exports run into billions of dollars and comprise nearly 50% of total revenues. Accepting all the vast differences in our domestic markets, our export performance is paltry. Drama will always be the most traded genre. The UK has neither found narratives that resonate in Europe nor the techniques and business model to support their production.[10] Our TV industry has consistently ignored the findings of the regular export surveys on the views of overseas buyers. This indifference to the potential economic contribution of the TV industry continues to frustrate. I have trouble understanding why this has not been recognised.

In the past decade I have worked a lot in both Europe and the US and learned much about the way different creative economies work. I have found little curiosity about this in the UK. But perhaps there's a simple explanation. Broadcasting is not really part of the 'economy' at all. It is part of our 'culture' and that comes first. I have already argued that our culture does not need protection. But perhaps there's a more insidious factor working here. The Westminster 'court' wants to maintain its primacy. Among the courtiers are highly intelligent, troublesome reporters and commentators who ask difficult questions and sometimes even bring down a minister. But they are part of the system that keeps the Westminster 'court' on our screens, indeed mandates that it stays there, and our politicians like both the exposure and the control. I fear reform is a lost cause.

About the author
David Graham was educated at Marlborough College, and Bristol and Indiana universities. He began as a radio producer in Toronto in 1967, joining BBC Radio in 1970 and moving to BBC Television in 1973, as a producer on *Nationwide*, *The Money Programme*, and *Panorama*. In 1981, David, with Peter Donebauer, set up Diverse Productions to make programmes for Channel Four. David is CEO of Attentional but the views expressed are his own.

Notes
[1] Unfortunately, Samuelson does not say much about entertainment. It is covered briefly under The Economics of Information, and emphasizes the difficulty of economic pricing in the internet age. (Samuelson, 2010).

[2] The seminal book for me was The Shadow in the Cave. Smith, Anthony (1973).

[3] There are detailed accounts of this which may still have some relevance and interest. See. Isaacs (1989) and Bonner (2004).

[4] See Graham and Clarke (1986).

[5] The 'series' rule, now current, is much too prescriptive for an Op-ed approach. 'This means more than one programme in the same service, editorially linked, dealing with the same or related issues within an appropriate period and aimed at a like audience. A series can include, for example, a strand, or two programmes (such as a drama and a debate about the drama) or a 'cluster' or 'season' of programmes on the same subject.' Broadcasting Code Guidance, Ofcom.

[6] A very detailed account of the negotiation of the 'terms' may be found in Darlow (2004).

[7] This was funded by a private consortium supported by the Department of Trade and Industry. The executive summary highlights problems echoed in successor reports produced by another company.

[8] This constraint is also inhibiting good discussion of 'big' issues like the evolution of the nation state (Bobbit, 2002)

[9] I wrote about the BBC in 2010 (Graham, 2010) in a paper for the Adam Smith Institute, just after the beginning of another economic crisis!

[10] Peter Ansorge, former head of Channel 4 drama, says something similar in *Broadcast*, Feb 12, 2016. 'You can't argue against HBO, AMC, Showtime being the new gold standard in TV drama. Even Germany has got in on the act with Deutschland 83…they are all original and contemporary works, with challenging things to say about their recent history…In contrast, the UK typically looks back or towards crime…'

References
Bobbit, Philip (2002) *The Shield of Achilles*, London: Penguin.
Bolton, Roger (1990) *Death on the Rock*, London: W.H. Allen & Co, p.113.
Bonner, Paul et al. (2004) *Independent Television in Britain, Volume 6*, London: Macmillan.

Darlow, Michael (2004) *Independents Struggle*, London: Quartet.

Graham, David (2010) *Global Player or Subsidy Junkie*, London: Adam Smith Research Trust.

Graham, David and Clarke, Peter (1986) *The New Enlightenment*, London: Macmillan.

Isaacs, Jeremy (1989) *Storm Over 4*, London: George Weidenfeld & Nicolson, p82-88.

Samuelson, Paul (2010) *Economics*, New York: McGraw-Hill, p222.

Smith, Anthony (1973) *The Shadow in the Cave*, London: George Allen & Unwin Ltd.

Vogel, Harold (2004) *Entertainment Industry Economics*, New York: Cambridge University Press, p111.

What's 4 for?

By John Newbigin

Has the channel fulfilled its purpose and become too marginalised to merit saving? Or is it uniquely placed to re-imagine public service broadcasting?

Channel 4 has always been a maverick institution. It was born with 'a licence to be different', not just in what it did but also in what it was. To the European Commission apparatchiks of Brussels it was a logical absurdity to have a publicly-owned broadcaster with a clear public service remit but an absolute dependence on commercial ad sales for its survival. At home it irritated, and still irritates, the more rabid end of the neo-liberal spectrum who see it not as an absurdity but as an evolutionary dead-end which has no future in the bracing climate of a strong-state-free-economy kind of world. That's strange because it is also quite possibly the most successful and cost-effective policy intervention by any government ever in the development of the creative industries. At no cost to the public purse other than a bit of free analogue spectrum, it can make a plausible claim to be the progenitor of an independent production sector that grew from a handful of querulous indie producers to become the most successful engine for new programmes and formats anywhere in the world of television, worth at least £1bn a year to the UK economy. There's no denying that, in Maggie Brown's felicitous phrase, it's a 'brilliant accident of history'.

Aside from its unconventional structure, Channel 4's purpose has also been to be different. Amongst other requirements, the 1980 Broadcasting Act required the infant channel to include 'a suitable proportion of matter calculated to appeal to tastes and interests not generally catered for by ITV' and to '...encourage innovation and experiment in the form and content of programmes and generally give the fourth channel a distinctive character of its own'. To 21st century eyes, attuned as we are to paranoid levels of mistrust between politicians and the media, such a *carte blanche* remit – so trusting and so optimistic – clearly belongs to different age. But not so. Twenty years later the Communications Act of 2003 still politely asked a now grown-up channel to 'demonstrate innovation, experiment and creativity in the form and content of programmes' and to 'exhibit a distinctive character'. Reflecting the changes in UK society in the intervening twenty years it was also asked to 'celebrate diversity'. It didn't even have to do it all on-air as a conventional broadcaster; Schedule 9 of the Act simply says it should 'make a broad range of relevant media content of high quality'.

Such a fabulously open-ended articulation of the remit has not made its fulfilment any easier. Edmund Dell, the first chairman, famously complained at an early board meeting that the channel seemed to be confusing 'alternative entertainment' with 'an alternative *to* entertainment'. In the same vein, its output has frequently been attacked as sensationalist, pointlessly provocative, lewd and crude, while its commissioning editors have indignantly, and sometimes rather naively, protested that they are simply doing their jobs by representing 'difference', 'diversity', 'alternative points of view' – and that being provocative is what they're supposed to be doing. From *Teen Big Brother* to *Benefit Street* what's been a refreshingly alternative take on the world for one viewer, for another has been proof of disastrously poor judgement and an institution that has completely lost the plot.

So it may appear difficult, from the perspective of 2016, to recall just how much 'difference' Channel 4 really has made. The first lesbian kiss and the broadcast of *My Beautiful Laundrette* are still trotted out by some old hands as evidence, even though both events, iconic as they may have been, occurred before half of today's viewers were even born. But however it is itemised, the record is pretty impressive: it's been a champion for diversity, sometimes exhaustingly and even tiresomely so when it comes to issues of sex and sexuality, but it has *inter alia* transformed the public perception of disability and Paralympic sport, not just in Britain but around the world, as the Rio Olympics are likely to show.

It has spent energy and money in attempts to broaden the diversity of a notoriously un-diverse industry in terms of ethnicity, gender and class. It has given a first and often a second and third break to hundreds of small indie production companies outside the charmed media circle of London and the South-East. It's been central to the dynamism of independent British cinema, combining creative risk-taking and successful talent development with enough Oscars to make any Hollywood major envious. It has been, and continues to be, a real pioneer of online services, most of which probably escape the notice of anyone over the age of 21. It also provides a significant quantity of educational content aimed, successfully, at kids who need it and, judging by the figures, appreciate it. It runs one of the most admired TV news programmes anywhere, commanding respect from across the political spectrum while successfully maintaining a radical perspective and highlighting international events in a way that most mainstream broadcasters are at pains to avoid. It cranks out current affairs documentaries in a way other broadcasters haven't been doing for a couple of decades. Notwithstanding the fact that it also produces its fair share of eminently forgettable and cringe-makingly awful programmes, it undoubtedly makes the UK's media world a little richer than it would otherwise be. And so it should. That's what it's there for. And its justification for remaining in public ownership is that it otherwise would not.

A shockingly long way to go

But do these things still need doing, even if they're not being done as well as they might be? The short answer must be 'yes'. British television still has a shockingly long way to go in addressing almost any aspect of diversity – and in terms of representing the nation's ethnic diversity on-screen is actually going backwards, as the actor Lenny Henry has pointed out. It needs all the help it can get. British independent cinema benefits hugely from having a variety of gateways for talent to be picked up and funded – every review of government film policy makes that point and every independent film producer knows it to be true. High quality content on-air and online to help young people make responsible life choices sounds like a good idea and the market is not exactly over-crowded with commercial providers. Are we so well served with news and current affairs that we don't need the exceptional quality of *Channel 4 News* and the great variety of documentaries brought to us by *Unreported World* and *Dispatches*? What's more, all these benefits come free to the public and are available on every major platform. With the end of analogue broadcasting and its protected spectrum, Channel 4 costs the public purse not a penny.

Would none of those things happen if Channel 4 were not in public ownership? The short answer must be 'no'. None of them are unique to Channel 4, though it would be difficult to argue that our media landscape is over-populated with any of them. Would these things be done better if the channel was in private hands? The argument is made that it is now too small to survive much longer in a world of mighty media giants. A big buyer would bring efficiencies of scale, would invest in better quality programmes and we would all be better off than we are today. All it would require would be for Ofcom to insist that the programme budget was protected and the job would be done. Or perhaps not. It requires a real effort of the creative imagination to see a private owner, almost certainly a large non-UK based conglomerate, being more rigorous than the present management in honouring commitments to 'creativity', 'experiment' and 'distinctiveness'.

Another argument is that the channel is unviable because its senior executives are paying themselves too much. If senior staff costs were reduced in the event of privatisation it would be an event without precedent in the entire history of privatisations. On the other hand, it could be taken as a certainty that overall staff costs would be reduced by stripping out such inessential functions as the fostering of relationships with new talent, new programme ideas, new production companies and public service style back-up services. To combine these arguments and suggest that a private owner would do all of the above: ring-fence the programme budget, enforce the remit, nurture new production indies, reduce executive pay – and still pay a dividend to all those shareholders who, presumably, would be as interested in getting a good rate of return on their money as getting the occasional good programme on their TV set at home – would stretch the talents of Derren Brown. It is not a credible scenario. Sooner or later creative risk would hit the brick wall of shareholder interest.

Twenty years ago the then chairman of Channel 4, Sir Michael Bishop, was able to persuade the government of the day, toying with the idea of selling off Channel 4, that to do so would kill the model. That was at a time when commercial TV companies had generous margins. Programme budgets, back-office costs, executive pay: none of them were under significant pressure. The media world, and television in particular, is in a very different place today. Margins are squeezed. Budgets, operating costs, staffing are all under real pressure. If Channel 4 is now too small to survive on its own and still be distinctive, Channel 4 as the privately owned subsidiary of a large international media empire would very soon either stop being distinctive, or just stop – and its meagre assets dissolved. A senior Channel 5 executive, when asked recently what the current owners, Viacom, thought of the channel, responded that he wasn't sure that Viacom were actually aware that they did own it but, if they were, it was pretty clear they didn't know what it did and didn't particularly care, as long as the financial projections stacked up.

Re-imagining public service broadcasting

Assuming Channel 4 survives, continues in public ownership, continues to generate enough advertising revenue to commission quality programmes and finds enough ways to generate revenue from its online and other activities to cover their costs, what should it do next? How can it fulfil its remit obligations to be innovative in form and content in a world that doesn't just have tsunamis of content on-air and online but in which 'the people formerly known as the audience' have the technology in their hands – literally – to be film-makers, commentators, composers, story-tellers and, most importantly, broadcasters in their own right? In these circumstances a few interesting programme ideas are not going to cut it when it comes to 'innovation', 'experiment' or 'distinctiveness': the whole concept of what it means to be a public service broadcaster with a clear remit (and Channel 4's remit remains very clear) needs to be re-imagined.

Many would argue that public service broadcasting doesn't merit re-imagining so much as euthanasia; that in fact it is already irrelevant and already on its death-bed, with all forms of live terrestrial television lying in the bed next to it. The demise of both has been announced at regular intervals over the last 20 years but they continue to flourish with audiences of an entirely different magnitude to most content in the online world. That's no proof of their longevity but it is evidence of the already well-proven adage that old technologies and consumer habits are not always killed off by the new, they simply learn to co-exist with them, as the publishing industry and the music business are finding out.

Furthermore, Snapchat, Instagram and YouTube are no substitute for an organisation whose stated purpose is to promote diversity, nurture new talent, bring new ideas from the margins into the mainstream, broaden people's horizons, provide news and analysis that holds public institutions and government to account, and give a voice to the unheard. All of these aspects of public life are essential to the well-being of a dynamic democratic society, but none of them are essential to the well-being of a transnational media empire or a social media platform.

Finally, concern about the creative commons, open sourcing and digital public space highlights the fact that the virtual commons of the online world are just as much under threat from powerful incumbents as the village commons of England were under threat from powerful landlords in the 18th century. They need to be actively defended by the citizenry and to do that the citizenry need powerful institutions of their own – which is what a 21st century public service broadcaster should be. The BBC, weighted down with almost a hundred years of accumulated baggage and, it seems, the undying enmity of significant sections of the Tory party (plus a handful of undying media moguls), is currently preoccupied with its own survival. ITV has developed an extraordinarily successful business model that produces great television but with barely a passing nod to the wider civic responsibilities of public service broadcasting. Forget Five. But Channel 4 has a track-record, an energetic cross-platform content strategy, a happy absence of production baggage by virtue of being nothing more than a publisher, a still viable business model and a sufficiently large group of youngish friends (its executives claim that more 16-34 year olds are 'registered' Channel 4 supporters than are registered to vote) to mean it could trigger another "brilliant accident of history" and surprise us all.

Margaret Thatcher's first government was responsible for the creation of Channel 4 and did so on the laudable grounds of giving a platform to the powerless, a good kicking to the powerful and a challenge to some creative people to try something different and take a few risks. A generation on, the powerless could still do with a platform, (and YouTube, on its own, isn't it) while the powerful need a good kicking more than ever. And since we now live in a country which politicians of all stripes love to tell us is the most creative on the planet, surely we should be in favour of giving creative people that chance to take a few more risks? Channel 4's task is not done. It has a licence to be different, not just in what it does but also in what it is. As the digital world throws up a stream of radical new ways of funding businesses, running businesses and managing businesses, of open-sourcing innovation and building collaborative creative partnerships, Channel 4 – a child of the digital age – needs to embrace its remit to be innovative in form and content more than ever. It could even be a smart way to prove to the world and ourselves that we really are a creative and confident nation. Flogging it off to Viacom would prove the opposite.

About the author

John Newbigin OBE is Chair of Creative England and of Cinema Arts Network. From 2000 to 2005 he was Head of Corporate Relations for Channel 4. Prior to that he was Special Advisor at the Department for Culture, Media and Sport. He is an Honorary Professor at the University of Hong Kong. In 2015 he was awarded an OBE for services to the arts and creative industries.

The remit and the risk factor

By Sylvia Harvey

The channel's public remit allows and requires it to take the risks that enable it to offer new pleasures to audiences and useful challenges to its competitors

In an interview in the *Sunday Times* in March 2016 the Conservative Government's Secretary of State for Culture, Media and Sport, John Whittingdale, indicated that he was still exploring options for the possible privatisation of Channel 4. He argued that this would be beneficial for the channel, bringing new opportunities for investment and expansion: 'Channel 4 is being restrained by not being privatised'. He also offered a reassurance that the channel's news, current affairs programmes and Film 4 would be protected should the broadcaster be sold. The legislative remit, or parliamentary purposes given to the channel, he considered to be 'rather fuzzy' and in need of clarification. Concern was also expressed about the 'lack of children's programmes' (Blazeby, 2016a). For those charged with commissioning innovative and creative content there are few 'how to' manuals available and a fuzziness in the remit could be an advantage. As Lord Inglewood, former chair of the Lords Communications Committee, noted:

> What's wrong with a fuzzy remit? The National Gallery isn't full of paintings by numbers. C4 is a cultural phenomenon in this country. It's not just a TV company, it's more like a parallel arts council. It's not about the remit being specific, it's about the output. (Blazeby, 2016b)

If we stop to ask the 'who's in charge here?' question, it is perhaps also worth noting that the Shareholder Executive that supervises various enterprises owned by Government – including Channel 4 – was moved in May 2015 from the custodianship of the Secretary of State for Business Innovation and Skills (Vince Cable's old department) to the Chancellor of the Exchequer and HM Treasury (Shareholder Executive, 2015).

In his guarded commitment to exploring privatisation options it could be that the Secretary of State had in mind a warning issued by Ofcom in a 2007 report that noted: '...the possibility that significant financial problems could emerge that would affect Channel 4's ability to deliver its remit'. C4 might need to request 'short term support' (Ofcom, 2007 p3-5). The banking crisis and financial crash that hit the British economy in the following year, 2008, rendered it highly unlikely that an institution hitherto entirely independent of state funding might simply request a public subvention.

Fortunately C4's financial health took a turn for the better, in part because of the risks it had taken in the early 2000s, developing a wider portfolio of services with the launch of several new digital channels. So although its main channel was attracting a modest 4.8 per cent audience share by 2014, this was outshone by an additional 6.1 per cent of viewing coming from the wider portfolio or family of channels – E4, Film4 etc. – giving them a combined UK audience share of 10.9 per cent (Ofcom, 2015a). This aggregate matched the figure of around 10 per cent of viewing that had been achieved from the original Channel 4 alone in the early 1990s in a world still relatively untouched by the multi-channel phenomenon (Channel 4, 1993 p18).

C4's share of the 2014 UK television audience brought with it significant income from advertisers who particularly valued access to the difficult-to-reach market of younger viewers: 28 per cent of all viewing to its main channel was claimed to come from 16- to 34-year-olds (Channel 4, 2015a p7). The overall share figure of 10.9 per cent in 2014 also places it among the top three most popular UK broadcasters, above the subscription-based Sky family of channels at 8.2 per cent but below the free-to-air portfolios of BBC and ITV whose shares are respectively at 33.1 per cent and 22.0 per cent (Ofcom, 2015b p198). It may be this success that makes C4 a tempting prospect for acquisition by a profit-distributing operator.

The channel itself has made the case that its ownership by the state and its 'social enterprise' model has enabled it to spend more of its income on making programmes than, for example, its shareholder-reliant competitor ITV. C4 claims that in 2014 two thirds or 66 per cent of its revenue was spent on content while its much larger rival ITV spent just over half or 52 per cent of revenue on making programmes.

In absolute terms it may be useful to compare the revenues received by Channel 4 and by ITV in 2014. Total revenue for C4 was £938m of which £602m was spent on all content production, including the buying-in of foreign series etc. Some 70 per cent of this content budget (£430m) was spent on UK-originated content (Channel 4, 2015a p8, p21, p24). By contrast ITV had a total revenue of £2.956 billion (three times as much as C4 in the same year), an investment of 'over £1bn annually in programming' and a commitment to providing an improved dividend for shareholders. The ITV content investment figure at nearer to one third of total revenue is clearly a smaller proportion of income than that spent by C4 (ITV, 2014 p5-6, p16-17).

In respect of choice and the quality of UK-originated programmes, the audience could have a lot to lose if Channel 4 goes into private, possibly

American ownership, with an inevitable shift of loyalty and resource towards the interests of shareholders. Most of its audience probably remains unaware of the privatisation proposal and its implications, though the independent production sector – suppliers of a large proportion of the channel's original programmes – has moved strongly and perhaps unsurprisingly behind existing ownership arrangements (Parker, 2015).

Riding the waves of change

There are currently at least four pieces of legislation which spell out the Channel 4 remit: the Broadcasting Acts of 1981 and 1990, the Communications Act of 2003 and the Digital Economy Act of 2010. Changes in structure and funding are also embodied in the legislation, for example the significant change that took place when the ITV companies no longer had the right to sell all advertising on C4, or when the old Independent Broadcasting Authority (IBA) relinquished its role as effectively the owner of the company. Following the 1990 Act C4 took on a new institutional existence, becoming the Channel Four Television Corporation in 1993. Retaining its status as a publicly-owned organisation, the corporation subsequently developed a number of subsidiaries and was also able to sell its own advertising for the first time. Some saw this a benefit; others as a handicap, as a new closeness to the preferences of advertisers might erode editorial independence and judgement.

Some ten years earlier, on the eve of Channel 4's creation, a Conservative Home Secretary with responsibility for broadcasting had foreseen and sought to avoid the danger that it might be constrained by too direct a relationship with the advertising sector (Whitelaw, 1979 p5).

The broadcasting world has seen great changes over the last two decades and it is clear that the advent of connected television sets, the use of internet-based catch-up services like the BBC iPlayer, the rise of a growing subscription-based video on demand sector (SVOD –Netflix, Amazon and others) and a great increase in online advertising, has led to the growth of new audience habits.[1] The satellite TV subscription sector, dominated by Sky, has take-up in 51 per cent of UK homes and wishes for more (Ofcom, 2015 p145). It is too soon to know how far non-broadcast providers will erode the model of watching live TV in the UK, but Channel 4 has already demonstrated considerable flexibility in recognising and riding the waves of technological and social change.

How has British legislation responded to and shaped change? The obligations laid upon all public service broadcasters (PSBs) by the 2003 Act are worth noting since these also apply to Channel 4. References include the following: concern with a '...high general standard' and the '...quality of the programme making' along with '...professional skill and editorial integrity applied in the making of the programmes'. Programming should reflect, support and stimulate '...cultural activity in the United Kingdom, and its diversity' as well as offering '...programmes that reflect the lives and concerns of different communities and cultural interests and traditions within the United Kingdom'. News provision should be 'appropriate for facilitating civic understanding and fair and well-informed debate on news and current affairs,' along with 'authoritative coverage of news and current affairs in, and in the different parts of, the United Kingdom and from around the world'. The schedule should have ambition and variety with '...programmes dealing with...science, religion and other beliefs, social issues, matters of international significance... matters of specialist interest', along with 'programmes about the history of different religions and other beliefs'. There should also be '...high quality and original programmes for children and young people'. Finally, it was expected that there would be '...an appropriate range and proportion of programmes made outside the M25 area' (a rather odd wording for the encouragement to make programmes outside London). In addition all PSBs must show a minimum 25 per cent quota of programmes made by independent producers and an appropriate proportion of 'original programmes' – the minimum proportion for each PSB channel to be determined by Ofcom (Communications Act, 2003 Sections 264, 277, 278).

In this last regard – the transmission of original content – the non-PSB channels can do more-or-less what they wish (though there are some relevant European regulations) and while they make up the majority of licensed channels, they are not among the most widely watched ones. Thus the freedom to avoid original UK content has allowed some providers and channels to be extremely profitable even without attracting very large numbers of viewers.

In Channel 4's case investment in original UK programmes in 2014 (i.e. those not bought in from elsewhere) represented some 70 per cent of total content spend, as already indicated (Channel 4, 2015b p13). Finally the 2003 Act requires all licensed channels to show impartiality in the presentation of 'matters of political or industrial controversy' and 'matters relating to current public policy' (Communications Act, 2003 Sections 319 and 320).

Architects of a new institution

Recalling the intensity of debates that preceded the establishment of Channel 4 in 1982 is like visiting a very foreign country and there are a number of useful sources and commentaries on that period (Smith 1976, Home Office/Annan 1977, Lambert 1982, Blanchard and Morley 1982, Isaacs 1989, Harvey 1989, Sparks 1994, Bonner 2003, Brown 2007, Hobson 2008). In the then three-channel world of BBC One, BBC Two and ITV, the creation of a new fourth channel seemed a matter of great moment.

Two countervailing forces might be identified. Firstly ITV believed that it was time for an ITV Two to match the BBC's enjoyment of such a second service. Secondly, dissatisfaction with the two existing broadcasting institutions led a range of people across the political spectrum to call for something new. In part this was a debate about free speech; in part an argument about the suppression of voices and aesthetic practices that seemed excluded from a rather complacent mainstream. Much of the intensity came from producers and film makers who, experiencing the current state of things, felt strongly that something better was needed to enable creative, challenging and innovative work. There were many architects of the new broadcasting institution; four will be mentioned briefly here.

Firstly Lord Annan's report, sponsored by the Home Office and published in 1977, called for the new fourth channel to be constituted as an Open Broadcasting Authority. The OBA should encourage productions which 'say something new in new ways' and it should function 'more as a publisher of programme material provided by others' than as a conventional broadcasting producer. The OBA would be funded from a variety of sources including spot advertising and operate with 'the maximum freedom which Parliament is prepared to allow' (Home Office 1977 p482-3). In the event, the OBA proposal was not adopted but it influenced the direction of debate. Secondly, Anthony Smith, a former BBC current affairs producer, subsequently a board member of Channel 4 and president of Magdalen College, Oxford, drew up a proposal for a 'National Television Foundation' (see chapter 10). The NTF would draw its programmes from many sources, aiming to break the stranglehold of the existing BBC/ITV duopoly; it would not offer a balanced evening's entertainment but be 'wedded to a different doctrine...of *openness* rather than to balance, to expression rather than to neutralisation'; it would identify and address specialised audiences not a 'homogeneous mass audience' (Smith, 1976; Lambert 1982 p48).

Thirdly, Jeremy Isaacs, former director of programmes at ITV's Thames Television, producer of *The World at War* for ITV and of *Ireland – A Television History* for the BBC, moved some of the details forward in his MacTaggart lecture of 1979. He was to be appointed Channel 4's first chief executive the following year. Interestingly, his speech assumed that the fourth channel would be an ITV2. Isaacs argued for a channel which 'extends the choice available to viewers...caters for substantial minorities presently neglected...builds into its actuality programmes a complete spectrum of attitude and opinion' (1989 p19).

Fourthly and finally, the Conservative Home Secretary William Whitelaw – responsible for making the final decisions about structure and remit - outlined the Government's plans some two weeks later. He had listened carefully and, contrary to many assumptions, decided that the new channel would be developed not by the shareholder-based ITV companies but rather by a public regulatory body, then the Independent Broadcasting Authority (IBA). The IBA would ensure that the newcomer offered 'a distinctive service of its own' with programmes 'appealing to...tastes and interests not adequately provided for on the existing channels'. Independent suppliers must receive 'a fair negotiated market price' and, perhaps most important of all for a new service in search of finance, the budget would '...not necessarily be governed by the revenue earned from the advertisements shown on that channel' (Bonner, 2003 p15-16). The IBA subsequently reached agreement with the ITV companies that in return for the right to sell all the new channel's advertising, ITV would provide a sufficient amount of income – guaranteed in advance – to ensure an adequate programme budget.

Within three years Channel 4 was generating sufficient advertising income to be self-supporting and persuading new audiences that it could deliver on the remit specified in the 1980 and 1981 Broadcasting Acts '...to encourage innovation and experiment in the form and content of programmes' with '...a suitable proportion of matter calculated to appeal to tastes and interests not generally catered for by ITV' (Broadcasting Act, 1981 Section 11).

Risk and reward

The quality of C4's best programmes (in drama, news, film, current affairs, documentary) also provides the best evidence in support of the case that the broadcaster should retain its publicly-owned status and its parliamentary remit. It has not been possible to explore examples here but the formal record is worth noting: 303 UK and international awards and four Oscar awards in 2014, with Steve McQueen's *12 Years a Slave* receiving the Oscar for Best Picture in March of that year. McQueen, a Turner prize winner, also received C4 investment and support for his earlier and arguably riskier projects, the feature films *Shame* and *Hunger*. There were also important documentaries and documentary series: *Syria: Across the Lines, Educating Yorkshire, Dispatches: Children on the Frontline, Kids in Crisis* and the internationally-oriented strands *Unreported World* and *True Stories*.

It is difficult to imagine a shareholder-sensitive company taking as many risks. But without such risk there is little serious innovation and few unexpected pleasures for audiences. To return to Lord Inglewood's National Gallery analogy, the production and display of cutting-edge work is vital for a nation of many faiths and none. And the art of television – at its best – reaches many more people than even the greatest London gallery. Moreover it reaches them in their homes, on their tablets and across all parts of the country.

**In memory of Alan Fountain (1946-2016),
first commissioning editor for independent film and video at Channel 4.**

About the author

Sylvia Harvey is visiting professor in the School of Media and Communication at the University of Leeds. She has published on film history and policy, on the political economy of media including Channel 4 and on broadcasting policy and regulation. She is a founder member of the Sheffield International Documentary Festival, and a trustee of the Showroom Cinema and of the Voice of the Listener & Viewer.

Notes

[1] Internet advertising now represents some 44 per cent of the value of all UK advertising, knocking television off its top spot and reducing the latter to a mere 27 per cent share with the Press at 18 per cent (ITV 2015 p10).

References

Blanchard, Simon and Morley, David (eds) (1982) *What's this Channel Four?* London: Comedia Publishing Group.

Blazeby, Miranda (2016a) John Whittingdale: privatisation would liberate Channel 4, *Broadcast*, 14 March. Available online at:
http://www.broadcastnow.co.uk/news/whittingdale-privatisation-would-liberate-channel-4/5101459.article, accessed on 20 March 2016. The *Sunday Times* interview was published on 13 March.

Blazeby, Miranda (2016b) Abraham hits back at Whittingdale's privatisation plans, *Broadcast*,15 March. Available online at:
http://www.broadcastnow.co.uk/news/abraham-hits-back-at-whittingdales-privatisation-plans/5101548.article, accessed on 20 March 2016.

Bonner, Paul with Lesley Aston (2003) *New Developments in Independent Television 1981-1992: Channel Four, TV-am, Cable and Satellite*, London: Palgrave Macmillan.

Broadcasting Act 1981. Available online at:
http://www.legislation.gov.uk/ukpga/1981/68
accessed on 25 March 2016.

Brown, Maggie (2007) *A Licence to Be Different. The story of Channel 4*, London: British Film Institute.

Channel 4 (1993) *Report and Financial Statements 1992*. Available online at:
http://www.channel4.com/media/documents/corporate/annual-reports/annual_report_1992.pdf , accessed on 25 March 2016.

Channel 4 (2015a) *Britain's Creative Greenhouse. A summary of the 2014 Channel 4 Annual Report and other key facts*. Available online at:
http://www.channel4.com/media/documents/corporate/annual-reports/C4_Brochure_Single_Pages_2ndJune15.pdf , accessed on 25 March 2016.

Channel Four (2015b) *Report and Financial Statements 2014. Britain's Creative Greenhouse*. Available online at: https://c4-cp-hosting.s3.amazonaws.com/annualreport/Channel%204%20Annual%20Report%20201 4_2.pdf , accessed on 26 March 2016.

Communications Act 2003, Chapter 21. Available online at:
http://www.legislation.gov.uk/ukpga/2003/21/contents , accessed on 15 March 2016.

Harvey, Sylvia (1989) Deregulation, Innovation and Channel Four. *Screen*, Vol. 30, Nos. 1 and 2, pp. 60-78.

Hobson, Dorothy (2008) *Channel 4. The Early Years and the Jeremy Isaacs Legacy*, London: I. B. Tauris.

Home Office (1977) *Report of the Committee on the Future of Broadcasting*. Chairman: Lord Annan, London: HMSO, Cmnd.6753 (The 'Annan Report').

Isaacs, Jeremy (1989) *Storm over Four. A Personal Account*, London: Weidenfeld and Nicolson.

ITV (2015) *Annual Report 2014*. Available online at:
http://www.itvplc.com/sites/itvplc/files/ITV%20Annual%20Report%202014.pdf , accessed on 25 March 2016.

Lambert, Stephen (1982) *Channel Four. Television with a Difference?* London: British Film Institute.

Ofcom (2007) *Channel 4 Financial Review*. Available online at: http://stakeholders.ofcom.org.uk/binaries/broadcast/reviews-investigations/psb-review/statement.pdf , accessed on 25 March 2016.

Ofcom (2015a) *PSB Annual Report*, TV Viewing Annex. Available online at: http://stakeholders.ofcom.org.uk/binaries/broadcast/reviews-investigations/psb-review/psb2015/PSB_2015_TV_Viewing.pdf , accessed on 20 March 2016.

Ofcom (2015b) *The Communications Market Report*. Available online at: http://stakeholders.ofcom.org.uk/binaries/research/cmr/cmr15/CMR_UK_2015.pdf , accessed on 20 March 2016.

Parker, Robin (2015) 'Indies rally behind Channel 4', *Broadcast*, 18 March. Available online at: http://www.broadcastnow.co.uk/news/indies-rally-behind-channel-4/5101593.article , accessed on 20 March 2016.

Shareholder Executive (2015) *Annual Review 2014-15*. Available online at: http://webarchive.nationalarchives.gov.uk/+/https://www.gov.uk/government/organisations/the-shareholder-executive , accessed on 25 March 2016.

Smith, Anthony (1976) The National Television Foundation – A Plan for the Fourth Channel, *The Shadow in the Cave*, London: Quartet Books.

Sparks, Colin (1994) Independent Production: Unions and Casualization, Stuart Hood (ed) *Behind the Screens. The Structure of British Television in the Nineties*, London: Lawrence and Wishart pp. 133-154.

Whitelaw, William (1979) Speech to the Royal Television Society. Reprinted in full in Hobson, Dorothy (2004 p5-7).

Be careful what you wish for

By Roy Ackerman

The Culture Secretary should think twice before cashing in a national asset that has been built on taking the kind of risks that shareholders hate

It started with a slow, almost inaudible rumbling. But, like a storm that you hoped was passing into a different valley, the thunder now feels perilously close. The government increasingly gives the impression it is hell-bent on doing something it has toyed with before – privatising Channel Four.

At first, I assumed that messing with the media was part of its mandate to govern without the irritating interference of those pesky Lib Dems. No, no reference to Channel 4 in the Conservative Party's manifesto or in any autumn statement. But, there again, Leicester City never announced they would be front-runners for the Premier League title. So maybe the government can ghost in on the blind side, sell it off, reduce debt, and keep Lord Grade, once so bitterly against taking Channel 4 into the private sector, happy.

What's the case made by the former Channel 4 CEO, one of the most talented media executives of his generation? Not the one some of the channel's critics cite: that it has diluted the remit (of which more later). No, Grade just wants to help the channel through tricky times. In the Lords recently he said: 'The current settlement for Channel Four is no longer fit for purpose and puts a risk on the public purse, because the taxpayers in the end are the shareholders of last resort. The world has changed dramatically and the commercial threats to Channel 4 are a hundred fold greater than they were when I was there and was part of the present settlement, and it is absolutely time that the channel has a new settlement that enables it to change its modus operandi and become a fully-fledged business.'[1]

So there we have it. Channel Four can't survive the stormy waters of the media market. We need to bring in private money. But, there's a logical hole at the heart of the privatisers' arguments, big enough to swallow up all of Horseferry Road and that other Westminster building that threatens its current status – and everything in between.

If Channel 4 is an impending financial basket case due to the challenging environment, nobody would deny that the biggest constraint on its profitability is the remit.

So, er, let's put it up for sale. Because, as we all know, private companies love a basket case – especially one with mandatory limits on how it can increase profitability. And the last thing a potential buyer would do is push to reduce the remit commitments to news and current affairs, diversity of supply and content, origination from British independents, support for talent, regionality and the rest.

Phew. Sorted.

Not.

Innovation, experimentation and creativity

I've spent 32 years working for Channel 4 as an independent producer and, from my perspective, privatisation would not make any sense for the UK – economically, creatively or culturally. Because I don't believe the channel's public service remit will ever be compatible with the concept of private ownership.

We have to ask, first, whether it is still delivering on that remit. There are a welter of statistics you can find in Ofcom reports which seem to show that, however much Channel 4 has changed since the heady days of 1982, it still meets its multiple obligations in terms of innovation, experimentation and creativity in form and content; appealing to the tastes and interests of a culturally diverse society; offering sufficiently distinctive and educational programmes – its support of the creative sector and talent and, in particular, a wide range of British independent producers.

The debate has always raged hot. We can all remember the stink around Shilpa Shetty on *Big Brother* in 2007, in the midst of a welter of attacks when big guns on all sides were arguing Channel 4 had ditched the remit. Even its natural supporters felt the golden age was long gone. Then there was the age of the begging bowl, when the channel claimed it needed a rescue remedy to avoid falling into bankruptcy. But, today, even if there may be evidence of less diversity in primetime and plenty of programmes that are as distinctive as grey skies in January, few would deny that Channel 4 *still* offers something different and, equally crucially, something that lies at the core of Britain's media ecology, which is envied by so many around the world.

I would argue, even if the schedule looks hugely different to how it was in the 80s and 90s, Channel 4 has been at its best when balancing the ratings-drivers with the risky and remit-worthy.

What I find most revealing is how the solidly commercial parts of the schedule (with few exceptions) have never lasted that long. One by one and in turn the 'bankers' fall away: C4's original soap opera *Brookside*, staple of the launch schedule; the first wave of US imports such as *Friends* and *Frasier* which kept the channel profitable, before the competition really kicked in for the latest hot US comedy or drama; *Big Brother*, the 90s 'Wall of Leisure' and the burst of innovative food programming built around celebrity chefs, Jamie, Gordon and Hugh; the Factual Entertainment hits such as *Wifeswap*; and, most recently, the wave of obs doc rig-shows.

They come, they conquer, they're copied and eventually lose their ratings edge. Out of the need to replace, often along come a bunch of programmes that fail or don't quite work, a load of angst about Channel 4 no longer being fit for purpose. And eventually something new – a *Gogglebox* – is rolled out and the channel is back on its distinctively angular rails.

And some of the most popular shows were in fact huge creative risks. When I took an opera competition open to all-comers to the channel in 2003, nobody knew if it would (a) work and (b) appeal either to aficionados, or to those unlikely to turn up to anything involving opera. Fortunately, it became one the most popular arts shows of the time, and launched a dozen culture contests, some even said a genre, of arts reality.

Is the business model really unravelling?

The next question is whether the channel is in need of the help that Lord Grade seems to be keen to offer. When US TV networks' share prices have been plummeting for more than a year and the evidence is increasing that young people, C4's core demographic, are fleeing from television, are we close to what analysts call a cutting of the cord and an unravelling of Channel 4's business model?

A report at the end of last year by Enders Analysis scrutinises how Channel 4 is likely to respond to the fragmenting media landscape. It paints a quite convincing and reasonably sanguine picture of a channel retaining its remit and its viability.

It says that the US and UK markets are 'apples and pears', that TV broadcast advertising revenues are holding up surprisingly well and that the 4 portfolio will hold up its share, especially with the removal of BBC3 from its TV slot. These, as well as developments in digital, airtime sales and sponsorship, lead the researchers to conclude that ad receipts will grow by 3% year on year, enough for sustainability. Ofcom also took a look when renewing Channel Four's licence during 2014 and came similar conclusions.

So, it's all good.

Perhaps. But, let's speak a little truth to power. Channel 4 is *so* far from perfect. Ask any producer and they'd produce a list of things they'd change about the broadcaster. It can drive you mad in so many different ways, as a viewer and a supplier. It can be defensive, arrogant and at times its claims about how and where it delivers the remit amount to little more than elegant sophistry. Some argue that it has become more parochial and less ready to trust its audience with complexity. And, excuse me for asking, but is this really the time to be challenging the suppliers' Terms of Trade that have allowed many independents to grow, but usually doing no more than make a sustainable margin, at a time when the programme tariffs for many genres haven't risen in decades?

And, yes, a channel created originally around unheard voices and minority ideas, has chosen (or been forced) to focus increasingly on *youth* and those hard-to-get 16-34s. Especially, to drive revenues, the affluent end of that demographic. To its over-34 viewers, many of whom have stuck with the channel since its early days, that has come across as a dilution in higher-brow 'grown up' programming.

But, blending truth with a touch of fairness, I think we are better served when Channel 4 offers a different, edgier product to the BBC, and that might often mean the opposite of the seemingly adult. And, take a look at how Vice has built a huge youth media brand, while offering hardcore journalism from faraway places. Young-skewing does not mean frivolous. Maybe some of Channel 4's critics are just a bit stuck in their viewing habits.

Risk and reward

Taken overall, Channel 4 remains, at the very least, definably different. The way the remit is delivered has had to change as society has changed. Launched in the heart of the Thatcher Revolution to shake up the cosy ITV/BBC duopoly and use up some spare analogue spectrum (what a very 20th Century word that is), it's surprised many with its continuing relevance. While the values that underpin the remit are much the same as in 1982, it's inevitable that the initial challenges and obligations it was set have had to visibly morph.

And, even though as a producer you can sometimes feel some of its commissioners almost paralysed by fear of your idea not being guaranteed ratings-gold, it still commissions so many programmes that other broadcasters would never dare to attempt. Sometimes these things work. Sometimes they don't – and I don't just mean reality shows that threaten the health of Olympic medallists. But, whether it's the Paralympics, dramas like *Humans* on the main channel, an online-gaming inspired young adult show on E4 or *Walter Presents* on the new All4 platform, innovation is definitely there.

But new ideas constitute risk, and shareholders are not that keen on risk. In his 2014 MacTaggart Lecture David Abraham, defending an institution that is commercial but has no shareholders, set out how he saw a profit-maximising Channel 4 would work. More acquisitions, repeats and ad-funded programmes, in-house production and anything to achieve fewer public service obligations. He should know – he's run commercial US networks.

Private sector operators and their shareholders demand profit. And why shouldn't they? Think about the thing we are many of us shareholders in – a pension. Those of us who have one will rely on it providing regular returns, as high as possible. Some of us may have enough scruples to choose a pension that doesn't invest in the arms trade, or tobacco companies. Beyond that, we don't stay awake worrying about the obligations of the company our pension invests in, as long as its returns can pay for whatever we are going to need in our retirement. Which potential shareholders in a privatised Channel 4 are going to give a flying four about how PSB its prime time output is, how many originations it takes from British indies or how much diversity it offers?

That's the point about owning shares. Profit often comes at a price, and the price in this case is likely to be an aversion to controversy, constant innovation and diversity. Yes, you can talk about how all the innovation of Silicon Valley is from the private sector. But media networks are totally different from mass market corporations producing uniform products, however clever and customisable they are.

A red-toothed ratings chase

In the end efficiency savings would do little to make Channel 4, with a current remit that the government has pledged to support, a profitable buy. A privately-owned Channel 4 would be forced to chase ratings in a much more red-toothed way than it already does. This is not always a guarantor of quality and innovation, to say the least. And the impact on other PSBs is also likely to be significant.

The government is keen to reassure us it can keep a privatised Channel 4 to its PSB responsibilities. Past evidence from ITV and Channel Five doesn't support the argument. Peter (*Wolf Hall*) Kosminsky recently wrote about how ITV's flotation preceded a long-term slide in its provision of a varied diet of classy, distinctive documentaries and drama. 'It's somehow accepted that ITV is a downmarket, stultifyingly cautious, broadcaster – as if it has always been thus. Well it isn't and it wasn't. It was done consciously and a small number of people got rich as a result. I was there. I saw it happen'[2]. So was I. I shared a desk briefly with Peter, working on the admired, long gone, ITV documentary strand *First Tuesday*.

Alter the incentives and things change – fast. Get rid of the channel's unique hybrid public corporate structure and you limit the amount of influence the state, or the regulatory body, can exert upon it. Yes, Ofcom could fine a post-privatisation Channel 4 for ignoring its commitments to the remit, but who's to say that its new owners wouldn't calculate that a hit of £5 or £10 million was worth paying if they were making an extra £30m from ditching expensive liabilities?

Ultimately, as a producer, my gravest concern would be the effect privatisation would have on the independent production sector and the wider creative economy. A privatised Channel 4 would almost certainly spend less money on programming. And might even look to move production in house.... At the moment, state ownership ensures all of the broadcaster's profits are reinvested in content. Last year, that meant £600m, of which £430m went to the British independent production sector. It is not just Abraham's view of a post-privatisation channel that is dyspeptic. It is hard to imagine a scenario that isn't catastrophic for us in the independent sector.

Last year Channel 4 invested more money with independents than ITV and Channel 5 combined. It has spent £10 billion with indies over its history, and its investment supports an estimated 19,000 jobs per year. 36 years on, the sector is strong but much of it still lives with margins on which few other businesses would survive.

I remember when building Fresh One Productions under a CEO who had been successful at Virgin and Body Shop. For a long time he could not understand why we kept agreeing to production deals with such low margins. After a while he understood, you only break into real profits if you make a hit that repeats and sells – and most of us know how rare that actually is. Having had a couple of hits, you learn to cherish them. British independent production still needs an independent Channel 4 with its unusual commitment to sustaining our sector.

Take the most likely outcome of privatisation – a foreign buyer; a search for profit leading to a reduction in the number of independents commissioned, especially smaller, newer ones; a very possible move into in-house production; a pressure to reduce new originations in prime-time. Any which way, that is going to take jobs out of this sector and the country. That's people losing livelihoods, not earning money, spending money, paying taxes. Instead, it's sitting in a shareholder's (probably US) bank account, gathering interest. Is it really worth losing that for a short term (and, in macroeconomic terms, fairly insignificant) cash injection into the Treasury's coffers?

So much for shareholder pressure

And then there are the job reductions (sorry, efficiencies), at Channel 4 itself. David Elstein wrote that 'without shareholder pressure to hold down costs, Channel 4's staff have attained salary levels that are the envy of the industry,' suggesting that shareholders in a newly privatised channel could scythe David Abraham's £800,000 pay package as part of a game-changing package of cuts. Meanwhile, the CEO of the privately owned ITV, Adam Crozier, earned £4.4 million last year, and £8.4 million the year before that. And over at Sky, CEO Jeremy Darroch netted a not insubstantial £17 million last year. So much for shareholder pressure keeping executive salaries down. No, shareholders' dividends would have to come from elsewhere. Programming budgets would be hit at some point.

Some time around 2007, I facilitated a seminar on Channel 4 with Gordon Brown's economist adviser Stewart Wood, when it had been reported that Brown was thinking of selling it to a commercial buyer. They took the idea for a long walk around the park – entailing a detailed financial review of the channel's whole operation. Then Ofcom chief executive Ed Richards concluded: 'When you do a financial review of Channel Four you end up thinking about the remit and its delivery. It is inescapable – the two things are related.'[3] The walk ended with a decision to give Channel 4 help with digital switch-over.

It takes a Conservative government to give this idea a run. Twice. John Whittingdale has been here before. Twenty years ago to be precise, when he tabled an amendment to the 1996 Broadcast Bill proposing privatisation (it *really* has been a long time since we last had a *real* Tory government). Now that he's Secretary of State, Whittingdale seems determined to go way further than take a gentle stroll with the private sector.

I think he should be careful what he wishes for. While he questions the idea of the BBC making too popular programmes (anyone wondered if that's a popular policy?), selling off Channel 4 guarantees a stormy reception.

We are talking about cashing in a unique cultural asset with a corporate structure and governance unusually effective at delivering public value – all for an estimate billion pound one-off fee. According to the Red Book, public spending in 2015-16 is set for £750bn. So that means that the privatisation premium will have gone in about one third of a working day. Now there's a burn rate to think about.

About the author

Roy Ackerman is a documentary producer of feature documentaries, documentary series and arts programmes. Among his hits *Operatunity, Dream School, Ballet Changed My Life* and award winning documentaries including *100% White, Richard Pryor: Omit the Logic, Mad Dog Gaddafi, The House I Live In, Trials of Henry Kissinger, Why We Fight, Gonzo, House of War, Tsunami 7 Hours on Boxing Day* and *Not Cricket*. He is Managing Director of Non-Scripted Television at Pulse Films. Formerly MD at Fresh One Productions & Chief Creative Officer at the Jamie Oliver Media Group, and Creative Director Diverse Productions, producers of *Man vs Wild*.

Notes

[1] *Hansard* 3rd February 2016

[2] *Guardian*, 5th January 2016

[3] OFCOM press briefing 14th June 2007

Maintaining choice

By Colin Browne and Sophie Chalk

For viewers it is the plurality of perspectives that counts. The channel should be given the stability to ensure that a range of distinctive, diverse programming is maintained

For the Voice of the Listener & Viewer, the only organisation in the UK wholly devoted to representing audience interests in broadcasting, the main issue at stake in any discussion of the future of Channel 4 is to ensure that we maintain audience choice. VLV supports a mixed broadcasting ecology which provides a plurality of perspectives; broadens our horizons; entertains and informs us with high quality content; confronts our prejudices; and rewards innovation.

We all want our favourite series to continue, but we also want to be surprised and engaged by the new, the original, the extraordinary. The word 'distinctive' – often used in the debate about the future of the BBC – is particularly relevant to any discussion of Channel 4, with its remit which places such a high value on innovation and originality.

The UK has an internationally-envied, complex broadcasting system with a range of remits, rewards and different funding options for our public service broadcasters. It supports an independent production industry which is thriving; it provides a range of high quality content which is free at the point of reception for audiences; and the system appears to be working well.

Our main concern is that audience choice should be maintained as a result of whatever broadcasting policy the Government decides to follow. Audiences patently have access to more media than they did in 1982, the year in which Channel 4 was launched. Alongside hundreds of radio and TV channels, we have virtually unlimited access to content on the internet, via subscription, OTT and VOD services. But has this proliferation of media platforms increased choice or simply overwhelmed us? Has the rise in the number of channels really created greater choice? As the market becomes more competitive, it is natural that the most popular formats and programmes are replicated as channels fight to survive and rush to the popular 'centre ground'. While each channel's marketing has to be distinctive in order to stand out from the crowd, there is a tendency to stick with tried and tested formulae. All channels are looking for hits and audience share.

In this context, to ensure choice is maintained, it is more crucial than ever that as a conscious public policy intervention our publicly owned broadcasters provide content which is original and innovative. They should set the bar high in terms of quality – forcing other broadcasters to maintain the quality of their output; they should be imaginative – devising new, exciting ways to engage us with the world around us; and they should encourage new talent, ensuring that we have a continual renewal of energy and ideas. This doesn't mean they should be forced only to deliver content which is not available elsewhere; it means they should have the freedom and the remit to expend time and energy working out how to refresh our viewing experience, to engage us with content and subjects commercial broadcasters wouldn't consider because they might appear too risky.

If we examine Channel 4's track record, it has for the most part achieved these goals. In some ways, what is surprising is that it has survived so long. Its remit specifically demands that it should challenge us, confront us and provide new, innovative content from which many other broadcasters shy away. Tricky, challenging content does not tend to be popular until it becomes so well known it is considered mainstream; audiences like what is comfortable and familiar; and innovation is an inherently risky activity.

The right to fail

The Channel 4 schedule is characterised by a mix of overtly public service content, cross-funded by more obviously populist programmes. We have *Channel 4 News, Dispatches,* and *Unreported World* alongside *Grand Designs* and other design/makeover programmes, and then hits like *Gogglebox* and, previously, *Big Brother*, which when they were first aired were considered highly original but became high-earning, mainstream, popular entertainment series. Not all the innovation works, of course, and, as Russell T Davies highlighted recently[1], an essential aspect of its remit is that Channel 4 has to be allowed the right to fail. As long as it succeeds more often than it fails, it will survive.

Its survival is testament to the subtle balancing act it performs: providing new content alongside crowd pleasers. As a result Channel 4 is doing better than surviving. According to Ofcom's recent review of the corporation as part of its 2015 PSB Review, it looks to be sustainable for the next decade.[2] Overall Ofcom ruled that since 2010 Channel 4 has been delivering its remit as set out in the Digital Economy Act. There are weaknesses in its performance – but overall it is doing a good job.

Channel 4, plays an important role in providing plurality of supply in key genres alongside the other PSBs, but most importantly it acts as a foil to the BBC. Viewer appreciation is high: Ofcom research shows that the public believes Channel 4 is more likely to cover ground and tackle issues other broadcasters tend to avoid and that it provides alternative perspectives.[3] It outperforms the PSB average for showing 'programmes with new ideas/different approaches/ideas' (58% vs average of 52%) and programmes whose style is 'different to what I'd expect to see on other channels' (57% vs average of 49%).[4]

Additionally, the main channel along with its portfolio channels plays an important role in attracting a broad range of viewers, especially younger adults. This is particularly important since research shows that this younger audience of 16-34 year olds is migrating from live television viewing and PSBs in general; the closure of BBC Three as a broadcast channel makes Channel 4's role more important than ever in this context.

We believe that C4 is particularly successful in its delivery of content which appeals to the tastes and interests of a culturally diverse society. Through documentaries, drama, comedy and entertainment, Channel 4 and the its portfolio channels promote alternative views and challenge established views. C4C and Ofcom research both suggest that minority groups highly rank C4C for tackling diversity issues and showing alternative lives.[5]

So what will we miss if Channel 4's operating model is changed and this, in turn, undermines the delicate PSB ecology we currently benefit from?

Fundamentally, if Channel 4's ability to deliver its remit is undermined by the need for greater commercialism or the need to pay a dividend to shareholders, we believe audiences' horizons are likely to be limited. This is because currently Channel 4 has the remit, and therefore the legitimate luxury, to approach content differently from other broadcasters. It is the only UK PSB with the remit to make us see the world differently. Often it seems more important for its content to cause debate, rather than appeal to the consensus view.

Channel 4 News consistently provides a different, indeed often idiosyncratic, approach to many of the mainstream stories of the day and covers stories that other mainstream bulletins ignore. Fixed-rig documentary series such as *The Tribe* have provided completely new and eye-opening insights into the lives of people that would otherwise remain remote from us. Channel 4 has also consistently mainstreamed issues which many of us shy away from because of political correctness or embarrassment. Its role in developing the profile of the Paralympics and disability in sport more generally has been outstanding.

Secondly, because of the large number of independent producers from which it commissions, C4C provides us with an opportunity to hear from a wide range of voices, some of whom are new to the industry and provide refreshing, innovative perspectives. These have a greater appeal to younger audiences than those of the other PSBs and this is key to the corporation's success, both in fulfilling its remit but also in attracting ad revenue.

Instability: Channel 4's challenge

The challenge the corporation now faces, as it has a number of times in the past, is to justify its operating model to the Government. The current uncertainty it is experiencing as a result of the Government's review is already destabilising it and making the commissioning of long-term projects difficult. This lack of certainty has been increased by the somewhat unfortunate circumstances that preceded the appointment of its new chairman, where Ofcom's original advice was not accepted. The new chair will face a difficult challenge in demonstrating his independence from government.

In order to support Channel 4 and all it offers audiences with its existing remit, we need to find a way to avoid these periodic proposals to privatise it. They divert energy away from programme making and innovation, and threaten its survival.

If it is to retain its credibility as a UK PSB with a very important role to play, it must ensure it plugs the existing gaps in the delivery of its remit as identified by Ofcom, so that its critics have little to complain about. It needs to continue to deliver its very challenging remit in the most engaging and innovative way possible. This is no mean task for the staff of the corporation to deliver, but we believe it can be achieved.

The best way to ensure the healthy survival of Channel 4 is for its existing licence, which is due to expire on 31 December 2024, to be considered as set in stone. The Government should respect the agreement which it signed up to in 2014. Perhaps when this licence is drawing to a close there can be a review of Channel 4 and its operating model, but until then it should be allowed to devote its energy and resources to coming up with great, innovative ideas and challenging the mainstream view for the benefit of audiences, instead of 'defending' itself from attack from its detractors.

As we said at the outset, VLV's principal concern lies with ensuring that audiences continue to receive the best possible range of high quality and diverse programming. While we understand the argument that this can be protected by a clear definition of remit and that the ownership of the company is irrelevant, it is our view that the culture and strategy of any company is deeply linked to its structure and in particular the way it is funded; and that a privatisation of Channel 4 would inevitably introduce pressures that would in turn lead to a significant change in the nature of its out output. At the very least, those who propose change need to be able to demonstrate clearly the advantages for audiences that change would bring. At the moment, privatisation looks like a solution searching for a problem that does not exist.

About the authors

Colin Browne has wide experience of broadcasting and the media. He has been chairman of VLV since 2012. He was director of corporate affairs at the BBC from 1994 -2000, having previously been director of corporate relations at BT. From 2000-2009 he was a partner and senior consultant at Maitland, one of the UK's leading financial and corporate communications consultancies. He currently has his own company providing strategic communications advice and is a non-executive director of the Centre for Effective Dispute Resolution (CEDR).

Sophie Chalk was a producer and director of news and factual programmes for a number of UK broadcasters including ITV, Sky and the BBC for 17 years before taking up broadcasting policy advocacy in 2006. She works as a consultant on policy issues for VLV and the International Broadcasting Trust.

Notes

[1] Russell T Davies speech to Broadcasting Press Guild Awards, 11 March 2016

[2] Ofcom, *Public Service Broadcasting in the internet Age, Ofcom's Third Review of Public Service Broadcasting* (2015:5.13)

[3] *Ofcom Review of Channel 4 Corporation's delivery of its media content duties* (2010-2013), (2014:4.56), p. 38

[4] *Ofcom PSB Annual Report 2015, PSB Audience Opinion Annex,* (July 2015, Figure 34)

[5] *Ofcom Review of Channel 4 Corporation's delivery of its media content duties (2010-2013),* (December 2014: 2.21), p. 10

References

Ofcom Review of Channel 4 Corporation's delivery of its media content duties (2010-2013), (15 December 2014)

Ofcom PSB Annual Report 2015, PSB Audience Opinion Annex, (July 2015)

Ofcom, *Public Service Broadcasting in the internet Age, Ofcom's Third Review of Public Service Broadcasting* (2 July 2015)

Northern exposure
By Alex Connock

Creatively, culturally and commercially, Channel 4's significant investment in programming from the North of England has paid off. Long may it continue

'Industrial policy.' There's a sexy phrase.

It will set the heart racing right up there with 'solutions provider' and 'constituency chairman'. It reeks of the 1970s: failure, *When the Lights Went Out* and historic government memos read by PHD students in Sussex between episodes of *Countdown*.

But the fact is that in our glossy, perhaps a little self-righteously autonomous UK television industry (see BBC debates past around regulation), we've always been part of, and massive beneficiaries of, a deliberate, multi-faceted, and incredibly successful industrial policy. It's no less thought thorough, or effective, or long termist, than China's entry into electronics over the past decade, or France's nuclear power generation.

TV workers in Britain should be thanking civil servants every morning before work for the benign environment we have been bequeathed – whether we are eating avocado on toast at the Soho House, or a Gregg's jumbo sausage roll in Sunderland.

The effective state-funding of the BBC – a deliberate industrial policy – was the pivotal contributor to Britain's global leadership in radio and TV technology and content across an almost 80-year span from the 1930s to the present day.

ITV was built by very impressive entrepreneurs in the 1960s, but they operated around the visionary policy architecture of state-mandated regional advertising monopolies. Those funded a federal content production operation that incubated regional creative expertise as improbable (at the time) as global investigative current affairs made in the imploding factory economy of Manchester, or global natural history programmes based from provincial, airport-free Norwich.

Into this mix came Channel 4.

It was created in 1982 – we should not forget – by Thatcherite free marketeers, working with civil servants, with the explicit remit of encouraging innovation, experiment and cultural diversity. Even if you did that same thing today, it would feel quite forward-thinking as an industrial policy. Launched by a Scots presenter with teeth twenty years ahead of his time (whatever happened to him?) the channel has brought us, besides much else, extraordinary Northern programming from *Shameless* to *Queer as Folk*, from *This is England* to *The Tube*, from *Brookside* and *Hollyoaks*, to much of *Dispatches*.

The public/private policy construct behind Channel 4 soon translated into the methodical creation, through commissioning, of a whole new and nationwide sector – independent production. It went on to put British formats and creators in a world-leading position, create thousands of jobs, and put a whole generation of lucky folk who sold hit-format-creating indie businesses in a decade-long global acquisition boom, into large mansions from Notting Hill to Glasgow's West End.

And after that Sky, as it now is, whilst powerfully free-market in origin, became the final major species in British TV's mixed woodland. We now have a rich ecology of production, commercial models, technology platforms and public service ideologies that is the absolute envy of the world, and not least for its sheer genetic diversity. In consequence as a nation we make some of the best content, we are one of the best content exporters, we have massive choice not only in what to watch on TV, but also in what kind of body produces it, where they are, and who owns it. By the time you add Netflix and Amazon too, it's hard to see any form of TV production choice we do *not* have – and you couldn't say that of the US.

Popping the London bubble

Britain's visionary TV industrial policy and its impact are not just historic either. Happily we still have an industrial policy that's a very good thing on the ground – and especially in the North of the nation.

'Far too much media exists in a London bubble,' said *BBC Newsnight* presenter Kirsty Wark at a recent Royal Television Society event. 'We need to get the BBC to reflect what's going on elsewhere.' That kind of thinking at the top level of the BBC put modern buildings in Manchester and Glasgow full of UK-wide productions, which have thrived as creative centres even whilst commissioning remained perplexingly London-based. Whatever tinkering government did with the licence fee, World Service and so forth during the period, the basic principle of a state-backed broadcasting behemoth that puts its footprint across the North is probably stronger than ever, and 5,000 TV jobs in Manchester alone, a significant economic footprint, speak for its success.

Creatively too, the North is on TV, from *BBC Breakfast* to *Happy Valley*, from *Coronation Street* to *Emmerdale*, for a concoction of reasons that owe easily as much to state-mandated industrial five-year plans as effervescent free market economics. If we think that cultural impact is worth having for society – which I do – we need to not forget that when thinking about policy going forward. It means not putting total faith in the Invisible Hand, and continuing state industrial interventions. And that, you will be happy to hear, now brings to an end the 1980s economics essay.

So what does Channel 4 contribute? And why does an industrial vision for the UK content production business matter when we talk about a potential privatisation?

Ofcom said in its recent Review of Public Service Broadcasting: 'Public service broadcasters' content forms the cornerstone of programme production in the devolved Nations and English regions outside London.'

It is absolutely right. Since launch, Channel 4 has spent £10bn on content and spends around £430m a year on UK original content. Channel 4 used 338 production companies last year across TV, digital and film and accounts for 36% of all spending on indies by the public service broadcasters (a higher proportion than BBC 1 and 2 combined, though I should for transparency say that these statistics came from Channel 4's own policy team rather than my own, otherwise tireless, research on the ground.)

More specifically, in the five years from 2010 to 2014, Channel 4 invested £720m in content *outside* London – a hefty 42% of its total content spend over that period. £351.6m of this was invested in commissions from the North of England, and that's an enormous percentage of the production market there. In 2014, Channel 4 spent £153m on production in the Nations and Regions, £62m of which was in the North of England. More than 50% of hours on the main channel were from Nations and Regions productions in 2014. You get the picture.

Interestingly too, even though Channel 4 could be argued to have missed the digital revolution first time around (in that it didn't find and back a Facebook), it has used a VC-style approach through its Alpha fund to back startups across the North, Scotland and Northern Ireland. (This is investment in a very loose sense, as it combines commissioning with investment, around a noble cause of building indie businesses.) Channel 4 has also been actually investing straight cash in up-and-running companies like Leeds' True North, with which it also trades creatively; True North is by far Leeds' most creatively and commercially visible indie.

Northern Powerhouse

Creatively, the particular ethic of Northern wordplay, no-nonsense humour (or whatever other *Phoenix Nights* clichés one pulls out of the toolbag) are profitably seen across Channel 4's output – not just historical, but also contemporary.

Cucumber, Banana and Tofu were the natural successors of *Queer As Folk*. Paul Abbott (now based in Venice, California but still with a powerful ear to the Northern voice) made *No Offence* in 2015. Warp Films of Sheffield made Shane Meadows' *This Is England* about life in the North in the 1980s and 90s, 'from the Stone Roses to the Thatcher Years and Madchester,' as Channel 4 described it.

Fresh Meat was both about Manchester (a thinly disguised MMU, Britain's largest university but strangely off the national radar) and filmed in Sharp Project, one of the city's amazing converted factory spaces for digital startups. If you don't believe that it's amazing go and see it – and it's a credit to Channel 4 that it was early to spot the space and the opportunity.

Perplexingly perhaps, Channel 4 has had a huge and positive impact in the North, even whilst it has never really been there on the ground as an administrative and commissioning body. The only complaint I could find amongst producers was that some commissioners are seen as having conducted SAS-style lightning raids on Northern cities, for instance taking a conference room in a five-star hotel for sequential 15-minute pitch meetings, rather than Channel 4 putting resident personnel *in situ*. As Kirsty Wark said, there is life beyond London, and regional boots on the ground are a good action point for Channel 4's board.

One place where Channel 4 did put in the ground war was Glasgow. If the phrase 'the North' were to be allowed to emcompass Scotland – a debate I neither embrace nor would ever win – Channel 4's Northern footprint would be even more impressive. It has backed indies from Raise the Roof to IWC Media, Tern Television and Firecrest Films, through various schemes. It has a strong record of backing digital and games developers like Edinburgh's *Realise Digital,* which works for C4 Education. *Reverse the Odds,* developed by Glasgow-based Chunk Games, won an international digital Emmy, and two Broadcast digital awards in 2015.

So if Channel 4's historic and ongoing contribution to the creative life and vibrancy of the whole North of Britain is not reasonably in any doubt, why does that pertain to its *ownership* structure?

Why not just privatise it and tell it to carry on as now? Wouldn't all this good stuff continue with Channel 4 in private hands?

I am an unabashed fan of shareholder ownership of creativity. I have worked constantly for the past 23 years for great, non-state-funded media companies, and have seen evidence throughout the period that creative endeavour and risk-taking sits perfectly well alongside the goal of building profit shareholder value. In fact, creativity and profit drive each other symbiotically.

But whilst shareholder value is by its nature geography-agnostic, Channel 4's model brings something extra and special to the mix: an industrial policy that specifically does target geographical diversity. It's a policy that helps the North in other words, and at the same time as pretty much everyone signs up to the strategic value of the Northern Powerhouse, but TV very often gets lost in the mix because everyone in suits is talking about trains and airports.

At one recent major conference, TV – a major industry in Manchester – was not even on the published agenda at any point. When I asked a council official why, he said: 'No one in local government understands how TV works.'

But Channel 4 does understand how TV works. It helped build the industry. It has an explicit industrial policy, going back to its original charter, to act (as its policy team put it) as a 'creative greenhouse – driving economic growth, creating jobs and supporting hundreds of SMEs across the UK.' Its rendition of shareholder value therefore goes beyond the targets of even the most corporate responsibility-minded profit/shareholder equity-driven corporation – not just because it is allowed to, but because it is *supposed to*. Channel 4 puts money into the regions because there is a public policy case, or a creative case, as well as, or even occasionally instead of, a good short term business case. And British TV is the better for it.

Is it possible, in 2016, to credibly combine an enthusiasm for unbridled creative and commercial free market entrepreneurialism – that's me – with an appreciation for the benefits of long term strategic planning and market intervention by government? Is it possible for the state to own assets that function commercially, incubate startup businesses, trade with profitable global corporations, create powerful export numbers and enrich creative value across the full spectrum of the nation, both geographic and cultural?

An emphatic yes. It's possible. That's what's happened in the UK television industry. Long may it continue. Let's keep Channel 4 as it is.

About the author

Alex Connock is managing director at Shine North, visiting professor at Manchester Metropolitan, Salford and Sunderland universities, visiting fellow at Manchester Business School and chairman of the RTS North West. He is also head of video at Manchester-based The LAD Bible, the UK's 12th most visited website.

Out of Utopia

By John Mair

The year is 2022. The BBC is half the size it was just 8 years ago, while ITV is entirely American-owned. And what has become of the term 'public service broadcasting'…?

Here in 2022, we can only look back at 1982 as a (near) Golden Age for British television. Two BBC Channels on form and producing classics like *Boys from the Blackstuff* and *Allo!Allo!*. ITV's fifteen companies are celebrating their regional roots and variety yet also producing national classics like *OTT* and *Coronation Street*.

Scarcity brought plenty.

On 26 April 1982, the Satellite Channel launched – later to become Sky. Then, on Tuesday 2 November, the arrival of a fourth (and noisy) TV channel with the plain words: 'Good afternoon. It's a pleasure to be able to say to you: Welcome to Channel 4.' That first night included *Book Four*, *Channel Four News* and *Walter*, a Channel 4-financed feature film.

It was a simple, regulated utopia. The audience were like Oliver Twist; they took the gruel broadcasters gave them. It worked for them.

Today, in Britain in 2022, broadcasting is a jungle; a competing cacophony of channels –hundreds of them – competing for audience attention on a wide variety of platforms. 'Traditional' (sit back) television is on a slow path to the grave, replaced by micro-viewing on phones, tablets, computers – even watches. Television watching *en masse* and *en famille* is reserved for big programmes like *Strictly* (still alive..) and big live events like the Tokyo Olympic Games two years ago and the Qatar World Cup this year.

But how have the other terrestrial channels fared in the revolutionary heat of the last decade?

The BBC, the grand-daddy, convulsed first in the 'great disruption' of 2017. Its charter was renewed for five years but with the size and scope of the corporation much circumscribed. In the parlance of the time, they got a 'good kicking' from David Cameron's Tory government, though one-time Culture

Secretary John Whittingdale did not survive the post Euro Referendum Cabinet clear-out in June 2016 to implement 'his' White Paper.

The TV licence fee settlement (or 'mugging') of 2015 by Chancellor Osbrone was bad enough: nearly 20% of BBC income removed from 2020 in one fell swoop with the Corporation having to take on paying the licence fees of anyone over 75 from HM Government. But the move proved even more costly than at first thought.

The original estimate was £750m per year but that has since been revised continually upwards to take account of the population ageing more. Modern medicine is working and the over 75s licence fee is fast becoming an albatross for Auntie. The BBC tried to assuage the impact by running an 'It's your BBC – pay back your licence fee..' campaign in 2019. It failed dismally.

Comfort won out over conscience.

The corporation had to severely tighten its belt from 2017. Out went entire services – some simply closed; others put on the internet with reduced budgets. After BBC Three in 2016, BBC Four followed in 2017, the BBC News Channel in 2018 and all digital radio channels the same year.

BBC News Online was cut back to a core news output, with no features or magazine items, no foreign language versions and no local news websites.

BBC local and regional services have become shadows of their former selves. The opt-out 'local' news programme is just fifteen minutes nightly before the network news: local radio reverted to the commercial radio default position of being music not speech based. All are now broadcast from regional hubs. Coventry and Hereford served by Birmingham. It is back to the future.

Oligarchs and idealogues

On the global stage, BBC Monitoring was closed in 2018. World Service radio had its 27 language services reduced to just 10 of strategic importance. World Service TV is now internet-only and available only in markets where it could demonstrably make money. World broadcasting had been ceded to those with deep pockets plus ideological drive like *CCTV* and *Russia Today,*

BBC staff numbers have been reduced from 17,000 in 2016 to 8,000 today. Lord Hall is just retiring after his second term as Director General having 'sorted' the BBC as best he could in the reduced straits.

Meanwhile ITV is coming up to its 70th birthday in 2025. The founding fathers – Bernstein, Forman, Grade (Lew) *et al* – would be turning in their graves to see it. Once the 1990 Broadcasting Act started removing elements of public purpose/public service in their licences, ITV companies became like snakes sloughing off all the skins they could and getting fatter and fatter. Integration and amalgamation became the order of the day. Regional commitments gone; religion gone; education and current affairs gone too. Regional news reduced to just five minutes a day as the BBC was no longer a serious competitor on the ground. ITV Production is now concentrated in London, Manchester and Glasgow or outsourced to independents.

Prime time on ITV 2022 starts at 5.15pm after the regional and fifteen minute ITV network news. It goes through to 11pm where *'News at Ten'* (as it was once called) now lives – at only fifteen minutes long. Domestic news only is covered after budgets were slashed. ITV Chairman Sir Peter Bazalgette left on principle in 2019 when the main evening news went to 11pm: a step too far even for 'Baz'.

In prime time ITV, each and every night is formatted and formulaic. There are few surprises. A soap or two (both *Corrie* and *Emmerdale* are still running); a big expensive drama (usually a co-production and on safe sellable topics like *Morse's* Oxford or *Mr Selfridge*); a big live event such as a rugby match; or occasional football highlights (the crumbs they had salvaged, along with the BBC, from the Sky table); and 'reality' and quiz shows filling the spaces.

There is a documentary strand – on the First Tuesday of each month at 11.15 for an hour.

You can set your watch by the format you are watching.

ITV had been fully taken over in 2017 by Liberty Global of the USA. There were no government or Ofcom objections. 'LibGlobal' imposed the American model on their British baby and used them as both a proving ground for new US series and a source of marginal income for the same when made.

Channel Five, *ab initio*, has never had much of a profile and presence. In 2022, it is now fully branded as *'Channel 5;the Viacom channel'* and it resembles in content and style a US cable channel of the 1990s.Very few of its programmes are British or even original.

Channel 4: remit no more

Channel Four was part privatised in 2017. A closed tender led to take over by a consortium led by Lord Grade which included Tim Hincks and Peter Fincham, with Luke Johnson and others financing it. Within a year, they had undertaken a 'strategic review' of the channel and gone back to Ofcom and The Treasury (into which the DCMS had been folded in 2017) to ask for 'easement'. They got it. *Channel Four News* went to 5pm for half an hour with a night (re)cap at 11pm for five minutes. Current Affairs was Dispatched, the Mitsubishi documentary hour reduced to one per week on Friday at 9pm when *Gogglebox* was not in season.

My colleague David Lloyd has used his insider knowledge of the channel to construct a perhaps not-fanciful future schedule in this book's final chapter.

Sky now firmly rules the British airwaves and living rooms. It has taken on all-comers and won. BT gave up the ghost in 2020 after spending billions on sports rights. It learned the hard lesson: 'Never take on Sky. Its pockets are deep. Losing is inevitable.'

Sky's income is now five times the size of its nearest competitor, the BBC. The satellite broadcaster's fortunes based now as in the beginning – 1989 when it properly started – on owning sports rights and charging viewers for them. There is a Sky channel for cricket, rugby, Formula 1, Golf, tennis and several for football-the Premier League, the Championship and the European leagues. There is a football fix every hour of every day for the Sky viewer.

Each marginal channel means a marginal extra subscription. Punters are paying dearly – subscriptions are now averaging £100 per month per household, though Sky is as ever at the forefront of developing mobile/on-the-go ways of viewing.

Sky had paid billions, especially for football rights (£1.4bn per year for the Premier League from 2016: £11million per match!) but now they are the only game in town.

Monopsony rules

So, Sky is now using its monopsonist's (monopoly buyer) position to negotiate those rights downwards. Under Sir Gary Davey and Sir James Murdoch, the company has the perfect business: rising income, falling costs, and more profit for the Murdoch family who had retaken control of all the shares in 2017 after the slight hiccup of the 2011 phone hacking scandal.

The rest of the Sky offering is much as it had been in 2015: films, some high grade drama (usually US oriented), plenty of mini-series with the two *Sky News* services (News and Sport) now inside the subscription tent. Everything makes money for the Murdochs. Plenty.

The new kids on the block – *Netflix, Amazon Prime, Vice TV* and *Google TV* – are making lots of noise and some money. But these hard subscription channels have never fully from Anonymous hacking their codes and allowing free access to all in 2018. Their paywalls are now porous. The US and other networks are freely available. *FoxNews* is omnipresent.

The 2018 Communications Act removed all questions of balance, impartiality and fairness in British broadcasting. The baby of a century of British broadcast regulation went out with the bathwater of laissez faire. Anything now goes.

Public Service Broadcasting, the idea of television as a common good or cultural product not just a selling medium as in the USA, is now one for the birds. It has had a long slow and recently accelerated death. Dame Patricia Hodgson's Ofcom has seamlessly made the 'journey' from tough regulator through light touch to simply soft touch.

So what is the wider general genre picture now?

In drama, there are plenty of high cost, high value series. Kevin Spacey is booked up for three years ahead. Too much of it is in the *Downton Abbey* comfort zone, portraying a world we are said to have lost in Britain. Too little of it is gritty, challenging and domestic. *The Boys from the Blackstuff* would be lucky to see even a pilot today; *Cathy Come Home* would be left homeless. The US owners of the big broadcasters are looking for long, returning run dramas with transatlantic appeal. Bangs for their invested bucks.

Reality TV in all its forms in like a rash over all the schedules. *Big Brother* is entering its second decade on *Viacom Channel five*.

The reality formats got sillier and more dangerous until a 'celebrity' got killed in *the Jump* on Channel 4 *in* 2017. The extremes have been pulled back, except for the one: *Wall of Death** on ITV, but the challenges to contestants no longer make for gripping television. (*Note that Channel 4 got their first – it broadcast a live *Wall of Death* on Easter Monday 2016).

Documentaries are rare on the main entertainment channels. On the serious channels, fixed-rig rules but the makers are running out of institutions on which to be flies on their wall. Their nadir was *Student flatmates* in 2018.

Comedy has become Americanised; broken and sitcoms rule. The formats have come East. Today *Allo! Allo!* would be *Goodbye! Goodbye!* to any commissioners at any channel.

It's the platforms stupid

The technological big bang was the phone/tablet revolution of 2018/19 when prices fell and the sales of mobile phone and tablets simply ballooned. Most people now had at least one of each. The broadband revolution went mobile and cheaper too. TV on-the-go became the order of the day. Television had to adapt. News is now packaged or repackaged in 30 second bites; documentaries are now 8 to 10 minutes long. Dramas too. It was serialisation by digits. Form has determined content. The big live events and shows were the last remaining hook for terrestrial television. Rights to them were at a premium. Simon Cowell was selling his properties – *X Factor* and *BGT* – to the highest bidders: Channel $ and 5. *Comic Relief* and *Sport Relief* were now on ITV. Summer Olympic rights were gold-dust though Channel Four retained a patina of their remit by still being 'The Paralympic Channel' (just).

All in all, British television has long ago come out of its utopia to a dystopia which pleases no one. Apart from American shareholders.
Progress? You decide.

Dark visions of the future

By David Lloyd

In later, unmissable episodes and in no correct order to protect the innocent .... Rome falls on truly hard times, audiences at the Colosseum fall to unprecedented low levels:... Commodus, last of the Antonines, arrives on an agenda to make the Empire 'more commercial' but he and his sidekick Lucius Verus, fail to locate the philosopher's stone, Pertinax comes and goes in short order, but decamps to Salford (in this account the is not murdered). The Empire is auctioned to the highest bidder, but Didius Julianus, the winner, holds none of the answers. Sentimentalists remember the brief but noticeable relief brought by Septimius Severus and Caracalla. The latter, though universally disliked across the empire, does at least bring some solvency to the proceedings. Finally, Jupiter chivvies up the Goths to trash the place. O tempora! O mores!

Standing on Richard Rogers' vertiginous walkway above the Horseferry Road foyer, gazing towards Victoria Street, it would have taken a seer or sybil of extraordinary powers to have judged that the channel's future was more likely to be governed by developments outside rather than inside this new building – most notably, the transfer of intellectual property and exploitation rights in its programmes from the channel to the production companies themselves; Michael Grade's pat retort – 'the channel pays for a programme so it should own it' – ran out of room, releasing a global, monetised, production industry to take wing.

The channel, under successive leaderships, could undoubtedly have related to this seismic development more intelligently but, more important, had a structure and culture robust enough to survive it, while allowing its fledglings to fly – to the benefit of Britain's tax base and balance of trade. Today the industrial sector to which it gave birth is worth an estimated £3 billion turnover[1]. Not bad for an initial public investment of £100. Can anyone tell me of a comparable Treasury success?

Not for the first time, the Channel 4 model had proved its sheer versatility; but that should not lead us to believe that it could survive privatisation, whether 'partial' or wholesale. As evidence of this I was Googling idly one afternoon when, from some cloud somewhere, the programme schedule of the first privatising owners dropped into my inbox. It was particularly instructive as an example of the gradualist change that any first owner would be likely to adopt in order not to gilt the C4 audience.

Monday-Friday- 1900-1930: *Channel 4 News.* **First Edition** (nb Jon Snow and Cathy Newman remain to take the two editions in turn for brand continuity and recognition, but the new owners have cut Krishnan and others to reduce the budget, while the new director of programmes is adamant that no loss of coverage or airtime has suffered in the new model.)

Wednesday- 2100-2130. *Twelve hours in A&E* (nb. again the new owners have faced budgetary pressures to sustain a recent favourite).

Thursday-2130-2200. *Location, Location* (one location has had to be sacrificed, both in title and in coverage, for reasons of cost and the properties featured have been reduced to 'nothing costing six figures' and, for the first time, rental accommodation to match the programme's changed demographic. Phil Spencer has been retained but Kirsty is now an avatar, allowing the new owner's PR to salute the channel's 'traditional search for technological innovation'.

Thursday-2200-2230. *Grand Designs* has been replaced by *George Clarke's Very Small Spaces*.

Friday-2230-2300 The new slot for *Dispatches*, allowing it to concentrate on more 'adult' stories, and those for grown-up consumers; the press have dubbed the programme the 'dodgy dildo show' but the new owners point to the fact that, against all odds, they have allowed the journalism to survive, and that for the first time, 'the show is making money, and 'returning a proper profit to investors'.

Friday-2300-2330 (and other weekday nights) *Channel 4 News: second edition.* The new owners are issuing regular press releases saluting the 'rise in audience for their new news strategy,' at no loss to 'immediacy of response around the newsclock', while Jon and Cathy are coming in for a great deal of criticism in the press for 'making this disastrous change acceptable'. Bruised by this unrelenting attack, Jon finally decides to call it a day...

Weeknights 2330-midnight. *Shameless* **repeats.** The new owners sign a 'major new deal' with Paul Abbott for the rights to his archive, and claim this as evidence of their 'continuing support for UK production' and testimony that they remain 'courageous and outrageous'. Abbott gets a slating in the press for the deal but tells them all to 'sod off and die'. *The Guardian* newspaper launches its 'don't press 4' campaign but whereas this has a damaging effect on audiences, advertisers refuse to be drawn. It also publishes a leak that the separate news and current affairs department is to be wound up and folded into Specialist Factorial. The director of programmes and creativity retorts that 'no one will miss the loss of head of news and current affairs on the screen'. At the first AGM under the new ownership investors and City journalists alike question the low profitability of the new enterprise; the US chairman is reported to mutter underneath his breath: 'would have been even lower if those fxxkers from Ofcom had made us run those shows for cripples and nancy boys!' The Channel 4 press office denies this absolutely but the remark was picked up on iPhones and goes viral on social media. Labour leader Hilary Benn demands a judicial enquiry into the conduct of the C4 Sale and the choice of winner, while launching a 'Whittingdale must go' campaign on the streets. An enquiry, conducted within Ofcom, concludes that the new owners of C4 are 'not fit and proper persons to hold a licence to broadcast'.

Certainly, there is no place for Whittingdale in George Osborne's first cabinet and he is put in charge of flood defence, as minister of state at Defra, with many judging he is lucky to have a government job at all.

As David Cameron steps down from No.10 in 2019, Steve Richards in the online *Independent* remarks sagely that 'for a man who so adroitly negotiated a special status for Britain in the EU to have dropped the ball on something so apparently trivial as Channel 4 will go down as one of the great political riddles of all time'.

Dark visions

For the 30th anniversary party we stood packed from floor to ceiling on the access ramp in the Horseferry Road restaurant as random celebrities like Gok Wan mingled with commissioners past, present and recent, and indies founding and global, listening to Sir Jeremy Isaacs describing the Channel as 'in good nick', which of course he was duty bound to assert to avoid raining on the parade.

Those in his audience will each have harboured their own thoughts and reflections. Mine were of two kinds. First of all the 'what ifs' flooded through my head: what if we hadn't lost the plot so completely without core audience; what if Luke Johnson as chairman had not taken Greg Dyke's suggestion to appoint Andy Duncan as chief executive; what if Duncan hadn't then cried doom from the rooftops about the future prospects of Channel 4, unintentionally reigniting the privatisation debate?

Predominantly though, my reflections were of sheer wonder that, against all odds, and despite seismic changes in the television industry together with monetising of independent production, this extraordinarily bold, Thatcherite oxymoron – of a commercially funded, not for profit, public service broadcaster – had survived for three whole decades with so much of its founding integrity intact. Of course, there had been mistakes along the way; the British governmental record at appointing suitable chairpersons and boards had been no less questionable at Channel 4 than at the BBC, and the defining gift of the channel's board has always been to choose the chief executive, which in recent years has proved to be quite some lottery (no reference to Camelot intended). But, beyond all else, Channel 4 has been this signal success, kick-starting the independent production industry and laying the template for one of the great, post-war industrial achievements of this country. My God, it has even rediscovered the British film industry when nobody else could, and continues to deliver films unmatched by the BBC. Even today, there is nothing whatsoever bust about this model, and there is absolutely no 'fix' that will consolidate it intact – least of all a sale, that would narrow the viewing choice within British television itself and jeopardise the solvency of other channels and content providers in what is now a subtly mature multi-channel and digital market.

In my final and darkest vision, the first owners give up on trying to reconcile remit with return and sell out to one of the truly predatory US multinationals who do a deal to forget the remit entirely in order to bolster the channel's capital base.

Returning on my last pilgrimage to Horseferry Road, I view the building as some kind of Palmyra, it is standing (just about) but is seriously the worse for wear, and the same is overwhelming true on the screen; On every EPG there is still a fourth channel. But there is no longer a Channel 4.

Notes

[1] PACT. Independent Production Sector Financial Census and Survey 2014
http://www.thecreativeindustries.co.uk/media/254048/pact_censusreport_2014_final-2-.pdf

Lightning Source UK Ltd.
Milton Keynes UK
UKHW020641070223
416609UK00011B/2642